Essays in Existential Psychoanalysis

In this brilliant and revolutionary collection of 14 major essays that draw from more than 25 years of painstaking research, M. Guy Thompson regales us with a stunning revisioning of conventional psychoanalysis that deepens our understanding of the human condition.

Integrating the most seminal existentialist philosophers, including Nietzsche, Heidegger, and Sartre, with the most forward-thinking psychoanalysts over the past century, including Freud, Laing, Bion, Winnicott, and Lacan, Thompson offers a profound yet deeply personal vision of what psychoanalysis can be in the 21st century. In this fascinating volume, Thompson explores such concepts as experience, authenticity, will, happiness, and agency by utilizing a wide range of thinkers, including the ancient Greeks, but always in his singular voice. Exquisitely lucid and engaging to read, Thompson deftly lures us into thoughtful and enlightening territory typically inaccessible to the general reader.

This compelling integration of continental philosophy and psychoanalysis will be of interest not only to psychoanalytic practitioners of all persuasions, but to psychotherapists generally and their patients, as well as philosophers, social scientists, and any student of the human condition.

M. Guy Thompson, PhD, is Founder and Director of the New School for Existential Psychoanalysis and a Personal and Supervising Analyst and Faculty Member at the Psychoanalytic Institute of Northern California, San Francisco. His two most recent books, *The Legacy of R. D. Laing* (2015, Editor) and *The Death of Desire* (2017, 2nd ed.), are also published by Routledge. Dr. Thompson is the author of numerous books and journal articles on psychoanalysis, phenomenology, and psychosis. He lives in Berkeley, California.

Philosophy and Psychoanalysis Book Series
Jon Mills
Series Editor

Philosophy and Psychoanalysis is dedicated to current developments and cutting-edge research in the philosophical sciences, phenomenology, hermeneutics, existentialism, logic, semiotics, cultural studies, social criticism, and the humanities that engage and enrich psychoanalytic thought through philosophical rigor. With the philosophical turn in psychoanalysis comes a new era of theoretical research that revisits past paradigms while invigorating new approaches to theoretical, historical, contemporary, and applied psychoanalysis. No subject or discipline is immune from psychoanalytic reflection within a philosophical context including psychology, sociology, anthropology, politics, the arts, religion, science, culture, physics, and the nature of morality. Philosophical approaches to psychoanalysis may stimulate new areas of knowledge that have conceptual and applied value beyond the consulting room reflective of greater society at large. In the spirit of pluralism, *Philosophy and Psychoanalysis* is open to any theoretical school in philosophy and psychoanalysis that offers novel, scholarly, and important insights in the way we come to understand our world.

Titles in this series:

'*Essays in Existential Psychoanalysis: On the Primacy of Authenticity* draws together 14 major papers written by Michael Guy Thompson. Their aim is to reconsider various foundational themes and assumptions within psychoanalysis from the focus point of existential theory. Always exciting to read, they are uniformly and clearly argued and presented. Thompson is rightfully renowned as an original theorist whose writing is both accessible and challenging, as well as to the point and passionate. These essays are intended to provoke and illuminate. Not only do they achieve this aim, in my view they surpass it thanks to the author's mastery of the material under discussion and, not least, his genuine enthusiasm in offering fresh perspectives on both psychoanalysis and existentialism.'

Professor Ernesto Spinelli, **PhD**, *author of* Practising Existential Therapy: The Relational World

'A unique and absorbing development of key commonalities between existential and psychoanalytic approaches to understanding clinical issues and the human condition. This book is a unique integration of existential philosophy and psychoanalysis, comprising Dr. Thompson's nearly thirty years of painstaking publications that have developed this perspective. As an existential psychoanalyst, Thompson explores concepts such as experience, authenticity, will, and agency by utilizing a wide range of thinkers from the ancient Greeks through to Nietszche, Freud, Heidegger, Sartre, and Laing. His thought-provoking existential perspective on psychoanalytic concepts such as free association, neutrality and working through makes this an invaluable and distinctive contribution to existential psychoanalysis.'

Douglas Kirsner, **PhD**, *Emeritus Professor, Deakin University, Melbourne, Australia; author of* The Schizoid World of Jean-Paul Sartre and R.D. Laing *and* Unfree Associations: Inside Psychoanalytic Institutes

'M. Guy Thompson knew and worked with some of the greats from the 20th century. Among these were R.D. Laing and Ernest Hemingway no less! And their influence is palpable. In this volume, Thompson's excursion through the interiors of existential psychoanalysis is exquisitely lucid and engaging—a revelation even to those of us schooled in its principles. Any reader wishing to understand the basis and importance of existential

Other books published by M. Guy Thompson

The Death of Desire
A Study in Psychopathology (1985)

The Truth About Freud's Technique
The Encounter with the Real (1994)

The Ethic of Honesty
The Fundamental Rule of Psychoanalysis (2004)

The Legacy of R. D. Laing
An Appraisal of his Contemporary Relevance (2015, Ed.)

The Death of Desire
An Existential Study in Sanity and Madness
(2017, 2nd ed.)

Essays in Existential Psychoanalysis

On the Primacy of Authenticity

M. Guy Thompson

Routledge
Taylor & Francis Group

LONDON AND NEW YORK

Designed cover image: M. Guy Thompson

First published 2024
by Routledge
4 Park Square, Milton Park, Abingdon, Oxon OX14 4RN

and by Routledge
605 Third Avenue, New York, NY 10158

Routledge is an imprint of the Taylor & Francis Group, an informa business

British Library Cataloguing-in-Publication Data
A catalogue record for this book is available from the
British Library

ISBN: 978-1-032-55124-1 (hbk)
ISBN: 978-1-032-55123-4 (pbk)
ISBN: 978-1-003-42910-4 (ebk)

DOI: 10.4324/9781003429104

Typeset in Times New Roman
by Apex CoVantage, LLC

Contents

Permissions

Acknowledgments

Earlier versions of the following chapters were previously published in journals. I acknowledge, with thanks, permission to publish them here:

An earlier version of Chapter 6 was previously published in *Contemporary Psychoanalysis* as "The Crisis of Experience in Contemporary Psychoanalysis," Volume 36, No. 1: 29–56, 2000. An earlier version of Chapter 7 was previously published in *Contemporary Psychoanalysis* as "The Sceptic Dimension to Psychoanalysis: Toward an Ethic of Experience," Volume 36, No. 3: 457–481, 2000. An earlier version of Chapter 9 was previously published in *Contemporary Psychoanalysis* as "Is the Unconscious Really All That Unconscious?: The Role of Being and Experience in the Psychoanalytic Encounter," Volume 37, No. 4: 571–612, 2001. An earlier version of Chapter 5 was previously published in *Contemporary Psychoanalysis* as "Vicissitudes of Authenticity in the Psychoanalytic Situation," Volume 42, No. 2: 139–176, 2006. An earlier version of Chapter 8 was previously published in *Psychoanalytic Psychology* as "Happiness and Chance: A Reappraisal of the Psychoanalytic Conception of Suffering," Volume 21, No. 1: 134–153, 2004. I want to especially thank the editor of the Philosophy and Psychoanalysis series at Routledge, Jon Mills, for inclusion of this volume in his series, and for his advocacy of this project and his encouragement.

Preface
What Is the Existentialist Sensibility?

What do we mean when we employ the term existential? What relevance does it have for clinical practice? By invoking it, what are we trying to convey about the way we conceive the therapeutic process? Psychoanalysis had someone, Sigmund Freud, to invent it. But no one is credited with inventing existentialism, as a philosophical school or simply as a concept. Yet, existential philosophy is the foundation for the various therapies that are identified with it, including existential therapy, existential analysis, Daseinsanalysis, existential psychoanalysis, and so on. I'll admit that I'm not too crazy about any of these designations. Just as there is no one philosopher who can be credited with having invented existentialism, there is no one who can be credited with having invented existential therapy. This makes it highly problematic to define just what performing therapy from an existential perspective should look like because there is no general agreement as to what existential philosophy is, nor what existential therapy should be.

On the other hand, psychoanalysis was created by Freud, and for a great deal of his lifetime, he was able to dictate what it was and what it was not. A number of Freud's followers, including C. G. Jung, Alfred Adler, and Otto Rank, broke with Freud when they began to develop ideas that were contrary to his, especially Freud's emphasis on sexuality as the *sine qua non* of the human condition. Because Freud got to define what psychoanalysis was, anyone who disagreed with him could be accused of no longer adhering to psychoanalytic principles as delineated by him.

Since Freud's death, however, this is no longer the case. There is wide latitude today as to what psychoanalysis is and who may call oneself a psychoanalyst. Yet, because Freud invented it and provided all of its fundamental concepts, including the unconscious and transference, analysts today are obliged to situate their perspective within the context of Freud's, to articulate those areas with which they are in agreement and those with which they are not. Even if what we call psychoanalysis today enjoys enormous elasticity (so long as the unconscious and transference are accounted for), Freud's writings nonetheless serve to provide the foundational texts from which all subsequent theories are derived, even if no one nowadays bothers to read Freud firsthand. This provides the psychoanalytic perspective, whatever it is and however defined by this or that practitioner, with a sense of integrity. The same cannot be said for therapies that are identified with existentialism. Existential therapy, or therapy practiced from an existential sensibility, can be more or less whatever anyone claims it is, which may account for why, as a therapeutic movement, it has not been nearly as successful or influential as psychoanalysis has been.

Existentialism became fashionable in the post-Second World War era, first in Europe, then gradually across the Atlantic to the Americas. As an adjective for *existence*, the word existential became a technical term that was descriptive of a philosophical school popularized by Jean-Paul Sartre with the publication of his *magnum opus*, *Being and Nothingness* (1954/1943) first published in France in 1943, two years before the end of the war. Though Sartre was the first philosopher to call himself an existentialist, he did not invent the label. The term was first coined by the French Catholic philosopher Gabriel Marcel in the mid-1940s, but it was Sartre with whom existentialism is most identified. *L'existentialisme* became the rage in Paris and served to epitomize the hip, *Bohemian*, Parisian café-set of intellectuals, *artistes*, and vagabonds who ushered in an age of non-conformity, a kind of societal and intellectual rebellion against chains, first imposed by the Germans during the Nazi occupation of France, then by any form of orthodoxy that presumed to dictate what people should believe and how they were to behave. Paris became a philosophical culture, and *l'existentialisme* dripped from the lips of anyone who presumed to be in the know and a member of the chic, *avant-garde* set of Parisian society to which everyone who was anybody wanted to belong. Sartre held center stage of this tribe of intellectuals at his favorite café, *Café' de Flore*, where he sipped espresso while crafting his most famous philosophical and literary works.

Sartre—along with his close friend, Maurice Merleau-Ponty, and lover, Simone de Bouvoir—may have made existentialism famous, but it anticipated them by more than a century. Though it is difficult to claim that any one person invented existentialism, it would be hard to contest that there were four principal philosophers who generated what came to be known as existential philosophy, each with his own singular contribution. The Danish nineteenth-century philosopher, Søren Kierkegaard, is generally credited as the first philosopher to articulate a philosophy that contained all the elements that we associate with this perspective. He did not, however, coin the label "existentialism" nor use it to depict his take on the human condition. Kierkegaard was followed by another nineteenth-century philosopher, the German Friedrich Nietzsche. It isn't clear whether Nietzsche ever read any of Kierkegaard's works, though he was aware of Kierkegaard and spoke of him. Both philosophers were opposed to the abstraction of traditional philosophy, epitomized by a German philosopher whom they detested, Georg Wilhelm Friedrich Hegel, and sought to emphasize the inherently personal aspects of philosophy and the importance of facing anxiety authentically, which is to say, head on. The twentieth-century philosopher Martin Heidegger was probably the most important thinker in the existential tradition due to the volume of his output, the radical nature of his ideas, and his emphasis on the role of existence in everyday human affairs. Unlike Kierkegaard and Nietzsche, Heidegger deliberately employed the term "existential" in his work and assigned it a specific philosophical meaning. Moreover, Heidegger was thoroughly steeped in both Kierkegaard's and Nietzsche's writings and made liberal use of both of them. Kierkegaard's views about anxiety, authenticity, and the nature of the self profoundly influenced Heidegger's thinking, and Heidegger's reading of Nietzsche, in turn, had a considerable impact on contemporary perceptions of Nietzsche's philosophy. Sartre's main philosophical work, *Being and Nothingness* (1954/1943), is almost a verbatim French version of Division II of Heidegger's *magnum opus*, *Being and Time* (1962/1927), which deals with concepts such as freedom and authenticity, though Sartre was also significantly influenced by Heidegger's teacher, Edmund Husserl (more about him later). It was Sartre who popularized existential philosophy and turned it into a cultural phenomenon which, in turn, brought Kierkegaard, Nietzsche, and Heidegger to the non-academic public's attention for the first time.

Another philosopher who is important in the development of existentialism is the German Karl Jaspers, a contemporary of Heidegger's and close friend of a woman who is closely associated with existentialism, Hannah Arendt, a student of Heidegger's with whom he had an affair. Jaspers was overshadowed by Heidegger's unprecedented celebrity, so he is better known as a psychiatrist who wrote a seminal work on psychopathology.

There are many more philosophers as well as literary authors who are associated with existentialism, including Spain's Miguel de Unamuno and Jose Ortega y Gasset, Franz Kafka, who was famous for his masterpiece, *The Trial*, and Albert Camus, another novelist famous for *The Stranger*. Others include Martin Buber, the philosopher and Jewish theologian, Paul Tillich, a Christian philosopher and theologian, the Russian Fyodor Dostoyevsky, Franz Fanon, Immanuel Levinas, and others too many to mention. This, of course, does not exhaust all the other names, non-philosophical novelists and artists, who can be included as having embodied what I am calling an existentialist sensibility, including the American writers Ernest Hemmingway, Dashiell Hammett, Jim Thompson, Philip K. Dick; the painters Pablo Picasso, Salvador Dali, Paul Cezanne, Francis Bacon, William Blake, Jackson Pollock, Andy Warhol; the poet Samuel Beckett; and filmmakers such as Ingmar Bergman, Luis Bunuel, Federico Fellini, Francois Truffaut, Alfred Hitchcock, Stanley Kubrick, and, of course, Woody Allen. We could spend all day compiling a list of twentieth-century artists, thinkers, and authors who embody an existential perspective, but I will spare you that. The second half of the twentieth century is dominated by this sensibility due to the two World Wars that preceded it, the Cold War that dominated the second half of the century, and the Industrial Revolution that preceded both. It was difficult to be a thoughtful person in the twentieth century and not be preoccupied with existential concerns.

So what *is* existentialism? What can we say about the existential perspective, or sensibility, despite so many philosophers who are associated with it? Because there is no orthodox encapsulation of what it means, I can only tell you what it means to me. Every philosophical perspective has its nomenclature, terms that set it apart from others, though there is often overlap. This is no less true for existentialism. The words I most readily associate with this perspective, though not exhaustive, are the following.

I will begin with the word *experience*. Experience is privileged in existential thinkers because it is inherently personal and not as abstract and academic as with other philosophies, which is what sets it apart from other philosophical schools. Though this sometimes makes existential philosophy more accessible to the layman, Heidegger's *Being and Time* is considered the most difficult to understand philosophical work ever written. Whatever else the existential perspective embodies, it is primarily concerned with *my* way of seeing things, which is the only way of seeing things to which I have direct access. The concept of experience was a favorite of R. D. Laing's and so important to him that it was included in the title of two of his books, *The Politics of Experience* (1967) and *The Voice of Experience* (1982).

Experience is closely associated with another term you see frequently employed by existentialists, but by no means exclusively: the word *meaning*. Things matter to me, which is another way of saying the world I live in *means* something to *me*. What it means is up to me to determine, and only I can do so. The search for meaning, specifically what my life is about, is probably the most basic topic explored in both existential therapies as well as psychoanalysis, each of which sees the therapeutic process as one of getting to know oneself in the most fundamental way possible.

Another is the term *authenticity*. All existentialist thinkers promote authenticity over inauthenticity, but there is little agreement as to what authenticity is. First and foremost, authenticity is a way of articulating what it means to be honest with oneself. Honesty was highly valued by Freud, and one could argue that he promoted authenticity in his patients' lives via the act of free association, disclosing whatever is on one's mind to another person. Both psychoanalysis and existentialism are concerned with becoming the person you are by dropping the pretenses we typically employ to please others. This is probably the single-most feature of both these disciplines that have made them so controversial. Each act as subversive elements in society by helping the members of that society separate themselves from the *status quo*. No group enjoys group members pissing on what that group is about, which is why groups are conservative in nature. Perhaps this explains why existentialists tend to be fiercely independent and avoid groups as a rule.

Authenticity is also closely linked to the existential preoccupation with the concept of *freedom*. This is a complicated and generally misunderstood concept. Like authenticity, various existential thinkers differ in how they see it. For the most part, to be free in the existential sense is to realize that I *choose* to be who I am at the deepest, most fundamental level of my being, though I usually deny this, a common ploy in psychotherapy. This doesn't mean I am always *conscious* of my choices, as they typically operate under the surface of awareness. This implies that I have *agency* in my actions, that I am behind my acts, impressions, and attitudes about the life I live and, therefore, I am responsible for who I am and what I do. I even choose my neuroses! A man in prison is unable to escape, but he nonetheless chooses how he reacts to being a prisoner, whether to become embittered or improve himself, or attempt escape.

Another term that is closely associated with the existential perspective is the German word *Angst*. We typically translate this as anxiety in English, but it can also mean anguish. Human beings are inherently anxious, and this is a fundamental aspect of our being. This is similar to Freud's contention that each and every one of us is an anxious creature who relentlessly seeks to minimize anxiety as much as we can, often to our detriment. Though the terminology adopted by existential philosophy and psychoanalysis differ, their respective ways of privileging anxiety as an ongoing problem with which all of us grapple are complementary. For the most part, they both agree that anxiety is a good thing and that we need to learn how to attend to and accommodate it rather than eliminate or minimize it. Naturally, when we *suffer* anxiety, we instinctively want to suppress it, but existentialism and psychoanalysis, like Buddhism, embrace suffering as a vital constituent of life that begs to be understood, without sedatives.

The last word I associate with existentialism is *alienation*, yet another term that is not used exclusively by existentialists. Humans are inherently *estranged* from, while being fundamentally *rooted in,* their environment. Alienation is also a key theme in Marxism but for different reasons. Marx argued that our alienation in society is due to the inequity of social classes and economic privilege. Existentialists locate our alienation in the encroaching power of technology that threatens to turn people into machines. Though this problem originated in the Industrial Revolution, it is also a popular theme among science fiction writers, such as Phillip K. Dick, who explored how the distinction between humans and machines may disappear in the not-too-distant future, in a world where, says Dick, "machines are more human than humans."[1] On a more basic level, we are alienated from each other because we can never really know each other or ourselves. We are inherent strangers to each other and mistake whom we take each other to be through the projections we confer on one another. Whether this is fixable or not varies among existential thinkers, some arguing there is no escape, others suggesting we are capable of bridging our estrangement from one another through love. The most basic problem, however, is our estrangement from ourselves because we do not really know ourselves any better than we know others, perhaps even less. This alludes to the problem of authenticity and how the inauthentic individual is estranged from himself but needn't be as long as he or she chooses to do something about it.

What all of these terms share in common is that they are perfectly ordinary terms that we use all the time. This is what made existentialism so popular in its heyday. Each of us grapples with these concerns throughout our lives. Any thinking person who has not encountered existential literature is, nonetheless, as it were, a closet existentialist—he just doesn't know it. It would be difficult to be a thoughtful human being and not be. Despite the variety of thinkers who are associated with an existential perspective and their diversity, what is the common outlook about life that links them together? In the main, all of these thinkers would agree that life challenges us, from the moment we are born, with pain, frustration, and disappointment and that it confronts us with tasks that are extremely difficult to perform and which leave scars that are impossible to erase. Though, as children, we are convinced things will become easier as we grow older, experience teaches us the opposite, that life becomes increasingly more difficult, and that this state of affairs persists throughout our existence until, finally, we are faced with the inevitability of our death. Whether you are religious or an atheist makes no difference in the existentialist's attitude about death. For the atheist, like Sartre, life has no intrinsic meaning and all we can say is that life is what we make of it, then we die. For a Christian existentialist, such as Kierkegaard, Gabriel Marcel, or Paul Tillich, believing in God may provide a measure of comfort, but because religious belief is rooted in faith rather than fact (it is a fact, for example, that I am going to die, but not that God exists) it means that, because I am human, I cannot escape those moments of doubt that *San Juan de la Cruz* depicted so well in *The Dark Night of the Soul* (2003). This is the despair I feel when I sense that I may very well be alone in the universe because God, if there is one, doesn't speak to me, or if He once did, has now abandoned me. Nietzsche's famous pronouncement that "God is dead" was his way of letting us know it is about time we take responsibility for our lives and stop leaning on external authorities to tell us what to do, or to save us. Despite Nietzsche's opinion on the matter, the existential position is that it is possible to do this whether or not one believes in God.

If there is one theme that pervades just about every existentialist thinker or artist, it is that we are unremittingly alone in this world, whatever I believe awaits me after I die, and this sense of aloneness is something I cannot nor should I deny. It is where I live in the deepest recesses of my self-identity. The ways that I cope with this aloneness make me the person I am and say more about me and who I am than the most detailed biography ever could. This is the basis of the despair that Kierkegaard described so effectively in *The Sickness Unto Death* (1980) and with which every existentialist philosopher has since identified. Is there a cure for this despair? Because despair is not a clinical diagnosis but a fundamental aspect of my nature, it is something that will always be a part of me. Some may react to it with an increase in anxiety or depression or give up and turn to drugs or other distractions to cope with the pain of it. Others may turn to philosophy, religion, or artistic endeavors to turn their despair into something meaningful that can paradoxically enrich their life and make it more valuable and rewarding. Others still may turn to psychoanalysis or other kinds of therapy, including existential, believing there is something the matter with them for feeling this way. Or they may recognize they are struggling with anxieties inherent in living and simply want someone they can talk to about it.

Before turning to the relationship between the existentialist sensibility and psychotherapy, I should say something about that other philosophical discipline which, though not identical with existentialism, is sometimes intertwined with it due to their intimate proximity, *phenomenology*. Unlike existential philosophy, phenomenology has a founder, a person who invented it, Edmund Husserl. Husserl, another German philosopher, was a contemporary of Freud's, so the evolution of both Husserl's and Freud's disciplines ran parallel courses and share some similarities. What distinguished phenomenology from existentialism is that existentialism, like other philosophies, entertains a view of the human condition, even if it is less systematic than most. Phenomenology has no such worldview because it is, for the most part, a *methodology* that, if followed, should take one closer to reality—in other words, to perceive things as they are. For this reason, phenomenology is almost exclusively rooted in epistemology, that branch of philosophy that is concerned with the nature of truth. Unlike Husserl, some phenomenologists are also existentialists and are sometimes referred to as existential-phenomenologists to distinguish them from strict phenomenologists, such as Husserl and Max Scheler, among others. Just as there are four principal existential philosophers, there are four principal phenomenologists: Husserl, Heidegger, Sartre, and Merleau-Ponty. Among the four most influential existential philosophers—Kierkegaard, Nietzsche, Heidegger, and Sartre—two of them, Heidegger and Sartre, are also phenomenologists. Other existential-phenomenologists of note are Maurice Merleau-Ponty, Hans-Georg Gadamer, Hannah Arendt, and Emmanuel Levinas. Some people would add Jacques Derrida to that list.

The number of philosophers identified with phenomenology is considerable, and while many of them are followers of Husserl, others lean closer to Heidegger's existential reinterpretation of phenomenology. What sets them apart? Husserl was interested in developing a method of investigation that was more radical than the empirical scientific method because he believed that science is too concerned with what it deems "objective" knowledge, a kind of knowing that is supposed to be free of subjective bias. Science isn't interested in the scientist's personal opinion about the object of investigation because it seeks a picture of reality that is not marred by emotional feelings that the scientist may have about what he is investigating. Doctoral students embarking on a dissertation are advised not to select a topic that is too close to their personal situation for fear it will bias the way they go about collecting their data. Say a psychology student, for example, wants to conduct a study of schizophrenia because her mother is so diagnosed, but she wants to prove that schizophrenia doesn't exist so that her mother will no longer be derided for her diagnosis. She would enter into this investigation with a bias, hoping to discover what she already hopes is the case. This is not science. The scientist wants to approach a topic without preconceived notions about what he will find and is open to whatever the data he collects tells him. In other words, he is free of subjective prejudice. Or is he?

Husserl believed that the scientist may not be as free of bias as we assume, and so needs to free himself of the biases he may not realize he entertains when conducting his investigations. Husserl developed a method of looking at things that were supposed to be free of presuppositions by employing a method he termed *epoché*, a word he lifted from the Greek Sceptics. By employing this attitude, one is supposed to bracket any bias and look at things with an attitude of naïveté, or innocence. Say a colleague refers a patient to me for psychotherapy and offers to send me his psychiatric records so that I can see how his previous treatments went. If I want to keep an open mind as to what I will see when I meet him, I must resolve *not* to read any case reports about him beforehand. That way, he comes to me as more or less a stranger, which in turn allows me to form my own opinion about him. This would amount to meeting him without presuppositions. Of course, it is far more complicated than that because what about my *own* biases that I bring with me into the consulting room, not about this patient but about the diagnostic process? This is a problem most psychoanalysts struggle with because they already have categories of diagnoses that they bring to bear when seeking to understand the patient before them, such as whether, for example, they suspect the patient is bipolar, borderline, schizoid, hysterical, psychotic, or what have you. Shouldn't I also bracket those categories as well and not think about concepts such as psychopathology if I want to be completely unbiased and, therefore, open to the phenomena before me? Husserl would say yes, and looking at this patient from such an unprejudiced frame of reference is what transforms the so-called symptoms before me into *phenomena*. Phenomena are what I see when I look at something using *epoché*, without bias or judgment. Phenomenology seeks to get in touch with the most basic things in my world by relying solely on my *experience* of them, without "looking" for something that a theory, for example, suggests I will find.

Husserl saw phenomenology as a discipline that could subvert the over-conceptualization of existence to which our era is prone by bracketing theoretical presuppositions and returning us to the ground of our native experience. According to Edie (1962),

> Phenomenology is neither a science of objects nor a science of the subject; it is a science of *experience*. It does not concentrate exclusively on either the objects of experience or on the subject of experience, but on the point of contact where being and consciousness meet. It is therefore, a study of consciousness as intentional, as directed towards objects, as living in an intentionally constituted world.
>
> (p. 19)

In other words, a genuinely phenomenological form of inquiry differs from conventional scientific investigation in that science isn't concerned with nor is it able to study experience, *per se*. Its manner of investigation is directed instead to objects of perception, the reality of which is presumed to exist *independently* of the person conducting the investigation. This is why science is unable to account for the experience of the subject who engages in the research because the subject's experience has to be separated from and, consequently, inaccessible to the object of investigation. Phenomenology seeks to examine the nature of the world *as experienced*, whatever object of inquiry we decide to explore, including one's self, one's thoughts, or one's experience of others. Instead of applying a theory that tries to account for what is happening "in" the patient I am treating, the phenomenologist goes directly to the person himself, by examining the therapist's experience of *his relationship with this person*. This means I need to resist speculating about what might be the matter with this patient by entertaining an inventory of possible diagnostic formulations and seek instead to determine the grounds of my relationship with this person as I notice that relationship transforming through the bond we share together, in common cause. The kind of truth I seek about this person isn't objective, but personal.

Following Husserl's call that we return to "the things themselves," a generation of phenomenologists, including Heidegger, Max Scheler, Sartre, Merleau-Ponty, Paul Ricoeur, and Levinas set out to investigate their experience of the world in a radically different way than the one with which scientists and other philosophers were accustomed. According to Safranski (1998), Husserl and his followers

> [W]ere on the lookout for a new way of letting the things approach them, without covering them up with what they already knew. Reality should be given an opportunity to "show" itself. That which showed itself, and the way it showed itself, was called "the phenomenon" by the phenomenologists.
>
> (p. 72)

Ironically, phenomenology resists definition because, like experience itself, its method is antithetical to theoretical and causal explanation; a method, however, tailor-made for investigating the relationships between *persons*. Its point of departure is the rejection of conceptualizing as well as objectifying tendencies typical of the hard sciences and even what we often find in the so-called social sciences. Laing and Esterson's study of families of schizophrenics, which they conducted at the Tavistock Institute and subsequently published in *Sanity, Madness and the Family* (1964/1971), is a perfect example of how a phenomenological study into families might be conducted. It was based exclusively on the conversations Laing and Esterson conducted with all the family members and what they made of those conversations. In his preface to his *Phenomenology of Perception* (1962), Merleau-Ponty suggested that phenomenology is necessarily difficult to define because it

> [R]emains faithful to its nature by never knowing where it is going. The unfinished nature of phenomenology and the inchoative atmosphere that has surrounded it are not to be taken as a sign of failure; they were inevitable because phenomenology's task was to reveal the mystery of the world and of reason.
>
> (p. xxi)

Phenomenology shares with psychoanalysis the view that explanation is inadequate to the task of understanding what is given to experience and shares with psychoanalytic treatment the task of determining the nature of anguish in a manner that doesn't objectify or categorize the sufferer. Instead of posing the scientific question of what *causes* a person to be this way or that, the phenomenologist asks, what does it *mean* to be the person I am treating, who is experiencing the world this or that way? Once the meaning question is substituted for that of causation, we enter the realm of phenomenology because in raising this question, we accept the inherent mystery of our existence. The phenomenologist isn't interested in *solving* this mystery but in deepening it.

The irony in all this is that Husserl believed phenomenology is in a better position to get to certainty than science after all the investigator's presuppositions have been bracketed away. This is the reason we find a split between phenomenology and existential-phenomenology. You can see from the above that, despite this split, there is a significant affinity between phenomenology and existentialism, especially in the way both privilege experience and meaning. Heidegger took Husserl's creation and turned it into a methodology that was more existential and, so, ambiguous. Heidegger wasn't after certainty because he doubted there is such a thing. His version of phenomenology is sceptical, and the outcomes of his questioning are necessarily ambiguous. Heidegger didn't use phenomenology to "know" more about things but as a way of being *more present* to the world in which we live, such as the world I share with my patient. In order to appreciate this argument better, it would help to know a little more about the prehistory that both existentialism and phenomenology share.

Both the existentialist and phenomenological perspectives have their origins in Greek thought, going back to Socrates. As mentioned earlier, Husserl borrowed his method of bracketing, the *epoché*, from the Greek Sceptics. The Sceptics came after Socrates,[2] and we can trace their origins to the way Socrates liked to engage the philosophers of his day in conversation, asking them how they knew the things they professed to know. No matter how astute his opponents were, Socrates always succeeded in humiliating them by showing they relied solely on theory and speculation, but not incontrovertible truths. Socrates professed to know nothing except that he was smart enough to recognize how ignorant he was, which was more than he could say about the philosophers he typically encountered, who were called Sophists. Because this method of conversing aimed to pare away false assumptions, this method planted the seeds for what would subsequently become the sceptic method of inquiry, the *epoché*, initiated by Pyrrho about a century after Socrates.

But Socrates was also the first existentialist in the manner he sought to separate philosophy from religion by looking for secular explanations about the meaning of life. In Plato's dialogues, Socrates ranges over all manner of topics, including the meaning of happiness, love, courage, integrity, morality, and so on, none of which rely on religious explanations as to what life is about. This was a radical and apparently dangerous position to take because everything that occurred in Greek culture was explained by the gods and goddesses on Olympus. Before Socrates, the Greeks believed that every human endeavor was supposed to have its origin in one's relationship with Greek deities. Though Socrates paid lip service to their existence, what distinguished philosophy from religion was its alternative, inherently secular worldview. Despite his efforts to placate the less sophisticated Athenian citizens, Socrates was eventually brought up on charges in his old age for allegedly corrupting the youth and preaching false religions (an allusion to Socrates' invention of mythological characters with which to buttress some of his arguments). Socrates could have avoided execution by apologizing for his misdeeds, but, being a man of integrity, he refused to do this and insisted he was doing his fellow Athenians a favor by educating their youth! This only inflamed his accusers further and, as he gave them no way out, Socrates was reluctantly executed. In death, Socrates became a martyr and epitomized the way subsequent philosophers sought to defend the truth as they saw it. Other philosophers in the centuries that followed were executed for similar transgressions. It is not coincidental that existentialists such as Nietzsche and Heidegger turn to the Greeks as the source of their own worldview, including the sceptic sensibility that Socrates epitomized.

Those phenomenologists who choose Heidegger over Husserl, including Gadamer, Arendt, Levinas, Sartre, Merleau-Ponty, and Derrida share with him the sceptic sensibility that is more existential than Husserl's version, because no existentialist believes in certainty (the sceptic sensibility is also a driving force in postmodernism).[3] This is why Heidegger privileges the *being* of human existence—e.g., what it is like for me to *be* a psychoanalyst, what it is like to *be* crazy, what it is like to *be* in a state of desiring—over what we can ever *know* about such questions, Husserl's preoccupation. Despite the overlap between the two traditions, their respective aims are not always compatible. For the purposes of this book, whenever I employ the term "existential" I am presupposing a relationship between it and the phenomenological method, but separating personal experience from scientific considerations. My exploration of desire, for example, is not a scientific one but rooted solely in my personal experience of the matter, including what I have learned from my patients and the life I am living.

We are now ready to look at those clinicians identified with the existential tradition, as well as some who are not but nevertheless demonstrate an existential sensibility. First, I should further clarify how I employ the term "existential" in this book. I do not make a direct correlation between this term and any one of the existential philosophers listed above, though I draw from many of them, including Heidegger, Sartre, Nietzsche, Kierkegaard, Scheler, Merleau-Ponty, and others. For the purposes of this book and the collection of essays that comprise it, I use the term broadly, sometimes figuratively. For example, there are a number of psychoanalysts whom I believe embody what I call an existential *sensibility* in certain, if not all, aspects of their clinical work. Apart from Laing and those analysts who explicitly identify themselves with the existential philosophical tradition, I include D. W. Winnicott, Wilfried Bion, Jacques Lacan, Hans Loewald, Stanley Leavy, Martin Bergmann, Harry Stack Sullivan, Otto Allen Will, Jr., Edgar Levenson, Eric Fromm, Frieda Fromm-Reichmann, Clara Thompson, and even Sigmund Freud as only some of the analysts who embody an existential perspective in their approach to clinical practice. I could go over each one of them and identify those aspects of their thinking that I identify as existential, but I don't think I need to bother with that because it should be abundantly clear how I would do this by the time you have finished reading these essays. I want to use the remainder of this Preface to highlight some of the general features of what I mean by an existential sensibility and how that is employed in this volume.

My own approach to clinical practice is a hybrid of psychoanalysis and the existential philosophical tradition. This is an odd combination, to say the least, and I may be among the few people in the world who see psychoanalysis as deriving from that tradition.[4] I first encountered Freud when I was 16 and looking for something to read about sex, a topic that was then at the forefront of my attention. I discovered that he had written a book titled *Three Essays on the Theory of Sexuality* (1905). It wasn't exactly what I was looking for, but the book held me spellbound and completely changed the way I understood sex. It so happened that while I was reading my first book by Freud, I had also stumbled upon a book by Sartre titled *Nausea* (1964). All I knew about Sartre at the time was that he was associated with existentialism. I hadn't a clue what existentialism was, but I was drawn to the word and wanted to know more about it. Because it whetted my appetite for more, I found another book by Sartre, titled *Sketch for a Theory of the Emotions* (1962). Somehow, as I was reading these three books simultaneously, I came away with a sense that both Sartre and Freud, existentialist and psychoanalyst, were talking about the same thing, though employing different terminology. They were talking about a lot of the things I was feeling at the time and with which I was struggling: anxiety, frustration, desire, disappointment, boredom. I decided then and there that I wanted to be a philosopher and that, somehow or other, this would be my vocation once I became an adult.

Unfortunately, I was stuck in a small town in Tennessee, and the only access I had to ideas was the local library which, you might imagine, was lacking in philosophical or psychoanalytic works. Tennessee was foreign to me, and I was not a happy camper. My family had moved to Havana, Cuba, when I was a year old due to a business venture that took my father to that faraway island. He was a chemical engineer and went to Cuba from New York, where we lived at the time, to build a textile plant. A year later, by the time the project was completed, my father had fallen in love with Cuban culture and decided to live there, so that is where I spent my childhood until just before my fourteenth birthday, when we returned to, you guessed it, Tennessee, where my parents were from. The culture shock from Cuba to Tennessee was devastating for a fledgling teenager. Cuba was an amazing and magical place for a child to grow up. Cubans were sexy, stylish, playful, intelligent, classy. Havana was breathtakingly beautiful and a playground for the rich or adventurous. As they were among the few ex-patriot Americans on the island, my parents were friends with Ernest Hemingway and his wife, Mary, and my father took me with him occasionally when he met Hemingway at the Floridita Bar for daiquiris. I adored Hemingway and loved to hear his stories about living in Paris and Spain, places I longed to visit. I didn't quite register this at the time, but he also spoke of a French philosopher and novelist who was a friend of his and happened to be visiting Cuba with his girlfriend, Simon de Beauvoir. It was only later, when I found Sartre's book in the Elizabethton, Tennessee library, that I realized this was the thinker Hemmingway had been talking about.

Trying to adjust to a tiny little town in East Tennessee after the exotic and sophisticated Havana threw me into an existential crisis. Who was I, and what was I doing there? I felt *Angst*, boredom, dislocation. A year after we returned to Tennessee from Cuba, two years before my encounter with Freud and Sartre, my mother, who struggled with depression all her life, killed herself. I was 14. My mother was everything to me, and I had thought I was everything to her. After leaving Cuba, she and my father divorced, and I stayed with her in Tennessee when my father returned to New York. The loss of my mother was devastating and, for some years, unhinged me. I blamed my father for her death, so instead of opting to live with him, I stayed in Tennessee and lived with my maternal grandparents, with whom I had always been close. It was during this hiatus, wondering what life had in store for me next, that I began looking for answers in this small-town library. It was around this time that John F. Kennedy discovered the Soviet Union had planted missiles in Cuba, initiating the Cuban Missile Crisis. Everyone was convinced we were about to enter a nuclear war with Russia and that once it commenced, every eligible American male from 15 to 50 would be drafted into service. The crisis passed, but soon after Kennedy was assassinated, and the world came apart all over again.

I'm just trying to paint you a picture, a portrait of what my life was like at the time I discovered existentialism and psychoanalysis, the two disciplines that were to dominate my adult life. The world, my world, was in chaos. Two years later, when I turned eighteen, the Vietnam War was beginning to evolve into something huge and scary. The media was all over it, and there was talk of drafting massive numbers of young men to fight in Vietnam. Though I had planned to leave Tennessee after high school and bum around Europe, where I hoped to find myself, perhaps in some of the cafés frequented by Sartre and Hemingway, I enrolled in the local university for no other reason than to avoid the draft. The Tennessee motto happens to be the *Volunteer* State. You can think of this as the motto of a state, or as a state of mind. This went back to the Alamo when Davy Crockett and other Tennessee adventurers went to Texas to fight in what was to become the Mexican-American War. Ever since, Tennessee prided itself in being the first state in the union to send draftees to fight in American wars, including the First World War, the Second World War, and the Korean War. The Vietnam War was no exception. I knew that without a college deferment, I would be conscripted, so I enrolled in college in September of 1965, but by December, I received my draft notice. I was told by the local draft board, led by a crazy old coot named Herman Banner, who had fought in World War Two, where a huge chunk of his head was blown away, that I had failed to fill out a form I had (allegedly) been sent, and so was reclassified to active duty status. Though I protested, I learned that there was no judicial system that controlled the Selective Service System, the government entity that drafted young men into the Army. They were a law unto themselves, so the only judicial body one could appeal one's draft to was the same local board that had drafted you. I appealed, and, as you would expect, the appeal was rejected. I decided to enlist in the Army so that I could have a choice of duty and where I would be stationed, though to do so meant serving an extra two years in the military, for a total of four. I was promised I would serve in the Army Security Agency, the elite military arm of the National Security Agency and principal intelligence unit of the Army, and that I would be assigned to their post in Great Britain, as far away from Vietnam as I could get. Upon completing boot camp in the summer of 1966, I was told that I would indeed be assigned to the Army Security Agency as promised but that my first assignment was to be Tan Son Nhut Air Base in Vietnam, just outside Saigon. When I told my commanding officer that I had enlisted for an additional two years in order to avoid going to Vietnam, he got a huge laugh at my naïveté. He said, "Never believe what an enlistment officer tells you." A lesson learned, and one I would never forget. It was at that moment that I lost my innocence.

While in Vietnam, I felt even more resentful, desperate, and alone than I had been in Tennessee. My wish to get out of Tennessee had come true, but as Truman Capote once cautioned, beware of answered prayers. Along with all my cohorts at the 509th Radio Research Group, the thinly disguised intelligence base masquerading as a pool of clerk typists, I was convinced that fate had taken me to Vietnam for a reason: to die. I was convinced I would never live to see the U.S. again and that all the anguish I had suffered the past five years was a presage to where I now found myself, in a war no one believed in, against an enemy no one understood. I set about preparing for death by reading everything I could get my hands on. This was when I first encountered Nietzsche, Camus, Kafka, and Heidegger; all sent to me by my family in Tennessee. In this most existential of places, I readily embraced this tragic sense of life that Sartre, Nietzsche, and Kafka articulated so vividly. I found this strangely comforting, and I am certain it was what got me through that year, counting each day toward the magic number 365 when, perhaps, by the intervention of some miracle, I might return state-side. Though I couldn't believe I would really make it, I couldn't stop myself from hoping that I would. In spite of all my cynicism and self-doubt, my desire to live and carve out a life for myself persisted, stronger than ever. I believed I had my existentialist bedfellows to thank for that.

Those years, from 14 to 19, were pivotal for me and shaped the direction I was to follow when I finally returned home from Vietnam. What I realized once our plane touched down to safety was that the *Angst* I had experienced in Vietnam wasn't specific to a war zone, where one's life is literally on the line. By now, my *Angst* had become a constant companion, and I realized that this *Angst* is a constant in life and a friend, not an enemy. I had decided at the ripe age of 20 that I was going to become a psychoanalyst and devote myself to engaging others in the same kind of dialogues that Socrates had, thereby tying my twin passions together, philosophy and therapy. The coalescence of all these factors, my ejection from Cuba via revolution, the search for meaning in small-town Tennessee, the catastrophic loss of my mother, the alarm and sense of doom that occasioned the Cuban Missile Crisis, my abduction from college by my own government to the Red Zone of Vietnam, all these had made existential philosophy my religion, and my deliverance.

After separating from military service, I moved to San Francisco to resume college and study psychology. In 1970, psychology was the rage in America, and San Francisco was ground zero for all the interesting things that were happening in that field. LSD, yoga, Buddhism, meditation, City Lights Book Store in North Beach, the center of the Beat generation's writers and poets, including Ken Kesey, Jack Kerouac, Lawrence Ferlinghetti, sex, drugs, rock and roll, Jefferson Airplane, Grateful Dead. It was all happening. From the ridiculous to the sublime, from the hell of Tennessee and Vietnam to the utopia of San Francisco, I felt I had earned it, maybe even deserved it. Yet, hippy San Francisco was an intellectual wasteland, and psychology, despite all the hip accouterments and bell-bottom trousers, was, ultimately, superficial to me. Psychoanalysis was in retreat, and you had to be careful who you told that you read Freud. To my dismay, there was no Heidegger on the curriculum, no Sartre, no Nietzsche. In those days, anyone interested in integrating existentialism and psychoanalysis had to make do with a collection of essays by mostly German and French psychiatrists who struggled to adapt the philosophy of Martin Heidegger into their psychodynamic perspective, led by two Swiss analysts, Ludwig Binswanger (1963) and Medard Boss (1963).[5] These efforts were so mind-numbing and esoteric that it was impossible to detect any element of an existential sensibility in their work. Then R. D. Laing entered the picture.

I hadn't discovered Laing until I moved to California when, walking along Muir Beach a few miles north of San Francisco in Marin County, I struck up a conversation with an interesting stranger about philosophy and my interest in Sartre. The young man unceremoniously pulled out a paperback copy of *The Divided Self* from his backpack and handed it to me, to keep. "Here," he said, "I think you're going to like this." I never saw that love child again, but this kind of generosity wasn't unusual in 1970s San Francisco. In the following two years, I read everything Laing had published and became obsessed with his thinking and way of articulating the incredibly dense ideas with which he had such an easy facility. In the autumn of 1972, Laing paid a visit to Berkeley on a national lecture tour that billed him as "The Philosopher of Madness." Seeing him in person and then meeting him after his lecture was all the encouragement I needed to leave graduate school and move to London in order to study with him.

Now I will briefly describe the scene that Laing had created under the auspices of his organization, the Philadelphia Association,[6] the same organization that founded Kingsley Hall. This was no ordinary clinic or training institute. Though Laing's colleagues liked to say that he had established a therapy training program that integrated psychoanalysis, phenomenology, and Buddhism, there was no curriculum nor apparent requirement for graduation or length of training. The structure was ambiguous, to say the least, because there wasn't one. It wasn't at all clear how to get in, and it wasn't any more apparent when or how you finished. This was, I realized, the perfect existential training scheme and possibly the only genuinely existential organization in the world. With an unlisted phone number, it seemed to everyone from the way it operated that it even doubted its own existence! One encountered ambiguity at every turn. If you couldn't hack the uncertainty, you were probably not temperamentally suited to train there. I saw some students who were so confused and frustrated that they threw up their hands and left. I pitied them because they had no idea what they were walking out on. Courses, if you could call them that—a *salon*, really, that met in people's living rooms and were called seminars—were convened by Laing and his closest colleagues, Hugh Crawford and John Heaton. Other meetings were labeled Study Groups and were convened by therapists who had already trained with Laing and his cohorts, the first cohort group to emerge from his training. You might have three or four meetings clustered around a central theme that was opened for discussion. The meetings were heavy with philosophy, texts by Heidegger, Sartre, Merleau-Ponty, basically all the existential philosophers I mentioned above and more, plus Freud, Winnicott, Klein, Guntrip, Bion, Lacan, including myriad texts from various spiritual traditions, including Chan and Tibetan Buddhism, Zen, I Ching, Nagarjuna, Mircea Eliade, Joseph Campbell, Dionysius the Areopagite, you name it. Everything was introduced conversationally, almost in passing, introducing and synopsizing the topic to be explored, followed by informal discussion. Some meetings, you were expected to prepare for, and others, you simply listened to the presentation and did your best to follow. No written assignments, exams, papers, or evaluations. The only assessment was made by your control case supervisor, who, with your other supervisors, decided when you had been cooked enough to stop. The outcome was sometimes ambiguous. Had you "graduated" or not? Most students elected to continue attending the seminars even after they had ostensibly completed their training, not certain they had really finished.

No two experiences of training were the same. Each, as it were, was tailored to what seemed appropriate in each case and what you negotiated with each of your supervisors. For myself, training included living in Portland Road for four years, one of the post-Kingsley Hall houses that had been established by a close friend of Laing's, his fellow Glaswegian, Hugh Crawford. My analysis with Crawford and the time I spent at Portland Road were so enmeshed that it is impossible for me to imagine doing the one without the other. Yet, I was the only person living at Portland Road who was also training as a psychoanalyst. Most of the students in training opted out of living in one of the houses, concerned they might lose their minds. If they went crazy, then what? But, for me, the two experiences were inseparable. Perhaps my year in Vietnam served me in this. By the time I had got myself to London, virtually nothing fazed me. Living with crazy people while working as the Association's administrator and training as a psychoanalyst? Why not?

The training program was not specifically billed as training in "existential therapy." Neither was it billed as training in psychoanalysis. Yet, it was, in effect, a training in existential psychoanalysis, with a concerted emphasis on phenomenology, a term that no therapist, as far as I knew, used in those days or even understood. When I asked Laing why he and his colleagues decided against identifying their perspective as explicitly existential, despite that being the philosophical tradition to which he, Hugh Crawford, and John Heaton subscribed, he said that to do so would effectively place their schema in a box. They would be identified with an existential theory, and before you knew it, there would be talk of an existential technique, with diagrams, flow charts, subcategories of this and subcategories of that and, who knows? Maybe they could start dispensing degrees and certificates of completion, etc. They might as well kill themselves and get it over with.

I don't know what I was expecting, but it wasn't *that*. I realized that whatever this was, it wasn't going to be remotely conventional or even identifiable as a recognizable "psychoanalytic institute," the prototype for the dozen or so other such psychoanalytic training schemes in the greater London area, going back to the founding of the British Psychoanalytic Society and its cousin, the Tavistock Institute, where Laing himself trained and with which he had been affiliated before founding the Philadelphia Association in 1965. Once I became familiar with the scope of the curriculum, it became more evident where this was going. The reason the program wasn't characterized as a specifically *existential* training was because the texts or topics that were directly related to authors usually associated with that tradition were relatively few. Although everyone, Laing's colleagues as well as the students, were there because of Laing, who had read some, if not all, of his books, there were no courses on Laing or his published writings. He was the beacon, the light that drew us there. Once there, the canvas presented covered the entire history of Western philosophy and virtually all of the major Asian spiritual traditions and practices. In addition to what I have already mentioned, the thinkers that we studied, beginning with the Greek era, included the pre-Socratics, e.g., Democritus, Parmenides, Heraclitus, Thales; then Plato, Aristotle, the Hellenistic era, e.g., Epicurus, Zeno, Cicero, Marcus Aurelius, Pyrrho (through the eyes of Sextus Empiricus and Montaigne). Then there was the Christian era to contend with, including Augustine, Abelard, Philo, Meister Eckhart, Thomas a Kempis; then the modern era with Descartes, Hobbes, Hume, Berkeley, Kant, Hegel, and on and on. And this was just the Western philosophical tradition. Courses also touched on Hinduism and various Buddhist traditions, including Chan, Zen, and Tibetan; then the occultists, Gurdjieff, J.G. Bennett, Alice Baily, Madame Blavatsky, Francis Mott, the Theosophists. The psychoanalytic texts favored no one in particular. Instructors had their favorites, but you were exposed to anyone that someone found of interest, including Freud, Ferenczi, Rank, Adler, Abraham, Rado, and Groddeck. The British tradition was comprised of the Kleinians and just about everyone in the Middle School, including the Balints, Rycroft, Coltart, Stewart, Limentani, Klauber, and

Symington; and finally, Anna Freud and her cohorts at the Hampstead Clinic. The only Americans of interest were Sullivan and other interpersonalists who collaborated with him, the one psychoanalytic school in America that Laing was affiliated with. No ego psychology. I had never even heard of this brand of American psychoanalysis until I began reading Lacan's scathing rejection of it in the last years of my stay in Britain. (Naturally, all of the prominent existential analysts who had adapted Heidegger to their integration of the existential and psychoanalytic traditions [introduced to American practitioners by Rollo May in his seminal 1958 publication] were included, but I found their adaptation to existential mores somewhat lacking, and too wordy and abstract to properly capture the spirit of the highly *personal* existential perspective. Laing's own integration of these traditions was more radical and relied on all of the existential philosophical tradition, not only Heidegger.)

What did all these thinkers and clinicians have in common? That was for you to decide. You were given the palette; it was up to you to pick and choose what appealed to you and run with it. Behind all this inquiry into the history of Western and Eastern thought, however, was a sensibility even more basic than existentialism. Laing, Heaton, and Crawford were sceptics, who were deeply identified with the Greek sceptic tradition, specifically Pyrrho. Contemporary scepticism has a bad press, and no wonder. Going back to Plato's Academy, after his death, it became the seat of sceptic philosophy, but one that was a far cry from Pyrrhonism. Pyrrho's conception of scepticism was so different from what the Academic sceptics made of it that it is probably misleading to even call them sceptics. The Academics were only interested in epistemology and the nature of truth. Following Socrates, they claimed that no one knows the truth because the truth is impossible to know. Many of the most famous philosophers we studied, including Descartes, Hume, Berkeley, Hegel, and Husserl, had all studied Sextus Empiricus, the principal source of scepticism that has survived, and excepting Hume employed the sceptic method of *epoché* in order to pare away all claims to knowledge that could be eliminated.

The Pyrrhonists, on the other hand, were not so dogmatic as to claim that no one could ever possibly fathom what is true. They simply pointed out that, as far as we know, no one has yet found it, but we are compelled to search for it all the same. It is our search for knowledge and the open inquiry it occasions that makes life so interesting, and potentially wonderful. The result of such inquiry, as practiced by Pyrrho and his followers, the

Pyrrhonists, is that you never settle on anything as being incontrovertibly so because every question leads to another, and then another, etc. But neither do you rule anything out. You can neither claim nor deny anything with certainty. This is why psychoanalysis can be interminable. You never really get to the end of your self-inquiry. Yet, inquiring into the meaning of things is what life is about. Scepticism gives us the tools for a non-judgmental attitude with which to deal with our relationships with others, our anxieties and our suffering, our fear of death and of intimacy, and so on. It was this attitude, this sceptic sensibility, that guided the seminars that Laing and his colleagues convened, that was the source of their psychotherapy training, and that imbued their interpretation of the existential, or phenomenological, perspective. This was not an indoctrination into a way of seeing things. It was a "cure" for all the things we had been indoctrinated into over the course of our lifetimes, including our formal education.

But Laing and his cohorts were also very savvy, and *cool*. This was not an academic environment like you would find in an institution of "higher learning." Anything but. Kerouac and Ferlinghetti were just as valued as Heidegger and Merleau-Ponty because they were hip. Laing loved drugs, and virtually everyone there smoked pot, tripped on acid, and invested most of their time exploring the nether regions of inner as well as social space. Laing reasoned, how could you possibly imagine what it is like to be crazy unless you have tripped on acid, not once but frequently? I remember when I once asked Laing what he thought the elements of psychoanalytic training entailed. He said there were three components that one should experience: begin your analysis, read the collected works of Freud, and drop acid, but in no particular order!

I know I haven't provided a perfectly crafted encapsulation of what the term "existential" means. I have alluded to it, and perhaps that is the only authentic way of approaching the matter by allusion. I hope I have at least provided an appetizer, a taste of more to come. The rest of this book will be drawing from a variety of existential thinkers, and I will try my best to explain how I wed each to the psychoanalytic tradition, indeed, how psychoanalysis, in its latency, *has always been* existential, in the manner that I conceive the term. There is no existential theory nor an existential technique, for there is not, nor can there be, anything remotely resembling an existential "how to" by the numbers. Given its inchoate nature, existentialism, and any derivative approach to therapy, can never be articulated from a theoretical perspective that will meet with universal agreement. This is why existential psychoanalysis can only ever be rooted in a *sensibility* which, in turn, is based on a manner of being with another person that helps the practitioner adopt an open-minded way of getting to his (or her) colleagues and his patients.

When all is said and done, the existentialist sensibility is nothing more than a style of engagement that is at once personal and elusive, that haunts every moment of the time we allot ourselves to engage in that most mysterious and perplexing of callings, the therapeutic process.

Notes

1 From the film, *Blade Runner*, based on Dick's novel, *Do Androids Dream of Electric Sheep?*

2 For a more complete treatment of the sceptic tradition, see my essay, "The Sceptic Dimension to Psychoanalysis: Toward an Ethic of Experience" in Thompson, 2000.

3 For more on the relation between scepticism and postmodernism, see my article, "Postmodernism and Psychoanalysis: A Heideggerian Critique of Postmodern Malaise and the Question of Authenticity," 2004.

4 I see certain features of the twentieth-century existential tradition as having derived from Sigmund Freud. For more, see my *The Truth About Freud's Technique*, 1994.

5 See also May, Angel, and Ellenberger, 1958.

6 *Philadelphia*, from the Greek meaning brotherly or sisterly love, but more specifically, friendship (*philia*).

References

Binswanger, L. (1963) *Being-in-the-World: Selected Paper of Ludwig Binswanger* (J. Needleman, Trans.). New York: Basic Books.

Boss, M. (1963) *Psychoanalysis and Daseinsanalysis* (L. Lefebre, Trans.). New York: Basic Books.

Edie, J. (1962) Introduction. In P. Thévenaz (Ed.), *What is Phenomenology? And Other Essays*. Chicago: Quadrangle Books.

Freud, S. (1905/1953) *Three Essays on Sexuality*. Standard Edition (Vol. 7, pp. 125–245). London: Hogarth Press.

Freud, S. (1953–1973) *The Standard Edition of the Complete Psychological Works of Sigmund Freud* (24 vols; J. Strachey, Ed. & Trans.). London: Hogarth Press (Referred to in Subsequent References as Standard Edition).

Heidegger, M. (1962/1927) *Being and Time* (J. Macquarrie and E. Robinson, Trans.). New York: Harper and Row.

Kierkegaard, S. (1980) *The Sickness Unto Death: A Christian Psychological Exposition for Upbuilding and Awakening* (H. Hong and E. Hong, Eds. & Trans.). Princeton, NJ: Princeton University Press.

Laing, R. D. and Esterson, A. (1964/1971) *Sanity, Madness, and the Family: Families of Schizophrenics*. 2nd Edition. New York: Basic Books.

May, R., Angel, E. and Ellenberger, H. (Eds.). (1958) *Existence: A New Dimension in Psychiatry and Psychology* (Various Trans.). New York: Basic Books.

Merleau-Ponty, M. (1962) *Phenomenology of Perception* (C. Smith, Trans.). London: Routledge and Kegan Paul.

Safranski, R. (1998) *Martin Heidegger: Between Good and Evil* (E. Osers, Trans.). Cambridge, MA: Harvard University Press.

Sartre, J.-P. (1954/1943) *Being and Nothingness* (H. Barnes, Trans.). New York: Philosophical Library.

Sartre, J.-P. (1962) *Sketch for a Theory of the Emotions* (P. Mairet, Trans.). London: Methuen and Co.

Sartre, J.-P. (1964) *Nausea* (L. Alexander, Trans.). New York: New Directions.

St. John of the Cross. (2003) *The Dark Night of the Soul* (E. A. Peers, Trans.). New York: Dover Publications.

Thompson, M. G. (1994) *The Truth About Freud's Technique: The Encounter with the Real*. New York and London: New York University Press.

Thompson, M. G. (2000) The Sceptic Dimension to Psychoanalysis: Toward an Ethic of Experience. *Contemporary Psychoanalysis*, Vol. 36, No. 3: 457–481.

Thompson, M. G. (2004) Postmodernism and Psychoanalysis: A Heideggerian Critique of Postmodern Malaise and the Question of Authenticity. In J. Reppen, M. Schulman and J. Tucker (Eds.), *Way Beyond Freud: Postmodern Psychoanalysis Evaluated*. London: Open Gate Press.

Chapter 1

Sartre and Psychoanalysis

The Role of Freedom in the Clinical Encounter

The relationship between psychoanalysis and existentialism has always been an uneasy one, for myriad reasons. The antipathy between psychoanalysis and philosophy generally is undeniable, typically delineated on the frontier between the science of the unconscious, on the one extremity, and the science of the conscious, on the other. From there, misunderstandings and snap judgements explode. Instead of obvious collaboration, we get competition and vitriol. And then there are the existential philosophers. Who can understand them? Though many existentialist thinkers are cited among the few psychoanalysts who read them, those that have had the most radical impact are Fredrich Nietzsche, Martin Heidegger, and Jean-Paul Sartre. All three figure prominently in this book. I will begin with Sartre.

Sartre's relationship with psychoanalysis is broad, for Sartre had a lot to say about it in multiple contexts. Given the breadth, I will limit my focus for now to its relevance in the clinical situation. My relationship with Sartre and psychoanalysis is complex and deeply personal. I discovered Sartre in my teens; the perfect age, looking back, to make his acquaintance. I grew up in Cuba in the 1950s, where my father, an American entrepreneur and chemical engineer, became friends with Ernest Hemingway, among the few American expatriates living on the Island. I was fond of Hemingway and remember his mentioning his friend, Sartre, who was about to visit Cuba with Simone de Beauvoir after Castro seized power. Hemingway thought that Sartre was something of a shit, the epitome of the French intellectual that Hemingway got to know when living in Paris in the 1920s. But he admired Sartre's writing, as well as his celebrity, and, most of all, he admired his fame and his success. Though Sartre was not awarded the Nobel Prize for literature until after Hemingway's death (which Hemingway won in 1954), they were bonded by Hemingway's impact on French writing, including Sartre's, and

DOI: 10.4324/9781003429104-1

their mutual admiration. They were both non-conformists, and they each insisted that the only way to live is authentically, no matter the cost. One of the things I admired most about Hemingway was that he knew how to *live*. He loved the life he was living and treated it as an adventure. Hemingway and Sartre were, as my Irish grandmother once suggested, a pair to draw to.

I was too young to read Sartre then, but a few years later, after my family had abandoned Cuba for their native Tennessee, I checked him out. Sartre introduced me to existential philosophy, and it became a sort of religion for me, if a secular one. This was also around the time I discovered Sigmund Freud, and I formed this surprising idea that Sartre and Freud were saying the same thing but in different languages. In the years that followed, I managed to get through Sartre's early philosophical works, but it was the section devoted to existential psychoanalysis in *Being and Nothingness* that riveted my attention. By the time I graduated from high school, I had decided I was going to become an existential psychoanalyst—whatever that was.

Life has a funny way of throwing us a curve now and then. Without warning, Tennessee drafted me into the Army and sent me to Vietnam in the summer of 1966. Like many of my compatriots there, I was convinced I was sent there to die. I was lucky, however, to be assigned to an intelligence unit in Saigon, and this afforded me the luxury of reading in my off time. I dove into Sartre and Nietzsche. They taught me that we are always dying and that the closer we get to death, the more precious life becomes. I think Sartre especially helped me live my death and survive it, and for that, I will always be grateful.

After I separated from the Army, I moved to San Francisco to study psychology. That was when I discovered R. D. Laing, the Scottish psychiatrist and existential psychoanalyst. By 1970, Laing was the most famous psychiatrist in the world due to his bestselling books and his groundbreaking work with schizophrenia. I was soon on my way to London, having abandoned my graduate studies in order to work with him.

Like me, Laing was passionate about Sartre. One may even read Laing's classic, *The Divided Self,* as an integration of Sartre's philosophy and object relations theory. This was unusual. Nearly all the psychiatrists who were drawn to existential philosophy after World War II embraced Heidegger, not Sartre. Perhaps this was because so many of them were German-speaking psychiatrists or because they were captivated by Heidegger's impenetrable prose. Or they may have been put off by Sartre, the bad boy of existential philosophy. Perhaps worst of all, Sartre was a Frenchman!

I think what bonded me to Laing was that we had both discovered Sartre in our youth, in the throes of rebelliousness and were each drawn to his contempt for everything *bourgeois* and conventional. This attitude is not typical of people who choose to enter the so-called mental health professions. As a class, I would characterize my colleagues as unremittingly conventional, uncommonly anxious, materialistic social climbers. I know this sounds harsh, even petty, yet some of my best friends are psychoanalysts. I love them all the same. But this is the kind of observation that Sartre inspired, perhaps the reason why few of my colleagues gravitated to him.

What I want to talk about here, however, is Sartre's relationship with Freud, epitomized by his critique of psychoanalysis in *Being and Nothingness*. Freud, too, was a bad boy, a troublemaker, and obsessed with sex. This was probably what drew me to him as a teenager. Sartre and Freud: *another* pair to draw to. So here I am, in the company of the three bad boys of the twentieth-century *avant-garde*: Sartre, Laing, and Freud. I was in heaven.

So, what is the relation between Sartre and psychoanalysis? I suspect some of you are familiar with what he says about this in *Being and Nothingness*, but if you aren't, we'll have to save that for another day. Instead, I want to focus on how Sartre's thinking transformed psychoanalysis into a truly human, which is to say, inherently personal, way of engaging clinical practice. In order to do this, I will explore three topics that are basic to understanding the therapeutic process. The first concerns Freud's conception of the *unconscious*. The second is Sartre's conception of *freedom* and the role it plays in psychoanalysis. And third, what do we make of the concept of *change*? How does this come about? And what, exactly, do we mean by change?

Freud's Conception of Psychic Reality

Let's begin with Freud's theory of the unconscious and the problems this concept continues to engender. Freud's first topography for demarcating a distinction between conscious and unconscious aspects of the mind concerned the nature of fantasy and the role it plays in neurosis. After he experimented with and subsequently rejected hypnotism, Freud surmised that each person is preoccupied with two kinds of fantasies: one I am aware of and the other I am not. Freud opted to label those that I am not aware of "unconscious" because we have no reflective experience of them. These so-called unconscious fantasies have been repressed and are inaccessible to us, but because they still reside "in" the unconscious, they engender psychic conflict, which manifests in our dream life as well as our psychopathology, including neuroses and psychoses.

Freud's first, topographical model of the unconscious was simple: one portion of the mind is conscious, and the thoughts it contains are in the forefront of awareness (i.e., *reflective experience*), whereas another portion of the mind is unconscious and composed of fantasies of which I am not consciously aware. Freud also included a third element in this topography, the preconscious, which contains unconscious thoughts and memories that can be recollected at will. Freud's topographical model served as a map of what he terms "psychic reality." Freud's depiction of psychic reality is necessarily contrasted by Freud with *factual* reality, which is investigated by the empirical sciences and readily available for study.

Yet, in what sense can one treat fantasies as "realities" when, after all, they are not real? Freud recognized that fantasies can be *experienced* as real in a similar way that objective reality is experienced. In other words, fantasies, though not literal depictions of the past, nevertheless convey meaning, and such meanings are capable of telling us more about our patients than the so-called facts of their history. By *interpreting* both fantasies and their consequent symptoms as meaningful, Freud was able to obtain truths about his patients that were otherwise hidden. His opposition between psychic and external realities served to juxtapose an inherently personal reality with a more concrete one. This isn't to say that concrete, or objective, reality is necessarily false, but it was Freud's genius to see that the truth about one's history can be derived from the communication of otherwise innocuous reflections by interpreting a patient's fantasies as disguised messages. The recognition that fantasies could be conceived as messages suggested there was something concealed in them that the patient neither recognized nor understood.

This means that fantasies serve a purpose: they disclose the intentional structure of our deepest longings and aspirations. *They tell us what we desire*. But Freud lacked a conception of intentionality that could explain how his patients were able to convey truths they didn't "know" in a disguised and indirect manner. In other words, his patients *unconsciously intended* their symptoms and the attendant fantasies that explained them—they weren't "caused" by their unconscious. Yet, Freud seemed conflicted as to the origin of such symptoms. He never entirely abandoned the idea that they must be *caused* by some traumatic something or other, a notion more popular today than ever. If not external reality, do they perhaps originate in the vicissitudes of our unconscious fantasy life?

Despite the recent development of relational analysis, which claims to approach the treatment situation from a more interpersonal perspective, contemporary psychoanalysts, with few exceptions, find it agreeable to use terms in which the *impersonal* aspect of the unconscious predominates. Analysts remain wedded to the notion that non-personal aspects of the mind account for the unconscious motives that guide us in our daily affairs, which in turn produce our psychopathology.

Sartre's Critique of the Unconscious

Whereas Freud depicted psychoanalysis as a science of the *unconscious*, it is impossible to deny that it is also a science—if we can call it that—which is preoccupied with *consciousness*, if only implicitly. Terms like truth, epistemology, knowledge, understanding, and comprehension pervade every psychoanalytic paper that is devoted to the unconscious as a concept. This is also the subject matter to which Sartre, Merleau-Ponty, Heidegger, and Ricoeur devoted a considerable amount of their philosophical writings: what is the nature of knowledge and what role does it serve in our everyday lives? Of all the phenomenologists, it was Sartre who took psychoanalysis the most seriously, even conceiving his own brand of "existential psychoanalysis" (1981).

In Sartre's critique of psychoanalysis (1962, pp. 48–55; 1981, pp. 153–171), he rejected Freud's topographical model for reasons similar to what Freud eventually rejected himself. In the topographical model, the only thing separating the system-conscious from the system-unconscious is the so-called "censor," which, according to Freud, regulates what is permitted into consciousness and, contrariwise, what is repressed into the unconscious. This means that the censor is aware of everything, that which is conscious and unconscious alike. Yet, because the ego is *unaware* of the censor, this model posits a *second* consciousness (the censor) that is both unknown and unknowable to the ego. Sartre's problem with this model is obvious: the so-called censor is the de facto "person" who is being analyzed and disclaims knowledge of all the shenanigans he employs in order to disguise what he is up to, an edition of what Sartre terms "bad faith," or inauthenticity. Freud also had problems with the implications of a "second thinking subject" and decided to discard this model for one that contained only one subject that *knows*—the conscious portion of the ego—and not one, but three subjects that do not know anything: the id, the superego, and the unconscious portion of the ego (which employs defense mechanisms).

Freud's subsequent revision of his earlier model, however, fares little better in Sartre's opinion. The topographical model is replaced with one that is less concerned with demarcating conscious and unconscious portions of the psyche than with determining the complex nature of psychic agency, or subjectivity. Sartre's complaint with the new model is that it still fails to resolve the problem of *bad faith*, the problem of a "lie without a liar." If anything, the new model gets even further away from Sartre's efforts to *personalize* the unconscious by instituting three psychic agencies that protect the conscious ego from any responsibility for its actions. *How would Sartre propose to remedy this situation, to account for those actions that Freud claimed the "conscious" patient is "unconscious" of devising, while holding the conscious patient responsible for performing them?*

Sartre accomplishes this by introducing two sets of critical distinctions into the prevailing psychoanalytic vocabulary. The first is a distinction between pre-reflective consciousness and reflective consciousness, and the second is between consciousness and knowledge. Sartre summarizes the basic dilemma in Freud's conception of the unconscious with the following questions: how can the subject not know that he is possessed of a feeling or sentiment that he is in possession of? And, if the unconscious is just another word for *consciousness* (Sartre's position), how can the subject not know what he is *de facto* conscious of? Sartre's thesis on pre-reflective consciousness is his effort to solve this riddle. Following Husserl, Sartre saw consciousness as *intentional*, which means it is always conscious *of* something. This means there is no such thing as empty consciousness, nor is there such a thing as a container or receptacle that houses consciousness. Instead, consciousness is always outside itself and "in" the things that constitute it as consciousness-*of* something. In Sartre's (1957) words:

> Intentionality is not the way in which a subject tries to make "contact" with an object that exists beside it. *Intentionality is what makes up the very subjectivity of subjects.*
>
> (pp. 48–49) [emphasis in original]

In other words, the concept of intentionality renders subjectivity as already a *theory of intersubjectivity*, since to *be* a subject is to be engaged with some thing "other" than one's self—even if this other something is merely an idea. Sartre elaborates on how this thesis would be applied to the social world in this famous passage:

> When I run after a streetcar, when I look at the time, when I am absorbed in contemplating a portrait, there is no *I* (or "ego"). There is [only] consciousness *of the streetcar-having-to-be-overtaken*, etc. . . . In fact, I am then plunged into the world of objects; it is *they* which constitute the unity of my consciousness; it is *they* which present themselves with values, with attractive and repellent qualities—but *me*—I have disappeared; I have annihilated myself [in the moment of conscious apprehension].
>
> (pp. 48–49)

This means that when I experience a rock, a tree, a feeling of sadness, or the object of my desire in the bedroom, I experience them just where they are: beside a hill, on the meadow, in my heart, in relation to myself and my beloved. Consciousness and the object-of-consciousness are given in one stroke. These things constitute my consciousness of them just as I constitute their existence *as* things through the act by which I perceive them and give them a name. And because naming things is a purely human activity, these things do not exist as rocks, trees, or emotions in the absence of a human consciousness that can apprehend them through the constitutive power of language.

Yet, such acts of apprehension don't necessarily imply *knowledge* of what I am conscious of. This is because Sartre distinguishes between the pre-reflective apprehension of an object and our reflective "witnessing" of the act. Ordinarily, when I am pre-reflectively conscious of a feeling, for example, I intuit the feeling of sadness and, in turn, reflectively acknowledge this feeling *as* sadness: I feel sad and experience myself as a sad person simultaneously. But I am also capable of feeling sadness, or anger, or envy without *knowing* I am sad, or angry, or envious. When this is suggested to me by my analyst, I am surprised by this observation. Initially, I may resist my analyst's interpretation and reject it. But I may eventually come to admit it because, once brought to my attention, I am also capable, upon reflection, of recognizing that this feeling is *mine*. Sartre argues that I would be incapable of recognizing thoughts or ideas that I claim no awareness of *unless I had been conscious of these feelings in the first place, on a pre-reflective level*. Though conscious, the pre-reflective isn't known. According to Sartre, it is *lived*.

In other words, what Freud labels consciousness, Sartre designates reflective consciousness (i.e., knowing *that* I am conscious of this or that), and what Freud labels the unconscious, Sartre designates as that moment of pre-reflective consciousness that, due to *bad faith*, has not yielded to reflective awareness and, with that awareness, knowledge of it. This is why I can be conscious of something that I have no immediate knowledge of, and why I can become knowledgeable about something that I am, so to speak, "unconscious" of, but am subsequently able to acknowledge. This implies that I can only actually *experience* something I have knowledge of, but not of what I am only pre-reflectively conscious.

The difference between Sartre's and Freud's respective formulations isn't that it merely substitutes Freud's terminology with Sartre's. On a more radical level, it eliminates a need for the notion of a second thinking subject *behind* or beneath consciousness and offers a way to personalize the unconscious in a manner that eluded Freud.

Sartre and Emotions

I now want to review Sartre's critique of the emotions and his transformation of a psychoanalysis rooted in psychology to one rooted in phenomenology. First, I want to ask, what *are* emotions? There is no shortage of theories that try to tackle this problem, yet no consensus on a definition. For some, emotions are distinct from cognition and judgment, while for others, our feelings are central to decision-making and even determine our judgments. It is undeniable that emotions tell us things that our cognitions often miss. Moreover, emotions are often the driving force behind our motivations, whether positive or negative. And what about the relationship between emotion and desire? Are emotions derived from desires, or are they determinants? Whatever they are, we cannot deny that we would not be human without them.

The term "emotion" dates back to 1579 when it was adapted from the French *émouvoir*, meaning "to stir up." It was first introduced to academic circles to replace a similar term, passion. Though the two terms have often been used interchangeably, passion is typically employed when referring to sexual feelings. There is also the problem with their respective etymology. Passion derives from the Latin *pati*, meaning to suffer or endure. One can see why the term passion began to take on different connotations than when simply feeling this or that. The French *émouvoir* appeared to solve the problem. Like the term "feeling" with which emotion is used synonymously, an emotion is of brief duration, whereas moods last longer. The more recent "affect," adopted by psychoanalysis, encompasses all three.

Psychoanalysis went a long way in explaining how human behavior is not orchestrated by random events because actions always have a motive, an intention, a specific end, even if we are ignorant of what the end is. Psychoanalysts were the first to emphasize the *significance* of psychic phenomena, that this seemingly innocent thought or emotion often stands for something else. The child who steals from his mother's purse is only trying to reclaim the mother's love. A girl who faints at the sight of parsley can't bring herself to recall a painful childhood incident when she was forced to eat vegetables. Yet, often as not, the psychoanalytic interpretation, if only surreptitiously, tends to privilege causal antecedents masquerading as interpretations in order to explain pathogenic behavior. History plays a crucial role in our lives, and this is just as true for people suffering from emotional disturbance. This is why I can project onto all women the quality of withholding because my mother was too depressed to comfort my needs. Each time I feel attracted to a woman, I find myself consumed with ambivalence, fear, consternation. The feelings I experience in these situations not only color my understanding of reality, but, to a significant degree, they determine *who I am.*

Freud's term for that traumatic moment every child is supposed to experience is the *Oedipus* complex. What makes this complex so compelling is the sense of betrayal that occasions it, feelings with which every boy or girl must eventually come to terms. I cannot say whether Sartre was influenced by Freud's dark assessment that love plays in our lives. Their respective views on the matter are remarkably similar and form the basis of Sartre's many plays and novels.

Emotions may be pleasing or painful. The pleasurable kind we don't question until they become self-destructive, but, even then, we rarely oppose them. The painful variety is more invasive, and problematic. Because they elicit distress, we can bear them for only so long. Like Jason clutching the Medusa, we divert our eyes and conceal our experience of them with magic, what Freud termed defense mechanisms. Our emotional life, always a mystery to us, inhabits a spectrum between desire and anxiety, each feeding the other. If we are creatures of desire, and anxiety is the price we pay for emotions, then they must be entangled inside those desires in principle.

Emotions are not merely barometers that tell me when my desires are satisfied or thwarted. They also possess an intelligence of their own that aims to make my life as agreeable as possible. That's not all. My emotions also shelter me from realities that are too painful to stomach. Sartre suggested that emotions are our way of magically transforming a situation we get stuck in, like a fly on a sticky mat, that we can neither accommodate nor escape. In other words, emotions provide a way of escaping situations that would otherwise drive me crazy. According to Sartre:

> When the paths before us become too difficult, or when we cannot see our way, we can no longer put up with such an exacting and difficult world. All ways are barred and nevertheless we must act. So then we try to change the world; that is, to live it as though the relation between things and their potentialities were not governed by deterministic processes, but by magic.
>
> (1962, p. 63)

The woman who faints at the sight of her attacker does so not because it reminds her of some previous event but because it removes her, albeit magically, from the present situation. She no longer has to face the immediate danger she is in. But this isn't to say she willfully faints with deliberation. She is seized by the situation, a situation that makes demands on her and with which she is unable to cope. Or rather, her manner of coping is so ingenious that it is unrecognizable, as such, to the unwary observer. The unlikelihood of finding a solution to the problem she faces demands that she invent a solution instead. If she can't take flight in reality, she can do so emotionally, which is to say, magically. Yet, an emotional response isn't just a substitute for other kinds of action, other ways of coping, because it isn't effectual. It doesn't act on the world but merely changes my perception of it.

On a more basic level, emotion is a structure of desire. It may be a way of enhancing a desire I enjoy, or a way of coping with a desire that is too risky, by fearing it. The person in danger wants to be somewhere else, so the fainting magically fulfills the wish to disappear. Similarly, if I want something I cannot have, my emotions can help remove the desire itself, allowing me to escape from bitter disappointment. Sartre invokes the sour grapes analogy as a common rationalization for this strategy.

Sartre's purpose in his early phenomenological study, *Sketch For A Theory Of The Emotions* (1962), was to show why behaviorism is incapable of explaining the phenomenon of emotions because behaviorism is stuck in a cause-and-effect universe that cannot account for the *intentional structure* of our motives, our folly, or our madness. Psychoanalysis goes further because it is sensitive to human agency but then ascribes our motivations to "unconscious" responses to trauma that, if we aren't careful, may be just as causal as behaviorism. At its best, what is often lacking in the psychoanalytic explanation is the personal dimension to motives because unconscious motives are not, strictly speaking, personal, so we cannot take responsibility for them.

Freedom and Choice

So, what are therapy patients supposed to make of this? How are they supposed to effect change in their lives? Isn't the purpose of therapy to change our manner of being in the world and improve it? How can this happen without turning the therapeutic situation into a *technology*? The essential task of existential psychoanalysis as envisioned by Sartre is hermeneutic, that is, deciphering the meaning of acts in relation to a synthetic totality underpinned by an original project of being, manifested in a fundamental choice. But what is choice, exactly? We ordinarily speak of choice as a volitional, deliberate act that is transparent to itself. This suggests that we are always ahead of our choices, that we weigh them in our minds and, having decided upon this or that option, execute them. Sartre is even sometimes accused of adopting this model, but it isn't that simple.

Say I want to go to the cinema. Which movie do I choose to go see? I look at the options and pick this one over the other. There! I have deliberated, weighed my options, and chosen the one most desirable. Or have I? One of the things that both Freud and Sartre share in common is that neither buys this explanation. Though separated by an enormous gulf in theory, temperament, and vocation, each concluded, as did Heidegger, that choices are free but not willful. Instead, they are predetermined. Something or other *predisposed* me to making that choice. Freud would say I did so unconsciously, whereas Sartre would argue that the choice occurred on a pre-reflective level. In both cases, it wasn't my ego or "I" that chose the action. The choice executed was rendered before the fact, beneath awareness, in my engagement with the world. The so-called *conscious* choice merely makes it official after the fact.

In other words, I cannot get ahead of my choices; I am always one step behind, as they guide me this way or that, so the choices themselves, and the reasons I make them, are often puzzling. This is why psychoanalysis, as envisioned by Freud, is always retrospective, not prophylactic. Only in behavioral psychology do we play the fiction of deliberating what we intend to do, and then execute the act. In psychoanalysis, the idea is to review *previous* actions and to learn something about ourselves from them. The actions reviewed may be buried in our childhoods, or they may have occurred moments earlier in the analytic session. In either case, we are not talking about an executive function but a *reflective* one.

This has led some commentators to conclude that Freud's conception of the unconscious was deterministic. If we don't make our choices "consciously," which is to say, *voluntaristically*, then our choices must be made *for* us—by our unconscious. This implies that there is no free choice in the matter if my choices aren't willfully executed. Psychoanalysts make this assumption because the unconscious is supposed to be *impersonal*, not personal. In Freud's tri-partite structure, it isn't "me" guiding my decisions, but the *id*, Latin for "it." This is the crux of Sartre's problem with the psychoanalytic conception of the unconscious, the problem of a lie without a liar, a thought without a thinker, an action without an actor.

What is at stake here is our notion of the self, what comprises the self, and how free the self is. For Sartre, there is no self, so to speak, no "I", not even a subject, if by subject we mean some sort of entity that, like the censor, orchestrates our lives *via* executive decision-making.

Unlike Freud, Sartre roots the person not in psychology, but in *situation*, in the world to which we belong, the world where we live and die. All of my choices derive from my engagement with that world, not in my psychology. That doesn't mean that I am determined by that engagement. I *am* that engagement. I have choices in the matter, and those choices are free, but that doesn't mean I am in control of the situation or the choices I make. The fact that my choices are free doesn't make me Superman. Freedom doesn't make me omnipotent. It isn't a freedom to rule, but a freedom to be me, and to ultimately embrace the me that I am.

This means that my choices are ontological rather than deliberate. Sartre suggests our neuroses go all the way back to a fundamental choice, in childhood, when we chose what our neurosis would be, on a pre-reflective level. In other words, we *intend* our psychopathology; we are not the consequence of this or that trauma. Contrary to behaviorism, or even psychoanalysis, nothing *caused* my condition. Rather, I *chose* to experience this or that incident *as* traumatic.

Given this thesis, how is therapy even possible? If I cannot will myself to health, then how does it come about? As Kierkegaard would say, through indirection. In this context, all my conscious, knowing mind is good for is to acquaint myself with the mystery of my existence and to plumb its depths over an unpredictable amount of time. I cannot will myself to overcome my fear of intimacy. I cannot compel myself to love more fully, behave more compassionately, or feel more alive. Yet, all of these transitions may and often do result from the analytic endeavor. How? We don't know, exactly. All we do know is that knowing oneself has the potential to change our lives in this way, to become who we are, authentically. If we are intrepid, over time, this process of self-reflection may result in a change of perspective and with it, a change in our selves, which is to say, our lives.

This can only happen indirectly, over time, *without ever knowing that we have made these changes until after having made them*—and without ever knowing why.

This is where authenticity comes into the picture. When I tell myself I hate the person I am, that I cannot give up my addictions, that I wish I could be more this or less of that, I am basically lying to myself. Because every choice I make is a free choice, and because everything that I am is a consequence of the choices I have rendered, I am always the person I wish to be. To be in conflict with myself is to pretend that something or other has "caused" me to be this way—something other than my free choice to be this way or that. This is inauthenticity, or bad faith, in its essence.

This also means that the goal of existential psychoanalysis is to *become* the person I am already, unreservedly, wholeheartedly, passionately, not ambivalently or reluctantly. This is not an ethical endeavor, to make me a "better person." I don't know if Sartre would agree with this, but it seems to me this form of radical self-acceptance that it aspires to is an act of love. It entails falling in love with the person I am and always have been, the same person who lived this life, and suffered its folly, up to this very moment in time. I hope Sartre will forgive me for this, but at the end of the day, existential psychoanalysis is nothing more or less than a cure through love.

Conclusion

In conclusion, how has this perspective affected my way of working with psychoanalytic patients? I think, perhaps like all analytic practitioners, I assumed early in my career, going back some forty years or so, that the therapeutic enterprise was all about change. This word has always haunted me. I remember thinking that I wanted to tackle this problem head-on, and to write a book about change, what it is, how it is effected, and so on. I abandoned this project once I realized that the very concept of change is problematic. We don't even know what it is. It was only later, when I had absorbed some insights from the existential philosophical tradition, that I finally came to realize that psychoanalysis isn't about change but rather becoming. Change implies that something that is should be discarded and replaced with something else. This works fine in the physical universe, where we readily change one flat tire for a new one, a house we no longer cherish for one more desirable, and so on. But you don't discard the person you are for a new, improved model. You are stuck with who you are, for better or worse, for life. This is when it came to me that we are always becoming, but not, strictly speaking, changing. In becoming, we are always what and who we are, but we are never finally that person until the end, until the day we die. Meantime, we are constantly, ceaselessly, becoming more and more ourselves. But this becoming isn't a panacea.

Without reflection, without care, and without concerted effort to reflect on our situation, we may very well simply become more and more miserable instead, more and more alienated from ourselves in order to escape the anguish of living. Existential psychoanalysis provides an opportunity to become something different than that. It offers the opportunity, with no guarantees, to become more and more the magnificent creature that we already are. Once on the road to becoming and embracing ourselves, we have a chance to be at peace with ourselves. When we are finally at peace with ourselves, we are at peace with the world.

References

Sartre, J.-P. (1957) *The Transcendence of the Ego* (F. Williams and R. Kirkpatrick, Trans.). New York: Noonday Press.

Sartre, J.-P. (1962) *Sketch for a Theory of the Emotions* (P. Mairet, Trans.). London: Methuen and Co.

Sartre, J.-P. (1981) *Existential Psychoanalysis* (H. Barnes, Trans.). Washington, DC: Regnary Gateway.

Chapter 2

Nietzsche and Psychoanalysis

The Fate of Authenticity in a Postmodernist World

In the past few decades, postmodernism has captured the attention of a generation of artists, intellectuals, and authors to such a degree that the term has even crept into the comparatively sober psychoanalytic literature, the last place one would expect to find it. Yet, any marriage between the psychoanalytic treatment perspective, with its painstaking, laborious pace, and postmodernism, with its premium on the arcane and the fashionable, is unlikely, if not altogether illogical. What would genuine postmodern psychoanalysis entail if indeed such were possible?

In addressing this question, I will explore how postmodernism insinuated its way into the contemporary cultural milieu, examine where the basic threads of the postmodernist impulse originate, and assess its impact on the theory and practice of psychoanalysis. I will argue that the postmodern perspective originated with Nietzsche and that contemporary characterizations of it are comparatively superficial and nihilistic departures from its original inspiration.

Nietzsche's Impact on the Postmodern Perspective

Although postmodernism was only recently introduced into philosophical debate by Jean-Francois Lyotard, it is commonly acknowledged that the concept alludes to a sensibility that has haunted Western culture since the nineteenth century, beginning with Nietzsche. In fact, many of the tenets that form the corpus of Nietzsche's philosophy are basic elements of the postmodern perspective. Yet, postmodernism is not a philosophical school that one can simply adopt or reject but a movement in culture that, like the object of psychoanalytic inquiry, sneaks upon us unawares, as though we had hardly been conscious of its presence.

DOI: 10.4324/9781003429104-2

Nietzsche was an unusual philosopher in that he didn't write systematic narratives on epistemology or metaphysics but instead wrote in aphorisms that resemble the pre-Socratic philosophers whom Nietzsche greatly admired. One of the reasons Nietzsche (1967) rejected questions about the nature of truth and reality was because he believed the foundations of philosophy should be overturned in light of his thesis that God is dead and that we are alone in the universe without an ultimate purpose or reason. Nietzsche's anti-foundationalism is a core of both his philosophy and the contemporary postmodern perspective. Nietzsche's (1994) real target in his attack on Christianity, however, was not God but the reliance on any authority that presumes to tell us how we should live our lives. In Nietzsche's estimation, anyone who needs universal values to guide his or her actions is simply being dishonest with themselves, or inauthentic. Similarly, Nietzsche rejected the worship of science and progress, which he viewed as palliatives for the masses that serve to keep them in line while saving them the trouble of assuming responsibility for their lives.

Like Montaigne and Schopenhauer before him, Nietzsche was a sceptic and disputed our capacity to know anything except our own experience—and even that is open to doubt! In contrast, most philosophers begin with a core of beliefs that are taken to be self-evidently true, such as the existence of a physical world. Such beliefs may be reasonable, but proving them, as many sceptics have demonstrated, is virtually impossible. The problem with such beliefs, though innocent enough in themselves, is that they lead to other assumptions that are also impossible to prove but are nonetheless employed to "explain" things that we cannot know, such as the purported "contents" of the unconscious. Ironically, Nietzsche is credited as one of the original proponents of the unconscious, but he used it as one of his weapons against science, which Nietzsche accused of pretending to explain everything. This anomaly implies that some conceptions of the unconscious are consistent with scepticism, whereas others are unabashedly dogmatic.

A favorite target of Nietzsche's scepticism was the Enlightenment, a cultural era that began towards the end of the seventeenth century. Though there is considerable debate as to what the Enlightenment was and whether we are still living in it, it has had a decisive impact on the role science and politics play in contemporary society. Nietzsche rejected the values of the Enlightenment and Enlightenment philosophers such as Descartes, who held that our capacity for reason is the basis of what makes us human. Other Enlightenment philosophers, such as Rousseau, emphasized the relation between reason and political progress. Like Descartes, Rousseau believed that humans are rational creatures whose capacity for reason makes them autonomous in their decision-making, manifested in the free and informed selection of political candidates in electoral democracies. Other Enlightenment philosophers, such as Kant, emphasized the relationship between reason and ethics. According to Kant, Enlightenment values gave Europeans an unprecedented degree of self-confidence in their pursuit of scientific, political, and moral progress, all fundamental tenets of the Enlightenment.

If fact, if the Enlightenment can be said to embody one value above all the others, it is epitomized by the belief in "progress." This value, in particular, defines the Modern era, more or less consistent with the Enlightenment. Following Darwin, the belief in progress assumes that all living organisms are in an inexorable process of evolution, though humans, due to their capacity for rationality, are able alone to influence the course that science and society follow. The Enlightenment's inherent Utopianism derives from the conviction that society will inevitably improve from one generation to the next and that scientific breakthroughs will make our material existence easier and, so, more rewarding. Nietzsche rejected this assumption and countered that, in other respects, our lives are actually getting worse because the more passionate side of our existence obeys neither science nor reason and is even suppressed by them, a view that anticipated and arguably influenced Freud's views about civilization. According to Nietzsche, every human being has to come to terms with the same problems that have beset human existence since the beginning of recorded history: how to be at peace with ourselves, how to live with others, and how to make the most of what life has to offer. In Nietzsche's opinion, our capacity to reason is not as objectively reliable as Enlightenment philosophers claimed because humans are driven by passion, the source of which is predominantly unconscious.

Another component of Nietzsche's scepticism is his historical relativism, which is consistent with his perspectivism. Relativism argues that all so-called truths are relative to a time and place and not eternal or objective but highly personal and fluid, whereas perspectivism is based on the idea that truth is wedded to the perspective of the person who promotes it. Because everyone's perspective is different, not merely from one person to another but from one moment or situation to the next, each of us abides by different truths at different times and occasions, so the task of ever knowing ourselves and others is constantly unfolding. Another, more contemporary way of putting this is that reality is what we interpret it to be and that our interpretations are more indebted to our passions than our reasons. Nietzsche's view that knowledge is culture-bound has also influenced contemporary philosophers of science, such as Thomas Kuhn (1962).

Yet another target of Nietzsche's assault on the Enlightenment was Descartes's belief in the "self." Disturbed by the rising influence of scepticism among thinkers of his generation, Descartes set out to determine at least one irrefutable truth that could resist sceptical doubt, which for Descartes was: I am certain I exist because I am capable of asking myself this very question, proving there is a mind that can question its own existence, if only my own. Descartes's *cogito ergo sum* led Western culture into a radical egocentricity that instantly transformed the nature of every individual's relationship with the world into a "problem" that needed to be solved. His next step was to imbue the self with qualities that define permanent aspects of a given individual's "personality." The Enlightenment definition of selfhood became rooted in the myth of a stable core in one's self-identity that defines who each person is. Nietzsche categorically rejected the concept of a stable ego and attributed its existence to nothing more than a trick of language. Because we are accustomed to using the personal pronoun in grammatical forms of address, we foster the myth that there is indeed such an entity as an "I" or a "me," what Nietzsche termed linguistic determinism. Just because we can say all sorts of things about ourselves and others grammatically—such as "I am brilliant" or "Harold is an imbecile"—we take these expressions to contain a truth about the person in question that isn't necessarily so. Nietzsche's scepticism helped him to realize that none of us can ever know ourselves or others with much accuracy, let alone certainty. Though we think, for example, that we know people when we love them, our love frequently blinds us to qualities in that person that are available to anyone else, epitomized by Freud's conception of transference. This is only one example of how transitory and impressionable our belief in our own self and the self of others can be.

Perhaps Nietzsche's most radical assault on the Enlightenment was embodied in his moral scepticism. The Enlightenment held that some morals are eternal and consistent with what it means to be civilized and that because humans are rational, they are capable of learning what it means to be moral and, with sufficient effort, to become so. Once God was out of the way, Nietzsche was in a position to argue that there is no ultimate foundation for morality and that the only morals that exist are arbitrarily chosen by a given society. History has shown that each era alters its perspective as to what our scruples should be, each assuming its values are more "enlightened" than the last, a view that was zealously embraced by Enlightenment thinkers. This assumption, however, assumes that humans are free to behave in whatever manner the current morality tells them to. Though Nietzsche blamed most of these assumptions on Christianity, it doesn't matter what one's views about religion are for Nietzsche's message to be compelling. Even among those who reject religion, there is a tendency to embrace a set of moral principles in dogmatic fashion, then condemn those who opt for a different set of values than their own. Nietzsche observed long before Freud that humans are duplicitous by nature and pretend to live their lives by one set of ideals while surreptitiously embracing another.

Nietzsche proposed to overcome these examples of moral hypocrisy by situating his philosophy in a pre-Socratic ideal that was in opposition to the subsequent Christian era that has dominated the Western world since the Roman Empire. In Nietzsche's estimation, pre-Christian Greeks lived their lives passionately and spontaneously and exemplified a Dionysian spirit that was subsequently suppressed by the weaker, more "democratic" Athenians, the prototypes for Christianity. He concluded that Modern Man is actually afraid of life and protects himself from his fears by overvaluing his Apollonian, rationalistic nature at the expense of his Dionysian spontaneity. While both qualities are aspects of every individual, Nietzsche argued that Western culture has emphasized the Apollonian to its detriment, culminating in what he foresaw as the collapse of Western civilization, though in hindsight, we have adapted handily to our moral hypocrisy by concealing our real feelings in neurotic compromise formations.

The Basic Elements of the Postmodern Perspective

So, what impact has Nietzsche's philosophy had on postmodernism? Perhaps the principal problem in addressing this question is that nobody knows exactly what postmodernism is. Although there is a tendency among contemporary authors to depict the postmodern perspective as antithetical to modernism, there is little agreement as to what even modernism entails. For some authors, it appears to be interchangeable with the Enlightenment, while for others, it is a twentieth-century phenomenon that originated with modern art and architecture. It is probably accurate to say that the single thread that ties all the postmodernist thinkers together is their condemnation of the progressive element of the Enlightenment and their sceptical orientation, views that were initiated by Nietzsche.

I will now review those aspects of Nietzsche's philosophy that presaged the postmodernist perspective and those that diverge from it. These can be listed as:

a. An *opposition to authority* characterized by an anti-foundational bias.
b. An inherent *scepticism* that permeates both Nietzsche's philosophy and postmodernism, exemplified by the *rejection of absolute truths* and any viewpoint that verges into *metaphysics.*
c. A *perspectivist* orientation that holds that truth is wedded to the perspective of the person who promotes it.
d. A moral and historical *relativism* based on the view that all so-called truths are relative to a time and place and, hence, neither eternal nor objective but highly personal and fluid.
e. A decentering of the *subject* that rejects the conventional notion of the self or ego as autonomous and in possession of its own volition.
f. An emphasis on *surface* instead of depth, a position which holds that there is no depth to the personality, as such, because we are what we *do,* not what we take ourselves to *be.*
g. An *emphasis on language* that permeates all the features of postmodernism listed above, deriving from sceptical doubt as to the accuracy of what language is capable of revealing about ourselves and the world we live in.
h. An opposition to *Enlightenment* values epitomized by the "grand narratives" of Utopian thinkers such as Hegel and Marx and the notion that civilization is in a constant state of "progression" toward an increasingly beneficial future.

Whereas Nietzsche was unequivocal that such progress has an unforeseen corrupting effect on our capacity for authenticity, postmodernists are equivocal about the role of technology and even embrace it as an essential component of the postmodern era, embodied in the cinema, television, media, and computer sciences. But whereas Nietzsche retained a romanticism about the superiority of Greek culture, postmodernists reject romanticism as an artifact of the Enlightenment.

So, was Nietzsche a postmodernist? It is evident from the above that there are important differences between Nietzsche's philosophy and contemporary postmodernism. Yet all of the principal proponents of postmodernism (e.g., Michel Foucault [1986], Francois Lyotard [1993], Jacques Derrida [1978], and Jean Baudrillard [1983]) have been profoundly influenced by Nietzsche. But Nietzsche also enjoyed an equally profound impact on phenomenology and existentialism, philosophical movements that are in opposition to postmodernism. Perhaps the principal difference between Nietzsche and postmodernist thinkers is Nietzsche's conception of authenticity, which postmodernists oppose.

Postmodernism and Authenticity

Although Heidegger was the first philosopher to employ authenticity as a technical term, Nietzsche's philosophy is the principal source for Heidegger's conception of it. For Nietzsche, authenticity characterizes the person who is not afraid to face up to the fundamental anxieties of living. Such an individual is embodied in Nietzsche's notion of the *Übermensch*, usually translated into English as overman or superman, who would appear someday in the future with the ability to accept reality for what it is, unbowed and unafraid. In other words, such a person would permit the more dynamic Dionysian aspect of his being to dominate over his more rationalistic and repressive Apollonian side.

Postmodernists have rejected Nietzsche's ideal as merely the latest edition in a long history of mythic figures (e.g., Marx's proletarian or Sartre's existentialist hero) that fails to take into account the severe limitations that human beings must contend with and ultimately accept. While there is some truth to this assessment of Nietzsche's hero, one would be mistaken to reduce Nietzsche's *Übermensch* to nothing more than an ideal that is out of step with the realities of living. Nietzsche predicted that the dominant Christian and scientific worldviews would collapse and a new kind of being, the *Übermensch*, would rise from the ashes and transcend the herd mentality to which modern civilization had succumbed. Though Nietzsche is rather vague on details as to how such a society would function, his vision was clearly modeled on the pre-democratic Greece of the pre-Socratics—a dubious political model, at best. The kernel of Nietzsche's basic idea nevertheless gripped the attention of Heidegger and other twentieth-century existentialists, who reframed Nietzsche's *Übermensch* into a modified characterization of authenticity.

The principal difference between Nietzsche's *Übermensch* and Heidegger's notion of authenticity is that, for Heidegger, there is no such person who epitomizes the "authentic hero" in juxtaposition to people who are inauthentic. Authenticity is characterized as a specific act or moment in any individual's life where the context in which a situation arises offers an opportunity to behave authentically or not. Heidegger was not talking about an ideal person who would someday emerge to replace the stereotypical contemporary neurotic but argued instead that *all* human creatures are necessarily inauthentic by their nature but that they are capable of behaving authentically when they can rise to the occasion. Moreover, every one of us is challenged to do so virtually every moment of our lives, but we are typically too anxious or distracted to bother. So how *do* we manage to act authentically in spite of our condition, and, more to the point, what would doing so entail?

In order to understand what authenticity entails, it is necessary to know what it means to be inauthentic. A central theme throughout Heidegger's early work is the relationship between the individual and society and how this relationship sets up a tension that the individual never entirely overcomes. This is because humans are existentially isolated from one another and, in their loneliness, crave the comfort of feeling at one with others, not unlike the "oceanic" experience Freud rejected in his *Civilization and Its Discontents* (1930). For Heidegger and Nietzsche alike, this sense of belonging is an illusion. We spend all our lives searching for a feeling of communion only to find our reward is always one more step out of reach. This quest is inconsolable because the only way of momentarily approximating this feeling is by selling out and abandoning an essential aspect of what we are about: our personal integrity. One characterization of succumbing to inauthenticity describes the human condition from which we cannot escape, whereas the other version becomes applicable when a person *tries* to escape his isolation by capitulating to social incentives to conform to the status quo. Yet, if we are condemned to *be* inauthentic as a fundamental facet of our existence, how can we also be granted a choice in the matter, to choose *not* to be so on certain occasions?

A good example of the inherent difficulty in recognizing this distinction was Heidegger's own fall into inauthenticity when he joined the National Socialist Party in Germany in the 1930s when he believed he was giving his soul in service to his country. Because sacrifice is an essential aspect of authenticity, Heidegger foolishly believed he was behaving courageously and resolutely when he abandoned the comfortable role of a sequestered academic for the more political and necessarily precarious role as a member of the Nazi Party. Later, Heidegger characterized his disastrous excursion into politics as an example of inauthenticity, an insight that only came to him in hindsight. So, why wasn't this apparent to him at the time he committed himself to the Nazi Party instead of later? According to Heidegger, one cannot always tell when one is behaving authentically or inauthentically *in the moment of doing so*. After the fact, Heidegger realized he was mistaken in believing that National Socialism (or, for that matter, any political platform) could serve as a vehicle for authenticity. Like so many others, he was caught up in the feeling of being at one with the German people and even saw himself as an instrument of National Socialism's success. Because any act necessarily exists in time, it is necessary to give one's actions the time they require to reveal, in their unfolding, what those actions were about *in hindsight,* a fundamental tenet of psychoanalytic investigation. Heidegger's conception of authenticity offers little in the way of reassuring, external markers that can discern the motives one is serving at the moment action is taken because our motives are always, to a significant degree, hidden or, as Freud would say, overdetermined.

Both Nietzsche and Heidegger recognized the terrible sense of anxiety that lies at the bottom of behaving authentically, but Heidegger was more adept at characterizing the precise features of this dread for what it is, the experience of simply being alive. Heidegger realized that because there is no ultimate foundation for our values or our behavior, we can never feel at home in the world. Yet because we are thrown into a world that is not our choosing, it is up to us to determine what meaning our lives will have. The inauthentic individual, like the neurotic, is incapable of accepting the anxiety and hardship that our everyday existence entails. Instead, he complains about his lot and the unfairness of the hand that is dealt him. For Nietzsche and Heidegger alike, the ability to accept life on its terms and suffer the day-to-day blows that are impossible to avoid or escape brings with it a reward that only authenticity can offer: the comfort of genuinely *being* oneself by learning to finally accept oneself, warts and all.

Like original sin, we are all inauthentic as a matter of course, but we also aspire to rise above our base motives by resisting the temptation of following the herd. Though Nietzsche was instrumental in our era's recognition of the illusory nature of the self, he argued that *because* the self is impressionable, it is imperative to find a way out of our congenital hypocrisy. This task is made difficult because it is impossible to know from one moment to the next what our motivations are and whose motives we are, in fact, serving. It is easy to see why this conception of authenticity was so troubling to Marxists (e.g., Habermas and Adorno), who scorned the very concept as a dangerous delusion. Consequently, Heidegger's critics argue that authenticity is just one more universal value that Heidegger, despite his rejection of modernity, succumbed to. In fact, Nietzsche's and Heidegger's depiction of authenticity is not a *universal* value because it has no foundation other than each individual's *conscience,* for better or worse.

Postmodernism and Psychoanalysis

So how does all this pertain to the relationship between postmodernism and psychoanalysis? The conventional perception is that postmodernism has influenced recent trends in psychoanalytic theory and technique, including hermeneutics, social constructivism, the French school, American relational theory, and intersubjectivity, that in turn constitute a paradigm shift in traditional psychoanalytic thinking. This view is predicated on the assumption that Freudian psychoanalysis is rooted in an outdated, modernist view of the human condition based on a one-person paradigm that is derivative of a Cartesian egocentrism. Like the postmodern phenomenon itself, the label "postmodernism" has been applied retrospectively to developments in psychoanalytic theory that have been in evidence long before postmodernism emerged as an identifiable theoretical perspective. Generally speaking, any psychoanalyst that can be said to have challenged Freud's sexual model has been enlisted as a representative of a new and postmodernist departure, including the views of such disparate analytic thinkers as Sandor Ferenczi, Melanie Klein, Michael Balint, Ronald Fairbairn, D.W. Winnicott, Wilfred Bion, Heinrich Racker, and Jacques Lacan. This list of analysts, distinguished for having disagreed with Freud on this or that matter, continues to grow in the form of so-called contemporary Kleinians, contemporary representatives of the British Middle School, and contemporary French and South American psychoanalysts. This group has been joined by contemporary American psychoanalysts who are avowedly anti-Freudian and in opposition to ego psychology.

The relationship between postmodernist thinking and the recent emergence of anti-Freudian theories in American and other cultures is uncertain.

Increasingly, proponents of the relational perspective, including but not limited to followers of Bion, have suggested that the "two-person" model is consistent with the postmodern turn in American and European cultures. I will now assess the validity of these claims.

I don't believe anyone would disagree with the observation that Freud was a creature of the nineteenth-century fascination with everything scientific and that he passionately embraced science and its empirical proclamations. Yet Freud also possessed a sceptical temperament that was continuously at war with his scientistic aspirations. Freud's scepticism notwithstanding,[1] there are five principal features of Freud's basic theory that are antithetical to the Enlightenment's reliance on science and the certitude it aspired to:

a. Freud's conception of the ***unconscious,*** which is a concept of mind that contemporary scientists emphatically reject. Although Freud wasn't the first to employ such a concept (Nietzsche had already discussed the notion at length), it was a radical concept when offered and brought considerable abuse against Freud from his medical, scientifically-trained colleagues.

b. Freud's adoption of the ***interpretative method,*** which follows from his conception of the unconscious, that the patient's speech acts are overdetermined and, as with Nietzsche, indicates that language is essentially metaphorical, so the meaning of what individuals say must be interpreted according to the context in which it is offered. Virtually all schools of psychoanalysis retain this model and build on it.

c. Barratt (1993) and others argue that Freud's novel conception of the ***free association method*** is antithetical to an empiricist view of data-gathering and presaged a central tenet of the postmodern perspective that much of our communication with others occurs unconsciously. The so-called revolution in the postmodern critique of language was anticipated by Nietzsche and is also a feature of Heidegger's conception of language, which in turn influenced Lacan and Derrida, as well as the existentialists.

d. Freud's conception of ***neutrality,*** a technical principle that continues to be a source of controversy. Contemporary analysts who are identified with the relational perspective (and sympathetic with postmodernism) show a surprising antipathy to this technical principle due to its alleged authoritarianism. In fact, this is the feature of Freud's treatment philosophy that was intended to *constrain* the analyst's authority, not inflate it. By Freud's definition, neutrality means nothing more than adopting an attitude of sceptic, open-ended inquiry by not imposing one's views on the patient.

e. The observation that *it is impossible to affect a patient's condition through appeals to rational argument or coercion,* an observation that permeates the entirety of Freud's treatment philosophy. Although Freud began his medical career learning methods that were rooted in nineteenth-century empirical practices, he had the flexibility to profit from his errors and gradually abandoned conventional psychiatric methods in favor of what evolved into psychoanalysis. All five criteria of Freud's theory are, as Barnaby Barratt (1993) observes, postmodern in spirit.

I have enumerated aspects of Freud's basic treatment philosophy that are both consistent with and anticipated elements of postmodernism, but what about those aspects of Freud's treatment model that continue to be rooted in Enlightenment values, as his critics allege? There is little question that while Freud's treatment philosophy was a farsighted and monumentally influential method of relieving human suffering, many of Freud's more fanciful theories were based on little more than his penchant for speculation that was oftentimes offered in a dogmatic fashion, sometimes alienating him from his most passionate disciples. The manner in which he offered interpretations to his patients was also frequently dogmatic, and Freud had a tendency to construe any rejection of his interpretations as resistance. Moreover, Freud's initial goal was to "cure" mental illness unequivocally in a manner that is reminiscent of the grand narratives found in Hegel, Marx, Kant, and other Modern philosophers. On the other hand, Freud's theories are not essential to his psychoanalytic method, which generations of innovators have subsequently demonstrated, so why fault him on his theory when one can substitute it with another without sacrificing the principles on which the method relies? Moreover, Freud was never satisfied with his theories and revised them throughout his lifetime. In this, Freud was a tireless sceptic, and, toward the end of his life (1937), came to the radical conclusion that a psychoanalytic cure of neurosis or any other form of suffering is impossible due to the fluid nature of the human predicament and our incurable sensitivity to circumstances that invariably disturb our equilibrium.

In fact, the question of theory was not only a problem for Freud but continues to bedevil contemporary psychoanalysts as well.[2] Were Freud a sceptic through and through, he would have recognized that theories are superfluous to the psychoanalytic instrument he fashioned, and he would have concluded that knowledge is not the aim of analysis but peace of mind.

Yet, how many contemporary psychoanalysts (even postmodern thinkers) have abandoned theory, even those who claim the search for knowledge is an artifact of the Enlightenment? There continues to be something suspiciously dogmatic about contemporary psychoanalytic theorizing, whose alleged virtue is its "superiority" over Freud's. But who, in the end, is able to judge who is right? It would serve the postmodernists well to take a page from the ancient sceptics, who recognized that if knowledge is in the eyes of the beholder, then it behooves us to abandon dogmatic claims entirely, including our self-certain condemnation of those with whom we disagree.

Because the language and sensibility of postmodernism are essentially a French phenomenon, it shouldn't be surprising that of all the psychoanalytic schools in the world, it would appear to have had the most influence on the French, principally Lacanians, but spilling over to non-Lacanian analysts as well, such as Kristeva. Notwithstanding the impact of both Nietzsche and Heidegger on Lacan's perspective, Lacan's conception of analysis has been championed by many postmodernist thinkers due to Lacan's theory of the "decentered-subject," his view that language constitutes subjectivity, and his exciting, if excessively complicated, critique of the unconscious. While there is much merit in Lacan's efforts to reframe psychoanalysis from a more philosophical perspective, there are many elements of Lacanian analysis that seem antithetical to the postmodern perspective, including his extreme reliance on theory, his claim to have found the "truth" about psychic processes, and his conviction that *his* psychoanalytic technique is superior to all the other technical principles that preceded it, especially ego psychology! Ultimately, Lacan is a dogmatist where his theories and pronouncements are concerned, a position that is antithetical to the sceptical sensibility that permeates the postmodern attitude, so the equation of Lacanism with postmodernism would appear to be no more consistent than with Freud, as we saw earlier.

Unlike the French, the American analysts most taken with postmodernism tend to emphasize matters of technique over theory. Elliott and Spezzano (1998, p. 73), for example, suggest that the work of Irwin Hoffman is postmodern due to his lack of certainty about what is going on between himself and his patients, in contrast to analysts who are more invested in pinning down what is supposed to be happening in the analyst's and patient's unconscious. This is a point well taken and consistent with the sceptical outlook in contrast to the dogmatic assertions of previous generations of analysts. Similarly, the work of Schafer is said to be consistent with the postmodern perspective when Schafer questions whether patients should be characterized as "deceiving" themselves simply because the analyst sees things differently. Of course, these features of Hoffman's and

Schafer's respective work could just as easily be characterized as existentialist in nature,[3] so they are neither necessarily nor essentially postmodern.

Whether such views are consistent with postmodernism and how practical they are clinically, I cannot say. There is an increasing tendency among analysts identified with contemporary perspectives to characterize the analytic relationship as one between equals, more or less collaborative in spirit, minimizing the tension that has traditionally characterized the patient's transference with the analyst. Yet none of these innovations are new, nor are they derived from the postmodern turn in contemporary culture. Matters of technique have been debated since the beginning of psychoanalysis, and there is a long history of disagreement between analysts who advocate a more authoritarian posture and those who opt for a "user-friendly" variety. While some analysts believe that technique should follow theory, others argue that practice is a creature of experience, a more sceptical position. I remain doubtful that recent so-called innovations in technique are anything new, whether or not they are consistent with the postmodern perspective. Psychoanalysis is such a flexible instrument that what finally matters is the person who employs it, not which theory or technical regimen the analyst is educated to follow.

What is the Matter with Postmodernism?

If there are positive components of postmodernism, what about those aspects of the postmodern turn that are irrelevant or even deleterious to the purposes of psychoanalysis? There is an expanding hegemony in the psychoanalytic world, evidenced by a movement toward standardization that parallels similar developments in global commerce, the internet, and the rapid disappearance of smaller, less orthodox psychoanalytic schools and organizations. The so-called global village, a quaint notion when the world was divided between the United States and the Soviet Union, now has the aura of a prison that encroaches on individualism and deviancy, if not eradicating them entirely. The decentering of the subject, while a compelling notion in theory, has fashioned a conception of the world not unlike that of the recent movie *The Matrix*, where individuals have become illusions, controlled by a vast network of computer intelligence in a not-too-distant, post-apocalyptic future run amok.

In a similar fashion, psychoanalysis has lost whatever edge it once enjoyed as a subversive element in society. Now it is part of the establishment, a tool of the "mental health professions," whose conception of psychic deviancy is listed in manuals of diagnostic nomenclature that are the bibles of the conventional psychoanalytic practitioner. There is something ominous about recent conceptions of treatment, where mandatory universal licensure is all but inevitable, where, any day now, confidentiality between patient and analyst will become an artifact of the past, along with other Enlightenment values that are suspect in an era of paranoia and suspicion. What role has the postmodern turn played in these developments? Does it question the efficacy of such values, or does it encourage them?

This is a difficult question to answer because by rejecting universal values altogether, the postmodernist wears the mantel of an observer, neither cheering nor condemning cultural mores. Perhaps this version of neutrality can be reconciled with a perspective that decries authenticity in principle, but the postmodern abhorrence of authenticity is both surprising and telling. Surprising because the authentic individual is not susceptible to the rewards of the people, and telling because it alerts us to the likelihood that, in its alleged rejection of values, postmodernism adopts values after all, but in the form of an anti-individualism that is, in equal measure, homicidal and suicidal. With no leg to stand on, even its own, postmodernism as it is currently envisioned appears to define itself as a paradigm of spiritual emptiness, a *cul-de-sac* that is impervious to either passion or purpose. Having abandoned any vestige of selfhood or history, it depicts a world that is, perhaps contentedly, finally alienated from its own alienation.

A culture that rejects any semblance of authority or tradition cannot help but impact the role that psychoanalysis aspires to. Psychoanalysis has always been the champion, *par excellence,* of the individual, a respite from the forces in every culture that demand obedience to the values adopted *en masse.* In this, psychoanalysis has offered a means to extricate oneself from such values, or, at least, to hold them in question, and to follow the beat of one's own drum —authenticity in its essence. Will psychoanalysis, like the culture at large, become a vehicle of the postmodern sensibility, or will it remain true to its original purpose of reconciling the individual to the muse of his own conscience? Only time will tell.

Notes

1 See Thompson, 2000, for a thorough discussion of Freud's debt to the sceptic tradition.

2 See Thompson, 2004, for a more detailed discussion of the phenomenological foundation to Freud's treatment method.

3 See Thompson, 1994, for an exhaustive examination of the existential elements of Freud's treatment philosophy.

References

Barratt, B. (1993) *Psychoanalysis and the Postmodern Impulse: Knowing and Being Since Freud's Psychology*. Baltimore and London: Johns-Hopkins University Press.

Baudrillard, J. (1983) *Simulations*. New York: Semiotext(e).

Derrida, J. (1978) *Writing and Difference* (A. Bass, Trans.). London: Routledge and Kegan Paul.

Elliott, A. and Spezzano, C. (1998) Psychoanalysis at Its Limits: Navigating the Postmodern Turn. In O. Renik (Ed.), *Knowledge and Authority in the Psychoanalytic Relationship*. Northvale, NJ and London: Jason Aronson, Inc.

Foucault, M. (1986) *The Care of the Self (Vol. 3 of The History of Sexuality)*. New York: Pantheon Books.

Freud, S. (1930/1961) *Civilization and Its Discontents*. Standard Edition (Vol. 21, pp. 59–145). London: Hogarth Press.

Freud, S. (1937/1964) *Analysis Terminable and Interminable*. Standard Edition (Vol. 23, pp. 209–253). London: Hogarth Press.

Freud, S. (1953–1973) *The Standard Edition of the Complete Psychological Works of Sigmund Freud* (24 vols; J. Strachey, Ed. & Trans.). London: Hogarth Press (Referred to in Subsequent References as Standard Edition).

Kuhn, T. S. (1962) *The Structure of Scientific Revolutions*. Chicago and London: University of Chicago Press.

Lyotard, J.-F. (1993) *The Postmodern Explained*. Minneapolis and London: University of Minnesota Press.

Nietzsche, F. (1967) *The Will to Power* (W. Kaufman and R. J. Hollingdale, Trans.). New York: Random House.

Nietzsche, F. (1994) *On the Genealogy of Morals* (C. Diethe, Trans.). Cambridge: Cambridge University Press.

Thompson, M. G. (1994) *The Truth About Freud's Technique: The Encounter With the Real*. New York and London: New York University Press.

Thompson, M. G. (2000) The Sceptic Dimension to Psychoanalysis: Toward an Ethic of Experience. *Contemporary Psychoanalysis*, Vol. 36, No. 3.

Thompson, M. G. (2004) *The Ethic of Honesty: The Fundamental Rule of Psychoanalysis*. Amsterdam and New York: Editions Rodopi.

Chapter 3

Logos and Psychoanalysis

The Role of Truth and Creativity in Heidegger's Conception of Language

In recent years, increasing interest in the relationship between language and psychoanalysis has gained influence in both philosophical and psychoanalytic publications. Yet, relatively little has been said about Martin Heidegger's important contribution to our understanding of the relationship between language and clinical practice and the role that creativity may lend to this endeavor. My aim in this chapter is to explore the relationship between truth and creativity through the lens of Heidegger's conception of language while exploring the enigmatic power of speech and the manner in which it is experienced by psychoanalysts and their patients.

According to Heidegger, human creativity should be understood as an act of revelation. The artist, for example, paints or writes in order to reveal something about the truth of our existence. The creative impulse is a means of unveiling what is ordinarily hidden from everyday awareness. Similarly, psychoanalysis is a means of revealing what is hidden, by chance or design, from ourselves—including the things that, unbeknownst to ourselves, we conceal from ourselves and each other. The creative act in psychoanalysis enables us to touch the mystery of our existence by disclosing something about its nature. In the main, this is achieved by means of telling stories. The kind of storytelling this entails, however, doesn't require a special skill or even a predisposition to employing words in a particular fashion. According to Heidegger, the tradition of storytelling to which each of us belongs requires nothing more from us than simply talking to each other. The act of self-disclosure that this entails isn't as simple, however, as it sounds because it requires talking in a certain way with a specific purpose in mind. First, I want to explore how Heidegger's conception of language helps to explain its liberating function, and then turn to his views on creativity and its relevance to the psychoanalytic process.

DOI: 10.4324/9781003429104-3

Heidegger rejected the view that words merely serve to "represent" things in nature, a conception of language that reduces the function of speech to a composite of signs and symbols, rules of grammar, and forms of syntax. Moreover, the representational conception of language emphasizes subjectivity to such a degree that the use of language becomes inherently self-referential, epitomized by contemporary education. In the context of science, for example, it is impossible to abandon oneself to language and to experience what it is about because words are systematically "appropriated" in order to serve utilitarian goals. Heidegger insisted that if we hope to grasp what language is about, we need to approach it from an altogether different perspective, by undergoing an experience with language in the act of using it—in the manner, for example, that you and I are doing at this moment.

According to Heidegger, the essential purpose of language is to reveal ourselves to each other. In other words, we use language to determine what we are about, to each other as well as to ourselves. That we are already always doing this anyhow (though we may not know it) helps explain why we already know how to participate in psychoanalysis the first time we try, because it entails the ordinary use of words that everyone employs each day of their lives. But what does it mean to actually undergo an experience with language? Does such an experience occur automatically? Or is it something we have a hand in, that we are able to either engage with, heart and soul, or resist? Finally, what role does experience play in the act of invoking language? Is our experience of language merely a means to an end, or is there something about the nature of experience that lends to language its power to transform? Heidegger (1971a) addressed some of these questions in the following excerpt:

> To undergo an experience with something—be it a thing, a person, or a god—means that this something befalls us, strikes us, comes over us, overwhelms and transforms us. When we talk of "undergoing" an experience, we mean that the experience is not of our own making; to undergo here means rather to endure it, suffer it, receive it as it strikes us and submit to it.
>
> (p. 57)

This highly condensed passage suggests something about the nature of experience and, in turn, how one's experience of language may be conceived. But what does it tell us about the nature of language itself, and what does it tell us about the nature of experience if our relationship with language is indeed rooted in experience and not in a theoretical formulation of it? For one thing, the above passage suggests that experience, whatever the nature of that experience may be, never occurs "automatically." Moreover, it implies that it is possible to *evade* an experience of a thing, person, or god—or, I might add, of language. On the other hand, if we undertake to undergo an experience with language, we will be obliged to approach it from an unsettling perspective by *submitting* to it. In so doing, we are "struck" by it, then suffer and endure it until we find ourselves overwhelmed and eventually transformed by it.

If all of this is entailed in what it means to genuinely experience something, does this imply that some people have never really experienced language, though they use it every day? As shocking as this may seem, this is precisely what Heidegger is saying. When we use language to describe, order, and calculate—even when we use it to express our innermost feelings in the context of psychotherapy or psychoanalysis—we're not necessarily "submitting" to language and experiencing it as such. Instead, we are often simply using it to deal with things that we typically hold at a distance. As a matter of fact, we are necessarily obliged to hold language at arm's length in order to use it. Of course, language is used by each and every one of us in a functional sort of way every day of our lives. It would be madness if we lost the ability to do so. The loss of functional usage of words is a common feature of schizophrenia. But this inherently utilitarian function of language, useful though it may be, is a relatively impoverished relationship with language when compared to the kind of experience with language we are all capable of having.

Undergoing an experience of this nature is not an esoteric affair that only the privileged few can obtain. Neither does it require specialized knowledge or training. Yet, the technical languages learned at universities and institutes, including medical, psychological, and even psychoanalytical, are even further removed from the kind of experience with language that Heidegger is talking about. Instead, he is referring to a dimension of language that each of us *already* inhabits, though we may not realize it. When we undergo an experience with language in the manner that each of us is perfectly capable of doing, *language shows itself to us and envelopes us.* At such moments we no longer use language in the conventional sense but enter "into" language by inhabiting it and succumbing to its power. According to Heidegger (1971a):

> If it is true that man finds the proper abode of his existence in language whether he is aware of it or not then an experience we undergo with

language will touch the innermost nexus of our existence. We who speak language may thereupon become transformed by such experiences, from one day to the next or in the course of time.

(p. 57)

In other words, it is impossible to really experience language by merely using it as a vehicle for information or communication, however sophisticated or complex such communication may be.[1] Being disturbed by something that language conveys when informing us about it, as when we hear a distressing piece of news, for example, isn't the same thing as undergoing an experience with *language*. In order to experience language, one must be touched by language itself, not the information it conveys. As Heidegger reminds us, when we experience language, we necessarily suffer and endure it because, once experienced, nothing is ever the same. Though most of us have never thought about language in these terms, we are no strangers to its effects upon us. We all intuitively share a sense of this dimension to language when we acknowledge, for example, the degree to which we fear the hold language has over us. Because language is able to disturb the slumber of our existence without warning, we typically hold it back by employing a variety of ways of ignoring what it has to say. Our intrinsic anxiety about language and the words it prompts us to divulge without warning is a feature of every analytic treatment, especially when it circumvents our resistance to revealing more about ourselves than we intend.

How are mere words capable of such power in the first place? And even if we manage to overcome our fear of it, how is it possible to beckon language forth, putting our resistances aside by inviting it to take us on a momentous journey of self-transformation? According to Heidegger (1971a):

In experiences which we undergo with language, language itself brings itself to language. One would think that this happens anyway, any time anyone speaks. Yet at whatever time and in whatever way we speak a language, language itself never has the floor. Any number of things are given voice in speaking, above all what we are speaking about: a set of facts, an occurrence, a question, a matter of concern. Only because in everyday speaking, language does not bring itself to language but holds back, are we able simply to go ahead and speak a language, and so to deal with something and negotiate something by speaking.

(p. 59)

In other words, language has to hold itself back in order for us to take from it what we require. Because language is always hovering on the periphery of our awareness, we find ourselves involved in a continuous dialectic of eliciting its presence through its absence, waiting for the proper moment to invite us in. Heidegger asks:

> But when does language speak itself as language? Curiously enough, when we cannot find the right word for something that concerns us, carries us away, oppresses or encourages us. Then we leave unspoken what we have in mind and, without rightly giving it thought, undergo moments in which language itself has distantly and fleetingly touched us with its essential being. But when the issue is to put into language something which has never yet been spoken, then everything depends on whether language gives or withholds the appropriate word.
>
> (p. 59)

If language were simply comprised of words, then the moment it escapes us would be when it is furthest away. But Heidegger proposes just the opposite: it is when words are most fleeting that the presence of language is felt. Though our experience of language occasions words, language cannot be reduced to words alone. That is why our experience of language is most poignant when words elude us because that is precisely when it takes hold of our attention in a manner we cannot ignore.

The art of presence making itself felt through absence is the kind of experience with language that psychoanalysts take for granted whenever they admonish their patients to speak with no particular aim in mind after invoking the fundamental rule of analysis.[2] The "emptiness" of experience this admonition engenders lends to language its latent power as a therapeutic agent and accounts for its power to transform. This is why Heidegger's views about language more closely approximate the conversations that occur in a psychoanalytic consulting room than the verbal conventions we typically employ in polite conversation, for example. Heidegger and Freud alike argued that civilized society has circumvented the latent power of language to disclose what we are about with customs of interpersonal discourse that inhibit spontaneous disclosure. What's more, over the course of the past three centuries, the evolution of science and technology has had such an incredible impact on culture that we have gradually lost something of the power words have traditionally enjoyed in the theatre and literature, for example. These age-old vehicles for self-awareness have been modernized and marginalized by a frenzy of electronic and other media that are hypnotic and mind-numbing in their ability to lull what is left of our minds into a slumber that we mistake for self-edification and self-knowledge. We no longer live in an Age of Enlightenment; we now reside in the Information Age.

This is one of the reasons why the means through which contemporary culture usurps the power of language occupies such an important role in Heidegger's philosophy.[3] Some of these developments are relatively recent while others can be traced back to the etymological roots of words that are so familiar we seldom give them a second thought. Whereas some of the modern corruptions of language have been affected by so-called instruments of communication, entertainment, and education, others go back to the Latinization (and, in Heidegger's view, corruption) of concepts that were Greek in origin. There is no better example of what Heidegger is referring to than when we look at the etymological roots of the English "word" and the respective applications that Greek and Roman cultures derived from this term.

The term word, for example, derives from the Old English *wordig,* which in turn comes from the Latin *uerbum* and *verbum,* both of which give rise to verb, verbatim, and proverbial. The Latin *verbum* is also cognate with the Latin *legere,* which literally means "to gather." More colloquially, *legere* is a collection of words, a story or a legend. A legend is literally a gathering or collection of words that produce a story. The words lesson, legible, intellect, and collect are also derivatives of *legere,* each of which pertains to how words come together to establish meaning. According to Heidegger, the Latinization of the Greek *legein* (from which *legere* is derived) has fostered an intellectual bias in the term that is evident, for example, in the English words lesson, legible, and intellect, all of which emphasize the cognitive and scholarly use of words, which we now associate with modern education—much, in Heidegger's view, to our detriment.

I will now compare what we just gleaned from the Latin *legere* with the Greek *legein* from which it originates. The Greek *legein* gives rise to the word *Logos* which plays a pivotal role in Heidegger's late philosophy. English words that are derived from the Greek *legein* and *Logos* include analogy, apology, eulogy, dialogue, and, surprisingly, the word "saying." Compared with the words that are cognate with the Latin *legere*—such as intellect—the Greek *legein* suggests terms that emphasize the simple utterance of words, often addressed to a group of people. Though the Latin *legere* and the Greek *legein* each literally means "to gather," the Latin emphasizes the relationship between words and mentation, whereas the Greek emphasizes the purpose for which words are generally gathered or grouped together in the first place: in order to be heard. A legend, for example, is a story—a gathering of words—that is told to a gathering of people, a story that is typically handed down through generations.

Heidegger was also struck by how the term *Logos* was used in the days of Heraclitus, who lived around 500 B.C. Usually translated as word, thought, or saying, in Heraclitus's day *Logos* also meant to lay down, to lay in order, to arrange, to gather oneself, or to lay asleep. So how did the notion "to lay" come to mean saying, talking, and discourse?

When we lay down to sleep, we gather ourselves before falling to sleep, in the same way, for example, that a diver gathers him- or herself before taking the plunge. Gathering isn't the same as merely amassing or jumbling things together, as in stuffing dirty laundry into a bag. Gathering involves a selection and sorting of that which we gather together. This explains why the words "laying" and "telling" both derive from the Greek *legein,* because when telling a story the appropriate words fall into place without our having to *think* of them.

Heidegger suggests that the essential relationship between words and language is disclosed in one of the most famous and enigmatic fragments of Heraclitus's writings. This fragment was the first in a collection of a hundred or so surviving sayings from which the entirety of his philosophy as we know it today is derived. The fragment reads:

When you have listened, not to me but to the *Logos,*
It is wise to agree that all things are one.

This fragment has spawned literally dozens of interpretations and even the translations from the original Greek into other languages are equally varied. The meaning that Heidegger gives *Logos* in turn formed his views about the nature of thought, poetry, and creativity. He interprets Heraclitus's fragment as meaning that when you truly *listen* to what words (*Logos*) have to say, you will be in agreement with the "order of things" and feel at one with creation, i.e., with Being. In other words, when we are genuinely attentive to language, what we hear isn't literally conveyed "in" the words that are transmitted between us or even by the speaker him- or herself. Instead, there is a higher truth that we instinctively seek from each other whenever we engage in dialogue. Ultimately, what we seek is a form of salvation, the kind we sometimes experience when reading a work of poetry. You might say it is spiritual.

Yet, we spend most of our time denying the very thing we long for the most. Oftentimes we speak to each other in a way that virtually ignores the *Logos*—we talk "about" things but don't speak to or really hear anybody. Heidegger calls this way of talking "idle chatter," or gossip. We pass words along with a complacency as to the truthfulness of what we are saying to each other. Moreover, we treat the words that we utter and that are uttered to us in turn as though they harbor no intrinsic significance. Instead of employing conversation to reveal what we mean to each other, we use it to distract ourselves from that which matters the most: *mutual recognition.* This is about as close as Heidegger gets to the concept of love in the form of intimacy.

What do these thoughts about the nature of language tell us about the nature of creativity, poetry, and psychoanalysis? Poetry and language are inextricably linked in Heidegger's philosophy and are fundamental to his views about the nature of art and the work art entails. But what is the "work" in question: the art object or the work entailed in creating the object? Remember that, in Heidegger's view, the purpose of language is to reveal the truth about our existence. According to Heidegger (1971b):

> The [art] work's createdness . . . can be grasped only in terms of the process of creation. Thus . . . we must consent . . . to go into the activity of the artist in order to arrive at the origin of the work of art.
>
> (p. 58)

In other words, the work of art, properly speaking, isn't the art object, *per se*, but the work that artists perform while creating the artwork. Creativity is embodied in the act of creation rather than the "thing" created, or even the talent that is utilized in creating it. The work of the artist—that which is "at work" in the artwork—is, according to Heidegger, an experience *(Erlebnis)*, or a "happening." Not just any happening; it is a happening of truth. This is why the truly creative person can never be reduced to someone who possesses a talent for painting pretty pictures or penning a catchy phrase, but rather someone who is able to say something truthful about what it means to be human.[4] This means that the revelation of truth and the act of creativity are mutually interdependent. But what does this tell us about the nature of creativity itself? According to Heidegger (1971b):

> To create is to cause something to emerge as a thing that has been brought forth. The work's becoming a work is a way in which truth becomes and happens.
>
> (p. 60)

How, then, does Heidegger's depiction of creativity complement one's capacity for undergoing an experience with language and, for that matter, an experience with psychoanalysis? For one thing, it deprives the artist of the illusion that she orchestrates the artwork by acts of will. In the same manner that experiencing language entails yielding to what we hear language saying, artists similarly *serve* the work that their creativity calls on them to perform. In the same way that words beckon us to hear, the artist is called upon to disclose through her work that which she is able to see. In other words, creativity is a manner of *seeing* and then speaking to what is seen.

Yet of all the arts, Heidegger believed that poetry was the highest because it exemplifies the achievement of what words, often in the most ordinary circumstances, are able to convey. Heidegger even proposed that all the arts are essentially poetic (i.e., *poiesis*), regardless of the medium employed.

> *All art,* as the letting happen of the advent of the truth of what is, is, as such, *essentially poetry.* The nature of art, on which both the art work and the artist depend, is the setting-itself-into-work of truth. It is due to art's poetic nature that, in the midst of what is, art breaks open an open space, in whose openness everything is other than usual.
>
> (p. 72)

Every art form endeavors to tell us something. But just as important as the speaking of that which we seek is the time we permit ourselves to elicit insight and inspiration. Art unfolds over time because it is a creature of time, evidenced not only by the eras to which we assign its treasures but also by our personal appreciation of art based upon our constantly evolving interpretation of it. Moreover, we take pains as a culture to protect the artwork over the passage of time and preserve it precisely because its relationship to time is so intrinsic to the value we confer upon it at a given moment:

> Art, as the setting-into-work of truth, is poetry. Not only the creation of the work is poetic, but equally poetic, though in its own way, is the preserving of the work; for a work is in actual effect as a work only when we remove ourselves from our commonplace routine and move into what is disclosed by the work, so as to bring our own nature itself to take a stand in the truth of what is.
>
> (pp. 74–75)

Art invites us to see what is already in front of us and implores us to take the time to hear what is always in the process of being disclosed. This, I would argue, is the principal goal of psychoanalysis as well: to take the time we give ourselves to reflect on what our lives are about by listening to what our words reveal to us about the enigmatic state of our existence.

To the degree that we are willing to allow, words hold the power to mesmerize, startle, bemuse, cajole, and ultimately deliver us to that singular form of experience that defines our discourse with others. For Heidegger, no one single individual epitomized the power that words are able to convey more persuasively than the German poet Friedrich Hölderlin. Hölderlin possessed an extraordinary capacity to lure his audience into spaces that were metaphysical yet perfectly natural—the kind of spaces into which every psychoanalyst aspires to lure his or her patients. Among English-speaking poets, Yeats probably comes closest to inspiring a similar effect: to both mesmerize and liberate us, if only momentarily, from the startling pace of the modern and postmodern eras that have taken over our lives.

If poetry has a discernible function, Heidegger would argue that it is to help us ponder the unpredictable manner in which each of our lives unfold by dwelling on it. In one of Heidegger's most frequently cited poems, Hölderlin says (cited in Heidegger, 1971b):

> May, if life is sheer toil, a man
> Lift his eyes and say: so
> I too wish to be? Yes. As long as Kindness,
> The Pure, still stays with his heart, man
> Not unhappily measures himself
> Against the godhead. Is God unknown?

Is he manifest like the sky? I'd sooner
Believe the latter. It's the measure of man.
Full of merit, yet poetically, man
Dwells on this earth. But no purer
Is the shade of the starry night,
If I might put it so, than
Man, who's called an image of the godhead.
Is there a measure on earth? There is
None.

(pp. 219–220)

Heidegger takes this to mean that our purpose on earth is to dwell on our existence and ponder its meaning in thoughtful consideration of the mystery that each person's life entails. In order to appreciate what life is about and experience it at the deepest level, we are obliged to let go of the willful conceits that characterize the world we live in by coming to terms with the unseen forces that manipulate and (to a degree we will likely never understand) determine our destiny. This device couldn't be more out of step with the technology-ridden zeal that has come to characterize modern science, including medicine, psychology, social media, and even certain aspects of psychoanalysis.

When Hölderlin proposes that "poetically, man dwells," he doesn't mean we are all poets, but that our existence and all it entails is basically a poetic affair, or at any rate, it can be, if only we take the time to dwell on it, without hubris. Poetry is the ultimate discourse because it captures what every attempt at discourse aspires to. In order for discourse to be poetic, we must permit the words that we utter to assume a life of their own. Poetry, says Heidegger (1971b), "is not the deliberate action of a subject, but the opening up of a human being, out of its captivity in that which is, to the openness of Being" (p. 67).

The selection of words that are gathered into a composition of poetry is no more "willful" than the colors envisioned by a painter. Words "come" to us, from the outer recesses of experience, when we invite language to speak and then get out of its way. This also describes how words serve their function in therapy. Words cannot work their spell if we get in "front" of language by ordering it about with plans, agendas, and treatment strategies, no matter how clever or ingenious such stratagems are. The more will we expend in our efforts to change our patients by manipulating their thinking, the more estranged from language they become and the less likely they will discover a way, their way, to come to terms with their suffering.

People seek therapy because they get caught in a web of despair that they can no longer bear, but the answers they want are elusive, and the solutions they obtain are fleeting. Psychoanalysts, like poets, offer a space where we are invited to collect our thoughts and to ponder what our lives are about. We take some time from our impossible schedules and, with no specific purpose in view, dwell on the things that concern us. We engage in conversation, yet the things we say are of no intrinsic importance. What is important is that we take what time we permit ourselves to take in what our experience has to say. And that we endure the discomfort of this process for as long as it takes.

Notes

1 For example, when patient and analyst talk to each other they are seldom "communicating" with each other, except when discussing fees or scheduling issues. Instead, they are conversing with each other, not merely communicating information.
2 For a more thorough exploration of this technical principle, see Thompson, 1998.
3 For a more thorough discussion of Heidegger's conception of language and its relevance to psychoanalysis, see Thompson, 1985, pp. 150–192.
4 For a more thorough discussion of Heidegger's conception of truth and its relevance to psychoanalysis, see Thompson, 1994, pp. 51–92.

References

Heidegger, M. (1971a) *On The Way to Language*. New York: Harper and Row.
Heidegger, M. (1971b) *Poetry, Language, Thought*. New York: Harper and Row.
Thompson, M. G. (1985) *The Death of Desire: A Study in Psychopathology*. New York: New York University Press.
Thompson, M. G. (1994) *The Truth About Freud's Technique: The Encounter with the Real*. New York: New York University Press.
Thompson, M. G. (1998, January) The Fundamental Rule of Psychoanalysis. *The Psychoanalytic Review*, Vol. 85, No. 1.

Chapter 4

What Is the Will?

On the Role of Desire in Psychoanalysis

The topic of this essay is *what is the will*? What does it mean to employ my will to do this or that? Or is Will something I can employ? Rather, does Will employ me? What, precisely, do we mean by this term, a word we use all the time without ever giving it a second thought? I hope to show that this much-used and abused term is more mysterious and complex than we typically suppose.

There are two fundamentally opposed conceptions of Will that persist to this day. One views Will as synonymous with desire, which for the most part is unconscious. The other views Will as synonymous with the ego, the rational part of our minds. We will explore both conceptions in depth and see where that takes us.

I will begin with the conventional definition of Will that most people nowadays typically embrace. It goes something like this: *Will is the faculty of the mind that selects, at the moment of decision, a desire among the variety of desires at my disposal. Will itself does not refer to a particular desire but rather the mechanism responsible for choosing from among this or that desire.*

There! What could be simpler? According to this definition, to will is to select, an executive function of the mind, always at our disposal, which puts us, so to speak, in the driver's seat. I can will this way or that, yes or no, and via my will I can make my desires come true. The more I exercise my will the more successful I am likely to be in the pursuit of my goals, yes? All it takes is to will it so: the more will, or willpower, the better. Do some have more Will than others? Is this what accounts for success in life, the person with the most willpower wins?

There are innumerable problems with this conception of the will. First, it implies that by force of Will I deliberately choose or select from among my

DOI: 10.4324/9781003429104-4

desires which one I decide to pursue. Then Poof! I pursue it. I more or less will my desire to come true. A second problem is the premise that I have a good deal of control over my Will. After all, if I employ my will to achieve my desires, then I am always ahead of my actions, always one step ahead of my desires, in control.

In fact, neither of these propositions is persuasive. Will is not necessarily or always conscious. I am never really in control of my will, nor do I select from among my desires which one I will opt for. My desires choose *me*. I do not choose my desires. How could we be so wrong about something so basic and ostensibly common-sensical? How could we be so confused about what this very simple word means? We say, "Where there is a will, there is a way." Yes. But what is Will?

Aristotle (1915) suggested that will may be voluntary or involuntary but argued that some people are better at it than others. Following Plato, he implies that no one chooses to do wrong, for example, they simply don't know they are choosing badly out of ignorance. So the key to the right use of Will is measured by the wisdom employed. Aristotle believed that the wise person always chooses rightly. In addition to wisdom, Aristotle also valued self-mastery. This may be where we got the idea that we are capable of becoming masters of our will, or potentially so. This notion has survived to the present.

The belief that we employ Will in order to do right was a popular idea among classical philosophers. A few centuries later, St. Augustine, who brought many of Aristotle's ideas into Christianity, refers to Will as "the mother and guardian of virtue" (Augustine, 2010). This implies that it is up to our will to be good Christians.

In the early Modern philosophical period, attention turned to whether Will is or is not free. The term "free will" was introduced as distinct from Will itself, as though one kind is free and the other isn't. Philosophers such as Hobbes, Spinoza, Locke, and Hume rejected this argument and attributed this misrepresentation to verbal confusion. They concluded that all will is inherently free. This opens the door to whether Will is entirely conscious, and what we mean by the word "free"? This is especially relevant to the question of ethics, and the degree to which we are free to do good instead of harm.

In the modern era, the nineteenth-century German philosopher, Arthur Schopenhauer (2012), was the first philosopher to situate the will in the unconscious, and to equate it with desire. His thesis fundamentally changed the way we conceptualize the nature of Will and whether it is something we can or cannot control.

Schopenhauer's most famous remark about Will goes something like this: "You can *do* as you will, but you cannot *will* as you will" (2012, p. 94). With this comment, Schopenhauer boldly claims that we have no control over our will, our desire. Rather, our desire controls us. He abandons the executive function of the will and situates it within a maelstrom of feelings, desires, and inclinations. When we become truly conscious of ourselves, says Schopenhauer, we realize that our essential qualities are comprised of endless urging, craving, striving, wanting, and desiring. All these are characteristic of what he calls the will.

Whereas his predecessors thought that Will depends on knowledge in the deliberate execution of our conduct, Schopenhauer argued that our will is primary and uses knowledge in order to satisfy its cravings. Ironically, Schopenhauer concluded that this means we are not free, because our actions are determined by our will, which according to Schopenhauer, is synonymous with desire. Because we are at the mercy of our desires we have no way of controlling them, no matter how hard we try. You only have to look at the drug addict to be persuaded of this thesis.

Nietzsche was profoundly influenced by Schopenhauer's conception of the will, but did not embrace his pessimism. Nietzsche (2001) claimed that his entire philosophy was encapsulated in the simple motto, "Will to Power," an enigmatic phrase that has no precise definition. I interpret it to mean "Desire to Passion," (will=desire, power=passion) meaning we are creatures of our desire. We may desire many things in life, but the grandest and most essential is the desire to live passionately. This is not a game for the timid. Nietzsche was nothing if not passionate. The notion that we can exercise control over our desires was the furthest thing from his mind.

Unlike Schopenhauer, Nietzsche equates desire with freedom. *The fact that we have no control over our desires is precisely what makes them free!* This raises the question: "Who" am I? My desires, or my capacity for rational thinking, my Ego? Nietzsche embraced the former. Our desires do not and cannot control "me," because I *am* my desires, the seat of my agency and selfhood. What could be more personal than what I want from life?

I now turn to the twentieth-century father of psychoanalysis, Sigmund Freud. Freud was profoundly influenced by both Schopenhauer's and Nietzsche's respective conceptions of the will. Unlike Schopenhauer and

Nietzsche, Freud (Thompson, 1994) situated the will in the conscious portion of the mind, the Ego. Yet, like Nietzsche and Schopenhauer, Freud conceives our desires (what he terms Libido, or the Id) as the *raison d'être* of our existence, firmly lodged in our unconscious. He equates the relation between our will and our desire as analogous to a rider on a horse. The horse is our id, or desire, and knows where it wants to go. The rider, our ego or will, tries his best to guide the horse where the rider wants to go but is not always successful in doing so. In order to get along they have to compromise. The happy person has come to terms with his desires and tries his best to serve them by not getting in their way. The neurotic doesn't trust his desires and tries his best to suppress them, out of fear.

Freud is sometimes accused of favoring the rational part of the mind over the passions that drive us, but it isn't that simple. Like Schopenhauer, Freud was pessimistic about the degree to which we can be in harmony with our desires, but he was no cognitive psychologist. The worst thing we can do, says Freud, is to repress our desires. The happy person recognizes them as her master and devotes her life to serving them. Psychoanalysis was intended to serve this very purpose, to give our desires more liberty in the conduct of our lives. Our will can either serve our desires or obstinately suppress them. More often than not, we choose the latter.

So what does this say about freedom and the will? What role does our rational mind play in achieving happiness, if not to guide and control our desires? Moreover, what are the implications for psychotherapy? Do we employ conscious will to make changes in our lives, or to simply discover what we are up to? Which makes more sense, to equate will with desire, or as the arbiter to our desires? And where do we locate choice? Is it a function of the ego, our rationality? Or is it a function of desire, which would render choice an unconscious activity?

For the answer to these questions I now turn our attention to the twentieth-century existentialist philosopher, Jean-Paul Sartre (Thompson, 2020), and the clinical perspective of R. D. Laing, who was profoundly influenced by Sartre's philosophy.

What difference does it ultimately make how we characterize the function of Will, whether we equate it with desire or whether we equate it with rationality, with the ego, so long as we are clear on how we define their respective functions? We know that human beings are driven by passion, the seat of emotions and desire, and have a capacity for rationality that serves as a kind of agent for our passions and a judge of appropriate action.

Let's suppose that our passions are the seat of our desires, and the ego is the seat of will, our capacity for rational judgment, and that they sometimes work in harmony and sometimes they are opposed.

I agree with Jean-Paul Sartre that human beings are fundamentally free and that their behavior is not determined by external causes, or their genetic structure, or even the mystification employed by their families and society. This means that all our actions are free, that every feeling, ambition, and attitude are the consequence of my free choice, even though these choices are not governed by my will, but by my desires.

Though separated by an enormous gulf in theory, temperament, and vocation, Freud and Sartre would have agreed that our choices are free but not willful. Rather, *our choices are instigated by our desires*. Freud would say that I render my choices unconsciously, whereas Sartre would argue that the choices are conscious but on a pre-reflective level. I only become aware of the choices I make after having made them. In both cases, it wasn't my ego or "I" that chose the action. The so-called conscious choice merely makes it official, after the fact.

This means that I can never get ahead of my choices, that I am always one step behind them as they guide me this way or that. This explains why I often do not know why I choose this over that, because my choices are not rational. This is why psychoanalysis is retrospective, not prophylactic. Only in behavioral psychology do we play the fiction of deliberating what we intend to do, and then execute the act. In psychoanalysis, the idea is to review previous actions and learn something about ourselves from them. The actions under review may be buried in our childhoods, or they may have occurred moments earlier, in the analytic session. In either case, we're not talking about an *executive* function of the mind but a *reflective* one.

This has led some to conclude that Freud's conception of the unconscious was deterministic. If we don't make our choices "consciously," which is to say, voluntarily, then our choices must be made for us—by our unconscious. This was Schopenhauer's position. This implies there is no free choice in the matter, if the choice isn't willfully executed. This conclusion is rooted in a misconception about the nature of choice, and whether we have conscious control over our decisions. We know from Freud's horse and rider analogy that it is the horse that drives the rider, and not the other way around.

Just because my choices are free doesn't mean I am in control of them. Freedom doesn't turn me into Superman, it doesn't make me omnipotent. My free choice isn't the freedom to dominate or overpower. It is a freedom to be me, and to embrace the me that I am, warts and all. Sartre suggests that our neuroses go all the way back to a fundamental choice, in our childhood, when we chose what our neurosis would be, on an unconscious, pre-reflective level. This means that we *intend* our psychopathology, we are not the "consequence" of this or that trauma. Nothing *caused* my condition. Rather, I chose to experience this or that incident as "traumatic." I am ultimately responsible for who I am, and how I became who I am.

Given this thesis, how is therapy even possible? If I cannot will myself to health, then how does change come about? When I asked Laing (Laing, 1979) this question in one of my supervision sessions with him, he answered with one word: *indirectly*. All my conscious, knowing mind is good for in therapy is to acquaint myself with the mysterious nature of my existence and plumb its depths, over an indeterminate amount of time. I cannot WILL myself to overcome the fear of intimacy. I cannot *compel* myself to love more generously, behave more compassionately, or feel more alive. Yet all of these dilemmas often improve as a consequence of the therapeutic endeavor to know ourselves. How? We don't know, exactly. All we do know is that, going all the way back to the Delphic Oracle's command to "know thyself," that knowing oneself has the potential to change our lives forever, to finally become who we are, authentically.

So how has behavioral psychology, and more recently Cognitive Behavioral Therapy (CBT), approached the role of will in the therapeutic process? Psychology, in its endeavor to appear more scientific than philosophy, equates Will with volition. Following the Stoics, behavioral psychologists situate the will in the conscious portions of our mind, and insist that all our choices are driven by rationality, not by desire.

According to this thesis, my will has the ability to decide upon and commit to any course of action. It isn't my desire that prompts me to make this or that choice, but rational thought processes. Will is defined as a *purposive striving,* and is one of four primary psychological functions, along with affect (emotion), motivation (goals), and cognition (or thinking). Volition and willpower are the same thing. In behavioral therapy, you decide to accomplish a task, such as overcoming the fear of flying, and over time you "will" yourself to overcome this fear by recognizing that your fear is irrational.

Does this work? Yes and no. As with other therapies, some people improve and others do not. But according to Laing, what probably helps CBT patients to actually change anything is always a function of their desire, not their will. They just don't know it and attribute their successes to willful engagements with their problems. According to Laing, it was probably the relationship with their therapist that eventually provided the desire to effect change, not willfully but indirectly, which is to say, unconsciously.

Laing was a committed existentialist and synthesized Freud's and Sartre's respective perspectives by situating our selfhood in our desires instead of our ego, synonymous with our character traits. This limits the function of the will to an agent of synthesis and repression, a view that was also embraced by Jacques Lacan. So how does this perspective show up in the context of a clinical situation? For a perfect example of how Laing believed that successful behavior always follows one's desire rather than Will, let us take a look at the drug addict. The addict may feel that he should stop drinking or drugging, because he should or because it is destroying his life. But unless he genuinely wants to, he will fail. The will is an executive function that can either serve desire or oppose it. When in opposition, the person is in conflict with his desire, but if he tries to control it with his will the result will be haphazard.

The addict tells himself that he needs to get "in control" of his addiction, as though he can steel himself against his desire to drink or eat too much by a force of Will. This is his dilemma: an obstinate refusal to genuinely want to give up this or that drug or behavior, but relies instead on an introjected mommy to make him do so. According to Laing, this never works. Yes, you can live your life this way, getting off and then back on the wagon, in and out of rehab, AA meetings, etc., but without ever really giving it up, both protecting your desire while fighting against it, as a way of life, without terminus.

At bottom, the addict wants to be free of the pain that is elicited by desire, so he medicates his pain with this or that drug. But you can never kill your desire, you can only redirect it. Because desire always entails risk and occasional failure, he suffers from an intolerance of the pain that the addiction momentarily relieves. This suggests that addiction is a form of suicide which occasionally succeeds in the deliberate or accidental overdose, organ failure, obesity, and waiting to die, or hoping to.

The same principle applies to any occasion when we galvanize the will to suppress the pain of desire, the pain of *living*. This is the most common circumstance that inspires a person to seek therapy. For some of us, our desire is so weak that all we have left is the will to carry on, but without joy. Having buried our desire, we nevertheless manage to eke out a measure of success, driven by Will alone, but are we happy? Will can sometimes lead to enviable wealth, yet leave us wondering why our lives are devoid of passion. The irony is you don't really need drugs to reduce anxiety. Your will can do it for you. Will and desire, more often than not, are at cross purposes regarding how much risk we allow in our lives. Though Will can be an instrument for change, more often it is not. To a surprising degree, Will resists change.

Genuine change only comes about when we want to change, not because we need to or because we should. Sartre's conception of psychic freedom is radical, and disturbing to those who fear our desires and are anxious to manage them. Laing believed what is missing in our lives is opening our hearts to risk. Unfortunately, life occasions risk, and fear is its greatest impediment. How much we are willing to risk is ultimately our choice, however much we may wish that it wasn't. The function of therapy is to use our capacity for reflection, our will, to assess why we always get in the way of our desires, and to put our defenses into question. We cannot will ourselves to let go of such defenses, but somehow—and how we do not entirely understand—engaging in such an inquiry often leads to change, even when we have no control over the matter.

References

Aristotle. (1915) *The Works of Aristotle, Vol. IX: Ethica Nicomachea* (W. D. Ross, Trans.). London and New York: Oxford University Press.

Augustine. (2010) *Augustine: On the Free Choice of the Wil, On Grace and Free Choice, and Other Writings* (Cambridge Texts in the History of Philosophy). Cambridge: Cambridge University Press.

Laing, R. D. (1979) Personal Communication.

Nietzsche, F. (2001) *Beyond Good and Evil: Prelude to a Philosophy of the Future* (Cambridge Texts in the History of Philosophy). (J. Norman, Trans.). Cambridge: Cambridge University Press.

Schopenhauer, A. (2012) *The World As Will and Representation* (E. F. J. Payne, Trans.) (p. 94). New York: Dover Publications.

Thompson, M. G. (1994) *The Truth About Freud's Technique: The Encounter With the Real*. New York and London: New York University Press.

Thompson, M. G. (2020) Existential Psychoanalysis: The Role of Freedom in the Clinical Encounter. In A. Govrin and J. Mills (Eds.), *Innovations in Psychoanalysis: Originality, Development, Progress*. London and New York: Routledge.

Chapter 5

Vicissitudes of Authenticity in the Psychoanalytic Situation[1]

One of the prevailing themes that has haunted the psychoanalytic discourse from its inception is the basis of the analytic relationship and the nature of the uneasy dialogue between analyst and patient. Whereas Freud characterized this discourse as one that both requires and enhances a unique capacity for honesty, I have increasingly found it more useful to characterize this relationship in terms of a quest for authenticity, a project that was first articulated by existentialist philosophers. Even when authenticity is not explicitly invoked by the person who aspires to it—which is usually the case in psychoanalysis—analytic patients and practitioners alike nevertheless allude to authenticity in the way they oftentimes characterize the goals of treatment and the demands that are made on both participants in the analyst-patient relationship.

Though authenticity is not a technical term in any conventional psychoanalytic text with which I am familiar, the idea of what I take authenticity to mean has pervaded psychoanalysis from its inception. For example, when Freud (Breuer and Freud, 1893–1895, p. 305) suggested that the goal of analysis is to "transform hysterical misery into common unhappiness," he was invoking authenticity as an essential, if undeniably ambiguous, goal of psychoanalysis. Similarly, when Winnicott (1989, p. 199) argued that "If we are successful [as analysts] we enable our patients to abandon invulnerability and become a sufferer," he was addressing the analysand's capacity to accept the inescapable reality of suffering and the need to embrace such suffering honestly, or authentically. And when Bion (1974, p. 13) says that whenever analyst and patient meet together that both of them should be experiencing fear and that, if they are not, they have no business being there, he was also invoking authenticity as an inevitable presence in every analytic encounter. Neither Freud nor Winnicott nor Bion, of course, employ

DOI: 10.4324/9781003429104-5

authenticity in their writing, but the sense of it pervades the corpus of their respective psychoanalytic sensibilities.

So why hasn't the term authenticity been incorporated in a more explicit way into the psychoanalytic discourse? I'm not sure I can provide a convincing answer to that question, as I continue to be puzzled by it myself. Of course, we know that authenticity was first employed as a concept by existential philosophers, not psychoanalytic practitioners. Though its sensibility can be traced back to Nietzsche and Kierkegaard, it was Heidegger who first coined the term and made it the backbone of his philosophical perspective. The term was subsequently adopted by other existentialist philosophers and soon after by psychoanalysts who became identified with the existential perspective. Ludwig Binswanger (1963), Medard Boss (1963), and R. D. Laing (1969) are only some of the many psychoanalysts who came to epitomize an explicitly existentialist approach to psychoanalysis in Europe, whereas, in America, mainstream analysts such as Hans Loewald (1980) and Stan Leavy (1980, 1988) were profoundly influenced by the writings of Heidegger. In recent years, other terms that were originally identified with existential psychoanalysis, e.g., hermeneutics, intersubjectivity, and social constructivism have filtered into the American psychoanalytic milieu, and authenticity has even been invoked in the recent contemporary relational literature (e.g., Mitchell, 1992). Yet none of the American analysts who have adopted these ideas would call themselves existentialists, and few of the Europeans who preceded them are cited in the psychoanalytic literature. There remains a profound cultural divide between European and American sensibilities when it comes to articulating the ends of the analytic treatment experience and it appears that the concept of authenticity occupies an uneasy role at the interface between them. For example, European cultures tend to view suffering as a source of strength and character whereas American culture tends to view suffering as a source of trauma and psychopathology.

Another obstacle to integrating authenticity in the analytic landscape is the aversion of the typical psychoanalyst to reading philosophical material, the source of authenticity as a concept. Still another obstacle is the ambiguous relationship between authenticity and morality. As I will argue, authenticity has no specific moral agenda, and while this may be acceptable to many psychoanalytic practitioners, others find this anomaly disturbing. But probably the most important obstacle to embracing authenticity as a treatment criterion pertains to the commonplace characterization of psychoanalysis as a way of increasing the patient's capacity for work and love—a characterization that is typically rejected by existentialists for being facile and market-oriented. While it is doubtful that Freud ever characterized more effectiveness in work and love as a specific goal of treatment or simply a common side-effect, the relatively pragmatic American analytic community has often invoked greater success with the neurotic's love life and career objectives as important treatment objectives—and among the few treatment goals that psychoanalysis is said to be good for!

Increasingly, the question of what psychoanalysis *is* good for is being debated in the American media, which usually consigns it to an antiquated, if quaint, treatment philosophy that isn't particularly adept at relieving the majority of ailments that typical therapy patients want relieved, including anxiety, depression, social phobia, low self-esteem, and so on. While many are prepared to allow that psychoanalysis is good at engendering self-understanding, I seriously doubt that analysis or even modified forms of analytic therapy are particularly effective at treating most of the disorders listed in the current edition of the Diagnostic and Statistical Manual. My reason for saying this is because what psychoanalysis is best suited for, more than any form of therapy I know, is greater authenticity in one's life.

Though there are contemporary and popularized versions of authenticity that reduce it to feeling states and forms of moral behavior (Taylor, 1991), for the purposes of this paper, I restrict the concept to three elementary attributes: 1) that it furthers behavior that is inherently *unconventional* or pertains to the road less traveled; 2) that it is the more difficult or *arduous* path and consequently more rewarding in a way that the less onerous path is often not; and 3) that it is *genuine*, but in a way that resists generalization because it is context-specific and consistent, for example, with efforts in the psychoanalytic literature to characterize aspects of the extra-transference relationship as *real* or honest, with a concomitant absence of subterfuge or contrivance. My aim is not to introduce a novel conception of authenticity into the analytic situation but to locate those elements of authentic relating that have been implicit in the psychoanalytic discourse since its inception.

With this brief introduction, I divide the following paper into four sections. In the first, I review the concept of authenticity in Nietzsche and Heidegger; in the second, I discuss the principles in Freud's treatment philosophy that are consistent with authenticity, including free association, neutrality, and abstinence; in the third, I explore the relationship between authenticity and the role of suffering in the work of Winnicott, Bion, and

Lacan; and in the fourth, I examine the role of authenticity in the so-called transference and countertransference relationship, specifically the real and genuine relationship in the analyst-patient interaction. I conclude with a brief discussion about the role of courage in the analytic situation.

I Authenticity in Nietzsche and Heidegger

Though Heidegger was the first philosopher to employ authenticity as a technical term, both Nietzsche and Kierkegaard were important sources for this component of Heidegger's philosophy. For Nietzsche (2002, 2003), authenticity characterized the person who is not afraid to face up to the fundamental anxieties of living. He saw this ideal person as one who would emerge one day in the future capable of "overcoming" the difficulties that his generation, Nietzsche believed, was incapable of facing. This special individual was embodied in Nietzsche's conception of the *Übermensch*, usually translated into English as a superman or, more literally, "over-man," a person who would come to grips with her fears and, in that sense, overcome the weight of her existence by accepting reality for what it is, unbowed and unafraid. Nietzsche rejected the Enlightenment view that society is in an inexorable process of evolution that will inevitably improve from one generation to the next with scientific breakthroughs that will make our lives more satisfying and countered that, in many respects, our lives are actually getting worse. In Nietzsche's opinion, our capacity to reason is not as objectively reliable as Enlightenment philosophers claimed because humans are driven by passion, the source of which is predominantly uncon-scious. Nietzsche's *Übermensch* was capable of recognizing this observa-tion and possessed the necessary courage to face it (Thompson, 2004d).

There are other qualities that the *Übermensch* embodies that are just as consistent with Nietzsche's rejection of contemporary society, includ-ing: 1) an opposition to authority that results in a fierce individualism; 2) a concerted scepticism that rejects absolute truths of any kind, embodied in Nietzsche's pronouncement that *God is dead*; 3) a perspectivism which holds that truth is wedded to the perspective of the person who promotes it, not fixed, immutable standards; 4) a moral relativism which holds that all truths are relative to a time and place and, so, neither eternal nor objective but highly personal and fluid; and finally, 5) a decentering of the subject which rejects the notion that the self is autonomous because, according to Nietzsche, there is no depth to the personality since we are what we *do*, not what we take ourselves to *be*.

So how does Nietzsche's conception of the *Übermensch* compare with Heidegger's notion of authenticity? Though Nietzsche's philosophy had a profound impact on Heidegger, one would be mistaken to construe Heidegger's authentic individual as nothing more than a twentieth-century edition of Nietzsche's *Übermensch*. One of the principal differences between Nietzsche's *Übermensch* and Heidegger's conception of authenticity is that, for Heidegger, there is no such person who epitomizes an "authentic hero" in juxtaposition to less endowed neurotics. Instead, authenticity is characterized by Heidegger as a specific act or moment in any individual's life where the context in which a situation arises offers opportunities to behave authentically or not. Unlike Nietzsche, Heidegger rejected the notion of an ideal person who would some day emerge to replace the stereotypical contemporary neurotic, an idea he thought was stuck in a modernist way of thinking. Heidegger argued that all humans are essentially inauthentic in their being but that they may, when challenged to, behave authentically on given occasions. In other words, behaving authentically isn't a process of cleansing ourselves of inauthentic character traits through a transformative religious or psychoanalytic regimen, like the perfectly analyzed person. Because we are inauthentic through and through, we cannot do anything to change our fundamental nature, which is to avoid anxiety as a matter of course. So how can we manage to act authentically in spite of our condition, and, more to the point, what would doing so look like?

In order to understand what authenticity entails, it may be helpful to ponder what it means to be inauthentic. In Heidegger's magnum opus, *Being and Time* (1962), he characterized inauthenticity as an incidence of "fallenness" (*Verfallenheit*), as when a person sells out to public opinion in order to curry favor. A preoccupying theme throughout Heidegger's work is the relationship between the individual and society and how it engenders a conflict that we can never resolve. This is because humans are existentially isolated and, in their loneliness, crave the comfort of feeling at one with others, not unlike the *Oceanic* experience that Freud describes in *Civilization and Its Discontents* (1930). For Heidegger and Nietzsche alike, this sense of belonging is an illusion. Though this quest is inconsolable, says Heidegger, the only way of approximating this feeling is by abandoning an essential aspect of what we are about, our personal integrity. Yet, if we are condemned to be inauthentic as a basic feature of our character, how can we also be granted a choice in the matter, to choose *not* to be so on certain occasions?

A good example of the difficulty we all face in recognizing when we have fallen from authenticity was offered by Heidegger himself, when he describes his own infamous lapse into inauthenticity when he joined the National Socialist Party in Germany in the 1930s (Safranski, 1998). Because sacrifice is an essential aspect of authenticity, Heidegger believed he was behaving courageously and resolutely—two ingredients of authentic choice—when he abandoned the comfortable role of a sequestered academic for the relatively precarious position as Rector of the German University system in the service of the Nazi Party. The fitful collaboration was short-lived and ended less than a year later. Many years after, in a famous interview (Heidegger, 2003, pp. 24–48) given shortly before his death, Heidegger characterized his excursion into politics as an incidence of inauthenticity, an insight that only came to him in hindsight. In other words, according to Heidegger, he wasn't able to tell he was behaving inauthentically *in the moment of doing so*. After the fact, Heidegger could recognize he was mistaken in believing that National Socialism (or, for that matter, any political platform) could serve as a vehicle for authenticity. Like so many others, he was caught up in the feeling of being at one with the German people and even saw himself as an instrument of National Socialism's success. Because any act necessarily exists in time, it is also necessary to give one's actions the time they require to reveal, in their unfolding, what those actions were about after the fact, a fundamental tenet of psychoanalytic investigation. This is why Heidegger's conception of authenticity offers little in the way of reassuring, external markers that can discern the motives one is serving at the moment action is taken, because our motives are always, to a significant degree, hidden or, as Freud argued, overdetermined. In other words, fate plays a role in whether our actions are authentic or not; it isn't just a matter of knowing right from wrong and exercising one's will accordingly. In the moment of decision, I effectively abandon my choices to forces that are beyond my ability to predict or even fathom. My authenticity isn't something I can perfect, no matter how compliant I am to the customs of my community, because my choices always harbor an element of uncertainty about them, and only time will reveal the full scope of what I intended the moment I acted on them.

So if this is how Heidegger characterizes inauthenticity, how does he articulate what it means to behave authentically? But first, where did Heidegger derive his views about authenticity from? Were those views original, or did he base them on precedents in Western philosophy? In fact, there are important antecedents to Heidegger's conception of authenticity in addition to Nietzsche, going all the way back to the Greeks, who influenced both of their philosophies. Guignon (2004) suggests that traces of authenticity begin with Socrates' dictum in the fourth century B.C. to "know thyself":

> To know yourself . . . is to know above all what your place is in the scheme of things—what you are and what you should be as that has been laid out in advance by the cosmic order. Only because finding your place in the scheme of things is what is truly important does it become worthwhile to assess your personal nature.
>
> (p. 13)

For Heidegger and Nietzsche, however, it is not Socrates or Plato who epitomize the roots of authentic relating but, as we shall see below, the Greek sceptics, whose lineage goes back even further to the pre-Socratics, especially Heraclitus.[2] After the Greeks, Augustine's *Confessions* represent the next important chapter in the pre-history of authenticity due to his account of a determined inner quest undertaken to shake off a life of carnal sin and wanton materialism. Unlike other impassioned religious conversions, Augustine's stands out for its naked honesty and contemporary relevance as well as its considerable impact on Heidegger's philosophical temperament. Though his confessions were to God, Augustine himself comes across as a "man's man" whose trials of the flesh and consequent soul-searching easily resonate with seekers of every generation, including our own.

Despite Augustine's singular impact, the rise of Christianity gradually brought a halt to the kind of impassioned search for answers "within" that men of the cloth taught could only be found through devotion to God. Perhaps this is why Augustine is the last great example of existential literature until the Renaissance that brought with it the rise of Romanticism and the rebirth of Greek scepticism. It is from this later, post-sixteenth-century era that many of the ideas we now associate with authenticity eventually crystallized, some of them veering off into a reified version of the self as inner substance, whereas the other trend—which was eventually embraced by Nietzsche and Heidegger—perceived the self as more fluid and less tangible. Most of our notions of authenticity today can be traced to the Romantic period when the self emerged as a component of the human personality, which imbued people with an inner core that is, in turn, composed of an ego or psychic substance. Consequently, many people in contemporary culture equate authenticity with getting in touch with their feelings or being true to their self, which, in turn, they believe is made up of their feelings and experiences.

The origin of this depiction of authenticity can be linked to Rousseau's rebellion against the Enlightenment's emphasis on rationality, epitomized by Descartes. Like Descartes, Rousseau believed there is a substantial self to get in touch with, but he disagreed about its nature. Whereas most Enlightenment philosophers equated the self with rationality, Rousseau and other Romantics equated it with non-rational feeling states, a perspective that became invaluable to artists, poets, and novelists. One of the implications of this argument is that subjective truth has precedence over objective, or scientific truth, and that the artist is in a more advantageous position to obtain such truths than scientists are. Moreover, the kinds of truths available was now open to debate. *Self*-discovery needed to be distinguished from, say, the discovery of new worlds across the oceans. For Rousseau, the most important task a man or woman could set for themselves is to discover who they are because we are opaque to ourselves and can only find ourselves by virtue of extraordinary effort and courage.

While the validity of Rousseau's conception of the self is open to debate, one can nonetheless recognize something of both Nietzsche and Heidegger's debt to the Romantic quest and their rejection of the Enlightenment's privilege of rationality over more subtle forms of experience. If nothing else, the emergence of the artist as a new authentic figure has its origins in the Romantic era and influenced both Nietzsche's and Heidegger's identification with art over science. As Guignon (2004) points out, our contemporary notion of the artist as an uncompromising, morally pure agent, so dedicated to his work and its inner truth that he refuses to "sell out" for the sake of becoming rich or popular, is a relatively recent phenomenon.

> The modern use of the word "artist" to refer to those engaged in the arts as we understand them first appears in English only in 1823 with the adoption of the French term, *artiste*. The very idea that there is something that painters and musicians and architects and poets and chefs have in common—something called being an artist—is relatively new in Western experience.
>
> (pp. 70–71)

The distinguishing feature of the so-called true artist contrasted with the pretensions of commercial artists rests precisely on the notion that the real article is authentic, that the work this artist is faithful to is a truth that is generated from somewhere "within," from an inner core of his or her being that cannot be accessed by skill or training, but rather some indefinable trial of suffering, *angst*, or unique something or other that belongs to this artist and none other. By this reckoning, we don't have to rely on Rousseau's or Descartes' conception of a tangible self, whether real or inner, to render legitimate the notion of the contemporary artist as we have come to know him. On the contrary, the artist has helped *us* learn something about the nature of authenticity itself, irrespective of which theory of the self (de-decentered or otherwise) we are partial to. It is this conception of the artist that inspired many of Heidegger's later writings about the relationship between language and poetry, epitomized by the German Romanticist poet, Friedrich Hölderlin (Heidegger, 1971).

But of all the literary figures who inspired Nietzsche's and Heidegger's respective nineteenth- and twentieth-century notions of authenticity, it wasn't Rousseau or Rilke or even Hölderlin, though all of them influenced contemporary notions of it to varying degrees. Instead, the person who should be given credit for serving as the link between the ancient Greek tradition of authenticity and the starker, more secular contemporary one derives from the sixteenth-century essayist and sceptic Michel de Montaigne. Montaigne's facility with the sceptic method of *epoché*, or suspension of judgment, as a means of accessing the deepest recesses of personal experience, served as the basis for entertaining a conception of authenticity that could dispense with notions such as selfhood, subjectivity, egoism, and the like (Montaigne, 1925, pp. 288–358).

Unlike Plato and Aristotle, who advocated rationality and the accumulation of knowledge as an intrinsic aspect of man's identity, the sceptics were so opposed to formal methods of rational inquiry that it is difficult to characterize their system as a *philosophy*, but more an attitude developed out of trends it inherited from pre-Socratic thinkers, such as Heraclitus and Democritus, including: a) an anti-realist bias; b) the turn to a more subjective attitude about truth; and c) the development of philosophy away from abstract epistemological inquiry toward the more practical goal of acquiring a state of serenity, or happiness.

Whereas Socrates and Plato offered what is arguably the first notion of authenticity rooted in a self that knows who it is by achieving a kind of wisdom that derives from self-knowledge, the sceptics advocated a method for overcoming the need to acquire such knowledge in the first place, treating such quests as symptoms of obsessional neurosis (Groarke, 1990). Instead of a knowing self, the sceptics envisioned an *experiencing* self that is capable of submitting to the world *as it is given,* in all its mystery and ambiguity. By suspending judgment about my ability to predict the outcome of events as they occur from one day to the next, the sceptic learns not to comprehend his experience in order to surmount it but to *suffer* it in order to accept it and be with it. The sceptics believed if you can overcome your obsessional quest for knowledge—including *self*-knowledge—a transformation in consciousness could occur, a kind of releasement or giving-way they claimed is free from worry (and a source for authenticity).

So, the question we need to ask ourselves is this: is authenticity necessarily incumbent on the concept of a self in the first place? One of the areas of contention among postmodernist thinkers regarding authenticity is the problem of the self, or subjectivity, which postmodernism rejects. As we have seen, popular literature on authenticity going all the way back to Rousseau and the Romantics situates authenticity in the notion of a feeling-self that is a version of the Cartesian ego but, in place of an ego that is based exclusively on rationality, the Romantics preferred a self imbued with feeling-states instead. In either case, the notion of a reified self that is substantial and constant is consistent with the idea of a hidden or true self that lies beneath an outer or social self, so this conception of authenticity degenerates into a private kernel of a self that is "inside" oneself, so to speak, and unconscious. While this conception of authenticity has been adopted by popular culture and American humanistic authors, it was summarily rejected by both Nietzsche and Heidegger. In fact, a great deal of Heidegger's efforts were devoted to addressing the problem of the nature of the self and how to conceive of authenticity without recourse to the notion of a substantial or reified self.

In contrast to Descartes' privileging of the ego's status as a thinking-subject *par excellence*, Heidegger argued that we live our lives in an everyday sort of way without thinking about what we are doing and, more importantly, without having to think our way through our activities as a matter of course. The place he assigned to reason is an after-the-fact operation that is not primary to our engagement with the world but secondary. It is only when our involvement with the world breaks down that we take the time to divorce ourselves from it for the purpose of pondering what has happened and why. According to Zahavi (2001):

At the beginning of his analysis of *Being and Time* Heidegger writes . . . that a subject is never given without a world and without others.

Thus . . . it is within the context of [every human being's] being-in-the-world that he comes across intersubjectivity.

(p. 124)

Whereas Husserl begins with the individual's relationship with oneself and goes from there to others, Heidegger begins with our relationships with others and then sets out to investigate how to determine or reclaim our relationship with ourselves (Thompson, 2001c). In other words, we dwell within a common public "totality of surroundings" that constitute us as individuals in a world *from* which all of our perceptions, sensibilities, and experiences derive. We are not principally occupied with perceptual objects in a remote theoretical way but rather with handling, using, and taking care of things in a manner that does not rely on our cognition of what we are doing when we are doing it. Heidegger is at such pains to emphasize the primordial structure of our being-with the world before we ever become individual subjects that he coins a new term for depicting each human being's essential status as a being. So, instead of using the familiar terms subject, ego, or self—each of which, in Heidegger's thinking, harks back to Descartes' solipsistic ego—he uses the German *Dasein*, which, unfortunately, has no English equivalent. In German, Dasein is a common, everyday term to which Heidegger gives his own meaning. The literal English translation would be "there-being," or the more common "being-there," a cumbersome and unsatisfactory rendition compared with what some translators have rendered as the more colloquial *existence*, which is also misleading because, after all, we are still talking about a *person*. Consequently, most translators simply retain the German Dasein without translating it and then, as I am now doing, are obliged to explain what it means.

Basically, Heidegger is drawing a distinction between what we typically depict as the subject or self, which, in his view, are constructs from a more fundamental way in which we exist in the world primordially. "I" exist first and foremost as a being of the world from which I cannot extricate myself very easily. The person I take myself to be is essentially an invention that I have a hand in creating, but the greater part of my self's authorship derives from what others make of me. In fact, I am so obsessed with what others think of me and how they see me that I want to make myself into the person they expect me to be, and, to a significant degree, that is who I am. Moreover, who I take myself to be is not just rooted in the past; "I" am also constantly in the making, every waking moment of my life. In Heidegger's view, we never really overcome this condition and are always looking to "them" to tell us what we should do and who we must become in order to be loved and acceptable. My ambitions play a pivotal role in the person I take myself to be because I am constantly striving to become someone who will be able to escape the awful feeling of never being completely accepted by others, no matter how much I try to meet their expectations.

This doesn't suggest that Heidegger ignores the past; it is just as crucial to him as it was to Freud, but, for Heidegger, the past is co-existent with the future to which I aim because I am always trying to correct perceived inefficiencies from my past life with possibilities I perceive ahead of me. Most of the time, I feel, to varying degrees, "thrown" into a maelstrom of competing notions and ambitions that others have a hand in constructing what I take my "self" to be. To make matters even more complicated, others are not everybody else but me, a totality from which I stand apart. Instead, they are me also, but from whom I do not customarily distinguish myself, despite my experience to the contrary. Dasein—this matrix in which I constantly dwell without necessarily ever knowing it—is something that can be, and usually is, *others*. Yet in everyday experience we do not ordinarily experience our "selves," nor do we ordinarily experience "others"—in fact, we are, for the most part, incapable of telling the difference between the two. According to Zahavi (2001):

> We do not experience ourselves in contradistinction to some sort of inaccessible foreign subjects; rather, our being-with-one-another is characterized by replaceability and interchangeability. We are there in the world together with others [so that] the "who" of the *Dasein* who is living in everydayness is therefore anyone, it is *they*.
>
> (p. 130)

My everyday relationship with others dissolves into my own Dasein wherein I "lose" myself in others and merge in and out of them, just as they merge in and out of me, relieving me of my responsibilities just as I relieve themselves of theirs. Zahavi concludes that "Dasein *allows* itself to be carried along with others, and its formation of judgment, its estimation of values, its self-apprehension, and its interpretation of the world are determined, dictated, and controlled by the publicness of being-with-one-another" (p. 130). My problem is not, as Husserl argued, one of how to establish a relationship with others in order to verify that others exist and occupy a role in my life; my problem is one of becoming my own person, with my own perspective, apart from others and what they would have me think and become.

From a Heideggerian perspective, the problem of empathy with which Husserl was so preoccupied—the problem of how an isolated subject can ever make contact with others—is a moot issue because we are with others in our primordiality to such an extent that we can never escape them. This is why my absorption in the world has the character of being lost, not in a desert but amongst others, in search of the self I genuinely am or can become. This is because I (or rather Dasein) do not possess a self-identity on which I rely, nor can I. Instead, I have to appropriate myself and because of this, once having done so can just as easily lose myself again, and eventually do, over and over again. Dasein's self, which is always in the making, can never be an objectively constituted entity, the culmination, one might wish, of a "thorough" analysis, but only a *manner of existing*. The manner in which I exist is either authentic or inauthentic; I am inauthentic, according to Heidegger, when I allow myself to be determined by others and what they expect me to be. This is the way we typically are except for those moments when we realize the degree to which we have compromised ourselves and lost ourselves in a socially constituted they-self.

So, if Heidegger's conception of authenticity is rooted in a rough and ready notion of a self that is inherently insubstantial, that lacks fixed characteristics, and exists in a state of yearning towards a future that it never reaches, then how can the essence of such a self be conceived, even when it is couched in this mysterious context that Heidegger calls Dasein? In Heidegger's earlier period, authenticity was articulated in the context of *resoluteness*, an attitude that characterizes the inherent difficulty that living on the edge entails. Later, language played a more important role in Heidegger's philosophy and influenced his thoughts about authenticity as well. By then, he saw human beings as basically language-bearing, story-telling creatures. Whereas postmodernists tend to view the self as a fragmented collection of episodic states of semi-consciousness that is constructed by the social and cultural forces constantly working on it, including economics, sex, politics, fashion, and media, Heidegger sees all of these elements as important influences, but none as important as the power that language has over our self-identity. Moreover, and perhaps even more importantly, we aren't merely shaped by language passively, like robots; we also *have a hand* in our relationship with the words that constitute our being and the kind of person we turn out to be. If my history plays a decisive role in the person I am, I also play a role in changing my history, adding to it, and arriving at new understandings of it through new interpretations of it every time I revisit and think about it. My past and my self are never fixed—they are alive to change and revision as long as I am capable of giving thought to the circumstances in which my life is rooted.

The function of language, from this viewpoint, is to tell stories, which we engage in every time we communicate with each other. From a narrative perspective, the self is not a static entity, like a character in a book whose personality is fixed in the mind of its author. It is instead a continuous, never-ending story that has no culmination until the moment of death, so our stories have this open-ended quality to them that defies clearly defined boundaries. Although this produces anxiety in each of us, it also elicits a sense of wonder and possibility, without which our lives would be unimaginable. It is this very sense of wonder that the psychoanalyst capitalizes on in the analytic process by utilizing language to discover approximately who the person being analyzed *is*, by reflecting on the significance of the communication patterns that spontaneously come to mind in the course of the open-ended conversations shared.

But if my self, or Dasein, is so insubstantial, if I am what I take myself to be in that moment that I wrest my identity from an inauthentic "they," that competes with me at every turn to determine who I am for me, and I have the freedom—the responsibility, even—to revisit my previous interpretations of myself with fresh eyes and perspectives to detect the fallacy of previously undetected corruptions in my earlier self-definitions, then what, ultimately, does anyone have to hang the hat of his or her self-identity on? What's to stop me from just changing my mind—and my self—at every whim and convenience whenever it suits me to do so? What's to stop me, in the name of authenticity, from giving myself over to a form of unbridled narcissism that surreptitiously seeks the easy way out at every turn, but does so in the name of authentic "unpredictability"? One of the German words that Heidegger employs for authenticity in *Being and Time* is *eigentlich*, which comes from the root meaning "own." Heidegger sees the authentic act as one in which I appropriate from the myriad of influences that I am constantly subjected to in my world and my history that which I choose to make "my own." Character traits, attitudes, opinions, and what have you become identified with who I take myself to be, not because of some reasoned argument, but arbitrarily and unconsciously. But, due to my powers of reflection, I am also able to survey these choices and, in a secondary sort of way, decide whether I want to commit myself to them and become them until such a time that I choose to revise them anew. The point Heidegger is making is that the committed person, which is to say, the authentic one, takes such choices seriously and views them in terms of building a structure or, in his later work, he would call it a "temple" to his or her relationship with being. As such, *who* each person is becomes something of a tradition and the seeds of a destiny that can be counted on, what we in America would call a person of substance or character.

Now all this may sound suspiciously narcissistic—and potentially criminal—to the person who is looking for evidence of a concept of authenticity that is tied to a standard of moral virtue that meets acceptable social mores, which, after all, is precisely what morality implies.[3] Postmodernists reject authenticity because they reject any pretension to a socially sanctioned code of ethics that can be imposed on the individual, which they mistakenly assume all theories of authenticity embrace. Like Nietzsche, Heidegger was opposed to the idea that society has the right to impose such standards willy-nilly except in the form of laws that are legislated and adjudicated in the courts, but he wasn't opposed to the idea of *virtue* in principle. The problem comes down to who gets to decide what virtue is and which virtues one should hold as most important, how religiously they should be applied, and how allowing we should be of individual imperfections. Remember that, for Heidegger, we are essentially *inauthentic,* fallen creatures, and that authentic selfhood is the exception, not the rule. Moreover, Heidegger refused to link authentic choices with ethical ones. Because ethics is a product of our relationships with others, we need a standard for our relationship with our *selves*, however insubstantial and inherently narcissistic the self may be. The concept of authenticity is intended to meet this standard. So when push comes to shove, how do we know when we are choosing authentically and when we are taking the easy way out? How can we tell when we are in touch with our own most being and when we are deluding ourselves with an act of momentary convenience?

Heidegger's answer to this problem is not so easy to grasp. It comes down to the observation that the authentic choice is never the easy one but always the road less traveled. If we're going to trust our conscience to be our guide, the inherent anguish that authentic choice entails should be as a reliable, if not perfect, foil to the folly that more crippling editions of narcissism often engender, yet consistent with the "destining" that Heidegger associates with authentic moments of importance. Contrary to the postmodernist who rejects values in principle because they cannot be universalized, the authentic person embraces values, however arbitrarily and subjectively chosen they necessarily are. And even if my values are different from yours, those values are nevertheless my own and an integral part of my authentic self-identity. In the end, because the self is insubstantial, the only thing I have to hold onto is what I make of myself, so the person I call myself stands for a tradition I have become, that I will continue to foster and tinker with for as long as I live. Certain views and character traits become precious simply because they are *mine*, because they are now part of this strange and indefinable yet indispensable "me." While I can always change who I am, the important thing is to determine whom, of all the people I can be, I resign myself to.

All this comes down to living with an awful lot of anxiety about who I am, why I do the things I do, and what I can possibly do to change the person I am when the person I have become is untenable. Both Nietzsche and Heidegger saw anxiety as a necessary and inevitable accompaniment to acting authentically. We are anxious due to a pervasive sense of alienation, the starkness of which is captured by Nietzsche's declaration that God is dead, or has abandoned us—meaning that in the postmodern era in which we live, there are no universal values to which we can cling, and the ground we walk on is no longer as solid as we once assumed. In Heidegger's phrase, we are thrown into a world that is not of our choosing, but we are nonetheless obliged to decide who we will be by the choices we make, even if our so-called choices are predominantly unconscious. This leaves us feeling alone in our decisions and the world in which we live, so we try to mitigate our anxiety by complying with what we imagine others want from us. The inauthentic individual, the contemporary neurotic, eventually discovers that compliance never meets with the kind of reward he longs for. Yet, he finds the alternative—the isolation of being his own person—equally untenable.

If, as Heidegger proposes, it is impossible to know from one moment to the next what our motivations are and whose motives we are serving at a given moment, then it isn't difficult to see why this conception of authenticity would be so troubling to conventional morality. If no one can set definitive standards for what authenticity entails, then how can we ever know whether we are being true to our selves or just acting from a convoluted strategy of compliance, on the one extreme, or a not-so-subtle form of conventional narcissism on the other? This is the question I now want to turn to in examining those aspects of authenticity that are readily evident in psychoanalysis.

II Authenticity in the Work of Sigmund Freud

In order to appreciate the importance of authenticity in Freud's treatment perspective, first, we need to examine his presuppositions about the nature of suffering and the role it plays in our lives. This topic is important because analysts and patients alike go into the treatment situation with their own views about what suffering entails and how much of it we can expect to diminish. There's no denying that Freud's take on the human condition is unconventional by contemporary North American standards. This is largely because it was born from a European, post-World War One, existential perspective that is anathema to the typical American mindset. Whereas, in this country, psychoanalysis was enthusiastically embraced as a tool of psychiatry in its never-ending war on mental illness, in Vienna and other European capitals such as Berlin, Paris, and London, psychoanalysis was marginalized by psychiatry and became a refuge for artists, writers, and intellectuals—and anyone wealthy enough to pay for six-times-a-week analysis. Many of Freud's patients came to see analysis as a means of facing the harsh realities of living instead of a device for the simple relief of their symptoms.

Yet, this paradox presented Freud's patients—most of whom came to him from all over the world—with a quandary: everyone goes into analysis in the first place because they suffer and want their suffering to diminish. In fact, without the motivation to sacrifice whatever it takes to effect a change in one's condition, the prospective analytic patient, Freud advised, should be refused treatment. Since the beginning of Western thought, philosophers, physicians, and religious leaders have been concerned with the nature of suffering, its ostensible causes, and its elusive relief. From earliest times, we have sought to understand what our suffering is about and how to relieve, accommodate, or accept it. Freud, though trained as a physician, was never willing to accept the strictly medical approach to suffering: to relieve it by any means possible, whatever the cost. Freud knew from personal experience that *life entails suffering*. The patients he treated suffered miserably yet seemed peculiarly intolerant of it. Because their desire for happiness caused them frustration, they instinctively suppressed desires they believed occasioned their suffering. How could psychoanalysis help them? Whatever kind of anguish analysis is suitable for relieving, Freud soon realized it could not be expected to relieve the kinds of suffering that life inevitably entails. This is because life subjects us to suffering. Life, in turn, eases the burden of suffering with momentary respites of pleasure and the promise of fleeting, if not lasting, happiness. In Freud's opinion, we are only capable of experiencing happiness in the first place because we suffer, but we compound our suffering even more because we aspire to happiness to unreasonable extremes. How can any person be expected to come to terms with this equation, which, by its nature, entails more suffering, not less?

In his most popular work, *Civilization And Its Discontents* (1930), Freud argued that neurotics find this equation unacceptable because they feel, to varying degrees, that life is systematically cheating them. They grow to resent their suffering and become increasingly desperate to rise above it. In their haste to relieve their suffering, however, they overlook what their anguish is trying to tell them. In effect, they become so preoccupied with diminishing their unhappiness they forget that if you reduce life to simply relieving your misery, you become so obsessed with it that the relief you covet becomes even more elusive. These were the kind of people Freud wanted to help but the way he decided to help them wasn't by diminishing their suffering but by increasing it, in Zen-like fashion!

Freud knew that if the patients he treated had any chance of success, he would have to reeducate them about the role that suffering properly plays in our lives. Taking from Aristotle, Freud believed that every human action is in pursuit of the good, but the problem lies in each person's conception of the good and such conceptions can serve us well or lead us to ruin. So, what conception of the good did Aristotle advocate? Aristotle believed that the good life can be equated with the pursuit of happiness, but he also observed that, for most people, pleasure is the focus of their lives and, consequently, how they conceive happiness. Aristotle believed there was a good far nobler—and in the end, more reliable—than pleasure, which is virtue, not because virtue serves utilitarian aims (such as relief from suffering) but because virtue is its own reward. In other words, whereas most people pursue happiness by accruing wealth and pursuing pleasurable activities, Aristotle argued that people of poor character will always be miserable while those of good character will be rewarded for it. Consequently, the virtuous person is happy—at any rate, *with himself*—while the person who pursues only pleasures is always in danger of losing them and, consequently, plagued with anxiety.

And what is the highest virtue? According to Aristotle, honesty—the capacity to be honest with others but, more importantly, the capacity to be honest, or more authentic, with oneself. Freud's problem was in persuading his patients to follow this counsel to the degree that it could make a difference in their lives. Like Aristotle, Freud believed that the capacity for honesty hinges on the strength of character each person is capable of developing. So, the first thing every analyst must learn is that you don't build character by conceiving of ways to relieve suffering, but by developing the strength to bear it. This makes the outcome of analysis and the drama that occasion's termination ambiguous and sometimes tragic. This is because the kind of suffering analysis is capable of relieving isn't the pain of suffering specifically but the alienation we experience when we know that the life we are living is a lie. The ability to overcome this lie, by becoming more honest with ourselves, can relieve the alienation but not the anguish that the slings and arrows of misfortune invariably exact from us.

It should be clear by now that the standard Freud is using for the outcome of analysis is far more complicated than the simple reduction of symptoms that we have become accustomed to in the rhetoric of contemporary psychobabble. In fact, he is talking about something most people probably don't ordinarily equate with relief from mental distress but something along the lines of character building, or personal integrity. What is peculiar to analysis is its singular approach to suffering, embodied in the rule of abstinence and the so-called classical technique, which holds that a certain quota of suffering should be endured in order to accrue the full benefit of what analysis can offer. While psychoanalysts have always experimented with *relaxing* this aspect of their treatment regimen, they never opted to entirely abandon it, so the question comes down to how much suffering are we talking about? What kind of suffering does psychoanalysis subject us to? And what are the varieties of contexts in which analytic patients are expected to encounter such suffering and surmount it?

I now want to focus on three components of psychoanalytic technique that are especially evocative of authenticity, the three technical principles that most poignantly characterize Freud's treatment philosophy: 1) The fundamental rule of analysis, i.e., the patient's acts of self-disclosure; 2) the rule of neutrality, i.e., the analyst's capacity for open-mindedness; and 3) the rule of abstinence, i.e., the patient's capacity to suffer. These three principles are hardly exhaustive. Most of the basic technical principles of psychoanalysis, including the use of countertransference and the admonition against therapeutic ambition, are concerned with authenticity, but I will only examine the first three in this context.

Basically, the fundamental rule is a contract that analytic patients are enlisted into during the early stages of analysis. Freud called this contract a pledge or a promise, so when patients agree to free associate, they essentially promise that they will. (Let's leave aside for the moment whether this pledge is explicit or merely implied, which is nowadays more typically the case.) On the other hand, the *act* of free associating is not a pledge but a spontaneous form of conversation in which patients are invited to participate by being unreservedly candid. To free associate in the manner that Freud intended requires nothing more complicated than the willingness to speak spontaneously and unreservedly, as we sometimes do when not the least self-conscious about what we are disclosing to another person. Obviously, Freud's conception of free association doesn't make much sense unless we appreciate the degree to which we ordinarily conceal most of what spontaneously comes to mind in the course of a typical conversation.

Free association is not, however, so much a *process* as a form of verbal meditation that entails speaking unreservedly while remaining attentive to what we are disclosing, something we do not ordinarily do. Most of us either speak impulsively without awareness of what we say, or we think through everything we are about to disclose before speaking. This is because patients instinctively want to censor things about themselves that they believe will lead the analyst to judge or dislike them. As we know, it takes a lot of courage to disclose things about ourselves that we customarily keep hidden, no matter how open-minded an analyst purports to be with his or her patient.

Yet, simply disclosing things about ourselves doesn't necessarily entail an authentic way of being. We may be "honest" in the strict definition of the word by verbalizing everything that comes to mind but not always in a fashion that is consistent with authenticity—in a manner that is heartfelt, considered, risky. The one isn't always or necessarily the same as the other. Freud was aware that some patients are content with engaging in a kind of verbal diarrhea by disclosing virtually nothing of significance, though technically "honest." What makes free associating potentially authentic is the way each of us faces the risk of exposing things about ourselves—to our analyst as well as to ourselves—that we are ambivalent about knowing. This is because, as Nietzsche observed, once such secrets are exposed, they change our perception of ourselves and the core of who we take ourselves to be. We may regret having said them and want to take them back, but we cannot. Once uttered, we have ingrained a piece of ourselves onto the fabric of the world for all to see. The analyst bears witness to our confessions and admissions, and however spontaneous and unconsciously intended they may be, they are no less true for being so.

Similarly, the rule of neutrality speaks to the analyst's capacity to be as authentic with her patients as her patients are trying to be with her. One of neutrality's most salient features was Freud's counsel to adopt a mode of evenly suspended attentiveness that is probably more familiar to practitioners of Buddhist meditation than to scientifically trained psychologists. For example, Freud advised analysts against trying to *remember* everything that patients tell them because by the act of trying to do so they select what they think is important instead of giving everything equal weight. This is hard to do because the most difficult thing analysts frequently encounter is how little they know about what is going on in the treatment and whether it is on or off the track. The typical treatment is no doubt off the track most of the time, yet patients somehow find a way to make the process work for them if the analyst can only learn to be patient—or, as Freud might have said, "neutral."[4] Unskilled analysts may inadvertently try to compensate for their lack of knowledge by pretending to know more than they do and acting accordingly, an incidence of what Freud called therapeutic ambition, in his view the most egregious example of countertransference, or inauthenticity.

Such behavior is inauthentic due to the analyst's unwillingness *to trust the process*. What this boils down to is the analyst learning to tolerate the patient's self-disclosures by abandoning the need to over-interpret. This was also a feature of Winnicott's (1989) later technique after he realized that his penchant for interpreting everything was actually interfering with his patients' free associations. Winnicott concluded that the principal task of psychoanalysis is to create a space where patients are free to explore their experience by speaking to it. From this angle, interpretations are not supposed to replace the patient's explanations with the analyst's but to subvert explanations altogether. Like Freud, Winnicott concluded that the most difficult thing analysts have to learn is to dispense with demonstrating how brilliant they are and instead give their patients the time they need to find their own voice.

But probably the most poorly understood technical principle in Freud's nomenclature is the rule of abstinence, the technical rule that pertains to the patient's relationship with his or her suffering. Patients expect analysis to relieve them of their suffering but soon learn that there is a kind of suffering they have to endure for the therapy to be of some consequence.

Whether we like it or not, therapy *hurts*. I don't think anyone disputes this statement in principle, though one of the most contested debates from the inception of psychoanalytic practice has revolved around the question as to precisely how much it ought to hurt in order to be effective.

Freud's position on the matter was typically ambiguous, saying only:

> The treatment must be carried out in abstinence . . . [so that] the patient's need and longing should be allowed to persist in her, in order that they may serve as forces impelling her to do work and to make changes.
>
> (1915, p. 165)

We are all abundantly familiar by now with the stereotype of the so-called classical analyst who never offers a word of encouragement or support, who sees the analytic process as a kind of deprivation chamber that is designed to inflict as much discomfort as legally permissible and who perhaps feels giddy with the knowledge that he actually has patients who are desperate or dependent enough to permit him to get away with such behavior. This kind of torture, however, is not what Freud envisioned, nor was it the way he conducted analysis with his patients. He was conversational, engaged, alive; if anything, he was over-involved with his patients by contemporary standards.

On the other hand, Freud was not warm and cozy. He saw the analytic process as an inherently painful affair that necessarily draws blood. This is because transference revolves around a kind of expectation that the analyst has the power to make the patient well, happy, improved—however you want to put it—instead of recognizing that the outcome of treatment ultimately hinges on the *work* that patients accomplish, and nothing more. The *person* of the analyst plays a role, to be sure, (which I examine in Section IV, below) but not necessarily the one the patient envisions. The rule of abstinence speaks to whether or not the analyst is in a position to help the patient in this endeavor *in the way* the patient expects the analyst to, or if the kind of help being offered seems more or less useless to the patient at the time and in the manner it is offered.

What all this boils down to is that the rule of abstinence is the technical principle that Freud conceived to say that it is through a kind of disillusionment that analysis ultimately has the power to effect change in a person's life. The term itself is perhaps unfortunate and would be better served, I suggest, by the term *authenticity* because what we are talking about is essentially our relationship to suffering and whether we are going to spend our lives trying to devise ways to turn away from it or determining how to face it and developing more effective ways of dealing with it.

III Authenticity and Suffering in the Psychoanalytic Experience

I have argued that authenticity originated in the existentialist observation that humans have a tendency to suppress their innermost being in order to relieve themselves of alienation by abandoning their principles and abdicating their agency to forces that pull them this way or that as long as the social incentives are sufficiently compelling. I have also suggested that one of the principal features of authenticity, as conceived by Nietzsche and Heidegger, is the wherewithal to *go against the grain* in one's day-to-day affairs by subjecting oneself to experiences that are undeniably painful yet rewarding. I now want to examine how this tendency applies to the patient's efforts to avoid as much suffering as possible and why the capacity to bear suffering is a necessary component of every analytic encounter. In psychoanalysis, as in existentialism, the capacity to bear suffering and the anxiety associated with being oneself are hallmarks of authenticity. My thesis is that this sensibility is already latent in psychoanalysis, although the term, authenticity, is seldom used to depict it.

Perhaps nowhere was Freud's authentic sensibility more aptly demonstrated than in the closing pages of his *Studies on Hysteria* (1893–1895, p. 305), where he proposed that the goal of analysis is to "transform hysterical misery into common unhappiness." One of the reasons Freud rejected happiness as a goal of therapy was the way he conceived of transference, that patients harbor fantasies about what the analyst will or should do to make them happy. In Freud's opinion, this amounts to eliciting the analyst's love, the easy way, he says, of obtaining momentary happiness, but without having to work for it, so it cannot endure. As every analyst learns, no matter how painful this lesson turns out to be, the analyst is ultimately obliged to *thwart* such longings instead of trying to make them come true. As we noted earlier, it is through *disillusionment* that analysis affects its power to transform the neurotic from a hopeless dreamer into an individual who is willing to take life by the horns and accept its conditions by fighting for what he wants or going without it (Thompson, 2004a).

Another way of putting this is that what we *ought* to do or *should* do, when it goes against what we *desire* to do, is almost always inauthentic.

This is consistent with Freud's conception of the superego, the seat of a pseudo-morality that is fixed by introjects from one's parents or immediate environment. Essentially primitive in nature, the superego acts against our capacity for desiring by prompting us to think of what others think of us at the expense of ourselves. While this arrangement is no doubt usually pleasing to others, it often becomes a blueprint for neurotic conflicts that systematically compromise our own chances for happiness. While there are situations when we are obliged to choose an inauthentic course for non-neurotic reasons, the analyst is concerned with those choices we make that are neurotic because the choices are predominantly unconscious.

Another example of authenticity in psychoanalysis is Winnicott's observation that the goal of analysis is to become a sufferer when he linked our fear of suffering with our wish to abolish it through omnipotence. Quoting Winnicott (1989):

> If we are successful [as analysts] we enable our patients to abandon invulnerability and [thereby] become a sufferer. [And], if we succeed, life will become precarious to those [patients] who were beginning to know a kind of . . . freedom from pain, even if this meant non-participation in living.
>
> (p. 199)

Enigmatic though this statement sounds, Winnicott apparently believed that *relief* from suffering was only a preliminary stage of analytic treatment that comes at a cost: non-participation in living. The real problem, as we know, is to prepare our patients for *post*-analytic existence, away from the sheltered container of the consulting room, where *life* and the anguish it occasions leads to new adventures that challenge them with unanticipated developments. But why is the ability to suffer a necessary component of authenticity? This may seem like a curious question to ponder when the purported purpose of psychoanalysis is to relieve suffering, not increase it. The problem comes down to the observation that there are two kinds of suffering, not one. The first is the kind of suffering that is incumbent on everyday life and consistent with Freud's dictum that neurotics need to learn to accommodate the reality principle by delaying their gratification long enough to achieve the goals they set for themselves. The second kind of suffering is the consequence of not accommodating the first. This second, pathogenic form of suffering is peculiar to neurotic and other forms of psychopathology and is the consequence of intolerable frustration or insurmountable trauma. In either case, we are left with the same painful choice of having to either look at the mess that our life has become and do something about it or continue with the folly to which we have become adapted. Either path is painful, but it was Freud's and Winnicott's respective conclusions that the more painful path is always the one less traveled—and the more therapeutic.[5]

Yet another example of authenticity in psychoanalysis is Bion's observation that "In every consulting room, there ought to be two rather frightened people; the patient and the psychoanalyst. If they are not, one wonders what they are doing there" (1974, p. 13)! Why the fear? Bion seemed to feel it has something to do with finding something out about ourselves that we would rather not know, the contrary of learning the truth about ourselves, i.e., being authentic with the instrument of analysis. One of Bion's earliest insights into the nature of transference came when he recognized that members of the groups he led wanted to deprive him of the freedom to think what he wanted to think and to speak his mind about them accordingly. In other words, they wanted to control what he thought and what he said about them, and he recognized that one of the features of countertransference is to succumb to this pressure by trying to meet such expectations by telling patients what they want to hear. Though Bion never used the term, this observation is a perfect example of how difficult it is to exercise authenticity in the analytic situation and why doing so is always uncomfortable and often exasperating. Like Freud, in his later period Bion also advocated a prodigious use of neutrality, but whereas Freud characterized it as adopting "evenly suspended attention," Bion conceived it in terms of "erasing memory and desire" (Bion, 1967). Both manners of putting it are characteristic of authenticity.

Still another example of authenticity in psychoanalysis is reflected in Lacan's famous "short session," a device he conceived as a way of thwarting the typical obsessional patient's attempts to control the analytic hour (Schneiderman, 1983, pp. 129–156). This device was consistent with Lacan's use of interpretation, which he believed should be measured in order to be optimally effective. For Lacan, the role of interpretation isn't to explain or to translate the unconscious but to take the patient by surprise by saying something startling, thereby unsettling the patient's narcissistic relationship with reality. In perhaps Lacan's most explicit allusion to authenticity, he advised analysts against trying to be helpful when help is asked, to abandon the wish to perform miracles, and to give up hope of terminating the treatment with the patient's gratitude for everything that has been done for them. The goal of analysis is to disappoint, and disappointment is necessarily painful and not immediately appreciated, though potentially liberating in the long run. Though there is something undeniably Stoic about Lacan's vision of psychoanalysis, one can also recognize his debt to the existential philosophical tradition to which he was wedded in his formative years and his resistance to following the more popular analytic herd.

Yet, the application of authenticity is a complicated affair, and analysts may opt to emphasize some of its features in their work while neglecting it elsewhere. Freud, Winnicott, Bion, and Lacan had remarkably different, even opposing, clinical styles, so the examples of their relationship with authenticity cited above shouldn't be taken to imply that the experience of being analyzed by one of them would be the same as being analyzed by another. Freud and Winnicott, for instance, permitted more of their personal relationship to intrude in their analytic space than Bion or Lacan did, who employed considerably more abstinence in their technique. Yet, each of these dimensions of the treatment situation, taken in isolation, is telling of what authenticity properly entails.

What all these examples share in common is the view that analysis contrives a situation in which analytic patients are able to finally abandon the fantasy that someone else—be it the analyst, a friend, lover, or benefactor—will rise from the shadows to solve their problems for them, like a parent who comes to the rescue of a child. No amount of reasoning or coercion will persuade us to abandon this fantasy; it is only relinquished through the nitty-gritty, day-to-day *experience* of bearing this disappointment while engaged in the work of trying to understand our resistance to it.

IV Authenticity in the Transference-Countertransference Relationship

We have discussed the philosophical and cultural underpinnings of authenticity and its roots in our relationship with suffering, how to contend with it, relieve it, and, when everything fails, face it, accept it, and let it be. We also examined the elements of authentic relating in Freud's technical principles and the clinical philosophies of D. W. Winnicott, Wilfried Bion, and Jacques Lacan. I now conclude our résumé of authenticity by examining its role in the so-called transference-countertransference relationship; in fact, the *extra*-transference and countertransference aspects of the analytic relationship.

There is a considered and even passionate debate in the psychoanalytic literature pertaining to distinctions between so-called classical technique and more contemporary, relaxed technical standards. The prevailing view is that the classical technique originated with Freud and found its culmination with American ego psychology, which is noted for an exaggerated use of abstinence and neutrality. This is confusing because classical technique, so defined, is actually foreign to the way Freud conducted psychoanalysis, as I have discussed elsewhere (1985, 1994a, 1994b, 1996a, 1996b, 1998a, 1998b, 1998c, 2000a, 2000b, 2000c, 2001a, 2001b, 2002, 2004b, 2004c). Freud's conception of transference lies at the heart of a dramatic shift in psychoanalytic technique that evolved in the post-World War Two era in the New York Psychoanalytic Institute by a group of European émigrés who began to publish articles critical of the way Freud conducted his analytic treatments. In an article that shocked many of his Chicago psychoanalytic colleagues, Lipton (1977) cited Freud's published treatment of the Rat Man to demonstrate the degree to which his psychoanalytic behavior diverges from contemporary "classical" standards using voluminous evidence of publications by analysts—virtually all identified with ego psychology—who roundly condemned Freud for the technique he employed in his treatment of the Rat Man.

All the analysts cited complained about the absence of strict adherence to proper analytic principles, e.g., that Freud was too personally engaged with his patient, gave him a gift, asked to see a photo of his fiancé, fed him a meal during a therapy session, failed to consistently analyze the transference, improperly asked his patient questions, engaged in extra-interpretative, conversational dialogues with him, etc. It has been widely reported by Freud's former patients how personally engaging he was as an analyst, that some even complained that he talked too much, that he invited some to accompany him on vacations, that he spoke openly of his personal problems with patients he was fond of, and so on. Freud did not report these "interventions" in his case reports[6] because he did not view them as *technical* interventions; they were part of his ongoing personal relationship with patients that he believed were not worth noting. The criticisms are surprising on two counts. First, because Freud's treatment of the Rat Man was successful and was used as a teaching tool in virtually every psychoanalytic institute in the world until Freud's death, it was only in the late 1940s that his analytic technique was deemed inadequate by so-called classical standards. Secondly, these criticisms suggest that the definition of classical technique changed after Freud's death into what is now defined as the standard for classical technique, yet this technique is erroneously attributed to Freud by contemporary authors who condemn this technique for its excessive use of detachment in the analytic relationship. What accounts for this shift in technique? I believe that the most telling feature of *revised* classical technique is its reconceptualization of transference by omitting from the analyst-analysand relationship all vestiges of the personal or real relationship. Moreover, I propose that the effort to defend the analyst from the personal elements of the relationship shared with patients serves as a source of inauthenticity and robs the relationship of genuineness, which patients experience and about which they invariably complain.

The situation is so confusing that Lipton proposed that this *newer*, post-World War Two technique that evolved during the late 1940s and early 1950s should be termed "modern" instead of classical in order to distinguish it from Freud's, which, because it came earlier, should be termed classical. This is not likely to happen, so we are left with the unfortunate dilemma of *two* classical techniques, one belonging to Freud and the other belonging to ego psychology but claiming to originate with Freud, though ego psychologists complain that Freud himself did not practice it (Thompson, 1994a, pp. 230–240)!

American ego psychology identifies itself with Freud and claims to be adhering to technical principles that he advocated but did not follow. The principal objection they raised concerns the way they perceived the interplay between Freud's *personal* relationship with the Rat Man and Freud's narrow *technical* interventions. Some analysts saw Freud's personal relationship with the Rat Man—e.g., feeding him a meal when he had apparently not eaten for days—as a *technical intervention* designed to manipulate the transference, but claim that Freud did not satisfactorily deal with this unconventional "intervention" and that, in hindsight, he should have refrained from doing so. It seems that none of these analysts were able to fathom what Freud had in mind with any of the personal asides he engaged in *unless* they were intended as expressions of technique; in other words, it was impossible to conceive his behavior as specifically personal in nature. Lipton concludes, "The essence of the difference between modern/classical technique and Freud's is that the definition of [this newer] technique has been expanded to incorporate aspects of the analyst's relation with the patient which Freud excluded from technique" (p. 262). In other words, Freud recognized both a personal relationship as well as a transference relationship that co-existed side by side during the

course of a patient's treatment. The personal relationship was not typically subjected to analysis or interpretation unless there was a compelling
reason for doing so.

In order to appreciate this distinction and why ego psychologists had
difficulty understanding Freud's clinical behavior, I will briefly review
the way Freud conceived the nature of transference and how this technical principle has evolved since his death. For Freud, transference was
essentially another word for love and ubiquitous to the human experience. It goes on everywhere, inside and outside the analytic relationship,
so the only thing that is special about the emergence of transference (the
patient's love for the analyst) in analysis is that instead of acting on such
feelings, they are examined and talked about, *without* acting on them.
Freud distinguished among three kinds of transference, positive and negative, and positive transference was divided again into two, erotic and
unobjectionable. Both negative and erotic components of transference are
unconscious and serve as sources of resistance, whereas unobjectionable
transference is comprised of conscious feelings of affection or positive
regard toward the analyst and the work both are engaged in collabora-
tively. Remember that, for Freud, analysis is about the *work* accomplished
and suffered. Transference can either further this process or engender a
wish that the analyst will cure the patient's ills through magic or infantile
love, manifesting editions of resistance that need to be interpreted and
worked through.

Now, love has a role, but a subtle one. To equate transference with love
is a complicated claim and demands a concerted exploration into its nature,
both its mature and regressive editions. Unlike most contemporary classical analysts, Freud believed that love plays a critical role in the outcome
of every analysis. Why, after all, would anyone put up with all the anguish
and heartache that the work of analysis demands from patients if it weren't
for the bond of affection felt for the analyst by the typical analysand? Freud
was aware that this kind of positive (unobjectionable) transference was crucial for a desirable outcome for the treatment, not because love heals, but
because without it, who would be willing to stay the course through all the
difficulty expected of them? Separating this form of love from the infantile
projections that urge the analyst to abandon all vestiges of abstinence is not
easy, but Freud expected that every analyst should be equipped to perform
this role with sufficient preparation and training. One form of love Freud
deemed personal, whereas the other he conceived as a technical component
of transference (Freud, 1915).

Perhaps, in order to make matters appear to be less ambiguous, Kanzer (1952) and Kris (1951) were in the vanguard of analysts who expanded the concept of transference to include the entirety of the patient's relationship with the analyst, so the idea of a personal—or what Freud termed unobjectionable—dimension to the analyst-patient interaction became moot. Until this development, it was common for analysts to engage in conversations with their patients and to make non-analytic comments of a personal nature, ask questions, even disclose information about themselves, and so on.[7] Now analysts are expected to speak only when giving interpretations and to otherwise remain silent. Why did this happen? Lipton suspects this developed by accident when Eissler (1953), in a paper condemning Franz Alexander's expansion of transference to include personal gestures by the analyst, advocated a revision of technique that encouraged a *minimum* of analytic interventions other than the use of interpretation. This paper had a decisive impact on the analytic community, partly because New York analysts were searching for a way to marginalize what they saw as Alexander's corruption of proper analytic technique.

In short order, all the other elements that we have come to associate with classical technique coalesced into its current form: 1) a concerted attention to the analyst's behavior instead of his purpose; 2) the exclusion of the analyst's *personality* from the treatment; and 3) the use of the analyst's silence as a mode of communication instead of a mode of listening. Ironically, efforts to eliminate the personal relationship from the analytic discourse are not only ill-advised but also patently impossible. Moreover, such attention to detail has the effect of placing too much weight on minor matters instead of major ones and lends to classical technique a prospective or prophylactic approach instead of a retrospective one. Instead of occupying himself with examining the meaning of his patient's associations, the analyst diverts a great deal of his attention to excluding interventions that would otherwise become the subject of future associations and discussion. This diverts the analyst's attentiveness from a neutral state of mind to a critical one. And what does the potential impact that working in this fashion have on the personality of a typical classical analyst? He is more liable to become shy, cautious, tentative, circumspect, and inhibited in his demeanor instead of bold, creative, adventurous, self-confident, and spontaneous. Even the selection process of analytic candidates in training institutes is more likely to favor obsessional types over hysterics, as history has demonstrated.

Presumably, most "modern" classical analysts recognized the impossible situation they put themselves in after removing the personal relationship because they were subsequently obliged to reinsert it in the guise of the so-called working or therapeutic alliance, which became not strictly personal in the conventional sense but a part of the technical, analytic relationship because it is subject to analysis and interpretation. Obviously, there is a difference between a dimension of a relationship that I have with a person that occurs naturally and spontaneously and one that I know is laden with hidden meanings and unconscious intentions, one that my analyst will always, after the fact, inform me of what I was really thinking or up to when such and such was said or shared between us. Lipton even suggests that utilizing a working alliance can be injurious to the analytic relationship:

> Devoting explicit attention to [the working alliance] encumbers the analysis with a series of dangers and disadvantages. It tends to foster artificiality; tends to give undue weight to the analyst's behavior; tends to expand technique beyond the area which the patient knows about and collaborates with; and tends to substitute for the genuine, personal relationship on which the analysis is based an idealized relationship in which the patient meets not another person but a sort of encompassing, technically-correct instrumentality.
>
> (p. 266)

In effect, all vestiges of the personal relationship shared with patients have been transformed into aspects of the patient's transference with the analyst, which the analyst is obliged to interpret accordingly. From the classical perspective, transference has become a rarefied, trance-like state of childlike hypnotic regression that places the patient in a one-down position from which she cannot easily extricate herself because she is always "in" transference, which she cannot get out of. This has the chilling impact of perceiving the analysand as never really being the author of his or her experience or a proper adult in an I-Thou relationship, but the "effect" of unconscious forces to which only the analyst is privy. In other words, the concept of transference has become a vehicle of defense against the realness of the person of the patient in treatment whenever it is convenient for the analyst to remove himself from the impact of proximity with his patients. So instead of using the transference/countertransference situation as a means of obtaining intimacy, of moving back and forth between the specific work of the treatment and the relationship shared between them, the so-called classical analyst rejects any vestige of extra-analytic engagement and interprets any incidence of closeness or informality as seduction, or "transference."

So, what are the criteria of the personal relationship so many analysts find so frightening that they have been factored out of treatment? Unlike technical aspects of the treatment situation, there cannot be universal standards for how a given analyst is going to use his or her person in the treatment with each patient. Freud wasn't even comfortable with mandating strict standards for the application of his technical principles, let alone the personal ones! As a rule of thumb, however, what is deemed personal should be obvious. It is both outside technique and subject to individual variation. It cannot be codified because, just as analysts differ from person to person, each analyst's conception of the personal relationship will vary as well. Moreover, analysts are liable to form different conceptions of what the personal relationship entails at different stages of their careers and with different patients, when they inhabit different moods, and so on. Even narrow interpretations need clarification and expansion, and such conversational digressions require a departure from strict interpretative speech. The many times that analysts must talk to their patients about matters such as whether the analysis is working for them, whether they should use the couch, disagreements as to matters of frequency, absences from sessions, increases in fees, and so on, have to be hammered out on a person-to-person basis that ultimately comes down to how credible the analyst is in the eyes of the patient. In my experience of these situations, the concept of a therapeutic alliance has been of little help in ironing these issues out.

For the personal relationship to be spontaneous, unpredictable, and authentic, it has to be free of contrivance and guile. Yet, sometimes it isn't so easy to tell when it is personal and when it is transference. Otto Will once told me a story of his analysis with Harry Stack Sullivan that may serve as an apt example. This was an uncomfortable period in his analysis, and Will was feeling frustrated with the progress of his treatment and with Sullivan, who could be difficult under the best of circumstances. Finally, one day Will blurted out that he felt angry with Sullivan. Will immediately felt guilty for his outburst and said in so many words that he was sorry for his behavior and supposed that this was evidence of his father transference emerging. Sullivan immediately corrected Will and said, "No, Doctor, that was not your father transference. It just so happens that right now you don't like me very much and I don't like you, but I'm sure if we persevere we'll get through it somehow" (Will, 1992). The distinction may seem arbitrary, but it is typical of the way Freud, Fenichel, Glover, Winnicott, and a legion of other analysts have typically distinguished between personal and transference communications between their patients and themselves, the one requiring interpretation, the other a simple acknowledgment of feelings that *analyst and patient feel for each other*.

The most common incidence of the personal relationship that exists in the analytic relationship is ultimately embodied in the forms of *conversation* that evolve between them. Classical analysts tend to reject the term because they argue that "conversing" has no discernible role in the analytic discourse. The patient speaks, and the analyst interprets; conversation, as such, is avoided. Yet, Freud conversed freely with his patients and engaged in straightforward dialogues with them, a form of speech that has subsequently become *verboten* to classical analysts (Racker, 1968, p. 35). This form of conversation is obviously gratifying for patient and analyst alike and is necessarily restrained by the rule of abstinence, but to abandon it entirely is artificial. It serves as an exemplary tool for furthering free association when employed skillfully, but it is also a humanizing aspect of the analyst's personal relationship with each patient, showing concern for each patient as a person with whom he or she is engaged, helping to prolong the treatment toward an optimal conclusion. Analysts reveal personal things about themselves to patients mature enough to contain them, and when patients make personal observations about their analysts, they are not always interpreted as projections but sometimes astute observations that may be taken as compliments or criticisms. Naturally, one monitors what occurs in such conversations and brings their content under scrutiny *when appropriate*, but not necessarily or systematically, as when addressing components of a technical regimen. Permitting one's personality to become part of the constellation of elements that patients experience serves as an invaluable source for authentic relating and complements the exercise of technical principles discussed earlier.

But probably the principal motive for engaging in a personal relationship with patients is that there is no good reason not to, because this is the context in which the analysand experiences genuine love for the analyst, not love as a projection or idealization or regression to infantile fixations, but the genuine or real edition of love that manifests itself in the course of just about every analysis, and without which a meaningful analysis is impossible to imagine. How could patients be expected to put up with the trials and tribulations they are subjected to during the course of their treatment if not for the love they come to develop for their analyst in the first place? It is relevant that few analysts talk about love or acknowledge its relevance to the analytic process, and most analysts go out of their way to insist that it has no role to speak of. Indeed, the concept of transference, once synonymous with love, is now viewed as little more than an algebraic equation, a place on the map occupied by one participant acting out a fantasy onto a blank screen whose function is little more than to interpret back as accurately as possible the etchings of the projections recorded. Anything of a personal nature is checked at the door and retrieved at the termination of treatment, if then.

In short, the capacity to acknowledge the existence of a personal relationship with patients, to accept it and freely engage in a manner of one's choosing that complements the needs of each patient, lends a dimension of genuineness to the relationship that has profound implications to the way the treatment is experienced, and even how the technical principles are construed. Intuitively, most analysts know this and conduct themselves accordingly. Recent controversies in analytic technique under the rubric of relational and contemporary perspectives have targeted these very issues, though some of the authors fail to recognize that the so-called classical technique they rightfully condemn has little relation to Freud's treatment philosophy or behavior, but is the creature of a more recent lineage.

V Conclusion

In conclusion, what do the foregoing clinical examples of authenticity share in common with the way the concept was conceived by Nietzsche and Heidegger? Although Freud, Winnicott, Bion, and Lacan never invoked the term as a feature of their analytic technique, the way they each reject the easier and undoubtedly more comforting strategy of doing everything one can to please one's patients in the hope this will elicit an easier treatment experience is a critical feature of how both Nietzsche and Heidegger characterized authentic being in the world. On the other hand, we have also seen how easily analysts just as frequently take the opposite tack in *doing nothing* to reach out to their patients, talking to them but holding them at arm's length in order to mitigate the anxiety they feel for being in close quarters with another human being. Their treatment is obviously not served by this. This isn't a moral position but a recognition that change is necessarily painful and requires sacrifice, so if analysts expect their patients to shoulder the quota of sacrifices they need to in order to benefit from the treatment, then the analyst has to be willing and able to shoulder the same measure of sacrifice himself.

What this comes down to is that the analyst instills the capacity for sacrifice in his patients *through his own example*. This instilling is not a matter of technique that can simply be "applied" from the comfort of detaching oneself from the process, but an *act of courage* that has to be suffered repeatedly and constantly throughout the treatment of every patient. This is why the wherewithal to endure the first kind of suffering discussed earlier in order to mitigate the second kind is what Freud, Winnicott, Bion, and Lacan had in mind when they concluded that not only life but analysis entails suffering. Though none of them used the term, the wisdom of submitting to suffering and making use of it makes little sense without at least an instinctive awareness of the role that authenticity properly plays in all of our clinical endeavors.

Notes

1 An earlier version of this paper was presented at the Northern California Society for Psychoanalytic Psychology in San Francisco on December 11, 2004.
2 We will examine the sceptic contribution to authenticity when we review the impact of Michel de Montaigne.
3 See Charles Taylor, 1991, for a conception of authenticity that embraces a moral perspective.
4 Actually *indifferent* in the original German.
5 For the relation between Winnicott's thesis of a true-self and false-self system and authenticity, see Jon Mills, 2003 and R. D. Laing, 1960.
6 The gist of these extra-analytic interventions were revealed in case notes that Freud typically destroyed after he published his cases but were left intact in the case of the Rat Man for some reason. Strachey included them in his translation of Freud's case report of the *Standard Edition*.
7 I am describing the way analysts who were identified with the classical approach of *Freud* tended to work. Analysts such as Melanie Klein developed a more austere form of analytic technique that dispensed with personally engaging with patients by employing abstinence to unprecedented degrees.

References

Binswanger, L. (1963) *Being-in-the-World: Selected Papers of Ludwig Binswanger* (J. Needleman, Trans.). New York: Basic Books.

Bion, W. R. (1967) Notes on Memory and Desire. In J. Lindon (Ed.), *Psychoanalytic Forum* (Vol. 2, pp. 271–280). New York: Science House.

Bion, W. R. (1974) *Bion's Brazilian Lectures-1*. Rio de Janeiro: Imago Editora Ltda.

Boss, M. (1963) *Psychoanalysis and Daseinsanalysis* (L. Lefebre, Trans.). New York and London: Basic Books.

Breuer, J. and Freud, S. (1893–1895/1955) *Studies on Hysteria*. Standard Edition (Vol. 2, pp. 1–305). London: Hogarth Press.

Eissler, K. R. (1953) The Effect of the Structure of the Ego on Psychoanalytic Technique. *Journal of The American Psychoanalytic Association*, Vol. 1: 104–143.

Freud, S. (1915/1958) *Observations on Transference-Love: Further Recommendations on the Technique of Psycho-Analysis III*. Standard Edition (Vol. 12, pp. 157–171). London: Hogarth Press.

Freud, S. (1930/1961) *Civilization and Its Discontents*. Standard Edition (Vol. 21, pp. 59–145). London: The Hogarth Press.

Freud, S. (1953–1973) *The Standard Edition of the Complete Psychological Works of Sigmund Freud* (24 vols; J. Strachey, Ed. & Trans.). London: Hogarth Press (Referred to in Subsequent References as Standard Edition).

Groarke, L. (1990) *Greek Scepticism: Anti-Realist Trends in Ancient Thought*. Montreal and London: McGill-Queen's University Press.

Guignon, C. (2004) *On Being Authentic*. London and New York: Routledge.

Heidegger, M. (1962) *Being and Time* (J. Macquarrie and E. Robinson, Trans.). New York: Harper and Row.

Heidegger, M. (1971) *Poetry, Language, Thought* (A. Hofstadter, Trans.). New York and London: Harper and Row.

Heidegger, M. (2003) *Philosophical and Political Writings* (M. Stassen, Ed. & Trans.). New York and London: Continuum.

Kanzer, M. (1952) The Transference Neurosis of the Rat Man. *Psychoanalytic Quarterly*, Vol. 21: 181–189.

Kris, E. (1951) Ego Psychology and Interpretation in Psychoanalytic Therapy. *Psychoanalytic Quarterly*, Vol. 20: 15–30.

Laing, R. D. (1960) *The Divided Self*. New York: Pantheon Books.

Laing, R. D. (1969) *Self and Others*. 2nd Revised Edition. New York: Pantheon Books.

Leavy, S. (1980) *The Psychoanalytic Dialogue*. New Haven, CT and London: Yale University Press.

Leavy, S. (1988) *In the Image of God: A Psychoanalyst's View*. New Haven, CT and London: Yale University Press.

Lipton, S. (1977) The Advantages of Freud's Technique as Shown in His Analysis of the Rat Man. *International Journal of Psychoanalysis*, Vol. 58: 255–273.

Loewald, H. W. (1980) *Papers on Psychoanalysis*. New Haven, CT and London: Yale University Press.

Mills, J. (2003) A Phenomenology of Becoming: Reflections on Authenticity. In R. Frie (Ed.), *Understanding Experience: Psychotherapy and Postmodernism* (pp. 137–160). London and New York: Routledge.

Mitchell, S. A. (1992) True Selves, False Selves, and the Ambiguity of Authenticity. In N. J. Skolnick and S. C. Warshaw (Eds.), *Relational Perspectives in Psychoanalysis*. Hillsdale, NJ: Analytic Press.

Montaigne, M. (1925) *The Essays of Montaigne* (4 vols; G. B. Ives, Trans.). Cambridge, MA: Harvard University Press.

Nietzsche, F. (2002) *Beyond Good and Evil* (J. Norman, Trans.). Cambridge: Cambridge University Press.

Nietzsche, F. (2003) *Writing From the Late Notebooks* (K. Sturge, Trans.). Cambridge: Cambridge University Press.

Racker, H. (1968) *Transference and Countertransference*. New York: International Universities Press.

Safranski, R. (1998) *Martin Heidegger: Between Good and Evil* (E. Osers, Trans.). Cambridge, MA and London: Harvard University Press.

Schneiderman, S. (1983) *Jacques Lacan: The Death of an Intellectual Hero*. Cambridge, MA and London: Harvard University Press.

Taylor, C. (1991) *The Ethics of Authenticity*. Cambridge, MA and London: Harvard University Press.

Thompson, M. G. (1985) *The Death of Desire: A Study in Psychopathology*. New York and London: New York University Press.

Thompson, M. G. (1994a) *The Truth About Freud's Technique: The Encounter With the Real*. New York and London: New York University Press.

Thompson, M. G. (1994b) The Existential Dimension to Termination. *Psychoanalysis and Contemporary Thought*, Vol. 17, No. 3.

Thompson, M. G. (1996a) The Rule of Neutrality. *Psychoanalysis and Contemporary Thought*, Vol. 19, No. 1.

Thompson, M. G. (1996b, January) Freud's Conception of Neutrality. *Contemporary Psychoanalysis*, Vol. 32, No. 1.

Thompson, M. G. (1998a, October) Manifestations of Transference: Love, Friendship, Rapport. *Contemporary Psychoanalysis*, Vol. 34, No. 4.

Thompson, M. G. (1998b, October) The Fundamental Rule of Psychoanalysis. *The Psychoanalytic Review*, Vol. 85, No. 5.

Thompson, M. G. (1998c) The Way of Neutrality. *Australian Journal of Psychotherapy,* Vol. 17, Nos. 1 and 2.

Thompson, M. G. (2000a, July) The Sceptic Dimension of Psychoanalysis: Toward an Ethic of Experience. *Contemporary Psychoanalysis,* Vol. 36, No. 3.

Thompson, M. G. (2000b, January) The Crisis of Experience in Contemporary Psychoanalysis. *Contemporary Psychoanalysis,* Vol. 36, No. 1.

Thompson, M. G. (2000c, Spring) Scepticism and Psychoanalysis. *Psychologist-Psychoanalyst,* Vol. 20, No. 2.

Thompson, M. G. (2001a) The Ethic of Psychoanalysis: The Fundamental Rule to be Honest. In A. Molino (Ed.), *Where Id Was: Challenging Normalization in Psychoanalysis* (pp. 73–86). London: Athlone Press.

Thompson, M. G. (2001b) The Enigma of Honesty: The Fundamental Rule of Psychoanalysis. *Free Associations,* Vol. 8(Part 3), No. 47: 390–434.

Thompson, M. G. (2001c, October) Is the Unconscious Really all that Unconscious? The Role of Being and Experience in the Psychoanalytic Encounter. *Contemporary Psychoanalysis,* Vol. 37, No. 4.

Thompson, M. G. (2002, January) The Existential Dimension to Working Through. *Journal of the Society for Existential Analysis,* Vol. 13, No. 1.

Thompson, M. G. (2004a) Happiness and Chance: A Reappraisal of the Psychoanalytic Conception of Suffering. *Psychoanalytic Psychology,* Vol. 21, No. 1.

Thompson, M. G. (2004b) *The Ethic of Honesty: The Fundamental Rule of Psychoanalysis.* Amsterdam and New York: Editions Rodopi.

Thompson, M. G. (2004c) Postmodernism and Psychoanalysis: A Heideggerian Critique of Postmodern Malaise and the Question of Authenticity. In J. Reppen, M. Schulman and J. Tucker (Eds.), *Way Beyond Freud: Postmodern Psychoanalysis Evaluated.* London: Open Gate Press.

Thompson, M. G. (2004d, July) Nietzsche and Psychoanalysis: The Fate of Authenticity in a Postmodernist World. *Journal of the Society for Existential Analysis,* Vol. 15, No. 2.

Will, O. (1992) Personal Communication.

Winnicott, D. W. (1989) *Psychoanalytic Explorations* (C. Winnicott, R. Shephard and M. David, Eds.). Cambridge, MA: Harvard University Press.

Zahavi, D. (2001) *Husserl and Transcendental Subjectivity.* Athens, OH: Ohio University Press.

Chapter 6

The Crisis of Experience in Contemporary Psychoanalysis

Now that we have closed upon the twentieth century and embarked on the next one, I feel an urgency to reflect on the monumental, and catastrophic, change that our world has suffered over the course of the last century. Advances in technology have made it possible to raise the standard of living for many human beings, especially in Europe and North America, to heights that were unimaginable when the twentieth century began. Technology also brought us to the brink of destruction when the unbridled arms race between the United States and the Soviet Union took us to the precipice of nuclear war.

Yet, for all their potential for danger, the greatest threat that faces us today are not war or even the famine and poverty that many continue to suffer; indeed, it is those of us who appear to be protected from such horrors that have the most to lose. What we are in danger of losing is not the material comforts to which we are accustomed but something much closer to our intrinsic humanity. I am thinking about the fragile condition of what was once taken for granted: *our capacity to experience.*

This may sound strange when, after all, our capacity to experience is something we generally take for granted. We invoke this term every day with such frequency that we seldom give it a second thought. Yet, philosophers have written voluminous treatises on the nature of experience, and many psychoanalysts have even included the term in the titles of their books, including Wilfried Bion (*Learning from Experience*, 1962, *Experiences in Groups*, 1959); Neville Symington (*The Analytic Experience*, 1986); Thomas Ogden (*The Primitive Edge of Experience*, 1989); and R. D. Laing (*The Politics of Experience*, 1967; *The Voice of Experience*, (1982). The fact that we use a term, however, doesn't necessarily ensure that we understand it, or that we treat it with the attention it deserves.

DOI: 10.4324/9781003429104-6

For the most part, philosophers remain ambivalent about the place experience occupies in their investigations. With the exception of the empiricists, who embrace experience as their most important philosophical principle, philosophers have tended to emphasize our capacity to reason over what is contrasted with the "senses." Inasmuch as philosophy is that singular discipline that celebrates our capacity to think, it is hardly surprising that the place philosophers typically reserve for experience is an afterthought, at best. Yet, many thinkers during the course of the twentieth century have expressed concern over the status to which experience has been relegated. Some have even warned that we are in danger of losing our capacity to experience altogether. Adorno (1992), for example, observed, "One may say that experience is the union of tradition with an open yearning for what is foreign; but the very possibility of experience is in jeopardy" (Vol. 1, p. 55).

Adorno's concern about the potential demise of experience was shared by many philosophers, historians, and intellectuals of his generation, including Walter Benjamin, who pointed to the increasing "poverty of experience" that seems to characterize our age (cited in Jay, 1998). Jay observed that the very concept of experience means so many things to so many people that the term is virtually unintelligible. Says Adorno (1992):

Although we can make attempts to communicate what we experience . . .

. . . only the subject really knows what he or she has experienced. Experience, to put it differently, cannot be defined, for to do so is to reduce it to other commensurable words or concepts, which is precisely what invoking the term is designed to forestall.

(p. 3)

Jay argues that there is an undeniable antipathy between academics and psychoanalysts on one hand and artists and common folk on the other concerning the place to which experience is allotted in our lives. I do not attempt a definition of experience *per se* but explore its relevance to psychoanalytic theory and technique. In so doing, I point to its singular absence in psychoanalytic theory and the gradual, if unwitting, decline of experience in its literature over the course of the century.

Though psychoanalysts, like everyone else, use this term all the time, the word "experience," as Jay observes, seems to have no specific definition. That being said, I offer the etymology of the term as a useful place to begin.

For example, the English word "experience" is derived from the Latin *peritus*, meaning peril. This lends to the term an ominous sensibility, implying that experience is something we may choose to embrace or resist, depending upon the experience in question. The Latin *peritus* also means "to try out" or "to test." On the other hand, the Greek root of "experience," which is older than the Latin, derives from the word *empeiria*, which gives us the word "empirical," a term that was adopted by the British empiricists (e.g., John Locke and David Hume) who reduced their philosophy to the study of *sensual* experience alone. According to Jay, the Greek *pathos* (or *pathe*) is yet another antecedent to what subsequently became "experience" in the English language, most notably when we think of experience as something that happens *to* us, passively. And finally, according to the *Oxford English Dictionary*, to experience something essentially means "to feel" or "to suffer" and even "to undergo" in the sense that what we experience is not of our own making. Also, the word "experience" gives us the term "experiment," which has been adopted by science as the means by which one may test a theory through practical application. In our century, the words "empirical," "experiment," and "experience" are often used interchangeably, though each has vastly different connotations when invoked outside of a scientific framework.

Over the past two centuries, the German language has offered particularly subtle variations on the types of experience of which we are capable, lending to the concept a diversity that the English language subsumes under the one term. It is perhaps not surprising, then, that German philosophers have dominated the nineteenth- and twentieth-century investigations into the nature of experience that subsequently spilled over to other European countries, including France, Great Britain, and Spain. I'm thinking specifically of Hegel, Nietzsche, Husserl, and Heidegger, each of whom elaborated on the notion of experience in great detail in their respective philosophies, giving the concept a central role in phenomenology and existential philosophy. These German philosophers influenced, for example, the French existentialists, including Sartre, De Beauvoir, Merleau-Ponty, and Marcel, as well as the Spanish philosophers Miguel Unamuno and Jose Ortega y Gasset. I say more about phenomenology later, but first, I want to say a few words about the German conception of experience and the etymology from which their designations are derived.

The first is the German *Erfahrung*, which derives from the word *Fahrt*, meaning "journey." *Erfahrung* suggests the notion of *temporal duration*, such as, for example, when one accumulates experience over time, including the accruing of wisdom that comes to those who live to old age. The other German term for experience is *Erlebnis*, which derives from the word *Leben*, meaning "life." The use of the word *Erlebnis* connotes a vital *immediacy* in contrast to the more historical notion of *Erfahrung*. When invoking *Erlebnis*, the speaker is emphasizing a primitive unity that precedes intellectual reflection.

I will now summarize the implications of what the etymological aspects of the word "experience" suggest and the many senses that the concept, whether of Greek, Latin, English, or German origin, seeks to convey. In the scientific community, the notion of experience suggests the accumulation of empirical knowledge through the use of experimentation, an inherently active enterprise. On the other hand, experience may also suggest something that happens to us when in a passive state and most vulnerable to stimuli, such as what occurs in a movie theater. It may also suggest the process whereby we submit to education, entailing the accumulation and memorization of knowledge over a considerable period of time. The term may also be used to connote a journey I have taken while traveling to a foreign country, perhaps in wartime when I am faced with obstacles and danger, the experience of which may have expedited my journey into manhood.

As you can see from this brief excursion into the etymology of this term, even while it offers tantalizing hints as to what the notion of experience in all its variety has been taken to mean, there still remains something that is essentially ineffable about the concept, defying categorization and even definition. This presents us with a paradox, for the word has often been used, according to Jay (1998), "to gesture towards precisely that which exceeds concepts and even language itself" (p. 3).

The word "experience" has frequently been used as a marker for what is ineffable and so private or personal that it cannot be rendered in words. One's experience of love, for example, is an experience that many insist is impossible to express or grasp in words alone, precisely because love is *experienced* long before it is understood, if at all. Even when I try to communicate what I experience to others, only I can possibly *know* what my experience is, and there are degrees to which even I am capable of acknowledging the full force of my experience to myself. Just as experience resists definition, our efforts to convey our experience are necessarily imperfect because it is impossible to reduce to words alone. This observation has enormous consequences for the experience of psychoanalysis for both patient and analyst, who rely almost exclusively on the passage of words between them.

What, then, does the essential nature of experience entail? Is experience antithetical to one's capacity for reason, as some have suggested? Or is our ability to reason *dependent on our capacity to experience* the very thoughts that our words endeavor to convey? Perhaps the greatest travesty to our commonsense notion of experience occurred among the humanistic psychologists of the 1960s, who sought to replace the intellectual bias of psychoanalysis with the curious exercise of "getting in touch" with their feelings. What they meant by "getting in touch" with them was never clear, but the insinuation was to dispense with the need for reasoning altogether by simply abandoning oneself to whatever feelings emerged, whether anger, sorrow, or desire. The vehicles through which this exercise was said to be accomplished were devices such as "encounter" groups and the like. For people who experienced difficulty in feeling anything at all, these exercises must have been powerful, indeed, though the therapeutic gain has been notoriously difficult to assess.

On the other end of the spectrum is the more recent state of contemporary philosophical fashion (I'm thinking of the French school),[1] as well as cutting-edge theories in psychoanalysis[2] that appear to assign experience *to nonintellectual activity*. As we know, many of this century's philosophers and academics have sought to reduce human activity to language, suggesting that the capacity to experience is mediated through words and, so, is secondary to the power that words possess. This view argues that preverbal experience is inconceivable so that even the experience of pain depends upon one's knowledge of what pain is. Many of the features of structuralism, deconstructionism, poststructuralism, and the postmodernist perspective argue that the notion of a conscious, sentient self, capable of determining its own truth, is an antiquated idea that should be replaced with a schema that views the subject, not in terms of an *experiencing* agent, but as an "effect" (or construct) of hidden forces.

One of the questions that naturally comes to mind is whether this perspective is symptomatic of a twentieth-century neurosis or whether we have struggled with this paradox in one form or another throughout the history of Western civilization. On reflection, it appears that our collective confusion about the role to which experience has been assigned goes all the way back to the origins of philosophy itself, starting with the impact that Plato and Aristotle have had on the evolution and development of Western culture.

The Greek Attitude About Experience

Overall, the place that experience enjoyed among the Greek philosophers was not as important as we might assume. The post-Homeric philosophical era began around 600 B.C. with Thales, who was followed in quick succession by Heraclitus and Parmenides (circa 500 B.C.), then by Socrates, Plato, and Aristotle, by far the greatest of the Greek philosophers (circa fourth and third centuries B.C.). The novelty of philosophy proper coincided with the abandonment of mythology and an inherently religious perspective in favor of a rationalistic and predominantly secular one. Though some of the early pre-Socratic philosophers and even Socrates himself continued to make reference to "gods" and "myths" with which to buttress their arguments, for the most part, the philosophers who succeeded them were committed to demonstrating man's capacity for reason, arguing that the origin of the universe and all it contained could be explained by what we today would call "science." In order to grasp where the Greeks were coming from, it is important to appreciate that, until recently, the terms *philosophy* (literally "the love of wisdom") and *science* (literally "knowledge") were used interchangeably. Both terms signified a departure from the Homeric era, when most people believed that human behavior could be attributed to divine intervention.

Though the Greek philosophers weren't necessarily opposed to religious faith in principle, where questions of human motivation were concerned they gradually developed a bias that favored the independence of the mind over the influence of deities. The most influential among them, Plato and Aristotle, professed that the capacity to reason was man's greatest achievement. Our other faculties (such as, for example, "sensual" experience and the knowledge we presume to obtain from it) were assigned a secondary status in comparison with the mind's capacity to reason its way to objective reality, unsullied by the "corruption" of the senses.

Though the pre-Socratic philosophers who came before Plato were not as wedded to reason as those who followed, Plato and his successors sought the absolute certitude that they believed rational, deductive thinking could provide over the inherently ambiguous and more uncertain features of *empeiria*, or experience. According to the American pragmatist John Dewey (1987), the classical philosophers distanced themselves from what they believed was the unreliable nature of experience due to three principal shortcomings:

1. They contrasted what they called empirical "knowledge"—which, in fact, they characterized as nothing more than "belief" or "opinion"— with scientific knowledge that could be apprehended with the mind.
2. They contrasted the "restricted" nature of *practice* with the relatively "free" character of *rational thought*.
3. They elaborated on what they deemed the "metaphysical" basis for the two defects of experience listed above: that sense and bodily action are confined to the realm of "phenomena," whereas reason is akin to *ultimate reality*.

Dewey goes on to argue:

[T]his threefold contrast thus implies a metaphysical depreciation of experience, an epistemological one, and, coloring both of the others and giving them their human value, a moral one: the difference in worth between an activity that is limited to the body and to physical things, originating in need and serving temporal utilities, and that which soars to ideal and eternal values.

(p. 74)

According to Jay (1998), "Plato had thought experience meant being enslaved by the past and habit rather than reason, [whereas] Aristotle restricted its use to the confirmation of universal laws," laws which, it should be emphasized, were derived exclusively from man's *capacity to reason* (p. 7). Whereas Plato elevated our capacity for reason to that of an "ideal" state that exists independently of the physical world (a world that, by definition, could never measure up to the "perfection" of ideas), Aristotle applied the generalizing tendency of reason for the purpose of developing an inventory of "sciences" that served to reduce the universe and everything in it to categories (e.g., politics, ethics, economics, physics, metaphysics) that have survived to this day, more or less intact. Though the sciences have developed in dramatic fashion over the course of the last two millennia, we can credit both Plato and Aristotle for having provided us with the foundation for the sciences as we know them today and even the means by which they are generally investigated.

Yet, contrary to what many assume, Plato and Aristotle were not the only Greek philosophers to have exercised such a profound influence on our age, even if the vast majority of commentary on the classical literature is devoted to their contributions. I'm thinking of the Hellenistic philosophers in particular, whose influence flourished after Aristotle: the Stoics, Epicureans, and Sceptics. Whereas the Stoics and Epicureans also favored the role of rationality over that of experience and more or less agreed with Plato and Aristotle that experience plays a secondary role to that of our capacity to reason, they shared with the Sceptics the goal of transforming philosophy from the accumulation of knowledge in principle (epistemology) to the more practical means of obtaining happiness (ethics).

Whereas the Stoics and Epicureans, however, were convinced that happiness could be attained through rational means alone, the Sceptics believed that each person must find her own means of obtaining happiness (or "equanimity") based on what she is able to learn from a critique of her experience.

The Sceptics flourished over a period of nearly seven centuries, beginning around 300 B.C. (during Aristotle's lifetime) and lasting until around 300–400 A.D. when they more or less vanished after the rise of Christianity. According to Groarke (1990), traces of the Sceptic attitude can be detected as early as Democritus and Socrates (circa 450 B.C.), when the Greeks formulated three philosophical trends that were subsequently incorporated into Scepticism: 1) an anti-realist bias; 2) the turn to a more subjective attitude about truth; and 3) the development of philosophy away from epistemological investigation in favor of an ethical criterion for obtaining happiness (i.e., "equanimity" or *ataraxia*). The origin of Sceptic philosophy is attributed to Pyrrho of Elis, who lived around 300 B.C.— about hundred and fifty years after Socrates—during the time of Alexander the Great, to whom Pyrrho was an adviser. Pyrrho's teacher, Anaxarchus, successfully employed sceptic arguments to convince Alexander that he wasn't a god, but not all monarchs were as receptive to his interventions. When Anaxarchus employed a similar argument with the king of Cyprus, he was put to death, proving that the attempt to shatter illusions can sometimes be fatal.

The Sceptics believed that most philosophers were of little use to the common man and, like Socrates before them, devoted their efforts to exposing the fallacy of what philosophers claimed to know. Their principal philosophical method was a state of mental attentiveness they called *epoché*, which entailed abandoning dogmatic assertions by suspending judgment on matters that were beyond their personal experience. By maintaining an air of open-mindedness,[3] a precursor to free association, the Sceptics sought to rid themselves of the search for certitude and its attendant anxieties by learning to take the largely unfathomable nature of life in stride. The Sceptics characterized the state of equanimity that resulted from such efforts as a state of gentleness or kindness, even open-heartedness. This may sound simplistic to our ears in the complicated era in which we live, but the method the Sceptics advocated was a precursor to the free association method conceived by Freud, probably transmitted to him through the essays of Michel de Montaigne, whom Freud is known to have admired.

Historically, the Sceptics were the first philosophers to emphasize the role of subjectivity in Western thought and *were the first philosophers to emphasize experience over reason* (Groarke, 1990). Although most people today share the mistaken assumption that the Sceptics were simply proponents of an inherently abstract argument that it is impossible to know anything, there were actually two schools of Scepticism, each with its own set of concerns: the Academic Sceptics, who took control of Plato's Academy and were concerned with the epistemological limitations of knowledge; and the Pyrrhonian, or therapeutic, Sceptics, who were concerned with the more practical task of determining the proper way to live.

Whereas most of the Classical philosophers saw their role as that of *thinkers* whose task was to reason their way to wisdom, the Pyrrhonian Sceptics saw themselves as *therapists* whose task was to help people obtain equanimity by learning to accommodate the inherently ambiguous nature of existence. It may be argued that the Sceptics were the first "psychoanalysts" because many of them, including Galen and Sextus Empiricus, were physicians whose treatment methodology relied on trial and error instead of theoretical explication. Despite its momentary disappearance, the Sceptical attitude has survived more or less intact to the present era and has even played a critical role in the way that psychoanalysis was originally conceived. This is exemplified in the observation that contemporary analysts would probably agree that it isn't "knowledge" per se that ultimately relieves patients of their conflicts[4] but the ability to access experiences that must be suffered[5] over time, the nature of which resists rational explication or indoctrination.

The Treatment of Experience in Modern Times

Our very notion of experience and the place it has occupied in our intellectual heritage may be credited to the Sceptics, without whom such recent philosophical movements as empiricism, the commonsense philosophy of Thomas Reid, and the phenomenology of Husserl and Heidegger may have never developed. Yet, after the emergence of Christianity and its adoption by the Roman Empire, Sceptic philosophy more or less vanished for a thousand years. Scepticism might have been lost forever had it not been for the discovery of some lost books of Sextus Empiricus in the fifteenth century, around the time the printing press was invented. Sextus's books were subsequently translated from Latin into other languages, and their method became the object of intellectual debate throughout Europe.

By this time, most philosophers were preoccupied with employing rational means in order to prove the existence of God, resorting to philosophical arguments that were said to confirm the "logic" of his existence. The Age of Rationalism dominated Europe to such a degree that some philosophers (e.g., Bishop Berkeley) even questioned the existence of the physical world, arguing that existence is essentially mental (i.e., "ideas") and that the world of perception is an illusion.

Francis Bacon was one of the first philosophers to argue against this view by proposing that reason alone can become a form of enslavement if philosophers fail to put their speculations to the test in order to verify their credibility. Bacon can be credited with reintroducing the importance of experience into the philosophical debate by countering that our capacity to reason is even more unreliable than what we are able to derive from our senses. It was Bacon who proposed that the claims of scientific theories should be "tested" by subjecting them to *experimentation*; by repeating such experiments (a corruption of "experience") over and over, the investigator is able to render his *subjective* experience *objectively* reliable. The philosophical school of empiricism subsequently became a dominant force in England, with John Locke and, later, David Hume serving as its principal proponents.

When the rebirth of Scepticism subsequently swept across Europe, Hume was one of the first philosophers to place it at the core of the scientific method, leading to the identification of modern science with what is, to this day, deemed the empirical method. Nevertheless, Hume doesn't appear to have appreciated the subtlety with which Pyrrhonian Scepticism was employed by the ancients. In order to make his brand of Scepticism scientifically respectable, Hume substituted the Pyrrhonian reliance on *subjective experience* with a more detached form of *objective experimentation*. In so doing, Hume virtually abandoned the essence of sceptic inquiry because of his failure to understand that, according to the Sceptics, *any claim to have obtained objective knowledge, empirical or otherwise, is a dogmatic argument, not a sceptical one.* The empiricists turned out to be just as devoted to the acquisition of objective knowledge as the rationalists; the two schools simply disagreed as to which was the more reliable, the mind or the senses.

Yet, elements of Pyrrhonian Scepticism infiltrated European culture despite Hume's efforts to render it more scientific and its influence became so pronounced in the seventeenth century that Descartes, who saw its increasing popularity as a danger, wrote his *Meditations* in an effort to refute it. The fact that most people today have never even heard of the Sceptics serves to confirm the antipathy that Western culture has typically displayed toward matters of the heart. Despite this philosophical bias, most of the existential philosophers who emphasize existence over rationality (e.g., Heidegger, Sartre, and Merleau-Ponty specifically) are, in this respect, sceptical in their thinking and owe much of their perspective to the Sceptics, either directly through Sextus Empiricus or indirectly through Montaigne.

The heritage of Pyrrhonian (what I am calling "therapeutic") Scepticism was not passed down by the empiricist philosophers but through men of letters, such as the French aristocrat Michel de Montaigne. Famous for his invention of the essay, a literary genre noted for its deeply personal and autobiographical style, Montaigne lived in France during the time of Shakespeare, who incorporated sceptic arguments into some of his plays. Montaigne loved another man dearly and, when his friend died, fell into a depression from which he was unable to recover. He subsequently retired to his castle outside Bordeaux and immersed himself in a study of the Sceptics, Stoics, and other ancient philosophers in hope of obtaining relief from his melancholy. Montaigne began to write *essai* for his friends and confidants for the purpose of unburdening himself of observations he had accumulated over the course of his life, including such topics as the nature of fear, the education of children, solitude, friendship, cowardice, cruelty, conscience, experience, and so on, more than a hundred in all. Writing the essays and sharing his intimate observations with others offered Montaigne a means for obtaining insight into his condition while providing him with a voice with which to express his feelings of anguish and torment. Whereas the simple revelation of his feelings for others to hear was probably what finally cured him, Montaigne credited his recovery to the Sceptic method of inquiry to which he became devoted.

Because of his aristocratic privilege, Montaigne was also active in community affairs, even serving as mayor of Bordeaux, which brought him to the attention of the king of France, to whom Montaigne subsequently became a counselor, or "psychotherapist." With this new commission, Montaigne applied what he gleaned from his study of the Sceptics to his therapeutic relationship with the king. Entire sections of his essays are devoted to the proper handling of such a delicate position, presaging many of Freud's technical recommendations by nearly three centuries.[6]

Even today, Montaigne continues to influence philosophers, writers, and thinkers of every persuasion, including phenomenologists, such as Heidegger and Sartre, and existential philosophers, such as Kierkegaard and Nietzsche. On a close examination of his essays, one may notice that Montaigne employed both senses of experience that are depicted in the German language as *Erfahrung* and *Erlebnis*, which were, in turn, subsequently incorporated by Hegel, Husserl, and Heidegger into their respective philosophies. Montaigne spoke at length about the quality of his experience in the sense of *Erfahrung*, the *accumulation* of experiences over time, as well as *Erlebnis*, the immediacy of having an experience that he could subsequently talk about and reflect upon, thereby revealing to him aspects of his personality. Both of these senses are faithful to our commonsensical notion of experience and reflect the way we typically employ this term every day. I may speak, for example, of being an experienced psychoanalyst because I have accumulated more than forty years of experience treating patients, but I may also speak of having an experience which is unique to me and me alone, in a sense that is more or less an outcome of my subjectivity. *What I experience and how reveals to the psychoanalyst, for example, the person I am.* Psychoanalysts make use of both kinds of experience as a matter of course, but I say more about this later.

The Contribution of Phenomenology

Both of these inherently commonsensical notions of experience pale when contrasted with the enormous contribution that phenomenology has made to our understanding of potential experience and what experience specifically entails. In order to appreciate the contribution of phenomenology to our understanding of experience, it is necessary to explore in greater detail the difference between the two forms of experience that are distinguished by *Erfahrung* and *Erlebnis*.

Phenomenology is concerned almost entirely with the nature of *Erlebnis*, in other words, with the question: *what does it mean to actually experience something*? As noted earlier, empiricist philosophers such as Hume separated experience from rationality by consigning to experience sensual data alone. Modern scientific methodology, which endeavors to combine the experience we derive from our senses with our capacity to think about and reflect upon the nature of such experience (through methodical testing via experimentation), is unable to account for the human subject's experience of ideas, thoughts, and imagination. In other words, philosophers have traditionally split the human being in half, assigning one portion of the human project to rationality (i.e., the mind) and the other portion to sense experience (i.e., the body). The closest they have come to bridging the gap between them, offered by Kant, was through our capacity to reflect upon our sensual experience. Yet, this doesn't explain how the two are ever finally connected, given the categorical split that separates them. Moreover, given the basis of this schema, the possibility of reconciling the two is practically impossible.

The singular contribution of Husserl at the turn of the century was to reconcile the split between sense experience and rationality by suggesting that what we experience and how is already inherently thoughtful because the nature of consciousness is *intentional*, which is to say, *the act of consciousness and its object are given at one stroke*. One is not "related" to the other because each is irrevocably dependent on the other for its existence so that neither can stand alone. As Buddhists have traditionally argued, the presumed split to which Western thought has been devoted is illusory because the two are actually One. This is why phenomenology is able to claim that there are degrees of experience I am capable of accessing, just as there are levels of awareness or consciousness, depending on how diligently I set out to "see" (rather than comprehend) what my experience is already always disclosing to me. This thesis is especially relevant to psychoanalysts who endeavor to direct the patient's attention to unformulated experience by interpreting the latent meaning of the patient's verbal utterances. Viewed from this angle, a good interpretation is never intended to explain one's experience but to *deepen* it, in the phenomenological sense.

Whereas Husserl was, like Hegel, invested in finding a means through subjective experience to absolute knowledge, or certitude, Heidegger rejected absolute knowledge in principle by adopting a more sceptical approach to what experience makes available for the subject who is undergoing it.

For Heidegger, experience is essentially the "revealing" of Being; in other words, my experience discloses (to me) who I am as well as the world I inhabit.[7] I am neither strictly constituted by the world (behaviorism) nor is my world simply constituted by me (idealism); rather, the two are mutually interdependent because each serves to constitute the other. Whereas Hegel believed that one's capacity to experience accounts for psychological change—that experience, for example, comes as a shock because it alters who I am—Heidegger (1959) suggested that my capacity to experience discloses (i.e., uncovers) truths I am always in the process of discovering about myself (see also Heidegger's, 1950, treatment of Hegel's conception of experience). The critical feature of experience from a Heideggerian perspective is its latent power to "shock" the world I inhabit at the roots, so that it is both transformative and transcendent in the most radical sense. According to Heidegger (1959),

> To undergo an experience with something—be it a thing, a person, or a god—means that this something befalls us, strikes us, comes over us, overwhelms and transforms us. When we talk of "undergoing" an experience, we mean specifically that the experience is not of our own making; to undergo here means that we endure it, suffer it, receive it as it strikes us and submit to it. It is this something itself that comes about, comes to pass, happens.

(p. 57)

My experience is never entirely passive because I always have a hand in it; I am able to anticipate my experiences with a specific aim in mind, thereby *making use* of my experience to gain insight into the kind of person I am. In other words, there are degrees to experience; it isn't all or nothing. This is why I am also capable of *resisting* experience, avoiding it, and even "forgetting" experiences that I repress when they are too painful to bear. In turn, the degree to which I am finally *able* to experience anything, whether a piece of music, a hazardous journey, even a psychoanalysis, is determined by how willing I am to *submit* to the experience in question. In fact, the notion of submission, a favorite theme in Heidegger (as well as Freud),[8] is vital to the role experience plays throughout my life, because it determines the uses I am able to make of it. Experience is my contact with the world and the only means by which I am able to apprehend reality.

Freud and Phenomenology

Now we might ask: what does the phenomenology of experience have to do with psychoanalysis? Some people would suggest: nothing. After all, psychoanalysis is concerned with exploring the unconscious, whereas phenomenology is devoted to examining the vicissitudes of personal experience as it is lived. Jay (1998) noted that the crisis of experience in the post-subjective age in which we live began with the erosion of subjectivity as a concept, bringing into question, *"who* can be said to experience something if there is no one *to whom* such experience can be assigned?" One of the principal features of the deconstruction of Derrida, the postmodernism of Lyotard, and the structuralism of Lacan is the disappearance of the traditional *subject who experiences* in favor of a decentered subject that is reduced to an "effect" of invisible forces, whether such forces are manifested in the guise of society, language, or the unconscious.

Jay pointed out that Nietzsche and Freud were in the vanguard of a trend at the close of the nineteenth century that has now, a hundred years later, taken center stage, a trend that questions the very existence of a subject who is capable of *experiencing* anything. I would be the first to allow that Freud has contributed to this trend and even played a principal role in it. But, to give Freud his due, it must be added that he was also ambivalent about this question and, so, inconsistent with the role to which he assigned experience in both his understanding of psychopathology and its treatment. Despite what Freud said about the ego no longer being the master of his own house, I submit that experience nevertheless plays a vital role in Freud's conception of both the treatment situation and the conflicts that analytic patients typically suffer. Yet, the direction that psychoanalytic theory and practice have taken over the course of the last century has diverged from Freud in significant ways. Basically, Freud believed that *our capacity to bear painful experiences* as children more or less determines whether we will develop neurotic symptoms (or worse) when we grow up. This is actually a Heideggerian conception of experience, though Freud never knew this. According to Freud, if a child is faced with an experience that is too painful to bear, the child simply represses it from consciousness, making the experience of frustration magically disappear (see Thompson, 1994, for a thorough discussion of Freud's conception of psychoanalysis). The only problem with this short-sighted solution is that the repressed[9] memory finds an alternate means of expression, transforming it into a symptom that the adult subsequently suffers and complains about but hasn't a clue what caused the symptom or what purpose it surreptitiously serves.

For Freud, the purpose of pathogenic symptoms is relatively straightforward: they serve to shield the individual from a painful disappointment that the individual desperately wants to escape. In order to evade the full force of such disappointments, the individual employs repression (or denial) in an effort to erase its incidence; but because the disappointment in question was only repressed, not actually eradicated, the individual instinctively *avoids experiencing similar disappointments and anything that may serve to remind him of them in the future.* The irony in this thesis is that so-called traumatic experiences aren't actually *experienced* as such but are deferred until a later date when, with the help of a psychoanalyst, perhaps, the repressed memory may be elicited and actually experienced, but for the first time.

Based on Freud's hypothesis, psychoanalytic treatment is nothing more than an investigation into the patient's experience suffered over the entirety of his or her life. Analysts seek to learn about the experiences—*Erfahrung*— that patients remember over the course of their history; they also seek to understand the patient's experience of the analytic situation—*Erlebnis*— which is to say, the patient's experience of his or her relationship with the analyst, the so-called transference phenomena, in the here and now. But analysts are also interested in eliciting what may be characterized as "lost" experience (what Heidegger would call "potential" experience) through the patient's free associations. Change comes about through the patient's ability to *speak* of her experience instead of concealing it, as she has in the past. In other words, giving voice to one's experience serves to deepen it, but only if the kind of speech elicited succeeds in plunging each patient to the depths of her existence via the gravity of circumstances it occasions.

So far, what I have said about psychoanalysis sounds a lot more like phenomenology than psychoanalysis, *per se.* All I can say in defense of this observation is that psychoanalysis *is* phenomenological, at least in the way that Freud conceived it. On the other hand, there is something about Freud's notion of the unconscious that is explicitly nonphenomenological when it alludes to things going on "in" a person's mind of which the person has no awareness. In fact, phenomenologists and psychoanalysts alike recognize that we are perfectly capable of engaging in acts of which we claim no awareness and, so, no experience either. Awareness and experience, from a phenomenological perspective, though not identical, are interdependent phenomena. According to Husserl, experience presupposes an "I" who *suffers* his experience. No matter how decentered or obscure one's "I" or "ego" may be, Husselr's conception of subjectivity is consistent with experience itself. Yet, we saw in Heidegger how it is possible to account for levels or degrees of experience, depending on whether we are prepared to undergo the suffering that is entailed in determining just what our experience is.

The proposition that there are levels of experience and, so, levels of consciousness as well, offers profound implications for what Freud depicted as unconscious motivation and intentions which, when interpreted, are seldom remembered by the patient to whom such intentions are attributed. Yet, there are undeniable moments in every treatment when the patient does remember or realize her part in a drama that had heretofore been erased from memory. Just because one has a thought, idea, or intuition does not guarantee that one will actually have a full-throttle *experience* of it. The phenomenologist accounts for this phenomenon by suggesting that (Freud's depiction of) the unconscious is nothing more than a mode of thinking (i.e., consciousness) that the patient is unaware of thinking. In other words, the patient has no *experience* of thinking the "thoughts" attributed to her because she did not *hear herself thinking* (and experiencing) such thoughts when they occurred. At the time the thoughts in question occurred, her mind was "somewhere else." The psychoanalyst says she was unconscious of what she was thinking, but the phenomenologist would say she simply failed to *listen to* and experience what was on her mind. The psychoanalytic experience is designed to reacquaint us with that dimension of our Being that we typically conceal. By listening to what we say to the analyst when it is uttered, we reflect upon our consciousness at the moment we share our free associations and, so, "hear" it for the first time, by finally *experiencing* it.

Whereas Heidegger would say that the nature of experience is inherently mysterious and should be regarded with a compatible frame of reference, Freud would say that our experience has been repressed and rendered "unconscious." In Freud's schema, something must be done to retrieve and, ultimately, return our repressions to consciousness *by giving voice to our experience as it occurs to us in the analytic situation*. The edifice from which psychoanalytic treatment derives assumes that neurotics live in their heads and have lost touch with what they think and how they genuinely feel about the issues with which they are in conflict.

Consequently, the purpose of psychoanalysis is to return the analytic patient to the ground of an experience from which she has momentarily lost her way, in order to finally claim her experience as her own, as she recounts it to her analyst.

It doesn't take much effort to recognize that the two ways of talking about the two perspectives in question—Heidegger's and Freud's—are perfectly compatible with each other and always have been. Yet, not everyone approaches Freud's conception of the unconscious phenomenologically; consequently, psychoanalysis has unwittingly contributed to the crisis of experience that has been occurring since the close of the last century. This reading of psychoanalysis is probably unfamiliar to most analysts because it is an inherently existentialist reading of Freud from the perspective of phenomenology.

Surprisingly, this reading of Freud, and, by extension, of psychoanalysis, is barely evident in the psychoanalytic literature, though there have been attempts to address the situation by incorporating some of the basic tenets of phenomenology into psychoanalytic theory (Loewald, 1980, p. viii; Leavy, 1980, 1988; Atwood and Stolorow, 1984; Schafer, 1976). In the main, however, these efforts have fallen short of reframing the corpus of psychoanalytic theory and practice along phenomenological lines, which would necessitate greater emphasis on the psychodynamics of what experience specifically entails. The mainstream of psychoanalysis has more or less factored the very notion of experience (in the phenomenological sense of the term) out of existence. Recent interest in the so-called intersubjective dimension of psychoanalysis, which borrows heavily from the interpersonal tradition, still employs an empiricist account of experience, not a phenomenological one.

The Demise of Experience in Contemporary Psychoanalysis

I now offer an example of what I mean by the crisis of experience in psychoanalysis and how the absence of experience as a technical term has affected the development of psychoanalytic technique over the past half-century.[10] Though I address my remarks in the context of Kleinian theory, it is an example that is nonetheless representative of the direction psychoanalytic theory and technique have been taking, irrespective of the school to which a given analyst belongs. R. D. Laing was the first psychoanalyst to incorporate the phenomenological perspective on experience into his treatment philosophy in the early 1960s when he had just completed his own analytic training at the British Psychoanalytic Institute in London. Melanie Klein was all the rage then, just as she subsequently became in South America and the United States, especially on the West Coast. Laing began his second book, *Self and Others* (1969),[11] with a critique of a paper by Susan Isaacs, who was explicating Klein's notion of "unconscious experience," a contradiction in terms for the reasons we just examined. Following Klein's thesis, Isaacs (in Laing, 1969, pp. 3–17) argued that the nature of the psychic world is such that every human being lives two parallel lives, one that is conscious and one that is unconscious. The conscious one we are all aware of and the unconscious one we have no awareness of and never can.

According to Isaacs, we must resort to *inferring* what is going on in the unconscious if we hope to determine what is there. Isaacs insisted that the unconscious has aims, wishes, and motives of which we are not, and cannot become, conscious and, in the sense that we have been discussing, could have no experience of, either. The nature of unconscious fantasy, says Isaacs, is such that we suffer "unconscious experiences" of which we are unaware but that determine what we are capable of experiencing consciously. The implications of this theory are considerable because what Isaacs proposes about the nature of experience says a great deal about the way in which many contemporary psychoanalysts view the experiences of their patients, their own experience of their patients, and the way analysts interact with their patients, in turn.

For example, the Kleinian conception of projective identification has not only displaced Freud's conception of repression as the prototypical defense mechanism but has virtually inverted conventional notions of transference and countertransference as well, or altered their original meaning to such a degree that they are virtually unrecognizable. Following Klein's thesis, Bion (1959) concluded that the only means the analyst has available to determine the patient's unconscious experience is *through the analyst's experience of his own countertransference*:

The experience of countertransference appears to me to have a quite distinct quality that should enable the analyst to differentiate the occasion when he is the object of a projective identification. . . . The analyst feels he is being manipulated so as to be playing a part . . . in someone else's phantasy. . . . From the analyst's point of view, the experience consists of two closely related phases: in the first there is a feeling that whatever

else one has done, one has certainly not given a correct interpretation . . .
I believe the ability to shake oneself out of the numbing feeling of reality
that is a concomitant of this state is the prime requisite of the analyst.

(p. 149)

In other words, Bion appears to believe that the patient's "unconscious"
experience—an experience that, according to Bion, is inaccessible to the
patient—is periodically *experienced by the analyst* via the analyst's experience of his own thoughts and feelings: thoughts and feelings that the analyst, according to Klein's theory, is obliged to construe *as originating in
the patient's unconscious*. Notwithstanding the speculative nature of interpretations that seek to determine whether such experiences originate in the
analyst or the analyst's patient, Bion's conception of experience is such that
it is rendered virtually meaningless by any philosophical perspective with
which I am familiar. In effect, experience can be said to mean anything
that the analyst wants it to mean, whether or not the interpretations that the
analyst attributes to the patient's (so-called) experience are subsequently
confirmed by the patient. Some of the implications of this technical innovation are discussed later, but first, allow me to summarize the gist of what
I have just said.

Freud believed that we repress intolerable experiences in order to deny
their existence. The goal of analysis is to contrive a situation in which
patients feel safe to speak their minds, eventually giving voice to the experiences that had at one time been "forgotten" (i.e., repressed). On the other
hand, Klein is saying that the nature of what is going on in one's unconscious has *always been unconscious and always will be*. So, the patient's
disclosures will never reveal in any direct way what is going on there. How,
then, from a Kleinian perspective, is one supposed to determine what is
going on there?

According to Klein (and Isaacs, and even the early Bion), it must be interpreted by the analyst to the patient since there are no other means available
for the patient to grasp it. In other words, whereas Freud says that the goal
of analysis is to make the unconscious conscious, Klein says that the goal
is for the analyst to interpret to the patient what the unconscious is harboring. Whereas the phenomenologist would say that the purpose of interpretation is to help one's patients get in touch with their experience, Bion
(following Klein's theoretical perspective) uses interpretation to "translate" to his patients what they are (presumed to be) "experiencing" in their

unconscious. On reflection, analysts working from a Kleinian perspective have no choice but to follow this model, given the developmental theory that Klein adopted.

Whereas Freud believed the critical stage of development that analysts should consider in their interpretations is clustered between the ages of three and five—a stage of development that most patients are able to recall— Klein believed that the critical stage of development is the first year, an age that no patient is able to remember. In Freud's schema, analytic patients are endeavoring to "remember" experiences that have been lost but have the potential for recovery. Moreover, it isn't until the child is able to *experience* his or her feelings (in the Heideggerian sense) that "trauma" can even occur because without foundational experiences, there would be nothing to repress. If experience is that feature of consciousness that the subject is capable of reflecting upon, then the developmental period of childhood that Klein is concerned with is not only prelinguistic but for the reasons we have discussed, is pre-experiential as well. In Freud's schema, psychoanalytic treatment is concerned with the recollection of (conscious) experiences that have suffered repression, whereas, in Klein's, the analyst is obliged to "experience" the patient's preverbal experience *for* the patient since the patient has no direct access to such experience himself. The implications of this thesis for analytic interpretation are at turns comical and heartbreaking, as I demonstrate in the following clinical vignette.

The following is what Bion (in Klein, Heimann, and Money-Kyrle, 1957) characterizes as "the essentials" of two sessions with a schizophrenic patient whom he had been treating for five years, five days a week, in psychoanalysis. This is offered as an example of how Bion makes use of interpretation, employing a Kleinian perspective. Interpretations, according to Bion, should be offered in language that is simple, exact, and mature:

Patient: I picked a tiny piece of my skin from my face and feel quite empty.
Analyst: The tiny piece of skin is your penis, which you have torn out, and all your insides have come with it.
Patient: I do not understand . . . penis . . . only syllables and now it has no meaning.
Analyst: You have split my word "penis" into syllables and now it has no meaning.
Patient: I don't know what it means, but I want to say, "if I can't spell I can't think."

Analyst: The syllables have now been split into letters; you cannot spell—
that is to say you cannot put the letters together again to make
words, so now you cannot think.

The following day, the exchange goes as follows:

Patient: I cannot find any interesting food.
Analyst: You feel it has all been eaten up.
Patient: I do not feel able to buy any new clothes and my socks are a mass
of holes.
Analyst: By picking out the tiny piece of skin yesterday you injured yourself so badly you cannot even buy clothes; you are empty and
have nothing to buy them with.
Patient: Although they are full of holes they constrict my foot.
Analyst: Not only did you tear out your own penis but also mine. So today
there is no interesting food—only a hole, a sock. But even this
sock is made of a mass of holes, all of which you made and
which have joined together to constrict, or swallow and injure,
your foot.

(pp. 229–230)

It goes without saying that clinical case material can be interpreted in any
number of ways. I am not, however, interested in whether Bion's interpretations are meaningful or meaningless, right or wrong, good or bad. No one is
in a position to make that determination with authority, and we cannot even
be sure how Bion's patient experienced these interpretations himself, even
if Bion is convinced they were right on the money. What I find remarkable
in these interpretations is the presumption with which they are offered, the
dogmatic nature of their delivery, and the lack of caution with which Bion
offers them, as though they were messages from the gods and he is the
Prophet who was assigned to divine their meaning.

Because the patient doesn't know why he suffers and is unable to make
sense of his own symptoms, Bion concludes that the analyst needs to compensate for what the patient doesn't know about himself by employing
frequent interpretations of the patient's unconscious drives and defense
mechanisms. Though Bion is concerned with determining what the patient's
experience is and how it is manifested in the patient's transference with the
analyst, he presumes that the patient is incapable of determining what his
own experience entails. Bion's analytic theories are complex, and many

of his followers would argue that to condemn his clinical behavior without recourse to their theoretical rationale is to ignore the most important aspect of Bion's contribution to psychoanalysis. Moreover, Bion modified his theories subsequent to this clinical example, so one could surmise that his clinical technique was also modified, though I have not been able to find any evidence to this effect. I submit, nonetheless, that it is possible to offer a compelling theory that has little relevance to how the analyst actually works. Bion's clinical vignette reveals more about his technique than anything he might argue theoretically, and this is the problem with theory in principle. After all, no matter what Bion may say about the role of experience "theoretically," his use of interpretation in the vignette demonstrates the role he assigned to experience in actual practice.

How Bion could possibly know, for example, that his patient's remarks are manifestations of his unconscious wish to tear Bion's penis to bits, I do not know. Neither do I know what his patient meant by his bizarre remarks. That, it seems to me, is the point: how can one know unless we take the time to incur the right conditions so that, in time, the patient can tell us himself? Following Kant, Bion adopts the notion that his patient is unable to experience his feelings because he lacks the concepts with which to experience them. Bion provides him with words that are presumed to depict that experience and, after invoking them, the patient is believed to be in a position to somehow "experience" them himself, if not consciously, then somewhere in the depths of his unconscious. Bion doesn't appear to be interested in *what* his patient experiences or *how* because he is so eager to apply (and demonstrate) his psychoanalytic theory to the treatment at hand. Because it isn't necessary that his patient confirm or disconfirm the value of the interpretations offered, it is virtually impossible for Bion (or you and I) to determine whether his interpretations are sound or absurd. Moreover, such confirmation is unnecessary because the theory that Bion adopts has eliminated the patient's experience as an object of investigation, replacing it instead with a model in which the analyst's *theory* effectively displaces the patient's experience of the treatment situation. Theory has assumed such precedence over technique in this schema that virtually anything the patient might do or say may be construed to "confirm" the theory under discussion. In his commentary on Bion's case report, Laing (1982) states that:

> It is difficult to imagine what the patient could say that could tell Bion anything he does not think he [already] knows. Bion's view is based on, and follows from, Bion's way of listening. . . . Anything anyone says can

be heard and processed in this very unusual way. It is difficult to imagine anything anyone could say which could possibly reveal to Bion that his constructions could be wrong, or [that] they are a grinding machine which reduces any sense to total nonsense. It is difficult to fathom the difference between Bion's psychoanalytic phantasies and what is usually called a psychotic delusional system.

(p. 52)[12]

Laing observed that if the reader didn't already know that Bion was the psychoanalyst, his remarks would probably appear just as delusional as the person with whom he is conversing. Indeed, without knowing who the two are, Bion's responses to what he believes his patient is "actually" saying to him could, in turn, be interpreted as the ravings of a paranoid schizophrenic. Of course, we know that Bion was not a paranoid schizophrenic but a highly respected analyst who both impressed and inspired a generation of analysts with his intellect and imagination, though he apparently suffered greatly himself. This makes it all the more distressing that he would conduct himself in this fashion. Had Bion been more in touch with (and accountable for) *his* experience, instead of ferreting about for (what he construes to be) the experience of his patient, perhaps he would have exercised greater sensitivity with the patient depicted in his vignette.

I don't single out Bion as though he is a reprehensible example of a psychoanalytic practitioner; I admire many of Bion's contributions and have benefited from them in my own psychoanalytic work. Neither do I have a bone to pick with Melanie Klein or Susan Isaacs; they merely exemplify a direction that psychoanalysis has taken over the course of the past century that has forgotten what the phenomenon of experience entails. What is the consequence of this dramatic alteration in Klein's, Isaacs's, and Bion's (and, by extension, virtually any psychoanalytic) conception of experience? Basically, it has done away with it. I am no longer conscious or in any discernible sense aware of what my most important experiences are and, according to Klein, I never will be. Consequently, I must rely on others to tell me what is going on in my own mind and explain to me the content of my experience in order to finally know myself. This development speaks to a crisis of experience in contemporary psychoanalysis because it has demolished any vestige of what we take subjectivity, experience, and personal responsibility to be, even in the most sophisticated sense of these terms.

Ironically, recent efforts to incorporate the phenomenological conception of intersubjectivity into the psychoanalytic landscape have misconstrued phenomenology's aim as that of doing away with the notion of subjectivity, or the person, altogether (e.g., Reis, 1999; Atwood and Stolorow, 1984; Stolorow, 1997; Stolorow and Atwood, 1992; Benjamin, 1990). Although Heidegger has been responsible for replacing the Cartesian preoccupation with subjectivity with a so-called decentered dimension to personal existence, Heidegger never did away with the subject or self entirely and even deemed it the instrument *through* which the vicissitudes of our personal existence must come into being. On the contrary, the specific focus of phenomenology is and always has been to delineate *the precise features of experience as they become manifest in the here and now of the situation one is in*, whether the situation in question is of a personal, clinical, or philosophical nature. Any model of intersubjectivity that proposes to dispense with this critical component of the phenomenological method ceases to be "intersubjective," properly speaking, and withdraws by fiat into a *socialization* of the therapeutic process that is closer to the interpersonal tradition than a, properly speaking, phenomenological one. The entire range of recent so-called intersubjective contributions to contemporary psychoanalysis are prone to committing this error.

The Crisis in Contemporary Psychoanalysis

I don't have to belabor the observation that psychoanalysis is in a state of crisis. This crisis appears to have affected the United States more than other parts of the world for reasons that are too complicated to go into at this time. In the United States, our culture is turning away from psychoanalysis and, as a consequence, there is considerable debate in the psychoanalytic community concerning what has accounted for this state of affairs. Though this trend began in America, it appears to be spreading to other parts of the world for reasons that are similar to those that have engendered this crisis in the U.S. Some blame it on managed care and less expensive and more accessible forms of therapy, while others blame it on the psychoanalysts themselves. This second group accuses psychoanalysts of having oversold analytic therapy in its infancy, thereby misleading people into expecting it would work miracles by making all of their woes and suffering go away. We all know that it cannot, and was never really intended, to do anything of the sort.

All that psychoanalysis has ever been good at is to help us get in touch with our experience by talking from our experience and about it while sharing it with another person who, no matter how misguided or crazy our account of our experience may be, is capable and willing to accept it all the same. In that acceptance and implicit recognition of who we are and who we are not, difficult choices can be made that will improve, if not our existence, then at least our relationship with ourselves.

Some see this as an indulgent preoccupation that hardly merits the enormous cost and time that is typically devoted to it. Others have countered that this simple exercise holds the potential to help us feel better about ourselves and, hopefully, more tolerant of the incredible frustrations and disappointments that are unavoidable in life. This isn't a novel idea; after all, it was being practiced by the Sceptics over two thousand years ago. But we have also seen how history has seen fit to take this notion, once a flourishing part of the culture, and bury it. If we are not careful, we will find ourselves guilty of doing so again.

Notes

1 See Roger Frie (1997) for a comprehensive treatment of the relationship between language and subjectivity and those contributors who have popularized its significance.

2 See Todd Dufresne (1997) for a comprehensive collection of essays that are representative of the trend in the second half of this century to conceive of the unconscious from the perspective of linguistics.

3 What Freud was to term two millennia later "evenly suspended attention." See Freud (1912, pp. 111–120) and Thompson (1994, pp. 145–154) for sceptical aspects of Freud's technical recommendations.

4 See my "The Sceptic Dimension to Psychoanalysis: Toward an Ethic of Experience" (chapter seven) for a detailed explication of the sceptical dimension to Freud's conception of free association and the rule of neutrality.

5 It should be kept in mind that the words "experience" and "suffering" derive from the same etymological root, *pathos*, so the notion of *suffering* one's experience or *experiencing* one's suffering is a tautology.

6 See especially Montaigne's essay "On Experience" for a detailed description of his therapeutic technique with the King of France.

7 The implication of Husserl's thesis is that experience is "given" directly, that it is more closely akin to a perception than a conceptualization. Merleau-Ponty (1962) subsequently developed this theme by depicting his phenomenology of experience as a "phenomenology of perception." See

also Thompson (1985, pp. 118–135) for an explication of Merleau-Ponty's phenomenology.

8 See Thompson (1994, pp. 192–204) for a discussion of Freud's reliance on passive aspects of experience when explicating his conception of working through.

9 For the sake of simplicity, I use Freud's conception of repression as the prototypical defense mechanism; the same can be said no matter which specific defense is in play: denial, splitting, projection, reaction formation.

10 For a detailed discussion of how the phenomenological aspects of Freud's technical recommendations were suppressed over the second half of this century see Thompson, 1994, 1996.

11 Laing's first book, *The Divided Self* (published in 1960), was devoted to a phenomenological critique of schizophrenia, whereas *Self and Others* (2nd Revised Edition, 1969) was devoted to a phenomenological critique of psychoanalysis.

12 See Thompson (1997) for an account of how Laing employed phenomenological principles in his treatment of psychosis.

References

Adorno, T. (1992) *Notes to Literature* (2 vols; S. W. Nicolsen, Trans.). New York: SUNY Press.

Atwood, G. and Stolorow, R. (1984) *Structures of Subjectivity: Explorations in Psychoanalytic Phenomenology*. Hillsdale, NJ and London: The Analytic Press.

Benjamin, J. (1990) An Outline of Intersubjectivity: Recognition and Destruction. *Psychoanalytic Psychology*, Vol. 7(Supp.): 33–46.

Bion, W. R. (1959) *Experiences in Groups*. New York: Basic Books.

Bion, W. R. (1962) *Learning from Experience*. New York and London: Jason Aronson.

Dewey, J. (1987) *John Dewey: The Later Works, 1925–1953, Vol. II, 1935–1937*. (J. A. Boydston, Ed.). Evanston, IL: Northwestern University Press.

Dufresne, T. (Ed.). (1997) *Returns of the "French Freud": Freud, Lacan, and Beyond*. London: Routledge.

Freud, S. (1912) *Recommendations to Physicians Practising Psychoanalysis*. Standard Edition (Vol. 12, pp. 109–120). (loc pub)

Freud, S. (1953–1973) *The Standard Edition of the Complete Psychological Works of Sigmund Freud* (24 vols; J. Strachey, Ed. & Trans.). London: Hogarth Press (Referred to in Subsequent References as Standard Edition).

Frie, R. (1997) *Subjectivity and Intersubjectivity in Modern Philosophy and Psychoanalysis: A Study of Sartre, Binswanger, Lacan, and Habermas*. New York and London: Rowman and Littlefield.

Groarke, L. (1990) *Greek Scepticism: Anti-Realist Trends in Ancient Thought*. Montreal and Kingston, London and Buffalo: McGill-Queen's University Press.

Heidegger, M. (1950) *Hegel's Concept of Experience*. New York: Harper and Row.

Heidegger, M. (1959) *On the Way to Language*. New York: Harper and Row.

Jay, M. (1998, November 14) *The Crisis of Experience in a Post-Subjective Age. Public Lecture*. Berkeley, CA: University of California.

Klein, M., Heimann, P. and Money-Kyrle, R. E. (Eds.). (1957) *New Directions in Psychoanalysis*. New York: Basic Books.

Laing, R. D. (1960) *The Divided Self*. New York: Pantheon Books.

Laing, R. D. (1961/1969) *Self and Others*. 2nd Revised Edition. New York: Pantheon Books.

Laing, R. D. (1967) *The Politics of Experience*. New York: Pantheon Books.

Laing, R. D. (1982) *The Voice of Experience*. New York: Pantheon Books.

Leavy, S. (1980) *The Psychoanalytic Dialogue*. New Haven, CT and London: Yale University Press.

Leavy, S. (1988) *In the Image of God: A Psychoanalyst's View*. New Haven, CT and London: Yale University Press.

Loewald, H. W. (1980) *Papers on Psychoanalysis*. New Haven, CT and London: Yale University Press.

Merleau-Ponty, M. (1962) *Phenomenology of Perception*. London: Routledge and Kegan Paul.

Ogden, T. (1989) *The Primitive Edge of Experience*. Northvale, NJ and London: Jason Aronson.

Reis, B. E. (1999) Adventures of the Dialectic. *Psychoanalytic Dialogues*, Vol. 9: 407–414.

Schafer, R. (1976) *A New Language for Psychoanalysis*. New Haven, CT and London: Yale University Press.

Stolorow, R. D. (1997) Principles of Dynamic Systems, Intersubjectivity, and the Obsolete Distinction Between One-Person and Two-Person Psychologies. *Psychoanalytic Dialogues*, Vol. 7: 859–868.

Stolorow, R. D. and Atwood, G. (1992) *Contexts of Being*. Hillsdale, NJ: The Analytic Press.

Symington, N. (1986) *The Analytic Experience*. New York: St. Martin's Press.

Thompson, M. G. (1985) The Death of Desire: A Study in Psychopathology. New York and London: New York University Press.

Thompson, M. G. (1994) *The Truth about Freud's Technique: The Encounter With the Real*. New York and London: New York University Press.

Thompson, M. G. (1996) The Rule of Neutrality. *Psychoanalysis and Contemporary Thought*, Vol. 19: 57–84.

Thompson, M. G. (1997) The Fidelity to Experience in R. D. Laing's Treatment Philosophy. *Contemporary Psychoanalysis*, Vol. 33: 595–614.

Thompson, M. G. (2000) The Sceptic Dimension to Psychoanalysis: Toward an Ethic of Experience. *Contemporary Psychoanalysis*, Vol. 36, No. 3: 457–481.

Chapter 7

The Sceptic Dimension to Psychoanalysis

Psychoanalysis is both a collection of ideas and a method based upon those ideas whose goal is the right way to live. This means that psychoanalysis is an "ethic" in the sense that it concerns the manner by which individuals conduct themselves. Derived from the Greek *ethike tekhne,* meaning "the moral art," *ethike* is in turn derived from the Greek *ethos*, meaning "character." Both the character of a person who aspires to behave ethically and the customs of a people by which one's standards are measured derive from the concept. Morality, a subsidiary of ethics, pertains to distinctions between right and wrong and good and bad, whereas ethics, according to the Greeks, concerns the pursuit of happiness, the nature of which produces a state of equanimity by obtaining freedom from mental anguish.

If psychoanalysis is an ethic whose goal is liberation from psychic conflict, then the nature of that conflict must have something to do with the way one lives, thinks, and behaves. While the character of an individual is no doubt decisive in the outcome of a patient's treatment, the psychoanalytic experience essentially revolves around a kind of work that is performed and accomplished, the outcome of which succeeds or fails. By analyzing the customs of a given patient—the manner by which that person lives—that patient is in a better position to change what needs to be changed and discover a better life. If psychoanalysis is an ethic, then what kind of ethic does it foster? What are the rules by which it is administered, and what is the basis of its method?

While most people today associate ethics with little more than a set of rules that govern one's behavior, in ancient times ethical behavior was situated in philosophical debates concerning the right way to live. The important thing was the consequence that derived from one's ethics and whether it obtained happiness or misery. In those days, philosophers didn't teach

DOI: 10.4324/9781003429104-7

in universities but earned their living by helping people sort out the troubles that contributed to their unhappiness. Unless they were independently wealthy, these philosophers were obliged to seek recognition as wise men in order to recruit followers who could support them. Like analysts today, philosophers offered any number of competing remedies for the relief of mental anguish. According to Hallie (1964), "What interested the Greeks primarily was insight into the proper conduct of life, practical wisdom for producing a happy life" (p. 6). Whereas most of their ethical prescriptions were rooted in rationalist principles, one philosophical school, the Sceptics, stood out from the others by arguing that the accumulation of knowledge was irrelevant to the relief of mental strife, or what we would call "mental illness." According to Groarke (1990),

> The most salient feature of the Sceptics' views was their rejection of the commitment to reason. . . . Thinkers who espouse this commitment extolled the human ability to discern the true nature of the world and proclaim the highest good to be the pursuit of rational inquiry. Plato exemplifies the spirit of such convictions when he writes that the sense of sight has given rise to number, time, and inquiry into the nature of the universe.
>
> (p. 3)

The Sceptics

The word "sceptic" comes from the Greek *skeptikos* meaning to inquire or to be thoughtful. Like psychoanalysts today, the ancient sceptics sought to inquire into the nature of experience by abandoning prejudice and claims to ultimate knowledge. As a form of "treatment," sceptic philosophy sought to deepen the weight of experience by inquiring into the forms of anguish we ordinarily seek to suppress. The sceptics were the first philosophers to organize those trends in Greek philosophy that emphasized subjectivity over objective knowledge. Consequently, they were more concerned with a person's character than what he claimed to know, how that person conducted his life, and how he was said to have faced his own death. The equanimity with which Socrates accepted his death without protest was an inspiration for sceptic philosophy and exemplified the ideal to which every sceptic aspired. By relying on personal experience instead of adopting what others claim to know, scepticism helped its adherents accept the intrinsic mystery of existence with a benign form of indifference. According to Hallie (1964), "Scepticism [was] the hope of living normally and peacefully without metaphysical dogmatism or fanaticism" (p. 7).

According to Groarke (1990), traces of the sceptic attitude can be seen as early as Democritus and Socrates (circa 450 B.C.), when the Greeks crystallized three philosophical trends that were subsequently incorporated into scepticism: a) an anti-realist bias; b) the turn to a more subjective attitude about truth; and c) the development of philosophy away from epistemological concerns toward practical means of attaining happiness (*eudaimonia*, or *ataraxia*).[1] Scepticism proper is attributed to Pyrrho of Elis, who lived around 300 B.C. (about hundred and fifty years after Socrates) during the time of Alexander the Great, to whom Pyrrho was an adviser. Pyrrho's teacher, Anaxarchus, successfully employed sceptic arguments to convince Alexander that he wasn't a god, but not all monarchs were as receptive to his interventions. When Anaxarchus employed a similar argument with the king of Cyprus, he was put to death, proving that the attempt to shatter illusions can sometimes prove deadly.

After Plato's death, the sceptics assumed control of his Academy and administered its teaching until its final demise, when they closed it because they believed it had become too "academic."[2] The movement flourished for nearly seven hundred years until after the middle of the fourth century A.D. when it virtually disappeared after the rise of Christianity[3] (Heaton, 1993). Scepticism vanished for more than a millennium until it resurfaced in the sixteenth century when a text by Sextus Empiricus was discovered, the only surviving document actually written by a sceptic. Pyrrhonian scepticism subsequently became the rage in Europe and served as an indispensable tool for intellectual debate. Erasmus, Montaigne, Mersenne, Gassendi, and Descartes are only some of the philosophers, scientists, and theologians who were either influenced by the sceptic method of inquiry or, in the case of Descartes, committed to refuting it (Popkin, 1979). Shakespeare was also influenced by Montaigne's essays, and many of his plays featured sceptical arguments (Heaton, 1993).

Since Pyrrho himself wrote nothing, nearly all of what we know about scepticism was derived from Sextus Empiricus. Sextus was a physician who lived in the second century, near the end of the sceptic era. Only three of his books have survived, loosely translated as *Outlines of Pyrrhonism*, *Against the Logicians*, and *Against the Mathematicians* (Annas and Barnes, 1994; Hallie, 1964). The sceptics believed that most philosophers were of little use to the common man and, like Socrates before them, devoted their efforts to exposing the fallacy of what philosophers claimed to know. Instead, the sceptics viewed philosophy as a therapy whose purpose was to obtain peace of mind, or equanimity (*ataraxia*). Many of the sceptics, like Sextus and Galen, were physicians who belonged to the Methodist school of scepticism, which employed sceptic methods in the treatment of physical ailments. Through the use of *epoché*, which entailed the suspension of judgment, the sceptics sought to rid themselves of speculation by adopting an inquisitive state of mind that entailed ceaseless, open-ended inquiry.[4] This use of the mind has been compared to certain schools of Buddhism that also advocate the suspension of rationality by effecting a meditative state of mind. For example, one of the common Buddhist devices for suspending judgement is to practice what is called the four lemmas:

There is not something.
There is not nothing.
There is not something and nothing.
There is neither something nor nothing.

Once the practitioner of Buddhism understands this riddle, he is said to have achieved enlightenment, or what the sceptics called equanimity. However, the sceptics cautioned that a state of equanimity is not something one "achieves" in the way that some people, for example, achieve great wealth or renown. Rather, it is something one aspires to in situations that tend to elicit anxiety, ill will, or despair. Because life is always taking us by surprise, and we never know when something may happen, eliciting disappointment or frustration, it is at such moments that the sceptic method offers a means—or "way"—to simply let the occurrence *be* without psychological defenses. Once one is able to allow such circumstances to occur without alarm (*epoché*), one has elicited, if only momentarily, a state of equanimity, or open-mindedness, what Buddhists term *acceptance*. Some sceptics have also depicted equanimity as gentleness, kindness, and open-heartedness. Like the modern psychoanalyst, the sceptics resisted the temptation to offer "solutions" to people's problems and concentrated their efforts instead on sympathetically exposing contradictions in the other person's beliefs.

Though some have countered that the simple rejection of objective truth offers no practical gain, such objections are rooted in a limited understanding of what sceptic practitioners did. For example, whereas most commentators tend to lump all the sceptics together, there were two groups of sceptics, the Academics and what I shall call the Therapists (i.e., the "Pyrrhonian" sceptics). The Academics were concerned with epistemological questions and spent their efforts refuting what philosophers claimed to know. This is the form of scepticism that most people are familiar with today, essentially a negative philosophy that claims one can never know anything for certain. Though it is impossible to prove the sceptics wrong on this count, such arguments ultimately lead to a *cul de sac* that offers little in the way of practical relief from one's suffering. Such arguments are frequently employed in debating societies wherein the position each party adopts is argued and then reversed and defended in turn, purely for the sake of argumentation. Quang Xi, the Chinese philosopher, employed a sceptic device when he posed the insoluble problem, "How do I know whether I am a man dreaming I am a butterfly or a butterfly dreaming I am a man?" This is an inherently academic question that fascinates simply because there is no conclusive answer.

The other school of scepticism, the Therapists, rejected epistemological questions in principle and devoted their efforts to developing an "ethic" (or therapeutic method) that they held could lead to happiness. This undertaking was a lengthy affair because it entailed an unusual, non-academic use of the mind, a precursor to free association. As most analytic patients soon discover, the replacement of one kind of thinking with another is disconcerting because it entails a transformation in the role that knowledge typically plays in our lives. Whereas academic knowledge emphasizes the application of theory and a facility for abstraction, the sceptics rejected rote learning in principle and emphasized instead the here-and-now of immediate experience.

The Epoché

The ability to attend to experience as it unfolds from one unpredictable moment to the next is what the sceptics termed *epoché*, the momentary suspension of judgement. In effect, the suspension of judgement requires that we abandon any theoretical, conceptual, or causal considerations that presume to explain why something is the way that it is by approaching the problem instead with an "emptied" mind—what Keats termed "negative capability."[5] Instead of claiming to know the answer simply because we have adopted a theory that sounds compelling, the sceptic adopts a form of

Socratic ignorance—or what Husserl termed naïveté—instead. The result is that the sceptic maintains a state of suspended inquiry open to the phenomena as it presents itself to experience. The rejection of knowledge to which the sceptics subscribed is so radical that even today, a concerted amount of debate persists among Classics scholars as to just how extreme their rejection of knowledge really was.

For example, does the *epoché* require the rejection of all claims to knowledge—even what we derive from experience—or is it limited to those sources of knowledge derived from deduction and inference? Some have argued that the sceptics never refuted knowledge, *per se*, but that they limited *claims* to knowledge to what they derived from their experience. Even so, experience is such that it is constantly changing, so limiting knowledge to this standard would necessarily entail qualification to time and place, and so on. Other commentators have argued that the sceptics rejected virtually all claims to knowledge, including what one derives from experience. But this position could be construed as simply another version of the former argument, depending on the degree of qualification one employs. It could even be argued that the sceptics not only rejected knowledge but even one's reliance on "faith" and "belief."[6] Moreover, the sceptic's rejection of theory was so total that it is virtually impossible to speak of a sceptic theory. Instead, we are obliged to debate our respective understandings of the sceptic perspective, sensibility, or method. But how is a method of inquiry that rejects belief as well as knowledge possible in the everyday world where we neurotics live?

The sceptics argued that each of us already rejects knowledge all the time but that we simply fail to recognize that we do so and to what degree. For example, in a commonsensical sort of way we (mistakenly) attribute what we (presume to) know to science, or theory, or to factual information we have accrued from education,[7] whereas the sceptics would say we actually rely on our experience instead. The problem is that many people have become so estranged from their experience they seek to buttress what they glean from it on some theory and lapse into an infinite regress that can be difficult to escape, even with the help of a therapist. This argument has profound implications for the education of psychoanalysts because many analysts claim that they rely almost entirely on theory in order to treat their patients, whereas others insist that they know little about how analysis "should" be practiced and that they rely on their experience to lead them. Some analysts even confess that the more experience they accrue, the less they know! According to the sceptics, even those analysts who claim that they depend almost entirely on theory probably rely on their experience in ways that they fail to appreciate. I will offer two examples of how experience is decisive in the way psychoanalysts conduct themselves in practice and the degree to which they rely on their experience.

The first example concerns the capacity to love. Most analytic patients (allow me this generalization) go into therapy because they suffer the absence of love in their lives.[8] Such patients frequently claim they don't know "how" to love or complain they no longer believe love is possible or even desirable. Yet, it is perfectly obvious to anyone with even a little clinical experience that reading about love doesn't provide a capacity for it; nor does it show how to obtain it. Many patients claim they don't know what love is, and those who presume to know often confess that they doubt whether they wholeheartedly love anyone, including themselves. No analyst would urge patients to read about love as a way to get in touch with it or counsel patients as to how they might obtain it. Indeed, the insistence that one must know "how" to love in order to experience it is symptomatic of obsessional neurosis.

For example, when I declare my love for someone, I wouldn't think of qualifying this statement with the proviso that I "believe" I am in love. Similarly, it wouldn't occur to me to insist that "I have no doubt whatsoever that I love you." Either of these qualifications would sound awkward and less than convincing because there are no proofs of love and no grounds for its certification. In fact, I never "believe" that I love someone unless I resort to deducing how I feel logically ("I must love her *because* we never argue," and so on). Similarly, to suggest that I know I love someone implies I have reason to love her and that I know for certain that I do, indubitably. In fact, I don't "know" or "believe" I love anybody. Love is something one *experiences* without ever ultimately knowing or having to know what love is. Were I to qualify my declaration of love with the insistence that I know or believe it is the case, I would cast doubt as to whether my declaration is genuine (an observation that psychoanalysts make all the time). If it were subsequently discovered that my declaration was duplicitous, it was because I sought to deceive the person to whom my declaration was addressed, or even myself (as in the case of a self-deception). When such deceptions are discovered, it isn't one's knowledge about love that makes the difference, but rather the genuineness with which one professes love to another. Moreover, when self-deceptions do come to light, it isn't because now I "know" what I had failed to earlier about what love is, but because now I am in touch with my experience of how I feel about this person, whereas previously I was out of touch with my feelings, and so on. It isn't the presence or absence of knowledge that determines self-awareness but the vicissitudes of my experience and what I take my experience to be.

The same can be said for how psychoanalysts are educated. Reading about psychoanalysis doesn't ensure that one will be adept at applying it. The more scholarly an analyst becomes in his grasp of psychoanalytic theory says nothing about that analyst's competence with patients. Erudition about theory has virtually no correlation to one's performance because the capacity to be a clinician entails the ability to be in touch with one's experience while developing sensitivity to the experience of the patients one is treating. It is a common sense convention that the more experience an analyst accrues, the more "seasoned," and the more accomplished. This isn't because older or more experienced analysts have had more time to acquire more knowledge but because they have grown more comfortable in their capacity to sit with their experience of working with patients. Over time, they suffer their share of failures and successes and, due to experience, are more adapted to the unpredictable nature of the treatment situation. These commonsense standards to which all of us incline derive from a sceptical sensibility, not a scientific one.

It should be noted, however, that the sceptics weren't necessarily opposed to learning theory in principle, nor did they claim that theories were useless. In fact, they held that it is necessary to learn theory in order to overcome it! The point they sought to emphasize in their queries about the human condition was whether knowledge is ultimately of any use in eradicating mental strife (i.e., "mental illness").[9] Their answer to this question was an unqualified no.

Only a little over a century ago, a contemporary version of the sceptic sensibility was incorporated by Edmund Husserl into his new philosophical method, phenomenology (Wachterhauser, 1996). Though scepticism and phenomenology are not identical, Husserl made certain aspects of the sceptic sensibility a cornerstone of the phenomenological method, even utilizing the term *epoché* as its principal feature. Husserl's phenomenological investigations subsequently influenced Heidegger, Sartre, and Merleau-Ponty, who in turn inspired existentialist philosophy. Traces of scepticism can also be detected in hermeneutics, deconstructionism, and contemporary anti-realist tendencies. The similarity of the sceptic method to some schools of Buddhism has also been documented, and it is common knowledge that Pyrrho visited India on a campaign with Alexander. It is unclear, however, whether Pyrrho was actually influenced by the Indian sages he met there or if the features that their respective philosophies held in common were coincidental (Groarke, 1990, pp. 81–82). Some have even suggested that Pyrrho may have influenced traditions of Buddhism that arose after Alexander's campaign, such as Chan and Zen and the Tibetan practice of "crazy wisdom."

Michel de Montaigne

The sceptical perspective was not only a source of phenomenology but was an important precursor to Freud's analytic method as well, presaging his conception of free association and its complement, the so-called rule of neutrality. Though a direct connection between Freud and the Pyrrhonian sceptics has never been documented, I suspect Freud owed a debt in the development of his psychoanalytic technique to Michel de Montaigne, a proponent of sceptic philosophy with whom Freud was intimately acquainted (Reidel-Schrewe, 1994, pp. 1–7). Famous for his invention of the *essai*, a literary genre noted for its deeply personal and autobiographical style, Montaigne was an aristocrat who lived in France during the time of Shakespeare. He loved a friend passionately, and when he died, Montaigne fell into a state of profound melancholy. Montaigne eventually retired to his castle outside Bordeaux and immersed himself in the sceptics, stoics, and other ancient philosophers in an effort to find a cure. He soon began to put his most intimate thoughts to paper and the resulting essays became not only a source of insight into his condition but, even more importantly, a voice with which to articulate the fruit of his discoveries. Comparisons with Freud's self-analysis are inevitable as the essays were nothing less than soul-searching inquiries into the trials and tribulations of every manner of human suffering,[10] just as Freud's correspondence with Fliess served a similar purpose. The simple revelation of his innermost feelings was probably what finally cured him.[11]

Due to his aristocratic privilege, Montaigne was quite active in community affairs and even served as mayor of Bordeaux, a great honor as it was the second largest city in France, after Paris. He soon became a favorite of the King, to whom Montaigne eventually became a counselor, or "psychotherapist." With this new commission, Montaigne set out to apply the fruits of what he learned from the sceptics to the manner with which he handled his relationship with the King. By this time, Montaigne had become increasingly wary of the "knowledge" that physicians based their prognoses on, and he grew increasingly sceptical of what scientists claimed to know. The sceptics believed that the only reliable source of wisdom is the trials and tribulations of personal experience because equanimity is derived through *self*-examination instead of following the advice of experts. If he had learned anything from his years of self-inquiry, it was to reject theory in principle by relying on common sense instead, a cardinal principle of scepticism.

Commonsense Experience

Commonsense experience is important to keep in mind when most philosophers and psychoanalysts alike are increasingly preoccupied with theories, the nature of which are speculative and complex. We should remember that Freud (1933) criticized philosophers for this very reason and saw psychoanalysis as a practical alternative to the questions philosophers typically muse about, endlessly (p. 161). Contrary to popular opinion, Freud didn't arrive at this assessment due to ignorance or a constitutional inability to study philosophy; he was schooled in the Classics, read Greek fluently, and even prided himself on his knowledge of Greek philosophy and mythology (Thompson, 1994, pp. 51–56). His protestations to the contrary, Freud apparently chose to keep one foot in antiquity and the other in science while not permitting himself the temptation of being dazzled by the latest theoretical fashion. Yet, I would be the first to admit that what most people conceive psychoanalysis to be is not remotely sceptical but dogmatic and abstract, and Freud is as much to blame for this situation as anybody.

If Freud's endeavor to situate psychoanalysis in science was not a total disaster, it was arguably a curse that served to compromise its credibility at the end of its first centenary. In the name of science, psychoanalysts spawn one theory after another, each insisting on its "correctness" at the expense of all the others. For the most part, students who continue to show interest in psychoanalysis and pursue analytic training are only too happy to adopt the latest theoretical argument, the nature of which is impossible for most students to grasp, let alone apply in a clinical situation. Since most students are incapable of assessing the veracity of what they are taught, they identify instead with whichever analysts they happen to admire and swallow their opinions whole. It shouldn't be any great surprise that the resulting relationship between the theories they adopt and their clinical behavior is fluid at best. Obviously, all of the theories offered cannot be correct, so it would seem that those who got it "wrong" would be ineffectual with patients while the ones who got it "right" should enjoy extraordinary success. Yet there is no discernible difference in the treatment outcome between one analytic school and another. On the contrary, it would appear that most analysts, whatever school to which they adhere, suffer the same proportion of failures and successes, despite their claims to the contrary.

Meanwhile, the relationship between the increasingly abstract theories that most psychoanalysts thrive on and the manner with which they treat their patients is, as far as I can tell, virtually nonexistent. This is, of course, a happy occasion for their patients because for the vast majority of analysts commonsense prevails over their penchant for theory. Yet, for the most part, analysts must be doing something right, even if many of them don't seem to know what it is. I like to think that most of us, with enough experience, simply become sceptics over time as we allow our common sense to teach us what even the most elegant theory is incapable of disclosing. It is my impression that analysts do not model their clinical behavior on a given theory but rather gravitate to the theory to which they are already (unconsciously) predisposed. Analysts who are preoccupied with aggressive tendencies may adopt a Kleinian model, analysts who are drawn to the enigma of love may adopt a Freudian perspective, analysts who sense the analytic community is against them may opt for a Lacanian paradigm, and so on.

Like it or not, we are every one of us creatures of experience, even if we fail to fathom what our experience is. At best, an adopted theory serves as little more than a calling card, a shorthand for how we wish to be perceived in the professional community to which we belong.

This is as it must be, since no theory could ever do justice to the mind-bending complexity and maddening inconsistency that characterizes our clinical experience. Even the practical gains that at least some of our patients exacted from their therapy experience remains unknown to us, simply because we have no way of determining how our erstwhile patients have gotten along with their lives after the termination of treatment. And even if we did have the opportunity to see them once again (as per Freud and Dora), we would share little agreement among ourselves as to how their (alleged) therapeutic gain should be assessed. Asking an "impartial observer" to do this for us only begs the question since we have no way of knowing that any criterion that is adopted is necessarily more reliable than the next. Like it or not, we are in no position to ever finally "know" about our patients' so-called progress in life, as much as we like to tell ourselves that what we do is surely beneficial.

The Sceptical Dimension to Freud's Technical Recommendations

Despite the dogmatic features of the typical psychoanalytic theory, I suspect the sceptic attitude surreptitiously insinuated itself into Freud's conception of psychoanalysis in the earliest days of its development, despite his efforts to situate it in science. To support my contention, I shall undertake to explore those elements of psychoanalytic technique that I take to be specifically sceptical: the free association method and the rule of neutrality. I would be the first to acknowledge that no one actually knows whether the sceptics influenced Freud's development of these technical principles or if, as Freud was so fond of saying, he "discovered" them himself. We do know, however, that Freud became acquainted with Montaigne around the time his technique took a decidedly sceptical turn—between 1912 and 1915—and that Montaigne's essays contain technical "instructions" that bear an uncanny resemblance to Freud's technical recommendations. First, I shall offer a selection of Montaigne's comments that I see as precursors to the free association method, and then I shall examine those technical recommendations of Freud's that strike me as inherently sceptical.

As noted before, at the peak of his powers and renown, Montaigne became an adviser to the king of France. One must assume that advising a king was a precarious affair that required extraordinary powers of persuasion and finesse, not unlike the conditions for conducting psychoanalysis. In one of his most famous essays, "On Experience," Montaigne reviewed the necessary qualifications for assuming such a task and the difficulties invariably encountered. For example, for those who would undertake to counsel (i.e., analyze) others, Montaigne cautioned:

> We need very good ears to hear ourselves judged of by others; and since there are few who can stand it without being stung, those who venture to undertake it must employ a peculiar form of friendship, for it is an act of love to undertake to wound and offend in order to benefit.
>
> (Montaigne, 1925, Vol. 4, p. 307) [Ives' translation slightly revised]

A sceptic in deed as well as in word, Montaigne tried to maintain a non-judgmental air when offering his counsel to the King, whether the counsel proffered was embraced or rejected. From experience, Montaigne had learned that the prospect of baring one's secrets to others is a necessarily painful affair because the counsel one receives, in turn, is bound to be more bitter than anticipated. The sceptics recognized that the intensity with which we typically attach ourselves to our beliefs is so strong that we resist examining them with all the forces at our disposal. Montaigne had even concluded that the passion with which we defend ourselves from the ordeal of examining our most sacred assumptions is the root cause of "psychopathology."

Whereas psychoanalysts are typically biased in terms of the importance given to the patient's past, the sceptics observed that most people live in anticipation of what they fear will happen to them and expend enormous amounts of energy avoiding their fate: the principal source of anxiety. On closer examination, however, this ostensibly contrary view is far more compatible with the psychoanalytic position than one would assume. If neurotics engage in defensive maneuvers in order to ward off the return of what was repressed, then surely it is the anticipation of a future discovery that accounts for their anxiety, not its mere recollection. Seen in this light, psychoanalysis is not so much invested in the "past" as in the movement of a latent temporality, the precise features of which we can never entirely determine (Merleau-Ponty, 1962, pp. 410–433; Thompson, 1985, pp. 118–135). The root problem for we neurotics is our insistence on harboring a belief (e.g., fantasy, wish, delusion) that is opposed to the reality of the situation. The sceptics concluded that if one can find a means of removing the belief, or at least its intensity, we "will remain unaffected in matters of belief and will endure only moderate suffering in respect to what [we] cannot avoid" (Sextus Empiricus, 1949, Vol. 3, pp. 325–326).

Such counsel is not only good scepticism, but good psychoanalysis as well.

Whereas psychoanalysts tend to focus on the past as the source of the patient's neurotic anxieties, Montaigne presaged (and in turn influenced) the modern existentialist view that the anxiety with which one anticipates the future is always the hidden source of the misery that neurotics inflict on themselves. On reflection, this view is not antithetical to the psychoanalytic bias but complements it, since the impetus to repress a painful experience in the first place is effected in order to avoid a disappointment that threatens to follow.[12] Anticipating obsessional neurosis nearly four centuries before Freud coined the term, Montaigne (1925) alluded to the obsessional character type when he observed,

> Men do not recognize the [un]natural disease of their mind: it does nothing but ferret and search, and is incessantly beating the bush and idly obstructing and impeding itself by its work, and stifles itself therein like our silk-worms; like a mouse in a pitch-barrel [Erasmus]. It thinks that it beholds far off I know not what glimmer of light and fancied truth. But while the mind hastens there, so many difficulties block its path with obstacles and new quests, that they turn it from the path, bewildered.
>
> (Vol. 4, p. 294)

The sceptic way was uniquely suited for overcoming just those features of resistance that are usually noted in the analytic literature, including the transference tendency to project onto the analyst a god-like ability to fathom the inherently ambiguous nature of one's difficulties and decipher them accordingly, preferably in a tidy package. Exhibiting a surprising sophistication in working with transference phenomena, Montaigne emphasized the need to maintain strict confidentiality in order to avoid splitting the transference. When turning to the qualities that are necessary for serving in this role, Montaigne advises that,

> Such a man would not be afraid to touch his employer's heart to the quick, dreading to lose the continuance of his advancement and income. . . . And furthermore, I would wish that such a position be given to one man only, since to dilute the privilege of such freedom and intimacy among many would engender a harmful lack of reverence. And finally, from any man that I would undertake to grant such a privilege, I would exact, above all, the fidelity of silence.
>
> (p. 308)

Montaigne concluded that if anyone hoped to benefit from therapy, one's counsel must be offered with honesty and tact. He recognized that therapy is necessarily painful and that the patient's willingness to suffer is essential to therapeutic change—just as the courage to inflict such suffering (in the case of abstinence) is a prerequisite for anyone who endeavors to serve in the role of therapist. Whereas the above example was at least partially indebted to Stoic philosophy (which emphasized the virtues of hardship), Montaigne was ingenious in his ability to weave a sceptic sensibility into views that were seemingly antithetical to it (a device that Freud adopted when co-mingling the rules of neutrality and abstinence).[13]

Because suffering is something that is necessarily experienced, we instinctively try to suppress an experience the moment we encounter the anguish it occasions. Montaigne recognized that if we expect to genuinely experience our suffering—to succumb to it; to *be* with it—we must submit to the suffering our experience engenders.[14] This observation served as the basis for the distinction Montaigne made between the Pyrrhonian and dogmatic (i.e., other philosophical) perspectives. Whereas the former argues that change is effected through the business of suffering one's experiences, the latter argues that change is the consequence of acquiring more know-how (or theory). Montaigne concluded that the only way change can ever finally be realized is by suffering our experience by experiencing our suffering and our pain, not by determining what we ought to believe or how we ought to behave, the essence of Sophistry. Montaigne concluded that the only reliable prescription for obtaining peace of mind is to "*Simply suffer!* [We] do not [have] to follow any other treatment" (p. 328). And for those who protest that suffering should be minimized and ultimately eradicated, Montaigne countered, "He who dreads suffering already suffers what he dreads!" (p. 329).

Montaigne's allegiance to the sceptic's fundamental rule—that experience is our only teacher and that we typically avoid it at every opportunity—comprised the entirety of his therapeutic method, which Freud subsequently subsumed under the rule of free association. It entailed nothing more complicated than exploring our experience with another person by relying on our capacity to remember past experiences while confiding them with candor and honesty. Yet, these represent only a selection of Montaigne's comments about the role experience plays in life and the peace of mind (equanimity) we can possibly obtain from it. The most striking feature of Montaigne's therapeutic recommendations is the virtual absence of anything even remotely resembling a technique. Rather, the sense conveyed is one of accrued wisdom accumulated from the trials of experience suffered over the course of a lifetime. For Montaigne, the ability to counsel isn't a skill that can be taught but a *manner of being* that employs nothing more fanciful than the art of conversation. Freud's free association method relied more or less entirely on the same principle of confiding to another person all that we have to say about ourselves: our experiences, hopes, and failures, virtually all that we are able to recollect, in short, the entirety of what comes to mind in the course of the analytic hour. Freud also recognized that we resist this simple instruction for the very reasons Montaigne observed: because the change experience occasions elicits a quota of suffering that we resist at every turn.

The Way of Neutrality

Perhaps even more sceptical in spirit than the free association method is Freud's ill-understood rule of neutrality; only now are we dealing with a principle that concerns the behavior of analysts instead of their patients. As with free association, Freud devised this technical principle gradually over time and only broached it explicitly in the technical papers he published between 1912 and 1915. Freud never actually used the term "neutrality" specifically, nor did he coin any other technical term for this attitude, probably because it isn't a technique in the proper sense of the word; it isn't a technique that can be employed but rather an "attitude" or frame of reference that must be cultivated over time. One of the terms Freud did use when depicting this technical principle was "indifference," which he invoked only once. Strachey translated the German *Indifferenz* into the English "neutrality" (*Neutralität* in German) because he thought it more aptly characterized the sense of non-committal open-mindedness that Freud endeavored to convey. Whether we like it or not, the word stuck.[15] In retrospect, analysts have subsumed any number of prescriptions under the term "neutrality," and this technical principle subsequently assumed a life of its own, much of it considerably removed from Freud's original intention.[16]

It is time to review what Freud observed about the mental attitude he believed analysts should follow, which, whether we prefer another term or wish to dispense with technical nomenclature altogether, is ingrained in the analytic lexicon as neutrality. There is no better source for what Freud had to say about this attitude than in the second of his technical papers, "Recommendations to Physicians Practising Psychoanalysis," published in 1912. No specific term was invoked in this paper to depict what he was alluding to, but the spirit of what was subsequently termed neutrality—or indifference—permeates the entirety of the paper. Though most analysts today typically characterize this rule as little more than the act of concealing one's thoughts and feelings from the patient, Freud's conception of it was surprisingly open-ended. The essential idea of adhering to neutrality is to: a) make no assumptions during the course of the treatment; b) abandon all pretensions to knowledge; c) allow the patient's experience to determine the course of the treatment with minimal interference from the analyst; and d) abandon all claims of scientific inquiry by adopting a state of "evenly-suspended attention" toward everything that is communicated by the patient. Virtually everything that Freud had to say about neutrality was elaborated from these four basic recommendations.

The most salient feature of analytic neutrality was Freud's counsel to adhere to a mode of open-minded attentiveness that is fundamentally foreign to academic inquiry. Ironically, Freud's conception of neutrality is probably more familiar to practitioners of Buddhist meditation than to scientifically trained physicians or psychologists. Any activity or preoccupation that interfered with one's capacity to adopt this mental attitude was considered anathema to psychoanalytic inquiry, as Freud conceived it. For example, in one of Freud's technical recommendations, analysts are admonished against striving to remember anything that patients confide to them because, says Freud (1912), "As soon as anyone deliberately concentrates his attention to a certain degree, he begins to select from the material [instead of giving everything equal weight]" (p. 112).

In other words, one cannot treat everything patients say with equanimity (i.e., neutrality) while selecting one thing as important and dismissing something else as irrelevant. In so doing, the analyst inadvertently selects from the material and introduces a bias into the inquiry. Besides, analysts who think they know what is important to remember and what isn't are invariably mistaken because, Freud (1912) continues, "The things one hears are for the most part things whose meaning is only recognized later on" (p. 112). Consequently, the analyst should be content to "simply listen, and not bother about whether he is keeping anything in mind" (p. 112).

Freud correlated this inherently sceptical mode of attentiveness with the act of free association, the disclosure of the patient's experience to the analyst. In Freud's view, the rules of neutrality and free association are inextricably linked, the one serving as a necessary complement to the other. He observed that if analytic patients are expected to take the fundamental rule seriously, then the analyst must, in turn, behave in a reciprocal manner. If analysts expect their patients to treat their (the patients') thoughts, feelings, and inclinations without prejudice by disclosing everything that comes to mind, then analysts must treat everything they are told in a reciprocal fashion, with an unflinching respect for the truth.

As we saw earlier, Freud characterized this state of mind as one of indifference, a sceptic term that Sextus Empiricus equated with equanimity (Groarke, 1990, pp. 87–92). In hindsight, one wonders why Strachey didn't invoke the term "equanimity" instead of neutrality since it approximates Freud's intentions precisely. According to the Oxford English Dictionary (Onions, 1973), equanimity means "impartiality, evenness of mind or temper, and the ability to remain undisturbed by good or ill fortune" (p. 673). It is difficult to conceive of a more apt depiction of the prescribed analytic attitude that Freud sought to convey throughout his technical recommendations.

Moreover, Freud argued that if analysts are to take the rule of neutrality to heart, then they need to abandon the practice of taking notes during the analytic session because such activity involves the critical use of the mind. Such preoccupations only serve to detract from the evently suspended attentiveness that neutrality is intended to foster by discouraging the tendency to obsess over what is or isn't being remembered. Whereas note-taking is a habit that is difficult for scientifically-trained practitioners to break, Freud was merciless in his insistence on this recommendation. Though a champion of science himself, it would probably surprise some of Freud's critics to discover that he dismissed the notion that analytic treatments could ever be subjected to anything like a "scientific" study or report (Freud, 1912, pp. 113–114). While he admired science enormously, Freud also recognized that the treatment experience should be protected from the potential for abuse that scientific institutions and physicians commit as a matter of course. Freud (1912) offered what is probably his most eloquent depiction of neutrality when arguing against mingling science with treatment objectives:

> Cases which are devoted from the first to scientific purposes and are treated accordingly suffer in their outcome; while the most successful cases are those in which one proceeds, as it were, without any purpose in view, allows oneself to be taken by surprise by any new turn in them, and always meets them with an open mind, *free from any presuppositions*.
>
> (p. 114; emphasis added)

And, for those analysts who take Freud's admonition against taking notes seriously, even the intention of publishing an analytic case in the future may contaminate the delicate balance of attentiveness and relaxation that Freud advised analysts to adopt (a lesson he probably learned from his treatment of Dora).[17] The point, however, is not that analysts should do whatever they must to avoid committing errors but rather to protect themselves from knowing too much about matters that are ultimately inconsequential, thereby encumbering themselves with details that may subvert their ability to cultivate the ideal of equanimity in themselves as well as their patients (Thompson, 1996a, 1996b).

Perhaps the most renowned feature of analytic neutrality in Freud's writings was his admonition against succumbing to "therapeutic ambition," which he alluded to when suggesting that analytic candidates should be analyzed in order to minimize the potential for countertransference. Though Freud cites therapeutic ambition in the context of the need to model oneself on (the demeanor of) the surgeon, this recommendation is usually taken to infer that Freud cold-heartedly suppressed any feeling of sympathy or concern for the patient's condition (actually a feature of abstinence, not neutrality). I shall review this recommendation more closely to determine whether such criticisms hold up. Freud (1912) begins with a passage that is familiar to virtually every psychoanalyst:

> I cannot advise my colleagues too urgently to model themselves during psychoanalytic treatment on the surgeon who puts aside all his feelings, even his human sympathy, and concentrates his mental forces on the single aim of performing the operation as skillfully as possible.
>
> (p. 115)

What is customarily omitted, however, is the rest of the recommendation, which explains what Freud had in mind. He continues:

> Under present day conditions, the feeling that is most dangerous to a psychoanalyst is the therapeutic ambition to achieve by this novel and much disputed method something that will produce a convincing effect upon other people. *This will not only put him into a state of mind which is unfavorable for his work,* but will make him helpless against certain resistances of the patient, whose recovery, as we know, primarily depends on the interplay of forces in him. The justification for requiring this emotional coldness in the analyst is that it creates the most advantageous conditions for both parties: for the doctor a desirable protection for his own emotional life, and for the patient the largest amount of help

that we can give him today. A surgeon of earlier times took as his motto the words, "I dressed the wounds, God cured him." The analyst should be content with something similar.

(p. 115; emphasis added)

When we examine the context in which Freud invoked the "model of the surgeon" analogy, it becomes obvious that he was merely admonishing analysts against the potential for committing hubris, the temptation of acting like gods who would aspire to shape the course of their patients' lives. Besides, preoccupations about the unforeseeable outcome of treatment only distract analysts from absorbing the entirety of what is happening in the here-and-now of the treatment situation. Psychoanalysts are ambitious people; they have to be in order to survive the sacrifice entailed in undertaking the necessary training and to survive the extraordinary demands of sustaining a viable income. Freud recognized, however, that this experience is just as likely to arouse hubris as to encourage the degree of humility that a psychoanalytic (and sceptical) attitude entails.

The sceptics believed that since we can never know what the truth is at a given time, it is impossible to predict whether a given course of action will culminate in success or failure. In the analytic situation, one can't even be certain what success or failure entails. Freud began his research into psychoanalysis with the conviction that he would be able to determine the causality of neurotic symptoms and, armed with this knowledge, develop a method for their resolution. But his technical writings and case reports suggest that he gradually abandoned this search on both counts. His case reports on Dora and the Rat Man, for example, failed to provide conclusive answers to the etiology of symptom formation, and by the time Freud wrote "Analysis Terminable and Interminable" (1937) at the end of his analytic career, he had summarily rejected the notion of a "cure" in the conventional meaning of the term.[18] What Freud was left with was an avowed sceptical attitude about the aspirations of psychoanalytic treatment, accrued from his tolerance of unresolvable ambiguities, not scientific certitude. Some commentators have taken this paper to exemplify a growing pessimism in Freud's views about the value of psychoanalysis. They apparently failed to appreciate the sceptical nature of his perspective. Freud's comments that the goal of analysis may be characterized as increasing "one's capacity for love and work" or reduced to the simple formula of, "where *id* was, there *ego* shall be," only beg the question since it is never finally determined in anyone's analysis whether (and to what degree) one's capacity for love has been realized, or even what love ultimately entails, or how to measure it. While it is commendable that many analytic patients discover after their analysis is over that they are able to work more productively and even enjoy an increased vigor in their capacity to love, these considerations can hardly be reduced to measurable "goals" of the treatment. The goal of analysis can only be what it has always endeavored to be since its origins: to increase self-knowledge by becoming more honest with oneself through one's relation with an interlocutor. Whatever effects one derives from this experience must be secondary to the spirit of unbiased, open-minded inquiry. How one can possibly measure such a goal at the completion of treatment and the degree to which it can be said to have been "successful" remains a mystery for every psychoanalytic practitioner, no matter how astute or accomplished a given analyst may be (excepting the occasional undeniable successes and failures, which are rare).

But, even if one were able to determine what success is comprised of, the sceptics would argue that failure is sometimes a necessary prelude to success and that success, if and when it occurs, is often temporary and always unpredictable, so the quest for equanimity could never rely on this standard. That doesn't mean analysts don't harbor opinions or that they should conceal the opinions they entertain—as long as they are treated as opinions and nothing more.[19] Ultimately, they must rely on the exercise of discretion as to whether to voice an opinion or stay silent. There is a fine line, however, between discretion and secrecy, and Freud recognized that silence can be just as manipulative as interpretation. Freud's treatment of the Rat Man indicates that he believed it is often better to offer opinions than conceal them, and to deal with the consequences later (Thompson, 1994, pp. 205–240).

Conclusion

In summary, what are the practical benefits of scepticism, and how does it inform our conception of psychoanalysis? By adopting the state of mind to which neutrality aspires, the sceptic sensibility[20] offers analysts the wherewithal to suffer their trials with their patients with equanimity, just as free association permits patients the opportunity to disclose the entirety of their experience by giving voice to it, whatever the consequences may be. Such permissiveness, however, exacts a price because analysts, no matter how conscientious they may be, invariably make mistakes. While many analysts nowadays seem concerned with minimizing errors and even aspire to eliminate them altogether, Freud accepted his mistakes without guilt and even argued it is unwise to conduct treatment with a view to committing as few errors as possible, as though this factor alone accounts for the outcome of treatment.[21]

The sceptics concluded that the only truths we ever finally approximate are derived from experience, so the truths we live by are subject to revision since our experience is constantly changing. This can prove unnerving to some because life is always taking them by surprise, and they can never be certain of the outcome. Some may try to escape the weight of experience by seeking objective (i.e., anonymous) truths instead. Once adopted, such truths tend to alienate them even further, culminating in a split that engenders even more desperate defenses and an increase in psychical conflicts and exhaustion. This, the sceptics believed, is the essence of mental anguish: *to be divorced from the ground of experience while searching further afield for a truth that is ultimately unobtainable.* Equanimity is compromised even further when we use knowledge to serve as a buttress against the suffering that experience necessarily engenders.

By keeping an open mind to their patients' experience and not imposing a bias of their own, analysts help them obtain relief from their anxious quest for knowledge. The sceptic sensibility helps overcome neurotic conflicts by abandoning the quest to ever finally "know" the self and embracing instead a benign acceptance of the self by letting one's self just *be*. In the end, analytic patients achieve equanimity by substituting one form of suffering for another: by replacing "symptomatic" suffering and its plethora of evasive maneuvers with the suffering that is simply a consequence of living, what Freud (1893–1895) termed "common unhappiness" (p. 305).

If it seems ironic that Freud would shun the pursuit of happiness while the sceptics pursued it, it should be remembered that there is no precise definition for happiness and that the respective languages used to invoke it are only approximate. Freud would have agreed with the sceptics that equanimity is ambiguous because its aim is not to eradicate suffering but to remain "unbothered" by it, by accepting it as a condition of life. By examining our condition with an equanimity we acquire, even without noticing it, a new attitude about what suffering and happiness entail is also acquired. The truly happy individual is one who can cope with life's problems without avoiding them, who can endure the anguish of living without cursing it. If this attitude is the essence of the analytic perspective, then the sceptics of old would undoubtedly be happy to see that their philosophy has made it all the way to the third millennium, despite its setbacks and hardships, still alive and more or less intact.

Notes

1 Whereas most ancient Greeks conceived happiness as a state of *eudaimonia*—a state of elation and well-being—the sceptics conceived it as a state of *ataraxia*, a state of equanimity that obtains freedom from psychic conflict. For a more thorough discussion of these principles see Groarke, 1990, pp. 55–56; 87–92; and Nussbaum, 1994, pp. 499–507.

2 I shall say more about the distinction between the Pyrrhonian and Academic schools of scepticism below.

3 There is some evidence that the Roman emperors were suspicious of philosophical schools in general and those that appeared to challenge faith in Christianity in particular. On the other hand, scepticism has generally flourished—as it did during the first three centuries after the birth of Christ—when there are many competing schools of belief and receded when challenged by a dominant belief system that was intolerant of heresy, as occurred during the fourth-century A.D.

4 There is some debate as to whether the sceptics sought to eliminate belief as well as knowledge or embraced beliefs dispassionately. See Frede, 1997, for a spirited discussion on this issue.

5 See Leavy, 1970, for a lucid depiction of Keats's conception of negative capability.

6 What the sceptics referred to as belief would include the modes of conscious and even "unconscious" fantasy emphasized in the psychoanalytic literature.

7 For more on the unreliable foundation from which scientific knowledge is derived, see Thompson, 1994, pp. 69–77.

8 I base this generalization on over forty years of clinical experience, in both psychoanalytic and in-patient treatment settings, in Europe and well as the United States.

9 For the purpose of this article, I do not wish to debate the use or meaning of the term "mental illness" or whether the psychoanalytic understanding of this term is consistent with the psychiatric one. The Sceptics and modern psychoanalysts are essentially concerned with relieving forms of mental suffering that, by their nature, are extraordinarily resistant to generalization and conventional norms of "treatment."

10 The word "essay," derived from the French *essai*, literally means "to try" as in an attempt to try something out (Partridge, 1958, p. 187).

11 For a more detailed account of Montaigne's and Freud's respective views about the nature of friendship and how Freud's relationship with Fliess influenced his conception of transference phenomena, see Khan, 1974 and Thompson, 1998.

12 See Thompson, 1996c, for a more thorough discussion of the relation between repression and anticipation.

13 For more on the antithetical nature of neutrality and abstinence, see Thompson, 1996a, 1996b.

14 See Heidegger, 1971, p. 57, for a detailed treatment of the relationship between experience and suffering.

15 In his study of Freud's technical papers, Ellman (1991) preferred Joan Riviere's translation over that of Strachey's, in part because she translated the German *Indifferenz* into the English "indifference;" Ellman's preference in this case has proved to be the exception to the rule.

16 See Thompson, 1994, pp. 230–240; 1996a, 1996b, for a thorough discussion of Freud's conception of neutrality.

17 See Thompson, 1994, pp. 93–95, for more on the dynamics of Freud's decision to publish this case.

18 See Thompson, 1994, pp. 93–132; 205–240, for a detailed discussion of Freud's treatments of Dora and the Rat Man, respectively, and Thompson, 1994, pp. 241–274, for an exhaustive account of Freud's views about cure.

19 Whereas the sceptics argued that "rules" are antithetical to the spirit of the kind of open-mindedness they sought, they advocated the employment of *epoché* (i.e., open-mindedness) as a palliative for psychic conflicts. The technical principles of free association and neutrality may be read in a similar light. Experience often suggests that the adoption of this attitude tends to foster a desirable result, though there is no guarantee it will work in every case. See Burnyeat, 1997, pp. 36–46, for a discussion on how the sceptics viewed their own aims.

20 In fact, scepticism and neutrality are more aptly characterized as "sensibilities" than methods since they share in common an attitude that one aspires to cultivate instead of a technique one is obliged to perform.

21 See Thompson, 1994, pp. 137–139 and Lipton, 1977, for more on this feature of the analyst's temperament.

References

Annas, J. and Barnes, J. (1994) *Sextus Empiricus: Outlines of Scepticism*. Cambridge: Cambridge University Press.

Burnyeat, M. (1997) Can the Sceptic Live His Scepticism? In M. Burnyeat and M. Frede (Eds.), *The Original Sceptics: A Controversy*. Indianapolis and Cambridge: Hackett Publishing Co.

Ellman, S. (1991) *Freud's Technique Papers: A Contemporary Perspective*. Northvale, NJ and London: Jason Aronson, Inc.

Frede, M. (1997) The Sceptic's Beliefs. In M. Burnyeat and M. Frede (Eds.), *The Original Sceptics: A Controversy*. Indianapolis and Cambridge: Hackett Publishing Co.

Freud, S. (1912/1958) *Recommendations to Physicians Practising Psychoanalysis*. Standard Edition (Vol. 12, pp. 109–120). London: The Hogarth Press.

Freud, S. (1933/1964) *New Introductory Lectures on Psycho-Analysis*. Standard Edition (Vol. 22, pp. 3–182). London: The Hogarth Press.

Freud, S. (1937/1964) *Analysis Terminable and Interminable*. Standard Edition (Vol. 23, pp. 209–253). London: The Hogarth Press.

Freud, S. (1953–1973) *The Standard Edition of the Complete Psychological Works of Sigmund Freud* (24 vols; J. Strachey, Ed. & Trans.). London: Hogarth Press (Referred to in Subsequent References as Standard Edition).

Freud, S. and Breur, J. (1893–1895/1955) *Studies on Hysteria*. Standard Edition (Vol. 2, pp. 1–311). London: The Hogarth Press.

Groarke, L. (1990) *Greek Scepticism: Anti-Realist Trends in Ancient Thought*. Montreal and Kingston: McGill-Queen's University Press.

Hallie, P. (1964) *Scepticism, Man, and God: Selections from the Major Writings of Sextus Empiricus*. Middletown, CT: Wesleyan University Press.

Heaton, J. M. (1993) The Sceptical Tradition in Psychotherapy. In L. Spurling (Ed.), *From the Words of My Mouth: Tradition in Psychotherapy*. London: Routledge.

Heidegger, M. (1971) *On the Way to Language* (P. Hertz, Trans.). New York: Harper and Row.

Khan, M. (1974) *The Privacy of the Self*. London: Hogarth Press.

Leavy, S. (1970) John Keats's Psychology of Creative Imagination. *The Psychoanalytic Quarterly*, Vol. 34, No. 4.

Lipton, S. (1977) The Advantages of Freud's Technique as Shown in His Analysis of the Rat Man. *International Journal of Psycho-Analysis*, Vol. 58: 255–273.

Merleau-Ponty, M. (1962) *Phenomenology of Perception* (C. Smith, Trans.). London: Routledge and Kegan Paul.

Montaigne, M. (1925) *The Essays of Montaigne* (4 vols; G. B. Ives, Trans.). Cambridge: Harvard University Press.

Nussbaum, M. (1994) *The Therapy of Desire: Theory and Practice in Hellenistic Ethics*. Princeton: Princeton University Press.

Onions, C. T. (Ed.). (1973) *The Shorter Oxford English Dictionary on Historical Principles*. 3rd Edition. Oxford: The Clarendon Press.

Partridge, E. (1958) *Origins: A Short Etymological Dictionary of Modern English*. London: Routledge and Kegan Paul.

Popkin, R. (1979) *The History of Scepticism from Erasmus to Spinoza*. Berkeley: University of California Press.

Reidel-Schrewe, U. (1994) Freud's Début in the Sciences. In S. L. Gilman et al. (Eds.), *Reading Freud's Reading*. New York: New York University Press.

Sextus Empiricus. (1949) *Adversus Mathematicus* (4 vols; R. G. Bury, Trans.). London: Loeb Classical Library, Heinemann.

Thompson, M. G. (1985) *The Death of Desire: A Study in Psychopathology*. 1st Edition. New York: New York University Press.

Thompson, M. G. (1994) *The Truth About Freud's Technique: The Encounter With the Real*. New York: New York University Press.

Thompson, M. G. (1996a/1966) The Rule of Neutrality. *Psychoanalysis and Contemporary Thought*, Vol. 19, No. 1.

Thompson, M. G. (1996b/1966) Freud's Conception of Neutrality. *Contemporary Psychoanalysis*, Vol. 32, No. 1.

Thompson, M. G. (1996c, December) Deception, Mystification, Trauma: Laing and Freud. *The Psychoanalytic Review*, Vol. 83, No. 6: 827–847.

Wachterhauser, B. (1996) *Phenomenology and Scepticism: Essays in Honor of James M. Edie*. Evanston: Northwestern University Press.

Chapter 8

Happiness and Chance

Once upon a time, there was a young prince who was inconsolably unhappy, and there was nothing the king could do to bring his son out of his doldrums. With some trepidation, the king's advisers reluctantly informed his majesty that the only thing that could cure the prince of his misery was to obtain the shirt of a happy man. After searching far and wide throughout the vast kingdom, they finally located a poor farmer who they determined was supremely happy. But much to their dismay, they discovered that this poor but contented soul did not even own a shirt.

The moral of this story can be interpreted in any number of ways, including the observation that wealth and power do not guarantee happiness. But all interpretations point to one inescapable conclusion: happiness is both enigmatic and elusive, and for all our efforts to obtain it, happiness always seems just beyond our reach, no matter how hard we try or how devoted to our quest we are. For some, the very idea of happiness is viewed as a form of denial or delusion, perhaps a manic episode. After all, mental health professionals are supposed to be concerned with healing sick minds, not improving healthy ones. Moreover, for all the prosperity Americans enjoy—a standard of living that has long been the envy of the world—all the money in this world, according to that old adage, cannot buy happiness. Each year, we spend billions of dollars on the latest antidepressant or anti-anxiety medication, but for all their success in relieving our suffering, they do little in the way of making us happier human beings.

Yet, the vast majority of people who come to psychoanalysts for help complain not about this or that ailment but about being unhappy in their lives. Whether we like it or not, there is an expectation among analytic patients that, somehow or other, psychoanalysis will succeed where all previous efforts to obtain happiness have failed. Perhaps the observation

DOI: 10.4324/9781003429104-8

that most of our patients leave their analysis no happier than when they began can be explained by a recent article in the *New York Times* ("Arts and Ideas," 2001) which reported that even though people today say they value happiness over money, they also admit that they don't want to work for it. Yet, the pursuit of happiness is not a luxury that only the prosperous or leisure class can enjoy. It is the driving force of every person's existence, no matter how poor, wealthy, educated, or simple-minded they are. According to Irwin (1999):

> We reveal our conception of happiness in so far as we articulate what we ultimately aim at in our lives, and which aims make it worthwhile to aim at the other things we aim at. Different people dispute about whether we are well off by enjoying ourselves, by devoting ourselves to the good of others, or by pursuing our own intellectual or artistic development. These disputes are disputes about the character and constituents of happiness.
>
> (p. 251)

In this chapter, I explore the question of whether psychoanalysis has anything to do with the pursuit of happiness by reviewing Freud's observations on the nature of happiness and, specifically, the relation between suffering and unhappiness. Freud devoted an entire book to this topic, published in English as *Civilization and Its Discontents* (1930/1961). Although this was Freud's most popular work, its title is widely acknowledged to be misleading.

According to Strachey (in Freud, 1930/1961, pp. 59–60), the original title Freud chose for this book was *Das Unglüück in der Kultur*, a rough translation of which would be *Unhappiness in Culture* or, better still, *Society*. (Perhaps a catchier title may have been *Misery and Society*!) A more literal translation of the German *Unglüück* into English would be misfortune or, simply, bad luck. In German, the concept of happiness is commonly conceived of as good fortune or a stroke of luck. Freud subsequently changed the German *Unglüück* in the title to *Unbehagen*, a term that Strachey noted is more difficult to translate into English but suggested that the French *malaise* (a state of discomfort or uneasiness) or even *dis-ease* would have made an apt choice. When the book was translated into English, however, in 1930, Freud proposed the title *Man's Discomfort With Civilization* to his translator, Joan Riviere. Ignoring Freud's recommendation, Riviere chose *Civilization and Its Discontents*, and for all its faults, this is the title we've been stuck with ever since.

Naturally, Freud's own culture played a role in his conception of happiness, though there is little evidence that either Viennese, Austrian, German, or Jewish cultures played a decisive role in his views about the human condition. In fact, his conclusions about this question were primarily rooted in the Europe of the late nineteenth century and the Greek classical literature that every educated European studied at university. Every culture in the world has its own term for happiness, and every culture in history has tried to find ways of obtaining it. Although every culture agrees that happiness is desirable, not all cultures agree as to what happiness entails. I want to examine Freud's views about happiness with a view to determining the role contemporary psychoanalysis plays in a typical patient's quest for it.

Virtually every psychoanalytic practitioner is familiar with Freud's enigmatic comment about the relation between psychoanalysis and happiness—that the aim of analysis is to "transform hysterical misery into common unhappiness"—but few analysts could name precisely where Freud made this remark. In fact, Freud made this cautionary statement about the limited role psychoanalysis plays in procuring happiness all the way back in 1895, in the book he co-authored with Josef Breuer, *Studies on Hysteria* (Breuer and Freud, 1893–1895/1955), buried on its very last page. Because we have all heard variations on what Freud was presumed to have said, it may prove instructive to see what he actually said and the context in which he said it:

When I have promised my patients help or improvement . . . I have often been faced by this objection: "Why, you tell me yourself that my illness is probably connected with my circumstances and the events of my life, [and that] you cannot alter these in any way. How do you propose to help me, then?" And I have been able to make this reply: "No doubt fate would find it easier than I do to relieve you of your illness. But you will be able to convince yourself that much will be gained if we succeed in transforming your hysterical misery into common unhappiness. With a mental life that has been restored to health you will be better armed against that unhappiness."

(Breuer and Freud, 1893–1895/1955, p. 305)

At the very least, one is liable to agree that Freud's statement about the relation between happiness and psychoanalysis is a surprisingly enigmatic way of ending a book whose purpose was to inform his suspicious Viennese colleagues about the nature of his novel treatment method, psychoanalysis.

More surprising, Freud waited until 1930—nine years before his death and thirty five years after his book on hysteria was published—to resume his query into the nature and causes of unhappiness. Obviously, he had a lot of time to think about it during the interim. By 1930, the world had suffered its first world war, arguably the most horrifying conflict in history, and life in both Germany and Austria had been profoundly affected by the war when Freud returned to this important subject. Yet his famous statement about unhappiness (and implicitly, happiness as well) and analysis had been made before The Great War, long before becoming identified with the alleged pessimism of his later years. Certainly, nothing happened in the interim that made Freud any less pessimistic about the human condition and what measure of relief from unhappiness psychoanalysis could be expected to offer.

Culture and Unhappiness

Before turning to Freud's views about the relationship between happiness and the outcome of psychoanalysis, I want to say something about Freud's intellectual and cultural environment. For the sake of argument, let us suppose that human suffering and unhappiness are the same thing. Later, we will take a closer look at Freud's distinction between psychological suffering—epitomized by, but not limited to, neurosis—and common unhappiness. Freud's views on happiness and unhappiness were derived from many of the great philosophers over the past two thousand years or so with whom Freud enjoyed some measure of familiarity, including Heraclitus and Empedocles in the pre-Socratic era; Plato and Aristotle, by far the West's greatest philosophers; the Cynics, Stoics, and Sceptics in the Hellenistic era; more recently, the sixteenth-century essayist and philosopher Michel de Montaigne; and more recently still, Schopenhauer and Nietzsche. Freud studied virtually all of these philosophers in his youth or later in his maturity. In the main, all of these great thinkers agreed that life challenges us from the moment we are born with pain, frustration, and disappointment and that it confronts us with tasks that are extremely difficult to perform and that leave scars impossible to erase. Though, as children, we are convinced things will become easier as we grow older, experience teaches us the opposite—that life becomes more difficult and that this state of affairs persists throughout our existence until finally, we are faced with the inevitability of our death.

In fact, so much of our lives are focused on one form of suffering or another that we spend a great deal of our time pursuing relief from the burdens that our trials thrust upon us, from one day to the next, and so on, in perpetuity. Freud, the great systematizer, believed we could cluster the devices we typically use for obtaining relief from such suffering into three categories: a) the first is what he terms deflections from our suffering, such as work and intellectual activity, which help keep us preoccupied from the weight of our misery; b) the second is substitutive satisfactions, characterized by the pleasure we derive from art and entertainment, which help to diminish our suffering; and c) the third involves intoxicating substances that render us insensitive to the pain and misery that are otherwise inescapable. All three figure to one degree or another in all of our lives, and all three are readily available to us. Yet, if we devote ourselves to just one at the exclusion of the others, we eventually become addicted to it, and the momentary relief from suffering it previously afforded us diminishes. Though Freud's formula is derived from the basic outline of his drive theory, it is perfectly amenable to just about any theoretical formulation you might substitute in its place. In fact, Freud's observations on the matter make perfect sense even without a supporting theory of any kind because we can confirm their efficacy from the fruits of our experience, including what we have learned as psychoanalytic patients or practitioners.

None of the methods Freud enumerates ever succeeds to the degree we would like, no matter how clever, resourceful, or enlightened we are in our pursuit to gain mastery over our emotions. This raises the inevitable question as to why life is so unremittingly difficult and, allowing that we agree this difficulty is intractable and more or less consistent with living, what purpose the trying nature of our troubled existence can ultimately serve. This is a question that has been examined from the beginning of recorded history, and we have yet to find a satisfactory answer. Of course, we are all familiar with Freud's dismissal of the religious argument that he outlines in *Civilization and Its Discontents* (1930) and its earlier companion publication, *The Future of an Illusion* (1927), which more or less suggests (depending on the religion in question) that human suffering is something of a test and a means of preparation for a future life that becomes available only if we are willing to endure our suffering on this earth with a benign sense of acceptance. Those who lack recourse to such a comforting solution are left to wonder what to do with their suffering and to ponder its effects on their attitude about life and, of course, death.

Naturally, the question of suffering is uppermost on the minds of everyone who turns to psychoanalytic treatment, as relief from suffering is the principal motivating factor that brings people to therapy in the first place. About this, I will say more in a moment, but first, what are the effects of a lifetime of pain and frustration on the human soul? How does such suffering affect us, and what does it inspire us to seek from life to relieve it, not only in spite of our suffering but because of it? For Freud (1930), the answer to this question was never in doubt: our suffering inevitably causes us to seek happiness, to want to become happy, and, ultimately, to remain so (p. 76). Suffering and happiness, then, enjoy a complementary relationship. It is because of suffering that we seek a happy state whose purpose is to alleviate it—and when we obtain happiness, we naturally want to preserve it as a means of insulating ourselves against the inevitability of suffering again. But the quest for happiness is not as simple as it appears because the nature of happiness is such that we typically experience it not as simply relieving our suffering but, more importantly, as a source of well-being in its own right, a point that Freud does not emphasize. In fact, we might ask ourselves if it is even possible to attain genuine happiness if our sole purpose in obtaining it is to serve a utilitarian relief from suffering at the expense of everything else.

Most of us would probably agree that relief from pain and the incidence of happiness are not the same thing, though it is probably the most difficult distinction that any human being is ever asked to consider—and one, I submit, that the majority of analytic patients struggle with throughout the course of their treatment experience.

The Sources of Unhappiness

But what are the principal sources or causes of our suffering? The first is perhaps the most obvious: our own body, which, according to Freud (1930), "is doomed to decay and dissolution" and even relies on pain and anxiety as warning signals (p. 77). Infirmity is a constant presence in all our lives, though some of us appear to suffer from somatic symptoms more than others, whether such suffering can be attributed to accident, constitutional factors, or hypochondriasis, the manifestation of which is a prominent feature of many therapy patients. In some cases, we take such suffering in stride, whereas in others, it is a source of unremitting and inconsolable misery. And though we probably don't give it much thought until disaster strikes us, we cannot deny that the external world is another ready source of suffering that, says Freud (1930), "[periodically] rages against us with overwhelming and merciless forces of destruction" in the form of hurricane, earthquake, flood, and the like (p. 77).

This source of suffering is closely related to the first because it inevitably affects us physically, but it is also a potential source of financial hardship or ruin, a threat to our physical and emotional health, and the cause of death or infirmity to loved ones. Though it is possible to minimize the potential for earthquakes or hurricanes or floods by living in areas that are impervious to them, we invariably substitute in their place other unavoidable disasters that are native to any geographical locale. Ultimately, there is no escape from such dangers, and wherever we live, we become reconciled to them and learn to live with the risks they entail. Both of these sources of hardship are undeniable causes of suffering, though I am reluctant to equate such suffering with unhappiness, *per se*. It is curious that Freud would include them in a discussion about unhappiness, except for the possibility that he sometimes equates suffering with unhappiness, while in other contexts, he separates them. His third category of suffering alerts us to a more ambiguous and, no doubt, axiomatic version of it. In fact, the most pervasive source of suffering in our lives is our relationships with *other human beings*, the consequence of which, says Freud, is more painful than any other kind of suffering we can endure.

Freud's emphasis on the third of the three sources of suffering is worth noting, not only because it is the only source of suffering on which psychoanalysis can have the slightest degree of influence, but because this is the one area about which Freud's critics claim he has the least to say. Despite his emphasis on biology—and his arguable overemphasis on the pervasive presence of sexuality in our symptoms—at bottom, Freud argued that our interpersonal relationships constitute the most painful experiences of which we are humanly capable, and the bedrock of what it means to be human. It goes without saying that we could write treatises enumerating the many ways in which human beings are capable of making others unhappy, but Freud reduced virtually all of his patients' complaints about their respective sorrows to one ineluctable foundation: the trauma of unrequited love. No matter what neurotics complain about during the course of their treatment experience, the prevailing tragedy from which all of them suffer is, at the bottom, that of the Oedipus complex. In one way or the other, Freud surmised, that is the one injury that we have not put to rest and the remaining obstacle to our chance for happiness. It is also apparent that the first two incidents of human unhappiness enumerated by Freud—bodily ailments and global catastrophes—are not related to unhappiness, *per se*, but to simple suffering. As we will see, the two, though related, are not identical.

It follows that all human beings seek to avoid suffering, and the ingenuity with which we are capable of engaging in all manner of scheming, denial, and vindictiveness is, as we know, legion. Some people opt to avoid relationships altogether—or at any rate, the most intimate forms of relation—in their abandon to protect themselves from being rejected, frustrated, or disappointed by others. Of course, this strategy is never entirely successful because there is also no greater source of happiness than in our associations with other people, whether they be lovers, spouses, friends, children, comrades-in-arm, or colleagues. Without them, we feel unremittingly unhappy, and because of the weight of isolation, alienation, and loneliness, we are eventually obliged to seek an alternative means of relief from our self-imposed isolation.

But why, one wonders, do our relationships with others cause such suffering in the first place? And, if Freud is correct, why should it be the one source of suffering that is unparalleled? What do other human beings promise that is, in every case, thwarted? Freud suspected that the answer to this question lies in a quest that endures throughout our existence and never ceases to compel: the so-called *oceanic* feeling that a friend of Freud described as the kernel of the religious experience. Consistent with certain forms of love or equanimity,[1] this feeling was described to him as something akin to eternity, a feeling, says Freud (1930/1961), "of an indissoluble bond, of being one with the external world as a whole" (p. 65).

Freud admitted to never having experienced such a feeling himself and even questioned whether it could be described as a feeling at all. It seemed more likely to him that the oceanic feeling is the consequence of an *idea* that one finds pleasing, which in turn results in the feeling it elicits secondarily. In fact, Freud found the notion that one could ever feel "at one" with society so alien to his experience that he wrote *Civilization and Its Discontents* (1930/1961) to offer an alternative explanation for the source of this alleged sensation. He concluded that the only experience any of us ever have of this feeling is during the earliest stages of infancy when the child is welcomed into the bosom of its family. As the child develops, however, and discovers that the paradise it enjoys with its mother is doomed, it seeks alternative sources for this feeling of oneness that had previously required virtually no effort on its part whatsoever.

On the basis of this formulation, Freud appears to reserve the word *happiness* for any experience that serves to return us to that original, momentary bliss that our relationships with others often promise but ultimately are unable to approximate. This characterization of happiness is obviously more ambitious than the mere cessation of suffering, but it is also a conception of happiness that Freud finds the most elusive and perhaps the most dubious. Happiness is fleeting because we experience it in contrast to the drudgery and frustration that our daily existence entails. Though we are loath to admit this, we cannot be happy all of the time. If we were, hypothetically, capable of preserving the happiness that we occasionally enjoy, our life would become an occasion for boredom, and the happiness we had previously cherished would evaporate into that familiar state of anxiety that characterizes the basis of our existence. Then the quest for happiness would begin all over again, only to be doomed to erosion the moment we succeed in approximating it again, and so on. This observation can best be summarized with the adage "no honeymoon can last forever," a phenomenon to which all analytic patients become reconciled when the honeymoon they once enjoyed with their analyst eventually disappoints. Even the manic episode suffers its terminus.

Neurotic Misery and Common Unhappiness

This somewhat gloomy portrayal of happiness, however, is not the whole story. Though Freud fancied himself a realist and believed that the analyst's role is to impress upon patients realities that they are wont to avoid, he also believed this bitter medicine holds out hope for a far richer existence than the neurotic had been capable of before therapy. By way of illustration, let's revisit Freud's earlier, enigmatic thesis that the goal of analysis is to prepare us for common unhappiness. It seems to me this comment—if it is to make any sense at all—hinges on Freud's distinction between hysterical (or, for all intents and purposes, pathological) misery and common unhappiness. The distinction between these two forms of suffering is more or less predicated on two other distinctions that are unique to psychoanalysis. The first concerns the distinction between the etiology of the respective *sources* of human suffering, and the second concerns a similar distinction between the respective *experiences* of each, which is to say, between pathological suffering and unhappiness. Unfortunately, Freud's impatience with philosophical reflection prevented him from examining his enigmatic statement about common unhappiness more thoroughly. But having made this statement, he raises an existential question about the nature of human misery and what, if anything, psychoanalysis can do about it. It is incumbent on us to examine this distinction more thoroughly and to correct Freud's oversight in the process of doing so.

Throughout Freud's analytic career, he confronted his patients with a choice: to either do something about the sorry condition they were in or accept it. The ability to choose one or the other and resign oneself to the choice one makes is, in Freud's estimation, the hallmark of mental health, even when the outcome often leads to an increase in suffering! We saw earlier that Freud assigned the possible causes of unhappiness to three principal sources: a) physical disability or infirmity; b) natural calamities; and c) our relationships with other human beings. Moreover, of these, our relationships with others are the source of the greatest unhappiness we can experience. But what do these three sources of unhappiness have to do with the motives that typically bring people into therapy? Of the three, only the third—one's relationship with others—serves as an ostensible motive, but difficulty with other people isn't necessarily evidence of psychopathology. Besides, these three sources of unhappiness ostensibly have little to do with the kind of suffering that patients initially complain about. In fact, when talking about unhappiness, Freud says nothing about the most common presenting symptoms with which every analytic practitioner is familiar, including alienation, depression, or anxiety—in other words, *unbearable feelings*. Why is anxiety, for example, or alienation not treated as a cause of unhappiness instead of merely symptomatic of it?

The answer to this question is no easy matter to explain if, in fact, neurotic (or pathological) misery should be distinguished from common unhappiness. In Freud's estimation, the neurotic has a problem with accepting the brutal choice all analytic patients, sooner or later, have to face in the course of their therapeutic journey. Freud made his most eloquent portrayal of the neurotic's plight in a relatively early paper, *Future Prospects of Psycho-Analytical Therapy* (1910), fifteen years after his enigmatic statement about the relationship between hysterical suffering and common unhappiness:

> A certain number of people, faced in their lives by conflicts which they have found too difficult to solve, have taken flight into neurosis and in this way won an unmistakable, although in the long run too costly, gain from illness. What will these people have to do if their flight into illness is barred by the indiscreet revelations of psychoanalysis? They will have to be honest, confess to the [forces] that are at work in them, face the conflict, fight for what they want, or go without it.
>
> (pp. 149–150)

Freud found that the typical analytic patient rejects this choice and devotes his efforts to devising a "third," but inherently magical, choice instead: to pine away his life in fantasy or bitterness, waiting for the day when fate—in the form of good fortune—will reward him for his obstinate refusal to face up to the realities (i.e., disappointments) of life. This so-called third choice, as all of us know, is the ingeniously fashioned neurotic symptom (or compromise formation), to which the neurotic clings. The neurotic solution provides a respite from unhappiness in the form of *anticipation* of what we long for but at a price that is more costly than we can afford: the consequent pathological conflict that we end up imposing on ourselves.

This formula for the etiology of neurotic conflict also explains why Freud makes a distinction between the respective sources of neurotic misery and common unhappiness. Freud perceived the causes of unhappiness to originate from *outside* the individual and, therefore, due to circumstances impossible to control. This is why he concluded that fate plays a decisive role in the etiology of happiness and unhappiness alike. On the other hand, neurotic and other psychological conflicts do not, strictly speaking, originate from outside but rather, in a manner of speaking, from "within." In fact, our conflicts are with *ourselves* and are self-imposed, though the inspiration for such conflicts derives from those very relationships with others that we cannot control, no matter how much we wish to.

Consequently, you may conclude that unhappiness may cause this or that person to become neurotic when he is unable, as Freud proposes, to either accept his unhappiness or, to the degree that is practicable, do something about it.

So the analytic task, on the basis of Freud's hypothesis, is to become more effective in *fostering our happiness* but, when this fails, to graciously accept our unhappiness with equanimity, and move on.

If the etiologies of common unhappiness and neurotic misery differ—the former being the result of circumstances beyond our control and the latter a creature of our own device—is the *qualitative experience* of each different or identical? Typically, the neurotic cannot tell the difference. But even if neurotics are incapable of making such a distinction, Freud expects that the psychoanalyst is able to, or should be, by extrapolating the respective sources of the patient's misery. Sometime after the fact, when a patient, for example, has succeeded in abandoning the "third choice scenario," he too will be able to discern the difference between ordinary frustration—common unhappiness—and the legacies of unreality and alienation that are the hallmarks of psychopathological suffering. These, in turn, are compounded by the guilt we unconsciously derive from being the instrument of our own suffering and the anxiety that our secret will be discovered. Even if patients do not leave therapy with the feeling that all of their aspirations have been met, they oftentimes enjoy a sense of serenity with the life they are living and a better understanding of the role they play in their misfortunes. In a word, they have arrived at *acceptance*.

Alternative Conceptions of Happiness

A nagging question persists in Freud's carefully wrought distinction between neurotic misery and unhappiness. Why is the newfound serenity that patients sometimes achieve as a consequence of their therapy experience not a feature of Freud's conception of happiness? In fact, isn't serenity—which is to say, being at peace with oneself—a valid characterization of happiness? Moreover, isn't this characterization of happiness one that is not at the mercy of fate and misfortune but one we can accrue for ourselves with concerted effort and perseverance? As we saw earlier, the German word for unhappiness, *Ungluück*, means misfortune, whereas the German word for happiness, *Gluück*, means fortune or good luck. The idea is to be lucky or fortunate in life, as when things are going one's way. Every culture has its own term for happiness, and although the etymology oftentimes derives from the same root, the respective meanings, nuances, and emphases can vary enormously. Moreover, history also plays an important role in a culture's conception of happiness. Periods of prolonged peace or war, for example, can alter a culture's notion of the good life, but not necessarily in ways we can predict. Although Freud never explicitly said so, his knowledge of ancient Greek culture and language, coupled with his fascination with history, gave him a sophisticated appreciation of what human suffering entails and how all cultures throughout history have grappled with the same dilemmas and misfortunes.

I want to take a moment to review other conceptions of happiness that are not limited to, or necessarily dependent on, good fortune and compare them with how Freud conceived the outcome of therapy. In other words, is the serenity Freud believed to be obtainable as a consequence of analysis consistent with other conceptions of happiness, either in present-day cultures or at earlier epochs in history?

In fact, there are two Greek terms that are usually translated into English as happiness. The more common is *eudaimonia*, the root meaning of which is to flourish or to make one's life a success. Some of the Greek philosophers are concerned with the experience of eudaimonia, whether it can be reduced to a feeling that comes and goes or a state or condition that is enduring, whereas other philosophers are concerned with the source of happiness, whether, for example, it depends entirely on external circumstances beyond our control or is something we can strive for and achieve, a consequence of effort. It is important to note that in contrast to Greek philosophers, most people today identify happiness with simply feeling happy, feeling pleased, so that happiness is identified with what is pleasurable. The equation of happiness and the feeling of pleasure was, with only minor qualifications, rejected by the Ancients and, according to Annas (2000, p. 40), is of modern origin.

Although its precise origin is unclear, Annas traces the contemporary equation of happiness with pleasure to the nineteenth-century British philosopher John Stuart Mill, who defined happiness as the feeling of pleasure and the absence of pain, now a popular American perception of happiness.

Given Freud's emphasis on the ubiquitous presence of the pleasure principle and the prominent role it plays in his metapsychology, it is tempting to surmise that Freud, too, reduces happiness to the feeling of pleasure. But this conclusion would be mistaken for the simple reason that Freud's conception of pleasure is more than a theory of affect but an ontological category that is concerned with a much larger question: what it means to be human. For Freud, pleasure is not merely a feeling but an underlying principle of human motivation. As such, it is largely unconscious, so whenever (the sensation of) pleasure becomes conscious, its manifestation often occasions feelings of anxiety, dread, longing, sacrifice, and the like.

With the exception of the Epicureans and Cyrenaics,[2] attributing happiness to the experience of pleasure was of marginal significance in the Greek literature on eudaimonia. In fact, one of the most protracted arguments among the Greek philosophers concerns the relationship between pleasure and eudaimonia. There are numerous arguments, for example, throughout Plato's (1963) dialogues where the nature of pleasure is discussed, including the relationship between pleasure and suffering and pleasure and happiness.[3] Plato anticipated a fundamental principle in Freud's conception of neurosis when he argued that in order to obtain pleasure one must be able to endure hardship. Moreover, Plato argues that happiness cannot be reduced to simple pleasures because happiness derives from the sense that one is in the game of life, so to speak, and not merely a bystander. Following Socrates, Plato emphasizes the capacity to reflect on one's life and the crises that accompany it and the ability to step back from the troubles of daily living by taking stock of how events have led one to where one is today and what sense can be made of it. According to Annas (2000):

> For the ancients this is the beginning of ethical thinking, the entry-point for ethical reflection. Once you become self-aware, you have to face choices, and deal with the fact that certain values, and courses of action, exclude others. You have to ask how all your concerns fit together, or fail to.
>
> (p. 41)

Plato's teacher, Socrates, argued that despite the importance pleasure occupies in our lives, genuine happiness is not incumbent on good fortune or the feeling of pleasure but follows from living a virtuous life, epitomized by a capacity for honesty and open-heartedness. Socrates argued that as long as a person is virtuous, it doesn't matter if his life is saddled with hardship and difficulty because virtue is impervious to external circumstances, so as long as one is virtuous, one will be happy. Indeed, it is when we are confronted with hardship that our capacity for virtue is most poignant. For Socrates, happiness cannot be reduced to a feeling because it is one's *life as a whole* that is happy (or not), whereas pleasure is episodic, something one feels now and then, here today and gone tomorrow. One cannot be happy one moment and unhappy the next because happiness is the ability to live life by a set of principles that serve to make one the person one is. Similarly, Socrates rejects the notion that happiness can be reduced to the consequence of achieving the conventional standard of success because such standards are driven by ambition, not character. This implies that happiness is not the result of achievement but the consequence of becoming self-aware. In other words, Socrates sees happiness (eudaimonia) as the ability to make sense of one's life by determining how its components come together to make one's life what it is (see Plato, 1963 [Gorgias, pp. 229–307]). Another way of saying it is that we are content with life when it has meaning, and we are troubled with life when it doesn't make any sense. A great deal of therapy is devoted to making sense of our suffering, even when we can do nothing about it, and such insights can serve as a vehicle to relieve the weight of disappointments with which we just have to live.

But this raises a critical question: can one obtain happiness through a form of ethical practice that is impervious to external events, or is happiness at least partially dependent on external circumstances, in which case we are always at the mercy of others for our happiness? This is the principal debate that runs throughout the classical literature on happiness. It is questionable, for example, how the capacity for virtue can necessarily make one happy in the face of unremitting pain or torture; virtue may serve as consolation for not behaving like a coward before a firing squad, but can such consolation be equated with *happiness*? Aristotle—whom Freud studied while a student of Franz Brentano at university[4] —integrated Socrates' and Plato's respective views about happiness and concluded that happiness depends on both living a virtuous life and external circumstances, or fate (Annas, 2000, pp. 48–50). In adopting this view, Aristotle agreed that pleasure is a necessary component of happiness but not sufficient for it. In his view, the greedy or narcissistic individual who looks out only for himself may obtain enviable pleasures, but he will never be happy because his relationships are self-serving, and the price of his success will eventually come back to haunt him with a commensurate loss of friends.[5]

Because Aristotle integrated the least controversial features of Plato's and Socrates' respective notions of happiness—that it is both the consequence of character and fate, effort as well as good luck—his views are the least radical and the most commonsensical of the Greek philosophers, and so the most popular and historically influential. Aristotle possessed an uncanny ability to make complex ideas appealing and was the most lucid and palatable of the Greek commentators on the nature of eudaimonia, which he characterizes as making one's life a success, what he calls *flourishing*. Though the emphasis Aristotle gives it sounds suspiciously conventional, Aristotle qualified his depiction of happiness by acknowledging that pursuing success by *any* means will eventually lead to guilt and more suffering so that to flourish, in the sense he intends, is considerably more difficult than it sounds.

Conscience plays just as pivotal a role as effort, and consideration for the feelings and respect of others is just as important as achieving personal success. In a sense, what one is achieving is a *life* which is never static or completed because it is always alive and in a process of unfolding, so we also possess the power to ruin it and render our earlier successes the instrument of a future downfall. There is a tension in Aristotle's reading of eudaimonia between what is beneficial for oneself on the one hand, and for the community we are a part of on the other, a formula that is so commonsensical to us today that we sometimes forget it is just one interpretation among many of what happiness can mean. Even if Aristotle's views on happiness are not the most radical among the Greek philosophers (Socrates or the Sceptics would get the credit for that), they have proved to be the most popular and enduring. It is also the standard for happiness that most impressed Freud's views about suffering, informing, for example, the tension he established between desire and conscience (i.e., id and superego) and the role the ego plays in orchestrating the most satisfying outcome.[6]

Despite his extraordinary impact on contemporary European and American cultures, Aristotle's views about happiness are not the most radical of the ones available to us, or even the most useful. After Aristotle's death, Greek philosophy entered the Hellenistic era, which endured until the rise of Christianity, around 300 A.D. The main philosophers in this period were the Stoics, Epicureans, and Sceptics. The Hellenistic philosophers are important because they were even more interested in the nature of happiness than Socrates, Plato, and Aristotle. They deemed ethical concerns to be so central to the philosophical temperament that they conceived philosophy as a therapy whose purpose is to heal the human soul, by determining the right way to live. It was also during the Hellenistic era that the second term for happiness I alluded to earlier (in addition to eudaimonia) came into prominence, *ataraxia*. Usually translated as serenity or equanimity, the Greek depiction of ataraxia, following Socrates' conception of eudaimonia, minimizes the role of both pleasure and environmental factors in the pursuit of happiness. The Hellenistic philosophers most preoccupied with obtaining ataraxia, or equanimity, were the Sceptics and Stoics, but their respective conceptions of it were not identical. They were nevertheless aligned in common cause in that both approaches distanced themselves from Aristotle's more pragmatic notion of happiness in favor of Socrates' argument that happiness culminates from moral virtue, so that virtue is the principal vehicle for happiness. Like Socrates before them, both schools emphasized the cultivation of character and freedom from suffering in preference over Aristotle's combination of good luck and success as the critical element in happiness. Moreover, whereas Aristotle advocated the integration of one's goals in tandem with the values of the society in which one lives, the Sceptics and Stoics taught that one should reject society's standard for happiness because the conventional standard of success is obtained by prevailing (through competition) over others. According to this view, competition elicits emotions such as envy, aggression, and hubris that are detrimental to achieving equanimity (see Irwin, 1999, pp. 250–277, for an excellent review of the Stoic and Sceptic respective conceptions of ataraxia).[7]

Some might argue this is rather like comparing apples and oranges because these respective notions of happiness—eudaimonia (flourishing) and ataraxia (equanimity)—are so different. Whereas eudaimonia is epitomized by a state of flourishing that derives from the adulation (or love) of others, ataraxia becomes accessible only when withdrawing from others in private meditation or communion with *oneself*. Even more than eudaimonia, ataraxia is predicated on the premise that one cannot be happy with one's life if one is not happy with oneself, so the Sceptic and Stoic emphasis on moral character entails a deepening of and transformation in one's relationship with oneself. If a person isn't happy with who he is, he may expend all of his efforts preoccupying himself with ambitious pursuits instead of examining the things about himself that make him unhappy, in the mistaken belief that he can change himself in and through the eyes of others. On the other hand, if a person is happy with himself, he is more liable to be happy with his life and, when that fails, more accepting of those incidents in his life that don't go his way. In this respect, the search for equanimity is open to the accusation of being more elitist than a simple state of flourishing, and even subversive, because the equanimity it offers cannot be derived from others or even enjoyed with them—but then the same could be said about psychoanalysis.

Despite all of the elements that the Sceptics and Stoics have in common in their pursuit of equanimity, their views about how to obtain it are quite different. The Stoics, for example, argued that the key is a life of contemplation and the ability to use one's powers of rationality over emotion. The ability to suffer without bitterness or resentment was such a prominent feature of Stoicism that today, we even equate the "stiff upper lip" syndrome with a stoic sensibility. Of course, the Stoics were more sophisticated than that. Perhaps the greatest Stoic of all, Epictetus, was a font of wisdom that inspired great thinkers throughout history, including Freud. Perhaps the greatest merit of Stoic philosophy is its emphasis on the ability to interpret the meaning of life for oneself instead of aping the community in which one lives. Some of the features of Epictetus' philosophy were so compelling they were subsequently incorporated into Christianity. His counsel for a happy life continues to inspire us today as much as when it was written, owing to his capacity to synthesize the elements of his philosophy into adages that could be remembered and called on when needed. Some typical examples follow:

Character means more than reputation.
Happiness can only be found within.
Spiritual progress is made through confronting calamity.
Seeking to please is a perilous trap.
Conduct yourself with dignity.
Be suspicious of convention.
Mind your own business.[8]

One can readily detect the Stoic influence on Freud's views about unhappiness—if one compares the way he contrasts happiness and unhappiness with the Greek distinction between eudaimonia and ataraxia—including the emphasis on rational means to better living. On the other hand, Freud was equally drawn to Aristotle's depiction of happiness as incumbent on motivation and fate and was not indifferent to the conventional pursuit of success. Indeed, Freud would have been suspicious of anyone who claimed to have risen above conventional notions of happiness as one who suffered from self-delusion or repression, a victim, no doubt, of the nirvana complex. Another point to consider is the Stoic rejection of eudaimonia with its emphasis on success (i.e., that things are going one's way) in favor of a more quiet and inherently passive sensibility that is impervious to disappointment and striving. This prospect, of course, would have exercised little influence on Freud, who believed that the irrepressible force of one's libido would not tolerate such a measure of quietude without savaging the very instincts that, given the right circumstances, make a person's life worth living. This is not to say that the Stoics shunned life, but there is no denying that when one paints the differences in emphases between Epictetus and Aristotle in broad strokes, the former emphasized a means for diminishing suffering and saw ambition as a vehicle of suffering, not happiness.

Like the Stoics, the Sceptics devoted themselves to the pursuit of equanimity, but they rejected rationality as the principal means of obtaining it and even rejected the Stoic characterization of equanimity as a state of unadulterated serenity. Moreover, the Sceptics claimed not to know the path to happiness for everyone; they simply observed that if one were to do such and such, the result was oftentimes a state of happiness, meaning peace of mind or peace with the world, which amounts to the same thing. The Sceptics even allowed that fate—or at any rate, happenstance—indeed plays a role in the experience of equanimity. Unlike the Stoics, who emphasized an attitude of contemplation, the Sceptics believed it best to adopt a quizzical, inherently befuddled frame of reference so that the less one anticipates things will go one's way, the less one will become disillusioned. Perhaps the most important aspect of sceptic philosophy is the counsel to stop trying to anticipate what will come next and to develop a capacity to court the unexpected instead.[9] In other words, instead of plotting your life according to a preconceived scheme, allow your existence to create a groove of its own that will, in turn, fit your temperament and allow you to flourish, but without striving for success. Unlike the Stoics, the Sceptics did not reject the pursuit of eudaimonia and even argued that one's chances for flourishing would increase once one had obtained equanimity.

Although the Sceptics never claimed to know the steps that should be followed to achieve happiness, they believed the therapeutic component of their philosophy could nonetheless lead to happiness, leading some commentators to see a contradiction in their argument. Ironically, this observation enjoys a remarkable similarity to contemporary psychoanalysts who don't claim to cure their patients but who nonetheless hold that analysis can be helpful. How is it possible, you might ask, to have it both ways? According to Nussbaum (1994):

> The sceptic's official answer goes like this. *Ataraxia* just comes by chance, *tuchikos*, as the result of a process he is following out of some non-dogmatic motivation—say, because it is his trade. He does not seek it out, he does not believe in it: it just happens to him.
>
> (p. 300)

In other words, happiness is a consequence of chance in that it happens of its own accord, by giving ourselves to what life asks of us. The sceptic notion of chance, however, is not the same as Aristotle's conception of fate. For the sceptic, my chance for happiness is not *determined* by fate because it only becomes available to me when I adopt the right frame of mind. The critical point is that I don't *expect* things to go my way, though I would like them to. If they don't, I'm not disappointed, and if they do, I'm pleasantly surprised. I neither expect things to go my way because I strive for them, nor do I hope things will come to me if I am "lucky." My life benefits from my efforts in mysterious ways. Although, much of what I want never comes to pass, a great many things do come my way that I never anticipated or imagined. If I am preoccupied with the things I strive for and measure my life by the endeavors I set out to achieve, I may ignore the things that happen to me incidentally and shrink my life accordingly. My attitude is crucial because by it, I can avoid the kind of bitterness and resentment that may lead to withdrawing from life instead of embracing it wholeheartedly. Similarly, psychoanalysis can be seen as a method for achieving happiness, but only in the sense that I position myself to court its likelihood—in other words, by taking chances, but without knowing if the outcome will be fortuitous or disappointing, the very attitude neurotics find most difficult to adopt. The person who is dedicated to minimizing suffering in favor of risking happiness will, perhaps, suffer less but will never enjoy the kind of happiness the Sceptics cultivated: the uncritical acceptance of one's life as it unfolds.

The sceptic sensibility is far more subtle than that of the Stoics, and more paradoxical— impediments to their transmission that are compounded by the absence of surviving source materials, except for Sextus Empiricus (1949), who lived some five centuries after the founder of scepticism, Pyrrho, died. The relative impact of the Stoics and Sceptics on contemporary culture has been difficult to assess, but it is undeniable that important features of many of the twentieth-century's most important philosophical developments, including phenomenology, hermeneutics, existentialism, deconstructivism, poststructuralism, and postmodernism, all have their origins in the sceptic tradition. On the other hand, the Stoics have had an enormous impact on our views about ethics and, after Aristotle, are the most important moral philosophers from antiquity.

Though the Sceptics were not as important an influence on Freud's conception of happiness as was Aristotle, their method for achieving equanimity, through the capacity to suspend judgment and expectations, had an impact on the two most important technical principles in Freud's treatment philosophy: free association and neutrality. Whereas the Sceptics equated the ability to rid ourselves of neurotic conflicts with happiness, Freud saw it as simply a means to reducing suffering, which, he observed, doesn't necessarily make us happier. So if equanimity is a kind of happiness, what form of happiness does it offer? The principal feature of equanimity is the ability to face life's frustrations and setbacks with what the Sceptics depict as "unperturbedness"—in other words, the ability to not become anxious or upset when something in one's life goes wrong. A famous example of this capacity is the serenity with which Socrates faced his own death, which subsequently served as the example on which both Stoic and Sceptic philosophers modeled themselves. The Hellenistic philosophers Anaxarchus and Seneca similarly met their untimely deaths with equanimity when, like Socrates before them, they were executed for simply teaching their students how to think for themselves. In each case, all of these philosophers accepted their deaths in the same manner by which they had lived their lives, free from fear or bitterness, irrespective of how life treated them. Whereas Freud's conceptions of free association and neutrality, which embody the ideal attitudes with which patient and analyst carry out their respective roles, owe much to the Sceptics (Reidel-Schrewe, 1994, pp. 1–7), Freud believed it unlikely that anyone is capable of obtaining such serenity as a permanent feature of his or her character, though he believed it was possible for momentary periods of time.

Happiness and Chance

Two thousand years later, philosophers are still debating whether it is possible to become happy by any means other than blind luck or chance. In Freud's case, he believed that fate plays the larger role, but he also advocated a state of equanimity—free association for the patient, neutrality for the analyst—as a means to guide us through the troubled waters of analysis. I now return to Freud's views on the matter and examine how his conception of happiness compares with the arguments we have explored from antiquity.

Though Freud was a creature of his culture and his views about happiness were rooted in his experience as a psychoanalyst, he was also an astute observer of cultural mores and viewed society as the principal source of our unhappiness. This observation is the premise of *Civilization and Its Discontents* (1930). The most telling aspects of how analytic patients use their search for happiness as a source of resistance to analysis are embodied in two pivotal themes in Freud's treatment philosophy, the patient's transference with the analyst and the problem of neurotic guilt.

One of the reasons Freud rejected happiness as a goal of analysis was the way he conceived of transference, that patients harbor fantasies about what the analyst will or should do to make them happy. In Freud's opinion, this amounts to eliciting the analyst's love—the easy way, he says, of obtaining momentary happiness, but without having to work for it, so it cannot endure. If we follow Freud's views about the role of abstinence in the analytic relationship to its logical conclusion, the analyst is obliged to *thwart* these longings instead of helping to make them come true. In other words, it is through disillusionment that analysis effects its power to transform the neurotic from a hopeless dreamer into an individual who is willing to take life by the horns and accept its conditions, by fighting for what he wants or going without.

Psychoanalysis promises us nothing except to know where we stand. It serves as both a hedge against hubris and a vehicle for reflection about the course our life is following, how we got to where we are today, and what we can do to make it better. More important, analysis helps us determine the role we play in our unhappiness and the role assigned to fate. It is only natural to seek love both as a source of happiness and as inoculations against unhappiness. Not surprisingly, this stratagem inevitably worms its way into the transference until the patient, eventually defeated, abandons all hope of procuring it, by which time, if he is lucky, this well-meaning dose of reality is accepted, not as a personal affront but as a challenge to face his needs realistically. Following Santayana's dictum, "he who lives in hope dies in despair," the analyst knows (from the experience of his own analysis) that he must avoid colluding with the neurotic expectation that love from another can ever finally compensate for one's shortcomings. If love is not only a source of happiness but perhaps the greatest source at our disposal, it is also the cause of our gravest sorrows. Transference is the stage where these cruel but necessary lessons are encountered and suffered, not once, but again and again until, through perseverance, we learn these lessons and move on. Although there is a measure of love that imbues every analytic relationship, it was Freud's observation that satisfying the patient's craving for it can never serve as a catalyst for emancipating oneself from one's narcissism. In Freud's estimation, it is the neurotic's *inability* to love that is the principal source of his unhappiness.[10]

As we have seen, love relationships and their relation to both unhappiness and psychopathology figure prominently in Freud's thinking. Even if Freud traces virtually all pathological conditions to the experience of unrequited love, he is reluctant to attribute the principal source of happiness to the gift of love. Perhaps this is because he sees love as a burden and responsibility that can never satisfy as much as we expect, or perhaps this says something about the era in which Freud lived and how times have changed, especially in America, over the past century. Increasingly, marital and other forms of intimate relations are seen as one's best hope for happiness, and the dissolution or loss of such relationships is the principal source of misery. So, why is the analytic relationship itself not an opportunity to fashion such a relationship, which in turn may serve as a prototype for future, post-analytic relations? Freud has his own answer to this question, rooted in the economics of libido, yet even analysts who reject Freud's drive theory agree that love is of limited value in the neurotic's quest for relief from mental conflict.

This is because psychoanalysis is more concerned with managing loss and frustration than with orchestrating success. Analysis is not prophylactic but retrospective in nature: its aim is to understand the past—including the immediate past that accrues from one's ongoing experiences—and to learn from it. So even if love is a source of happiness in every person's life, the inability to accept losses and put them behind one serves to mitigate the potential to love again, the prototypical picture of the contemporary neurotic.

Similarly, Freud's views about guilt offer equally important insights into our unhappiness and, by extension, our resistance to therapy. Society, Freud observes, is concerned not with supporting our endeavors but in spoiling them. As Freud (1930) puts it,

What we call our civilization is largely responsible for our misery. . . . [Moreover], a person becomes neurotic because he cannot tolerate the amount of frustration which society imposes on him in the service of its cultural ideals. . . . [Therefore, any] reduction in those demands should result in a return to possibilities of happiness.

(pp. 86–87)

Later, he adds, "[in other words], the price we pay for our advance in civilization is a loss of happiness through the heightening of . . . guilt" (p. 134). And in a footnote citing Shakespeare, he gravely concludes, "Thus conscience does make cowards of us all" (p. 134).

Freud's principal thesis about guilt is that once we internalize the guilt society imposes on us, our conscience becomes our worst enemy. Of course, our conscience helps to keep us in line, and this serves the motives of others very well, but often at the sacrifice of our own happiness. As one would imagine, Freud was dubious of moral philosophers who promote self-effacing contributions to society, not out of benevolence but because of the (internalized) social pressure to do so. The line between generosity and guilt is notoriously difficult to draw, and even the most successful analysis cannot inoculate us from the relentless pressure to conform. If we can overcome at least some of the guilt that society imposes on us, says Freud, our chances for happiness can only increase. Freud wasn't insensitive to our quest for happiness, nor did he believe that happiness, by any definition, is impossible; he simply observed that it is elusive and that our efforts to procure it are only partially successful. This, of course, is the most difficult line to straddle as a psychoanalytic practitioner: to encourage patients to pursue their ambitions and even their folly while taking care never to promise that all—or for that matter, any—of their aspirations will come true.

As we have seen, the Greeks placed considerable importance on the experience of happiness as well as the means of obtaining it. Their arguments about the nature of pleasure, though complicated, no doubt influenced Freud's thesis that life is governed by a striving for pleasure. On closer examination, however, Freud's conception of pleasure—more an ontological category than a simple emotion or drive—includes the experience of pain and the capacity to delay gratification in order to further one's prospects for happiness. Unlike the Epicureans, Freud did not equate happiness with pleasure.

A few years before he wrote *Civilization and Its Discontents* (1930), Freud revised his views about suffering and replaced the pleasure principle with the "life" or love principle—Eros— which he juxtaposed against Thanatos, his controversial thesis of a death drive. In this formulation, individuals who are incapable of bearing frustration "deaden" their capacity for pleasure to minimize the pain of disappointment, whereas healthy individuals are able to bear hardships to maximize their chance for happiness. The capacity for risk and the courage to take chances play a pivotal role in becoming a more viable person and a happier one.

On this note, it is interesting that the etymological root of the English term *happy* derives from the Middle English *hap*, meaning chance. This observation can be taken in two ways. The first is consistent with the commonsense understanding of happiness as good fortune or a stroke of luck—in other words, a chance happening. We also characterize the unlucky person as one who is hapless. But the other meaning of happenstance emphasizes the element of risk in life and the chances we invariably take in our endeavors. Freud saw the neurotic as a person who typically plays it safe to minimize the risk of disappointment. Seen in this light, psychoanalysis offers the neurotic a second chance at happiness by coming out of his self-imposed exile and placing his future prospects at risk. As early as 1885, during his long engagement to Martha, Freud discovered the dynamics of the neurotic personality engendered by a society that restricts its members to gratifications it deems appropriate. In a letter to his then-fiancée, Freud wrote:

We [neurotics] economize with our health [and] our capacity for enjoyment. . . . We save up for something, not knowing ourselves for what. And this habit of constant suppression of natural instinct gives us the character of refinement. . . . Why do we not get drunk? Because the discomfort and shame of the hangover give us more "unpleasure" than the pleasure of getting drunk gives us. Why don't we fall in love again every month? Because with every parting something of our heart is torn away. . . . Thus our striving is more concerned with avoiding pain than with creating enjoyment [happiness].

(Reiff, 1959, pp. 309–310)

This makes for interesting commentary on those analysts—as far as I can see, the majority of them—who see the psychoanalytic setting as a *safe harbor* with an emphasis on security. Perhaps one of the reasons for Freud's decline in popularity among contemporary analysts is that they feel he was unnecessarily reckless with patients and because so many of his analyses, including some of his ostensible successes, are considered failures by contemporary standards. Implicit in Freud's technical writings is the view that to increase our chances for happiness, we must place ourselves at risk, including our chances at love, the risk neurotics fear most. From this angle, happiness depends not on the quota of our successes but on the satisfaction derived from knowing that we are willing to *be* at risk, in the first place, win or lose, or as Plato put it, to simply be "in the game."

Conclusion

There are three distinct conceptions of happiness I have reviewed and contrasted: a) the first equates it with a feeling of pleasure or well-being that is episodic and depends principally on fate; b) the second is the satisfaction of having done something with one's life and the consequence of both personal effort and good fortune; and c) the third is a state of equanimity that depends on the cultivation of character and relatively impervious to misfortune. These forms of happiness are not, however, mutually exclusive. We can accept all three as an intrinsic part of our existence and pursue the ones that are responsive to our efforts while developing a means within ourselves of reacting with serenity when fate deals us one of its inevitable blows. Moreover, all three enjoy a place in the psychoanalytic situation and are just as applicable to the analyst as they are to the patient.

In the final analysis, happiness is never solely dependent on the degree to which a life flourishes or the passive happenstance of Lady Luck smiling upon us, but on the virtue of participating in the game of life to which all of us have access . . . and playing the game the best we can.

Notes

1 Christianity recognizes three forms of love: *eros* (erotic love), *philia* (brotherly love, or friendship), and *agape* that are drawn from the Greeks. *Caritas*, a Latin term, was introduced to Christianity by Augustine.
2 The Cyrenaics qualified their conception of pleasure so extensively that it was no longer reduced to a simple *feeling*, whereas the Epicureans conceived pleasure as the reduction of pain, a notion of pleasure that Freud would have characterized as neurotic.

3 Some of these dialogues include *Gorgias*, 494d; *Laws*, 2.662e; and *Philebus*, 47b (for the pagination references cited, see Plato, 1963).

4 Freud was so taken with Brentano's courses on Aristotle while a student at university that he confided to a friend, "Under Brentano's influence I have decided to take my PhD in philosophy and zoology" (Vitz, 1988, p. 52).

5 See Aristotle's *Nicomachean Ethics* (2000, pp. 3–22) for his views on the nature of eudaimonia.

6 See Thompson (2001, pp. 400–410) for a detailed explication of Freud's views about the role the ego plays in the exercise of conscience.

7 See also Sextus Empiricus (2000, pp. 172–177) for his treatment of sceptic and Stoic conceptions of happiness.

8 See Lebell (1995) for a synthesis of Epictetus' philosophy and Long (2001, pp. 179–201) for a more general overview of the Stoic conception of happiness.

9 The notion of "courting surprise" as a vehicle to a state of well-being has also been noted by Stern (1997).

10 See Thompson (1998) for a more exhaustive treatment of the role love plays in the analytic relationship.

References

Annas, J. (2000) *Ancient Philosophy: A Very Short Introduction*. Oxford, England: Oxford University Press.

Aristotle. (2000) *Nicomachean Ethics* (R. Crisp, Trans.). Cambridge, England: Cambridge University Press.

Arts and Ideas. (2001, May 19) *The New York Times*, pp. A15–A17.

Breuer, J. and Freud, S. (1893–1895/1955) Studies on hysteria. In J. Strachey (Ed. & Trans.), *Standard Edition of the Complete Psychological Works of Sigmund Freud* (Vol. 2, pp. 1–305). London: Hogarth Press.

Freud, S. (1910/1957) Future Prospects of Psycho-Analytical Therapy. In J. Strachey (Ed. & Trans.), *Standard Edition of the Complete Psychological Works of Sigmund Freud* (Vol. 11, pp. 139–151). London: Hogarth Press.

Freud, S. (1927/1961) The Future of an Illusion. In J. Strachey (Ed. & Trans.), *Standard Edition of the Complete Psychological Works of Sigmund Freud* (Vol. 21, pp. 3–56). London: Hogarth Press.

Freud, S. (1930/1961) Civilization and Its Discontents. In J. Strachey (Ed. & Trans.), *Standard Edition of the Complete Psychological Works of Sigmund Freud* (Vol. 21, pp. 59–145). London: Hogarth Press.

Freud, S. (1953–1973) *The Standard Edition of the Complete Psychological Works of Sigmund Freud* (24 vols; J. Strachey, Ed. & Trans.). London: Hogarth Press (Referred to in Subsequent References as Standard Edition).

Irwin, T. (Ed.). (1999) *Classical Philosophy*. Oxford, England: Oxford University Press.

Lebell, S. (1995) *The Art of Living: Epictetus*. San Francisco: HarperCollins.

Long, A. A. (2001) *Stoic Studies*. Berkeley: University of California Press.

Nussbaum, M. (1994) *The Therapy of Desire: Theory and Practice in Hellenistic Ethics*. Princeton, NJ: Princeton University Press.

Plato. (1963) *Collected Dialogues* (Bollingen Series, LXXI) (E. Hamilton and H. Cairns, Eds.). Princeton, NJ: Princeton University Press.

Reidel-Schrewe, U. (1994) *Freud's Debut in the Sciences*. In S. L. Gilman, J. Birmele, J. Geller and V. D. Greenberg (Eds.), *Reading Freud's Reading* (pp. 1–22). New York: New York University Press.

Reiff, P. (1959) *Freud: The Mind of the Moralist*. New York: Viking Press.

Sextus Empiricus. (1949) *Adversus Mathematicus* (Vols. 1–4; R. G. Bury, Trans.). London: Heinemann.

Sextus Empiricus. (2000) *Outlines of Scepticism* (J. Annas and J. Barnes, Trans.). Cambridge, England: Cambridge University Press.

Stern, D. B. (1997) *Unformulated Experience. From Dissociation to Imagination in Psychoanalysis*. Hillsdale, NJ: Analytic Press.

Thompson, M. G. (1998) Manifestations of Transference: Love, Friendship, Rapport. *Contemporary Psychoanalysis*, Vol. 34: 543–561.

Thompson, M. G. (2001) The Enigma of Honesty: The Fundamental Rule of Psychoanalysis. *Free Associations*, Vol. 8: 390–434.

Vitz, P. (1988) *Sigmund Freud's Christian Unconscious*. New York: Guilford Press.

Chapter 9

Is the Unconscious Really All that Unconscious?[1]

There is little question in the minds of every psychoanalytic practitioner that Freud's conception of the unconscious is the pivot around which psychoanalysis orbits, even if the particulars as to what the unconscious comprises have been debated by every psychoanalytic school that has followed in his wake. Yet, despite the controversial nature of this concept, there is a pervasive agreement among analysts that whatever the unconscious is, it is certainly not a form of *consciousness*. That being said, this is precisely the dilemma that philosophers have found most troubling about the psychoanalytic conception of the unconscious and the reason why so many have questioned its efficacy. In a recent book, Grotstein (1999) addressed a fundamental and, as yet, unresolved difficulty in prevailing conceptions of the unconscious, which follows when we attempt to assign the very core of our being to a hypothesized unconscious agent that we can never know directly, and whose existence we must infer and believe to be so, as an article of faith. Grotstein concluded that we are still, after one hundred years of trying, unable to account for this persistent yet obstinate contradiction: that the unconscious knows all, but is "known" by no one.

Like many, I have been haunted by this anomaly over the course of my analytic career. For the purposes of this chapter; however, my concern is not a theoretical one but one of approaching the problem phenomenologically, which is to say, from the perspective of the psychoanalyst's lived experience, what has been depicted by the interpersonal school as an experience-near paradigm. Therefore, I do not intend to offer a new theory about the nature of the unconscious but rather explore the relationship between the alleged existence of the unconscious and one's experience of it. In the course of my exploration of this problem, I address a number of critical questions: does it make sense, for example, to speak in terms of

DOI: 10.4324/9781003429104-9

one's capacity to "experience" the unconscious if the very concept of the unconscious refers to that which is beyond experience? Moreover, does it make sense to talk in terms of suffering "unconscious experiences" if one is not aware of the experiences one is presumed to be suffering? And finally, allowing that experience is, at its margins, tentative and ambiguous, how does one account for those phenomena on the periphery of experience, whether such phenomena are characterized as unconscious (Freud), ambiguous (Merleau-Ponty), mysterious (Heidegger), unformulated (Sullivan), or simply hidden?

I do not claim to have found the answers to these questions, nor even a preliminary step in that direction. Instead, I merely seek to explore some of the problematics that the psychoanalytic conception of the unconscious has obliged us to live with ever since Freud formulated it over one century ago. First, I shall review Freud's depiction of the unconscious in relation to his conception of psychical reality and then turn to some of the philosophical problems that derive from his characterization of the "two types" of mental functioning: primary and secondary thought processes. Finally, I shall review some of the implications that derive from the psychoanalytic conception of the unconscious by employing a phenomenological critique of its presuppositions and exploring the role of Being and experience in Freud's conception of the psychoanalytic encounter.

Though my concern is not a theoretical one, it is nonetheless philosophical because the questions raised are of a philosophical nature. While I am aware of the fact that numerous psychoanalysts since Freud have endeavored to situate his conception of the unconscious in the light of subsequent theoretical developments, my purpose is not to assess these developments with a view to contrasting them with Freud's. Instead, I shall review the problematics of Freud's thesis in the light of those philosophers whose perspective is at odds with the very notion of an "unconscious" portion of the mind and who endeavor to situate the phenomena that Freud deemed unconscious in the context of consciousness itself, or, in the case of Heidegger, one that dispenses with the conscious/unconscious dynamic altogether. To this end, I will propose that the Freudian unconscious is a form of sentient, nascent "consciousness"—implied in Freud's own depiction of it—but a form of consciousness that is unavailable to experience. I characterize the purpose of the psychoanalytic endeavor as one of bringing those aspects of consciousness that lie on the periphery of experience to experience, to the degree that is feasible in each case.

Freud's Conception of Psychic Reality

Freud's first topography for demarcating the distinction between conscious and unconscious aspects of the mind concerned the nature of fantasy and the role it plays in the life of the neurotic. As a consequence of his experiments with hypnotism, Freud surmised that every individual is driven by two kinds of fantasies: one of which one is aware and the other of which one is unaware. Freud opted to term those of which one is unaware "unconscious" because we have no conscious experience of them but are nonetheless capable of discerning their existence when hypnotized. Such so-called unconscious fantasies have been repressed, but because they reside "in" the unconscious, they engender psychic conflict, the manifestation of which accounts for psychopathology, dream formation, and parapraxes.

Freud's first, topographical, model of the unconscious was relatively simple: one portion of the mind is conscious and the thoughts it contains are in the forefront of awareness (or conscious experience), whereas another portion of the mind is unconscious and is composed of fantasies that have suffered repression (or more primitive defense mechanisms). Freud also included a third element in this topography, the "preconscious," which contains thoughts and memories that, though not immediately conscious, are nonetheless available to consciousness in principle. Freud's earlier topography is essentially an outline of the vicissitudes of the individual's psychic life, what Freud termed "psychic reality." Freud's depiction of psychic reality is not, however, predicated on the kind of factual reality that is investigated by the empirical sciences because it is a kind of "reality" that one *experiences* in the form of fantasy, delusion, or hallucination. Quoting Freud (1913):

> What lie behind the sense of guilt of neurotics [for example] are always *psychical* realities and never *factual* ones. What characterizes neurotics is that they prefer psychical to factual reality and react just as seriously to thoughts as normal people do to realities.
>
> (p. 159)

Yet, in what sense can one treat such fantasies as "realities" when they are not real? Freud recognized that fantasies can be *experienced* as real in the same way that objective reality—which is to say, that which is not our invention—is typically experienced. In other words, fantasies, though not literal depictions of the past, nevertheless convey meaning, and such meanings are capable of telling us more about our patients than the so-called facts of their history. By interpreting both fantasies and symptoms as meaningful, Freud was able to obtain truths about his patients that were otherwise hidden. His opposition between "psychic" and "external" realities served to juxtapose an inherently personal reality with a more literal one. This isn't to say that literal or objective reality is necessarily false, but it was Freud's genius to see that the truth about one's history can be derived from the communication of otherwise innocuous musings by interpreting a patient's fantasies as disguised messages. The recognition that fantasies could be conceived as messages suggested there was something "hidden" in them that the patient neither recognized nor appreciated.

So fantasies serve a purpose: they disclose the intentional structure of the individual's deepest longings and aspirations. But Freud lacked a conception of intentionality that could explain how his patients were able to convey truths they didn't "know" in a disguised and indirect manner. In other words, his patients unconsciously intended their symptoms and the attendant fantasies that explained them—they weren't "caused" by their unconscious. Freud nevertheless suspected the existence of an unconscious form of subjectivity that was capable of intending symptoms when he coined the term "counter-will" in one of his earliest papers. Leavy (1988) brought attention to Freud's difficulty in grappling with the notion of an "unconscious subject" in a study of the development of Freud's psychoanalytic theories:

> One of Freud's earliest ways of presenting the idea of unconscious motivation was as "counter-will" (Gegenwille), a word that is worth keeping in mind whenever we say "the unconscious". Will, so rich in philosophical overtones, has been played down by psychoanalysis. Being a verb as well as a noun, the word will always implies a subject. When I do something that I claim I didn't want to do . . . it does no good to plead that blind, impersonal, unconscious forces "did" the act: *they* are *me*.
>
> (p. 8; emphases added)

Leavy's use of the term "will" is not, of course, limited to the conventional usage of conscious will, any more than Freud's expression "counter-will" is. The term "will" refers to an intentional act that often alludes to *pre-reflective* (or "unconscious") sources of motivation. Freud (1892) first used the term counter-will in a paper on hypnotism where he referred to an idea of which the patient is unaware but was brought to conscious awareness under hypnosis. Freud continued to use the term in a variety of contexts for some twenty years. The last time he apparently used it was in a paper on love and sexual impotence that was published in 1912. Leavy notes that the term seems to have disappeared thereafter. According to Leavy (1988),

Probably the generalization fell apart into concepts like resistance, repression, unconscious conflict, and ultimately, drive. But the gain in specificity was accompanied by the loss of the implication of a personal "will."

(p. 12n)

As Freud pursued his project of establishing the empirical "causes" of symptoms, his earlier notion of the unconscious as a subtle agent, or anonymous ego, or counter-will, receded into the background. Yet the tendency to depersonalize the unconscious into impersonal drives, forces, and instincts has not met with universal acceptance, even in psychoanalytic circles. The term "instinct" and "drive" were scarcely used before 1905, though the concepts were there under other guises. Yet, expressions like "affective ideas" and "wishful impulses" clearly convey more subjective nuances than the terms "instinct," "drive," or "excitations," for example. With all the current debate over Strachey's translation of Freud into English—especially the translation of *trieb* into either "drive" or "instinct"—neither the use of *trieb* nor drive alters Freud's understanding of the concept.

Whichever term one prefers, whether drive or instinct, psychoanalysts, with few exceptions, find it agreeable to use a term in which the impersonal aspect of the unconscious predominates. One of those exceptions, in addition to Leavy, was Hans Loewald, who took considerable care to explain how his use of the term "instinct" was intended to convey a human quality. According to Loewald (1980):

When I speak of instinctual forces and of instincts or instinctual drives, I define them as motivational, i.e., both motivated and motivating. . . . [For me] instincts remain relational phenomena, rather than being considered energies within a closed system.

(pp. 152–153)

Terms such as "motive" and "relational" lend a clearly personal nuance to the term instinct, and even the word "phenomena" sounds more personal than "forces." If Freud's shift from counter-will to instinct lent credence to his claim that psychoanalysis, at least in appearance, deserved the status of a science, it is nevertheless a science more similar to that of academic psychologists who "study" rats or physicists who "measure" energies. However much some analysts may strive to measure the psychoanalytic experience in specifically scientific terms, the legitimacy of one's fantasy life can only be grasped metaphorically and experientially in terms that remain personal in nature.[2]

Freud's Formulation of Two Types of Mental Functioning

After Freud formulated his theory of the structural model in 1923, his ear-lier allusions to the unconscious as a "second subject" that behaved as a "counter-will" gradually disappeared. The precedent for this revision was predetermined even earlier by Freud's distinction between primary and sec-ondary thought processes. The publication of Freud's (1911) "Formulations on the Two Principles of Mental Functioning" in 1911 roughly coincided with his final reference to the unconscious as "counter-will" in 1912.

In this formulation, Freud conceived the primary thought processes as essentially "unconscious." They account for such psychic phenomena as displacement, condensation, the ability to symbolize and apprehend time and syntax, as well as dreaming. Since the primary thought processes are supposed to be governed by the pleasure principle, they are respon-sible for that portion of the mind that "strives toward gaining pleasure" and withdraws from "any event that might arouse [pain]" (Freud, 1911, p. 219). More to the point, Freud held that unconscious processes were "the older, primary processes [and] the residues of a phase of development in which they were the only kind of mental process" that was available to the infant (p. 219). Whatever the infant wished for, says Freud, "was simply presented in a hallucinatory manner, just as still happens today with our dream-thoughts each night" (p. 219).

However primitive the primary thought processes may seem, they are nonetheless perfectly capable of sensing that when the infant's hallucina-tory anticipation of pleasure fails to materialize, another means of obtaining gratification must be substituted in its place. Moreover, the primary thought processes are also presumed to be capable of "experiencing" disappointment, leading to the necessity for another means of engaging the world. Quoting Freud (1911):

It was . . . the non-occurrence of the expected satisfaction, the disappointment *experienced*, that led to the abandonment of this attempt at satisfaction by means of hallucination. Instead of it, the psychical apparatus *had to decide* to form a conception of the real circumstances in the external world and to endeavor to make a real alteration in them. A new principle of mental functioning was thus introduced; what was presented in the mind was no longer what was agreeable but what was real, even if it happened to be disagreeable, [thus paving the way for] setting up the reality principle.

(p. 219; emphases added)

Freud's conception of the unconscious is based more or less entirely on the distinction between these two principles of thinking. Now the secondary thought processes, governed by the reality principle, assume responsibility for the individual's relationship with the social world, including the capacity for rationality, logic, grammar, and verbalization. It doesn't take much reflection to see that there is something unwieldy, even contradictory, about the way Freud unceremoniously divides facets of the mind between these two principles of mental functioning. For example, if the primary thought processes are only capable of striving toward pleasure and avoiding unpleasure, and the secondary thought processes are in turn responsible for delaying gratification while formulating plans in pursuit of one's goals, to what or to whom is Freud (1911) referring when he suggests that it is the "psychical apparatus" that "decides to form a conception of the real circumstances" encountered, and then "endeavors to make a real alteration in them" (p. 219)? Is the so-called "psychical apparatus" the primary or the secondary thought processes?

We can presumably eliminate the secondary thought processes from this logical conundrum since Freud just explained that the psychical apparatus (whatever that is) was obliged to bring these very processes *into being* in the first place. On the other hand, we can also eliminate the primary thought processes from contention since Freud proposes the need for a more realistic mode of thinking than already existed precisely because the primary processes are, by definition, incapable of executing them.

Many of the questions that Grotstein raises in response to Freud's formulation of the two types of mental functioning are devoted to the need to find a resolution to this problem, and there has been no shortage of subsequent analysts who have raised this point. For example, Charles Rycroft (1968) questioned Freud's conception of the "two types" of thinking in his 1962 paper, "Beyond the Reality Principle" (pp. 102–113). There he questions whether it makes sense to insist that the primary thought processes necessarily precede the secondary ones. Rycroft notes that even Freud doubted it since, according to a footnote in his paper on the "Two Principles of Mental Functioning," Freud himself admitted:

> It will rightly be objected that an organization which was a slave to the pleasure-principle and neglected the reality of the external world could not maintain itself alive for the shortest time, so that it could not come into existence at all. The employment of a fiction like this is, however, justified when one considers that the infant—provided that one includes with it the care it receives from its mother—does almost realize a psychical system of this kind.
>
> (Quoted in Rycroft, 1968, pp. 102–103)

Freud might have added to this "fiction" the notion that the infant is as helpless as Freud suggests before it elicits the "protection" of its developing ego. Rycroft (1968) observes,

> Freud's notion that the primary processes precede the secondary in individual development was dependent on . . . the helplessness of the infant and his having therefore assumed that the mother-infant relationship . . . was one in which the mother was in touch with reality while the infant only had wishes.
>
> (p. 103)

Again, we cannot help being struck by the notion that the infant needs somebody else (in this case, the mother or, later, an ego) to grapple with the social world *on its behalf*. Rycroft concurs with the view of many child analysts that infants aren't as helpless as Freud supposed. According to Rycroft (1968):

> If one starts from the assumption that the mother is the infant's external reality and that the mother-infant relationship is from the very beginning

a process of mental adaptation, to which the infant contributes by actions such as crying, clinging, and sucking, which evoke maternal responses in the mother, one is forced to conclude that the infant engages in realistic and adaptive behavior [from the very start].

(p. 103)

Rycroft concludes that the secondary thought processes probably operate earlier than Freud suspected and that they even coincide with primary process thinking. Even if Freud was right in proposing that infants are indeed ruled by primary thought processes, what if those processes happen to include those very qualities he attributed to the secondary, such as rationality, judgement, and decision-making—even an acute grasp of reality? Wouldn't such a scenario, in turn, negate the utility of the ego's so-called "synthetic" powers? If Freud's original formulation of the ego is retained—that it is essentially defensive in nature—then the so-called "unconscious" id, which is governed by the primary thought processes, could be conceived of as a form of consciousness. Freud's wish to distinguish between two types of thinking could be retained, but only after remodeling their capacities and functions. Paradoxically, what I am proposing would, in many ways, reverse Freud's schema. The primary thought processes—which I propose are "conscious" but pre-reflective and consequently not experienced, properly speaking—enjoy a spontaneous relationship with the social world, while the secondary thought processes—those employing the tasks of *reflective* consciousness—determine the individual's relationship with him- or herself.

The nature of subjectivity has always puzzled philosophers and psychologists alike. Freud's depiction of an "unconscious" agency whose designs need to be interpreted in order to be understood was his singular contribution to our age. But his theories could never explain what his intuition was capable of perceiving. Freud hypothesized some sort of self or agency prior to the formation of the ego. This was supported by his theory of primary thought processes and, in another context, by his conception of primary narcissism. We know that the id is capable of thought because, after all, it decided to form an extension of itself—the ego—in order to insulate itself against the anxiety of being in the world.

In practical terms, the division between the id and the ego is a false one. As Freud himself acknowledged, the ego is merely an "outer layer" of the id; it was never conceived as a separate entity. If we expect to be consistent with the ego's origins, then that ego—following even Freud's reasoning—is nothing more than a "reservoir" of anxiety; in fact, our experience of anxiety itself.

Sartre's Critique of the Unconscious

Given all the attendant problems that Freud's conception of the unconscious has elicited, it is surprising that there is little, if any, attention paid to the prevailing conception of consciousness it presupposes. Whereas Freud depicted psychoanalysis as essentially a science of the unconscious, it is impossible to escape the observation that it is also a science—if we can call it that—that is preoccupied with consciousness itself, if only implicitly. Terms like truth, epistemology, knowledge, understanding, and comprehension pervade virtually every psychoanalytic paper that is devoted to the unconscious as a concept. But isn't our fascination with the unconscious and our failure to resolve questions about its nature a consequence of our obsession with "consciousness" and the epistemological bias it engenders?

These are among the questions that phenomenologists such as Jean-Paul Sartre, Maurice Merleau-Ponty, Martin Heidegger, and Paul Ricoeur devoted the bulk of their philosophical writings to: what is the importance of knowledge and what role does it serve in our everyday lives? Of all the phenomenologists, it was perhaps Sartre who took psychoanalysis the most seriously, even conceiving his own brand of "existential psychoanalysis" (1981). Fascinated with Freud the man as well as his project, Sartre was also a Frenchman and, like all French philosophers, was preoccupied with the nature of rationality, a legacy of Descartes. Yet Sartre's fascination with Freud alerted him at a very early stage of his intellectual development to the problems I have summarized above.

Sartre (1962, pp. 48–55; 1981, pp. 153–171) rejected Freud's topographical model for similar reasons that Freud did. In Freud's earlier topographical model, the only thing separating the system-conscious from the system-unconscious is the so-called "censor," which serves to regulate what is permitted into consciousness and, contrariwise, what is repressed into the unconscious. So, the censor is aware of everything, that which is conscious and unconscious alike. Yet because the ego is unaware of the censor, this model posits a "second consciousness" (the censor) that is both unknown and unknowable to the ego in principle. Sartre's problem with this model is obvious: the so-called censor is the *de facto* "person" who is being analyzed and who disclaims knowledge of all the shenanigans he employs to disguise what he is up to, "bad faith" in its essence. As we saw earlier, Freud also had problems with the implications of a "second thinking subject" and decided to discard this model for one that contained only one subject that knows, the conscious portion of the ego, and not one but three subjects that do not know: the id, the superego, and that portion of the ego that is responsible for defense mechanisms.

Freud's subsequent revision of his earlier model, however, fares little better in Sartre's opinion. The topographical model is replaced with one that is less concerned with demarcating conscious and unconscious portions of the psyche than with determining the complex nature of psychic "agency" or subjectivity. Although the two models are not completely complementary, it is easy to recognize those elements of the second model that were intended to remedy the problems engendered by the first. Now the id more or less assumes the role of the system-unconscious, whereas the ego more or less assumes the tasks of the system-conscious. Ironically, the system-preconscious does not enjoy a direct parallel with the third agency in Freud's new apparatus, the superego; instead, the superego adopts some of the functions of the now-abandoned *censor* due to its ability to prohibit those wishes and desires it deems unacceptable. Sartre's principal complaint with the new model is that it still fails to resolve the problem of bad faith, the problem of a "lie without a liar." If anything, the new model gets even further away from Sartre's efforts to personalize the unconscious by instituting three psychic agencies that protect the conscious ego from any responsibility for its actions. How would Sartre propose to remedy this situation, to account for those actions that Freud claimed the "conscious" patient is "unconscious" of devising while holding the conscious patient responsible for performing them?

Sartre accomplishes this by introducing two sets of critical distinctions into the prevailing psychoanalytic vocabulary. The first is a distinction between pre-reflective consciousness and reflective consciousness, and the second is between consciousness and knowledge. Sartre summarizes the basic dilemma in Freud's conception of the unconscious—contained in both the topographical and structural models—with the following questions: how can the subject (a divided "subject" notwithstanding) not know that he is possessed of a feeling or sentiment that he is in possession of? And if, indeed, the unconscious is just another word for *consciousness* (Sartre's position), how can the subject, even by Sartre's reckoning, not know what he is "conscious" of? Sartre's thesis of "pre-reflective" consciousness is his effort to solve this riddle. Following Husserl's thesis, Sartre saw conscious-ness as intentional, which means it is always conscious *of* something. There is no such thing as "empty" consciousness, nor is there such a thing as a "container" or "receptacle" that houses consciousness—a formulation that rejects not only Freud's thesis but Melanie Klein's "part-objects" hypoth-esis as well. Rather, consciousness is always "outside" itself and "in" the things that constitute it *as* consciousness-of something. In Sartre's (1957) words:

> Intentionality is not the way in which a subject tries to make "contact" with an object that exists beside it. *Intentionality is what makes up the very subjectivity of subjects.*
>
> (pp. 48–49) [emphasis in original]

In other words, the concept of intentionality renders subjectivity as already and in its essence a theory of *intersubjectivity*, since to be a subject is, by necessity, to be engaged with some thing "other" than one's self—even if this other something is just an idea. Sartre elaborates on how this thesis would be applied to the social world specifically:

> When I run after a streetcar, when I look at the time, when I am absorbed in contemplating a portrait, there is no *I* (or "ego"). There is [only] con-sciousness *of the streetcar-having-to-be-overtaken*, etc. . . . In fact, I am then plunged into the world of objects; it is *they* which constitute the unity of my consciousness; it is *they* which present themselves with val-ues, with attractive and repellent qualities—but *me*—I have disappeared; I have annihilated myself [in the moment of conscious apprehension].
>
> (pp. 48–49)

When I experience a rock, a tree, a feeling of sadness, or the object of my desire in the bedroom, I experience them just where they are: beside a hill, in the meadow, in my heart, in relation to myself and my beloved. Conscious-ness and the object-of-consciousness are given at one stroke. These things constitute my consciousness of them just as I constitute their existence *as* things through the act in which I perceive them and give them a name. And, because naming things is a purely human activity, these things do not exist as rocks, trees, or emotions in the absence of a human consciousness that is capable of apprehending them through the constitutive power of language.

However, such acts of apprehension do not necessarily imply knowledge of what I am conscious of. Sartre makes a distinction between the pre-reflective apprehension of an object and our reflective "witnessing" of the act. Ordinarily, when I am pre-reflectively conscious of a feeling, for example, I intuit the feeling of sadness and, in turn, reflectively acknowledge this feeling *as* sadness: I feel sad and experience myself as a sad individual more or less simultaneously. But I am also capable of feeling sadness, or anger, or envy without *knowing* I am sad, angry, or envious as such. When such a state is pointed out to me by my analyst, I am surprised to be alerted to this observation. Of course, I may resist the analyst's intervention and reject it, but I may also admit it because, on being alerted to this possibility, I am also capable of recognizing this feeling as *mine*. Sartre argues that I would be incapable of recognizing thoughts or ideas that I claim no awareness of unless I had been conscious of these feelings in the first place on a pre-reflective level.

In other words, what Freud labels consciousness Sartre designates "reflective consciousness" (i.e., knowing *that* I am conscious of it), and what Freud labels the unconscious Sartre designates as that moment of pre-reflective consciousness that, due to resistance, has not yielded to reflective awareness and, so, "knowledge" of it, after the fact. This is why I can be conscious of something of which I have no immediate knowledge, and why I can become knowledgeable about something of which I am, so to speak, "unconscious" but am subsequently able to recognize as mine when a timely interpretation alerts me to it. I can only *experience* something of which I have knowledge, but not of what I am merely conscious. The power of analysis, according to Sartre, lies in its capacity to "arrest" time for the patient by allowing the neurotic (or psychotic) the opportunity to slow the pace of her anxiety-ridden experience in order to ponder what that experience is in its immediacy.

Of course, the decisive difference between Sartre's and Freud's respective formulations isn't that it merely substitutes Freud's terminology with Sartre's; on a more radical level, it eliminates a need for the notion of a "second thinking subject" behind or beneath consciousness, and ultimately offers a means for personalizing the unconscious in a manner that Freud was unable to do. There are still problems, however, even with Sartre's formulation. Because Sartre shared with Freud an obsession with the nature of consciousness, he went even further than Freud and eliminated the need for an "unconscious" altogether, replacing Freud's formulation with a model that was rooted solely in a theory of consciousness, a solution that was even more rationalistic than Freud's. Sartre even acknowledged late in life that his earlier project had been too indebted to Descartes and suffered from being infused with rationalism, as though "comprehension" is the final arbiter to psychic liberation.

Ironically, despite Freud's preoccupation with epistemology, he moved away from his earlier bent toward intellectualism and subsequently adopted the more sceptical position that knowledge, *per se*, plays a limited role in the psychoanalytic experience. The move away from interpretative schemes toward transference (and, more recently, relational) conceptualizations of psychoanalysis reflects the growing influence of phenomenology, scepticism, and hermeneutics on psychoanalytic practice. If we want to find a philosophical model that can integrate all these influences, however, we will not find it in Sartre but in someone who was a mentor to him in the earliest days of his intellectual development: Martin Heidegger. I now want to review those elements of Heidegger's philosophy that appear to solve the problem of the unconscious that neither Freud nor Sartre were able to decipher.

Heidegger's Conception of Being and Experience

Although he was never all that interested in psychoanalysis, and what little he knew of it dismayed him, there are many aspects of Heidegger's philosophy that are sympathetic with it. Unlike Sartre and Freud, Heidegger was not interested in the nature of consciousness, *per se*, because he thought it tended to psychologize our conception of human experience instead of getting to its roots. Heidegger's reasons for taking this position were complex but at the heart of them was a conviction that epistemology is not a viable means for getting to the bottom of what our suffering is about. Of all the phenomenologists of his generation, Heidegger was alone in conceiving philosophy as a therapy whose purpose is to heal the human soul. This made Heidegger unpopular with academic philosophers but a valuable resource to a group of European psychiatrists and psychoanalysts who saw in his work a humanistic alternative to Freud's penchant for theory. Ironically, many of them, including Medard Boss, Ludwig Binswanger, Eugene Minkowski, and Viktor Frankl, threw out the baby with the bathwater in their haste to separate themselves from the psychoanalytic zeitgeist by replacing it with Heidegger as the basis for their clinical theories. This culminated in the impoverishment of both traditions, and only a handful of psychoanalysts (e.g., Hans Loewald, Stanley Leavy, Paul Federn, and R. D. Laing) sought to integrate elements of Heidegger's philosophy into Freud's conception of psychoanalysis.

Heidegger is probably most famous for his decision to root his philosophy in ontology, the study of Being, instead of epistemology, the study of knowledge. This is irritating to philosophers and psychologists alike because it discards epistemological questions in favor of a fundamental critique of what human existence is about. This is a topic that most people would prefer to leave alone, for why question the "why" of our existence when it is patently obvious that we, in fact, exist? But Heidegger was not simply interested in why we exist but how, and to what end. For example, when I pause to take stock of myself by asking, "who am I?", I am asking the question about the *meaning of being*. In fact, we submit to being all the time but without knowing it. Whenever we are engaged in writing a paper, painting a picture, driving a car, or riding a bicycle, we "let go" of our rational and conscious control of the world, and in that letting go, we submit to being, an experience that, by its nature, we cannot think our way through. Arguably the most radical critic of Descartes's rationalistic constitution of subjectivity, Heidegger countered that we live our lives in an everyday sort of way without thinking about what we are doing and, more importantly, without having to think our way through our activities as a matter of course. The place he assigned to reason is, in effect, an after-the-fact operation that is not primary to our engagement with the world but secondary; it is only when our involvement with the world breaks down that we take the time to divorce ourselves from it for the purpose of pondering what has happened and why.

Contrary to both Husserl and Sartre, who believed it is possible to employ the conscious portion of the mind in order to fathom the bedrock of who I am in tandem with the choices that determine my subjectivity, Heidegger countered that it is impossible to ever get "behind" our constitutive acts in such a way that we can determine the acts we intend to embark on *before* committing them. Whereas Sartre argued that I "choose" the person that I am and can always change who I am by choosing to be someone else, Heidegger observed that my ability to comprehend the choices I make necessarily occurs after the fact, so that I am always endeavoring to "discover" (or disclose) the acts I have already made in a world that is not my construction but always "other" to my intent or volition. This is because I am always embedded in a situation that is imbued with moods and feelings that conspire to "determine" my choices before I am ever conscious of having made them. So, my experience of myself is one of having been "thrown" into the situation I find myself in and then collecting myself in order to fathom how I got here and what my motives have been, afterwards.

More primary for Heidegger than the comprehension of the world (Descartes), the search for pleasure (Freud), or relief from anxiety (Klein) is the need to *orient* ourselves at every moment in time by asking ourselves where are we, what are we doing here, and to what do we belong? It is my sense of "who" I am to ask this question that constitutes me in my existence. Although the question of who-ness is the foundation of Heidegger's philosophy, it is important to understand that this is not a psychological question of identity, as per Erikson, but an ontological question of being, because who or what we are as human *beings* is bigger than the psyche or the self. At bottom, this question is presupposed when we query the role of the unconscious, but it replaces Freud's psychologization of this question with an existential one. If one removes these questions from a strictly philosophical context and inserts them into one that is specifically clinical, one readily recognizes that Heidegger is raising the same questions that our analytic patients are struggling with, only they lack the means with which to ponder them.

Because Heidegger rejected epistemology, his philosophy is inherently sceptical,[3] not in the sense of doubting that I can know anything but because knowledge doesn't get to the heart of what my life is about. Moreover, this attitude is easily adapted for the purposes of psychoanalytic inquiry, as any number of contemporary psychoanalysts have recognized. The novelty of this perspective has also insinuated its way into the thinking of many disparate (including "classical" as well as contemporary) psychoanalytic practitioners, some by virtue of their acquaintance with Heidegger's philosophy (Leavy [1980, 1988], Laing [1960, 1969]), some by virtue of Sullivan's interpersonal theory (Levenson [1972, 1983, 1991], Stern [1997], Bromberg [1998], Langan [1993]), and others through the influence of classical psychoanalysts such as Hans Loewald (1980), a self-identified Freudian analyst who studied with Heidegger in his youth. What holds such disparate theoretical outlooks together is their respective conceptions of experience. Heidegger's movement from epistemology toward ontology led to his abandoning concepts like consciousness and even intentionality (as it was conceived by Husserl) in favor of a critique of our relationship with Being and the manner it is disclosed to us in the immediacy of everyday experience.

How, then, does Heidegger conceive of experience, and why is this an ontological question instead of an epistemological or psychological one? From a strictly Heideggerian perspective, psychoanalysis is already concerned with our manner of Being and has been from the start. People go into analysis because they are not satisfied with the manner of Being they embody and want to change it. But in order to determine what our manner of Being is about, we have to give ourselves to it, through our experience of it. In its essence, psychoanalysis gives us the opportunity to give thought to our experience by taking the time that is needed to ponder it. Heidegger would have agreed with Freud that there are indeed "two types" of thinking that we typically employ, though he wouldn't formulate them in the way that either Freud or Sartre proposed. Heidegger not only rejected Freud's conception of the unconscious but also avoided employing the term consciousness in the convoluted manner that Sartre did, opting instead to focus his attention on two fundamental types of "thinking": calculative and meditative. Basically, Heidegger believed that the nature of consciousness is so inherently mysterious that it is misleading to equate it with synonyms like "awareness" or "knowledge." We have seen from the thicket of contradictions that both Freud and Sartre entertained about the distinction between a conscious and unconscious portion of the mind that such a distinction ultimately dissolves into a well of confusion.

Whereas analysts are abundantly familiar with the observation that their patients frequently resist thinking about certain topics because they are distressing and would prefer to think about those topics that are more pleasing or interesting to them, Heidegger observed that one manner of thinking (whatever the topic may be) is inherently comforting while the other is more liable to elicit anxiety, or dread (*angst*). We tend to avoid thinking the thoughts that make us anxious and abandon ourselves to thoughts, speculations, and fantasies that are soporific. The prospect of enduring the kind of anxiety that genuine thought entails is distressing, and the tactics we employ to avoid it are universal. The task of analysis is to nudge our thinking into those areas we typically avoid so that we can access a region of our existence that we are loathe to explore but which lies at the heart of our humanity. This is effected by experiencing what our suffering is about and allowing such experiences to change us not by virtue of knowing more than we already do about ourselves, but by helping us accommodate a dimension of our experience that we avoid at every turn. When we succumb to such experiences, we are thrown into a different manner of experiencing ourselves and what we, as "selves," are about.

In order for this to make any sense, we must understand why Heidegger distinguished between my manner of *being* and beings generally, a distinction that Heidegger calls "the ontological difference." "Beings" are "entities" and, as such, are the object of scientific investigation, including our everyday perceptions: trees, houses, tables, feelings, and so on. In other words, beings refer to things as they seem at first blush. Heidegger, however, transforms these "things" (beings or entities) into *being* by recognizing the *temporal* dimension in which we exist, that "beings" necessarily exist *in time,* in a temporal flux of past-present-future: what we ordinarily call "now." This temporalization of beings into being, however, can only be achieved by a *human* being who is privy to a relationship with his or her objects of reflection via the capacity to think about them and interpret what they mean. Our relationship with time reveals what the being of "beings" share in common: the world as it is disclosed or "illuminated" *to a person* by virtue of his or her capacity to experience the object in question. In other words, beings (things, objects, perceptions) are transformed into being when they are experienced by virtue of my capacity to interpret their significance for *me*. This observation sheds light on what psychoanalysts have already been doing whenever they employ interpretations to help their patients realize that everything they experience is unique to them alone because everything they are capable of experiencing contains an historical component. Where Heidegger parts company with most analysts, however, is that such realizations are not intended to merely help patients "understand" themselves better, but to *experience* who and what they are, essentially. Like Heidegger, the analyst "temporalizes" the patient's experience by interpreting its historical antecedents, and that act of temporalization helps the patient's world come alive. This is what Heidegger calls doing "fundamental ontology."

Thought—And the *Experience* of Thinking

As noted earlier, in Heidegger's later thought, he emphasized a form of thinking he characterized as meditative, a kind of thought that is usually dismissed as irrelevant by scientists and academics who employ a manner of thinking that Heidegger depicts as calculative. But what kind of thought does meditative thinking entail? J. Glenn Gray (1968) suggests it is helpful first to understand what Heidegger does not mean by meditative thinking:

Thinking is, in the first place, not what we call having an opinion or a notion. Second, it is not representing or having an idea (*vorstellen*) about something or a state of affairs. . . . Third, thinking is not ratiocination, developing a chain of premises which lead to a valid conclusion. . . . [Meditative] thinking is not so much an act as a way of living or dwelling— as we in America would put it, a way of life.

(pp. x-xi)

Offering a different perspective on this enigmatic proposition, Macquarrie (1994) proposes:

"Meditation" suggests a kind of thought in which the mind is docile and receptive to whatever it is thinking about. Such thought may be contrasted [for example] with the active investigative thought of the natural sciences.

(pp. 77–78)

In comparison, Heidegger characterizes calculative thinking as the conventional norm and a byproduct of the technological age in which we live. Though its roots go all the way back to Plato, its impact on culture was not fully formed until the scientific revolution that was inspired by Descartes in the sixteenth century. The tendency to perceive the world in the abstract and conceptual manner that calculative thinking entails took an even sharper turn in the twentieth century with the birth of the computer era and the amazing gains that technology has enjoyed over the past century, evidenced in the development of housing, transportation, medicine, and so on. The question of technology is a complicated one and remained the focus of Heidegger's attention throughout his lifetime. Though it would be extreme to say that Heidegger was opposed to science, there is little doubt that he believed science had overtaken our lives to such a degree that we have now forgotten how to think in a non-scientific manner. One of Heidegger's most infamous statements about the status of science is that "science does not *think*" and that the thinking science employs is an impoverished variation of it, epitomized by the credence given to scientific "research" and the like, which Heidegger dismisses as thought-less and thought-poor.

One of the consequences of the technological age is what has recently been depicted as the "postmodern condition," the ultimate expression of our contemporary obsession with technology and the technology culture it has spawned. This is a culture that, from Heidegger's perspective, is fundamentally ill in the sense of being "ill at ease" with itself, a product of the pervasive emptiness that characterizes the twentieth-century neurosis. Heidegger saw psychoanalysis as the inevitable response to the malaise in which Postmodern Man is imprisoned because once we created this dire situation, it was necessary that we fashion a cure for it. What, in Heidegger's opinion, is the cure for such malaise? To simply remember *how* to think in the manner that we have forgotten. In fact, this is the kind of thinking that Freud, despite his penchant for science, stumbled upon on his own, not by engaging in scientific research but by examining his own condition.[4] As we know, his efforts culminated in the radical treatment scheme that lies at the heart of the psychoanalytic endeavor, epitomized by the free association method and its complement, the mode of "evenly suspended attentiveness" (neutrality) that he counseled his followers to adopt.

Whereas in Heidegger's earlier period, he emphasized the region of our everyday activities that we perform as a matter of course without recourse to having to think our way through them, the period of his development in which he distinguished between calculative and meditative thinking entailed a "turn" in his thinking that focused on the kind of experience we are capable of obtaining once we are cured of our obsession for knowledge. Though Heidegger abandoned terms such as intentionality and consciousness in his later period, he emphasized to an even greater degree than before the importance of attending to experience and argued that the only means we have of "touching being" is by pondering what our experience tells us from this novel perspective.

To summarize, whereas Sartre distinguishes between pre-reflective and reflective modes of consciousness, Heidegger distinguishes between a region of our existence that is unavailable to experience and the capacity we have to access this region by giving ourselves to it. Whereas Freud's conception of the unconscious conceives it as an "underworld" of hidden aims, intentions, and conspiracies that shadow the world we are conscious of (i.e., the world in which we live), Heidegger reverses this thesis in favor of one that dispenses with the psychoanalytic notion of the unconscious altogether. Instead, Heidegger sees a cleavage between the acts we commit without thinking (i.e., which we have no knowledge of when we commit them) and the acts that become available to experience by giving them thought. Conversely, it is the world I inhabit without thinking where I reside, not the one (as per Freud) of which I am conscious. Indeed, this is the world I bring to awareness in analysis, but a world that I will never, no matter how much I try, be fully conscious of, at least not in the obsessive way that the neurotic would have it.

R. D. Laing's Critique of 'Unconscious Experience'

Much of this, I imagine, is probably familiar to you, not because you have studied Heidegger but because, with enough experience of your own, you have already adopted a phenomenological perspective but without knowing it. This is one of the virtues of phenomenology: since we are only capable of grasping it intuitively, many people stumble upon it on their own, as Freud did, without formal instruction. In many respects, despite his pro-testations to the contrary, Freud was a closet phenomenologist, and many of his ideas about psychoanalysis, including the bulk of his technical rec-ommendations, were faithful to the phenomenological perspective. In fact, Heidegger recognized that Freud's conception of free association and the analyst's endeavor to effect a state of evenly suspended attentiveness was compatible with the kind of meditative thinking Heidegger was advocating.[5]

Given the parallels between Heidegger's and Freud's respective concep-tions of meditative thinking and the analytic attitude (i.e., free association, neutrality),[6] it is all the more surprising that Heidegger's influence has not been more evident in psychoanalytic circles. Despite his influence on a gen-eration of Continental psychiatrists following the Second World War, there has been little effort among psychoanalysts to critique Freud's conception of the unconscious from a Heideggerian perspective. A singular exception is the work of R. D. Laing, who studied Heidegger before he trained as a psy-choanalyst and published his first, Heideggerian inspired, book during his analytic training (1960). Laing's first two books, *The Divided Self* (1960) and *Self and Others* (1969/1961), were inspired attempts to apply some of Heidegger's insights to the psychoanalytic conception of the unconscious and the relation it bears on what is given to experience.[7]

In Laing's *Self and Others*, he confronts some of the problems with Freud's conception of the unconscious (noted earlier) in a critique of a paper by Susan Isaacs, a follower of Melanie Klein. Though Isaacs's paper is mostly related to Klein's technical vocabulary, one of the themes in Isaacs's study that caught Laing's attention originated with Freud and has been adopted by virtually every psychoanalyst since: the notion of "uncon-scious experience," a contradiction in terms for the reasons we reviewed earlier. Indeed, Laing (1969/1961) avers:

It is a contradiction in terms to speak of "unconscious experience," [because] a person's experience comprises anything that "he" or "any part of him" is aware of, whether 'he' or every part of him is aware of every level of his awareness or not.

(p. 8)

Laing's thesis is that the psychoanalytic notion of unconscious experience alludes to a more fundamental contradiction with which Freud's conception of the unconscious begins: that there is such a thing as an unconscious portion of the mind that one is capable of experiencing (see "Freud's Formulation of Two Types of Mental Functioning" previously in this chapter). Indeed, Freud's decision to conceive a separate portion of the mind that the (conscious) mind has no awareness of sets up a series of false theoretical dualities between inner experience and outer reality that land one, in the words of Juliet Mitchell (1974), "in a welter of contradictions such as the notion that 'mind' is a reality outside experience—yet is the 'place' from which experience comes" (p. 254). Mitchell observes that "This problem is peculiar to psychoanalysis . . . because the 'object' of the science . . . *experiences* the investigation of the scientists" (p. 254).

The heart of Laing's (1969/1961) argument revolves around the difficulty that every psychoanalyst faces if he or she believes that the psychoanalyst is in a position to know more about the patient's experience (conscious or unconscious) than the patient does:

My impression is that most adult Europeans and North Americans would subscribe to the following: the other person's experience is not directly experienced by self. For the present it does not matter whether this is necessarily so, is so elsewhere on the planet, or has always been the case. But if we agree that you do not experience my experience, [then] we agree that we rely on our communications to give us our clues as to how or what we are thinking, feeling, imagining, dreaming, and so forth. Things are going to be difficult if you tell me that I am experiencing something which I am not experiencing. If that is what I think you mean by unconscious experience.

(pp. 12–13)

Even when one allows that the psychoanalyst is investigating the experience of the analysand, the analyst must remember that he has no direct access to the patient's experience other than what the patient tells him, whether the patient's account of his experience is reliable, and to what degree. Yet, it seems that the analyst is not content with the limitations of the situation that is imposed on him and prefers to engage in wild speculations and inferences as to what he "supposes" is going on in the patient's mind, of which the patient is presumed to be unaware:

> Beyond the mere attribution of agency, motive, intention, experiences that the patient disclaims, there is an extraordinary exfoliation of forces, energies, dynamics, economics, processes, structures to explain the "unconscious." Psychoanalytic concepts of this doubly chimerical order include concepts of mental structures, economics, dynamisms, death and life instincts, internal objects, etc. They are postulated as principles of regularity, governing or underlying forces, governing or underlying experience that Jack thinks Jill has, but does not know she has, as inferred by Jack from Jack's experience of Jill's behavior. In the meantime, what *is* Jack's experience of Jill, Jill's experience of herself, or Jill's experience of Jack?
>
> (Laing, 1969/1961, pp. 14–15)

The subtle interplay of how one's experience of others affects one and, in turn, how one's reaction to this effect elicits behavior that affects others' experience as well was a major theme in Laing's writings throughout his career. The book in which Laing's critique of Isaacs' paper appeared was a full-scale examination of the effect that human beings have on each other in the etiology of severe psychological disturbance, fueled by the acts of deception and self-deception that characterize our most seemingly innocent exchanges with one another. Heidegger's influence on Laing's clinical outlook was explicitly acknowledged by Laing when citing Heidegger's essay "On the Essence of Truth" (1977) in that work. Noting Heidegger's adoption of the pre-Socratic term for truth, *aletheia* (which conceives truth as that which emerges from concealment: what is dis-covered), Laing put his own twist on Heidegger's thesis by emphasizing the interdependency between candor and secrecy in the way that one's personal truth emerges and recedes in every conversation with others, an innovation that owes just as much to Sartre and Freud as to Heidegger's ontological preoccupations.

Many of the terms that Laing introduced in that book for the first time— e.g., collusion, mystification, attribution, injunction, untenable positions— were coined for the purpose of providing a conceptual vocabulary that could help explain how human beings, in their everyday interactions with each other, are able to distort the truth so effectively that they are able to affect each other's reality, and their sanity as well. It was just this vocabulary that Laing suggested was missing in Freud's psychoanalytic nomenclature. In the language of psychic conflict, Laing agreed with Freud that people who suffer conflicts are essentially of two minds: they struggle against the intrusion of a reality that is too painful to accept on the one hand, and harbor a fantasy that is incapable of being realized on the other. Consequently, their lives are held in abeyance until they are able to speak of their experience to someone who is willing to hear it with benign acceptance, without a vested interest in what one's experience ought to be.

Like Heidegger, Laing avoided employing terms such as consciousness and unconscious and situated his thinking instead in the language of experience and how experience determines our perception of the world and ourselves. Instead of characterizing what we do not know as that which has been repressed into one's "unconscious," Laing was more apt to depict such phenomena descriptively, as that which I am unconscious *of*, or better, as that which is not available, or given, to experience, even if in the depths of my Being I intuitively sense I am harboring a truth that is too painful or elusive to grasp. Laing also adhered to Heidegger's thesis that my experience of the world is dependent on what I interpret the world to be, so that if I want to change my experience of the world, I have to reconsider my interpretation of it (Laing, Phillipson, and Lee, 1966, pp. 10–11).

It should be remembered that these words were written over fifty years ago, long before the subsequent development of hermeneutic, relational, constructivist, and intersubjective schools of psychoanalysis that have, in turn, noted some of the same problems that Laing presaged but for which he gets credit rarely. One possible explanation for this oversight is that Laing's commentary is still, fifty years hence, radical in comparison with contemporary treatments of this theme. Space does not permit me to compare and contrast Laing's contribution to this discussion with more contemporary versions of it; my concern is limited to that of assessing Freud's conception of the unconscious and some of the problems that inhere from its presuppositions. I include Laing in this discussion because of the emphasis that he, more than any other psychoanalyst, has reserved for the place of experience in the psychoanalytic encounter and the problems that derive from it. That being said, there are aspects of Freud's conception of experience that are surprisingly consistent with Heidegger's and are compatible with the ontological dimension of human experience.

Freud's and Heidegger's Respective Conceptions of Experience

I now want to review those aspects of Freud's conception of the unconscious that are compatible with Heidegger's philosophy and the respective importance that each assigns to the role of experience in our lives. Over the past two centuries, the German language has offered perhaps the richest and most subtle variations on the kinds of experience that English subsumes under the one term. It should not be surprising, therefore, that German philosophers have dominated the nineteenth- and twentieth-century investigations into the nature of experience that subsequently spilled over to other European countries, including France, Great Britain, and Spain. I am thinking of Hegel, Schopenhauer, Dilthey, Nietzsche, Husserl, and Heidegger specifically, each of whom elaborated on the notion of experience in their respective philosophies, granting the concept a central role in both phenomenology and existential philosophy. Before exploring their impact on phenomenology, however, I shall say a few words about the German conception of experience and the etymology from which the terms they employ are derived.

The first is the German *Erfahrung*, which contains the word *Fahrt*, meaning "journey." *Erfahrung* suggests the notion of temporal duration, such as, for example, when one accumulates experience over time, including the accruing of wisdom that comes with old age. The other German term for experience is *Erlebnis*, which derives from the word *Leben*, meaning "life." The use of the word *Erlebnis* connotes a vital immediacy in contrast to the more historical perspective of *Erfahrung*. When invoking *Erlebnis*, the speaker is emphasizing a primitive unity that precedes intellectual reflection.[8] In the scientific community, the notion of experience suggests the accumulation of empirical knowledge through the use of experimentation, a supposedly objective endeavor. On the other hand, experience may also suggest something that happens to us when in a passive state and vulnerable to stimuli, such as what occurs in a movie theater. It may also suggest the process whereby we submit to education, entailing the accumulation and memorization of knowledge over a considerable period of time. Finally, the term may also be used to connote a journey I have taken while traveling to a foreign country, perhaps in wartime when I am faced with obstacles and danger, the experience of which may have expedited my journey into manhood.

You can see from these distinctions between the two types of experience we are capable of having that, even while offering tantalizing hints as to what the term means, there remains something ineffable about the concept itself. This presents us with a paradox because the word is often employed, according to Martin Jay, "to gesture towards precisely that which exceeds concepts and even language itself" (1998, p. 3). In fact, the word experience has frequently been used as a marker for what is ineffable and so private or personal that it cannot be rendered in words. One's experience of love, for example, is an experience that many insist is impossible to express or grasp in words alone, precisely because it is experienced long before it is understood, if then. As Laing observed earlier, even when I try to communicate what I experience to others, only I can know what my experience is. Our efforts to convey our experience are imperfect because it cannot be reduced to words. This observation has enormous consequences for the experience of psychoanalysis for both patient and analyst, who rely almost entirely on the passage of words between them.

So, what does the essential nature of experience entail? Is experience antithetical to our capacity to reason, as some have claimed, or is our ability to reason dependent on our capacity to experience the very thoughts that our words endeavor to convey? As we know, many of the last century's philosophers and academics sought to reduce human activity to language, suggesting that one's capacity to experience is mediated through words and secondary to the power that words possess. This view implies that pre-verbal experience is inconceivable so that even the experience of pain relies on one's "knowledge" of what pain entails. Many of the features of structuralism, deconstructionism, post-structuralism, and the postmodernist perspective argue that the very notion of a conscious, sentient self that is capable of determining its own truth is an antiquated idea that should be replaced with a schema that views the subject, not in terms of an experiencing agent, but as an effect, or "construct," of hidden forces.

In order to appreciate the contribution of phenomenology to our conception of experience, it is important to note that, historically, empiricist philosophers such as Hume separated experience from rationality by consigning to experience sensual data alone. Modern scientific methodology, which endeavors to combine the experience we derive from our senses with our capacity to think about and reflect upon the nature of such experience, is unable to account for the experience of ideas, thoughts, and imagination. In other words, philosophers have traditionally "split" human beings in half, assigning one portion of the human project to rationality, the mind, and the other portion to sense experience, the body.

The singular contribution of Husserl at the turn of the century was to reconcile the split between sense experience and rationality by suggesting that experience is already inherently thoughtful because the nature of consciousness, according to Husserl, is intentional, so that the act of consciousness and its object are given at one stroke. One isn't "related" (as per object relations theory) to the other because each is irrevocably dependent on the other so that neither is capable of standing alone. As some Buddhists have argued, the presumed split to which Western thought has been devoted is illusory because the two are actually One. Heidegger concluded that there are levels of experience—just as there are levels of awareness or consciousness—depending on my capacity to interpret to the depths what my experience discloses to me.

This thesis is especially relevant to the psychoanalyst, who endeavors to direct the patient's attention to his or her experience by interpreting its meaning. Viewed from this angle, a good interpretation is never intended to explain one's experience, but to deepen it, in the phenomenological sense. Alternately, *what the patient experiences and how reveals to the analyst the person that the patient happens to be.* As Laing noted earlier, patient and analyst alike are interested not only in their own experience of the situation they share together but in what each takes the other's experience to be, however imperfect the ability to understand the other's experience may be.

This is why Heidegger sees experience as the "revealing" of being. Because experience discloses who I am as well as the world I inhabit, the two are inextricably connected. I am neither strictly constituted by the world, nor is the world I inhabit my invention: the two are interdependent because each serves to constitute the other. The distinctive feature of experience from a Heideggerian perspective is its capacity to shock the world I inhabit at the roots because experience does not only reveal things that are hidden, it is also capable of changing, by virtue of such revelations, who I am. Hence (Heidegger, 1971),

When we talk of "undergoing" an experience, we mean specifically that the experience is not of our own making, [so that *in order* to undergo experience] we [must] endure it, suffer it, [and] receive it as it strikes us, and [finally] submit to it.

(p. 57)

By anticipating my experiences with a specific purpose in mind, I can make use of them in order to gain insight into the person I am. Moreover, there are degrees to experience; it isn't all or nothing. This is why I am also capable of resisting experience, avoiding it, and even forgetting experiences that (due to repression) are too painful to bear. In turn, the degree to which I am able to experience anything—a piece of music, the essay you are now reading, even a psychoanalysis—is determined by how willing I am to give myself to the experience in question.

What, then, does the ontological structure of experience have to do with the unconscious? Some would argue nothing. After all, psychoanalysis is concerned with exploring the unconscious, whereas Heidegger's conception of phenomenology is devoted to the revelation of Being through the critique of one's experience. Despite what Freud said about the ego "no longer being the master of its own house," experience nevertheless plays a vital role in Freud's conception of analysis and the conflicts that patients typically suffer. Basically, Freud believed that our capacity to bear painful experiences (*Erlebnis*) as children more or less determines whether we will develop neurotic symptoms, or worse, when we grow up. This is actually a Heideggerian conception of experience, though Freud never knew this. According to Freud, if a child is faced with an experience that is too painful to bear, the child simply represses it from consciousness, making the child's experience of frustration disappear. As Freud realized, it isn't the actual experience of frustration that is repressed but the knowledge (or as Heidegger would say, the "interpretation," of what one takes the case to be) of the incident that elicited the experience in the first place. After this piece of knowledge (i.e., interpretation) is suppressed, the individual continues to experience moments of sadness or anxiety, for example, but has forgotten why. The only problem with this solution is that the repressed memory finds an alternate means of expression that transforms it into a symptom, which the adult subsequently suffers and complains about, though he hasn't a clue what caused the symptom or what purpose it serves.

For Freud, the purpose of pathogenic symptoms is to shield the individual from experiencing a disappointment of traumatic proportions that the person who suffers the symptom (that replaced the original trauma) wants desperately to suppress. Since the disappointment in question was repressed (or disavowed, projected, etc.) but not entirely eradicated, the individual instinctively avoids experiencing similar disappointments and anything that may serve to remind him of it in the future. Analytic patients are loathe to risk disappointment because to really *be* disappointed is not only transformative but necessarily painful. But such disappointments are transformative only and to the degree to which they are finally experienced at the heart of one's being, in the give-and-take of the treatment situation.

Just because one has a fleeting thought, idea, or intuition, for example, doesn't guarantee that one will have a full-throttle experience of it. The phenomenologist accounts for this phenomenon by suggesting that Freud's unconscious is nothing more than a mode of thinking (consciousness) that the patient is unaware of thinking. In other words, the patient has no experience of thinking the thoughts attributed to him because he failed to hear himself thinking the thoughts in question. At the moment such thoughts occurred to him, his mind was "somewhere else." The psychoanalyst says he was unconscious of what he was thinking, but the phenomenologist would say he simply failed to listen to, and experience, the thoughts in question as they occurred to him.

Based on this hypothesis, psychoanalytic treatment is nothing more than an investigation into the patient's experience suffered over the entirety of one's life. Analysts seek to learn about the experiences (*Erfahrung*) that patients remember over the course of their history, just as they seek to understand the patient's experience of the analytic situation (*Erlebnis*), i.e., the patient's experience of his relationship with the analyst: the so-called transference phenomena. But analysts are also interested in eliciting what may be characterized as "lost" experience (what Heidegger would call "potential" experience) through the patient's free associations. Change comes about through the patient's ability to speak of his experience instead of concealing it, as he has in the past. In other words, giving voice to experience deepens it, but only if the experience elicited plunges the patient to the depths of his suffering.

Concluding Unscientific Postscript

What does Heidegger's emphasis on the ontological dimension of experience tell us about the psychoanalytic conception of the unconscious? Does it do away with it entirely or does it offer another way of conceiving of it? How, in turn, does it relate to Sartre's distinction between reflective and pre-reflective consciousness? Are Heidegger's and Sartre's respective views compatible or are they hopelessly irreconcilable? And finally, is it possible to be "conscious" of something of which one has no experience, or is it necessary to experience something in order to know it, even "pre-reflectively"? Or contrariwise, is there a dimension to experience that one is not *aware* of experiencing, or is it essential to be conscious of experience in order to construe it as experience, as such, whether one is referring to *Erlebnis* or *Erfahrung*?

Recall that Sartre makes a distinction between pre-reflective consciousness and reflective consciousness (i.e., that which we ordinarily term "conscious awareness"). Even while Sartre is indecisive on this point, for Heidegger, Sartre's notion of pre-reflective consciousness only makes sense if it is conceived as a form of nascent awareness that is not immediately available to experience, properly speaking. Only when I *reflect* on my pre-reflective acts of consciousness am I capable of experiencing them and being with them. This is why, from a Heideggerian perspective, there is no such thing as "unconscious experience," despite the views of Melanie Klein, Wilfried Bion, Harry Stack Sullivan, and so on. If Sartre's conception of pre-reflective consciousness is simply another term for what Freud calls primary process thinking, then *the unconscious should be conceived of as a form of consciousness that is not yet available to experience.*

As we saw earlier, Heidegger lost interest in exploring the distinctions between consciousness, awareness, and intentionality because he felt they were inadequate concepts for describing the nature of thought and why it is available to my experience in some situations but not others. Our very capacity to experience is the final arbiter for what it means to inhabit the world and to be-in-the-world authentically, as the person I genuinely am, because experience, whatever form it assumes, is irrevocably my own. Heidegger finally rejected the primacy of consciousness because he was concerned with how one comes to *be* who one is and the weight of guilt and anxiety that being oneself inevitably entails.

If Freud's conception of the unconscious is finally a scientific one, it is nevertheless imbued with ontological overtones that are evident, for example, when he characterizes the way we stumble upon it in our dreams, parapraxes, and symptoms. From this perspective, the unconscious is nothing more than an algebraic "x" that serves to explain that which is not immediately given to experience. Moreover, one can discern parallels between Freud's and Sartre's (as well as Heidegger's) respective depictions of "two types of thinking," which, when treated phenomenologically, betray ontological connotations to Freud's intuitions, if not his theoretical conceptualizations. What Freud depicts as primary thought processes may be conceived of as a version of Sartre's notion of pre-reflective consciousness, and what Freud depicts as secondary thought processes are editions of what Sartre terms reflective consciousness. Seen from this angle, the primary thought processes are a form of consciousness but lack the reflective capacities that the ego is only capable of obtaining after the acquisition of language. Another way of understanding the distinction between *Erlebnis* and *Erhfarung* is to conceive the former as a form of pre-verbal experience (i.e., the experience of the infant), whereas the latter pertains to the child's (and later, the adult's) capacity to reflect on his or her experience after having acquired the capacity for language. The child's ability to learn from experience will evolve and develop, just as the capacity to experience will also evolve, from the most primitive aspects of *Erlebnis* to the more sophisticated editions of *Erfahrung*. Freud's topographical and structural models are indeed scientific, but only to the degree that psychoanalysis is a theoretical science that presumes to explain that which is inaccessible to experience. As a theoretical construct, it may be accurate or not. We do not know, nor can we, whether and to what degree they are accurate, which probably explains why the history of psychoanalysis is littered with a seemingly endless array of alternative formulations to Freud's, each of which is just as feasible (or not) as the next. Whosever's theory one opts for—whether Klein's, Sullivan's, Bion's, or Lacan's, for example—however compelling or attractive or elegant it may be, it is still just as theoretical, abstract, and impossible to prove (or disprove) as Freud's.

From Heidegger's ontological perspective, the unconscious is not a theoretical construct, nor is it "in" my head, but out there, in the world, a dimension of being. The unconscious is my abode, my past, and my destiny converged so that "I," the one for whom the unconscious comes into Being, am simply the experience of this tri-partite intersection. We apprehend it as an enigma, a dimension of our existence that lies hidden one moment, then slips into view the next, only to disappear again, in perpetuity. If our only access to it is through the vehicle of interpretation, it is not the interpretation (i.e., translation) of this or that psychoanalytic theory into a language of the consensus but the kind of interpretation we render each moment of our lives by virtue of giving things a name and a significance. This is because everything we are capable of experiencing conveys meaning, and the only way to understand what something means is to determine what it means for me, when it is experienced, and how.

Consequently, the unconscious is never unconscious for me but a living presence in my world. This is why the purpose of analysis is not to finally "know" the unconscious but to return the analytic patient to the ground of an experience from which he has lost his way in order to claim it as his own.

Notes

1 An earlier version of this paper was presented as the Presidential Address at the Eleventh Annual Interdisciplinary Conference of the International Federation for Psychoanalytic Education, Chicago Illinois, November 4, 2000.
2 For a more thorough treatment of Freud's conception of psychic reality, see Thompson, 1994, pp. 1–50.
3 See Thompson, 2000b, for a discussion on the sceptical dimension of Heidegger's and Freud's respective conceptions of the human condition.
4 See Thompson, 1998 and 2000b, for a more detailed exploration of how Freud developed the principles of free association and neutrality.
5 See Medard Boss' account of Heidegger's take on Freud in Boss, 1988, pp. 9–10.
6 See Thompson, 1996a, 1996b, and 2000b, for a more detailed exploration of Freud's conception of free association and neutrality in light of the sceptic and phenomenological traditions.
7 The theme of experience preoccupied Laing throughout his lifetime. Two of his other books, *The Politics of Experience* (1967) and *The Voice of Experience* (1982), even contain the word experience in their titles. (See more on the history of experience in Western Culture in Thompson, 2000a.)
8 Whereas Sartre would imply that pre-reflective consciousness is a form of experience (*Erlebnis*), Heidegger would argue that in order for knowledge to be available to experience it must be *thought*; so, for Heidegger, pre-reflective consciousness is not actually *experienced*, per se. For this reason, Heidegger disputed the notion of *Erlebnis* as a feature of experience, properly speaking, although he would have no problem with employing this term so long as it connotes an act that is reflectively conscious to the person at the moment it is experienced. For more on this point see Heidegger, 1970.

References

Boss, M. (1988) Martin Heidegger's Zollikon Seminars. In K. Hoeller (Ed.), *Heidegger and Psychology, A Special Issue of the Review of Existential Psychology and Psychiatry* (pp. 7–20). Seattle, WA: Review of Existential Psychology and Psychiatry.
Bromberg, P. (1998) *Standing in the Spaces: Essays on Clinical Process, Trauma, and Dissociation*. Hillsdale, NJ and London: The Analytic Press.

Freud, S. (1892/1966) *Case of a Successful Treatment by Hypnosis*. Standard Edition (Vol. 1, pp. 115–128). London: Hogarth Press.

Freud, S. (1911/1958) *Formulations on the Two Principles of Mental Functioning*. Standard Edition (Vol. 12, pp. 215–226). London: Hogarth Press.

Freud, S. (1912/1957) *On the Universal Tendency to Debasement in the Sphere of Love*. Standard Edition (Vol. 11, pp. 177–190). London: Hogarth Press.

Freud, S. (1913/1958) *Totem and Taboo*. Standard Edition (Vol. 13, pp. 1–161). London: Hogarth Press.

Freud, S. (1953–1973) *The Standard Edition of the Complete Psychological Works of Sigmund Freud* (24 vols; J. Strachey, Ed. & Trans.). London: Hogarth Press (Referred to in Subsequent References as Standard Edition).

Gray, J. G. (1968) *Introduction to What is Called Thinking?*, by Martin Heidegger. San Francisco: Harper and Row.

Grotstein, J. (1999) *Who is the Dreamer That Dreams The Dream?* London: Karnac Books.

Heidegger, M. (1970) *Hegel's Concept of Experience* (Harper and Row, Trans.). New York and London: Harper and Row.

Heidegger, M. (1971) *On the Way to Language* (Peter D. Hertz, Trans.). San Francisco: Harper and Row.

Heidegger, M. (1977) On the Essence of Truth. In D. F. Krell (Ed.), *Basic Writings* (pp. 113–142). New York and London: Harper and Row.

Jay, M. (1998, November 14) *The Crisis of Experience in a Post-Subjective Age*. Public Lecture. Berkeley, CA: University of California.

Laing, R. D. (1960) *The Divided Self*. New York: Pantheon Books.

Laing, R. D. (1969/1961) *Self and Others*. 2nd Revised Edition. New York: Pantheon Books.

Laing, R. D. (1982) *The Voice of Experience*. New York: Pantheon Books.

Laing, R. D., Phillipson, H. and Lee, A. R. (1966) *Interpersonal Perception: A Theory and a Method of Research*. London: Tavistock Publications.

Langan, R. (1993, October) The Depth of the Field. *Contemporary Psychoanalysis*, Vol. 29, No. 4.

Leavy, S. (1980) *The Psychoanalytic Dialogue*. New Haven: Yale University Press.

Leavy, S. (1988) *In the Image of God: A Psychoanalyst's View*. New Haven: Yale University Press.

Levenson, E. (1972) *The Fallacy of Understanding: An Inquiry into the Changing Structure of Psychoanalysis*. New York and London: Basic Books.

Levenson, E. (1983) *The Ambiguity of Change: An Inquiry into the Nature of Psychoanalytic Reality*. New York: Basic Books.

Levenson, E. (1991) *The Purloined Self: Interpersonal Perspectives in Psychoanalysis*. New York: Contemporary Psychoanalysis Books.

Loewald, H. W. (1980) *Papers on Psychoanalysis*. New Haven: Yale University Press.

Macquarrie, J. (1994) *Heidegger and Christianity*. New York: Continuum Publishing Company.

Mitchell, J. (1974) *Psychoanalysis and Feminism*. New York: Pantheon Books.

Rycroft, C. (1968) *Imagination and Reality*. New York: International Universities Press.

Sartre, J.-P. (1957) *The Transcendence of the Ego* (F. Williams and R. Kirkpatrick, Trans.). New York: Noonday Press.

Sartre, J.-P. (1962) *Sketch for a Theory of the Emotions* (P. Mairet, Trans.). London: Methuen and Co.

Sartre, J.-P. (1981) *Existential Psychoanalysis* (H. Barnes, Trans.). Washington, DC: Regnary Gateway.

Stern, D. B. (1997) *Unformulated Experience: From Dissociation to Imagination in Psychoanalysis*. Hillsdale, NJ and London: The Analytic Press.

Thompson, M. G. (1994) *The Truth About Freud's Technique: The Encounter With The Real*. New York and London: New York University Press.

Thompson, M. G. (1996a) The Rule of Neutrality. *Psychoanalysis and Contemporary Thought*, Vol. 19, No. 1.

Thompson, M. G. (1996b, January) Freud's Conception of Neutrality. *Contemporary Psychoanalysis*, Vol. 32, No. 1.

Thompson, M. G. (1998, October) Manifestations of Transference: Love, Friendship, Rapport. *Contemporary Psychoanalysis*, Vol. 34, No. 1.

Thompson, M. G. (2000a, January) The Crisis of Experience in Contemporary Psychoanalysis. *Contemporary Psychoanalysis*, Vol. 36, No. 1.

Thompson, M. G. (2000b, July) The Sceptic Dimension to Psychoanalysis: Toward an Ethic of Experience. *Contemporary Psychoanalysis*, Vol. 36, No. 3.

Chapter 10

The Demise of the Person in the Psychoanalytic Situation

The Deconstruction of the Personal Relationship

The demise of the person in the psychoanalytic process may seem like a strange choice of subject matter as the words person and personal are not technical terms in standard psychoanalytic nomenclature. Both terms are typically invoked, if at all, in a strictly offhand way when referring to non-transferential and non-technical behavior or experience in the context of the psychoanalytic treatment relationship. For the majority of analysts, so-called personal aspects of the treatment situation have little, if any, role to play in the psychoanalytic process as it is typically conceived. For many, it is the absence of a personal engagement with patients that distinguishes psychoanalysis from its more user-friendly cousin, psychodynamic psychotherapy. It has become increasingly commonplace that contemporary psychoanalysts of virtually all persuasions reduce the psychoanalytic process to the analysis of transference, resistance, and, more recently, enactments. This has resulted in the general assumption that virtually all of a patient's reactions to the person of the analyst should be treated as transference manifestations. Similarly, most, if not all, significant interventions by the analyst in response to transference phenomena are informed by whichever technical principles a given analyst elects to follow. This is a view typically held, for example, by Kleinian, classical Freudian (i.e., American ego psychology), and most contemporary relational analysts, all of whom tend to deconstruct the very notion of a person-to-person engagement out of the psychoanalytic process. Such analysts often concede that interactions of a personal nature invariably occur during every analytic encounter, but such occurrences are usually deemed irrelevant and even impediments to the analytic process and are scrupulously avoided or, when unavoidable, systematically analyzed.

DOI: 10.4324/9781003429104-10

As a topical example of just how far this attitude has evolved, I cite a recent article in *Psychoanalytic Psychology* (Maroda, 2007), which was subsequently discussed in the New York Times, that questioned the efficacy of analysts treating patients in their home office. The author of the article, Karen Maroda, offered that such arrangements may serve as "keyholes" into the analyst's personal life and consequently "over stimulate and overwhelm" the patient. She argues that any contact with the analyst's personal life will inevitably result in an unsettling, even harmful experience (if, indeed, knowledge of a personal nature about one's analyst is inherently traumatic).

Even a cursory survey of the psychoanalytic literature over the course of its long history shows how surprisingly recent the trend to "depersonalize" the psychoanalytic relationship, in fact, is. An extraordinary number of seminal contributors to matters of technique—including Freud, Ferenczi, Reik, Fairbairn, Winnicott, Lomas, Erikson, Loewald, Stone, Fromm, Leavy, and Lipton, among many others—believe, on the contrary, that the personal relationship between patient and analyst should be acknowledged in order to accommodate the unpredictable nature of the *total* psychoanalytic encounter. These analysts argue that a wide assortment of object relations, in addition to transference phenomena, occur over the course of every psychoanalytic treatment and that the astute handling of such non-transference and non-technical interactions is an indispensable component of the proverbial analytic process. On the other hand, Ferenczi, an important advocate of informal technique, may inadvertently serve as a confusing model for a more personally engaged way of conducting psychoanalytic treatments. For example, Ferenczi was noted for his gregarious and affectionate personality in the way he typically behaved with patients. Ferenczi also engaged in a series of *technical* experiments that were designed to make the psychoanalytic process more democratic and less authoritarian. Ferenczi is often cited by contemporary relational analysts (Davies and Frawley, 1991; Ogden, 1994; Mitchell and Black, 1995) as the first advocate of a two-person psychology, yet his inherently outgoing personality traits are typically confused with his more deliberate technical innovations so that both are erroneously conceived as aspects of technique, in the strict sense of the term. Consequently, the specifically spontaneous, unpredictable attributes of a given psychoanalyst's personality have been incorporated into deliberate, circumscribed technical recommendations that effectively compromise the uniquely personal component of the analyst's participation in the process.

Another example of this development can be found among relational analysts who take umbrage with the more classical characterization of transference phenomena as distortions of the patient's real or realistic perception of the analyst's behavior. Relational analysts argue—in my opinion, correctly—that such perceptions *may* (or may not) be accurate and even insightful observations of the analyst's behavior, about which the analyst may be unaware. Yet, in so doing, these same relational analysts tend to treat such ostensibly accurate perceptions as aspects of the patient's transference. Consequently, such perceptions are not conceived as components of the ongoing *personal* relationship but, rather, as an "expanded" notion of how classical analysts typically conceive the transference situation. For instance, whereas Hoffman (1983) advocates for more spontaneity and truthfulness in the analytic relationship, his principal concern is a technical matter, that analysts should encourage their patients to reflect upon and verbalize how they are experiencing their relationship with their analyst. Hoffman points out that analysts have traditionally not been taught to perform such interventions. Moreover, he believes that many of the analysts (e.g., Stone, Loewald, Strachey, Greenson, Langs, Kohut) who have emphasized the importance of the real or personal relationship existing alongside the transferential do not encourage their patients to verbalize their experiences about their relationship. He also chides these analysts for adhering to the traditional depiction of transference phenomena as "distortions" of what is really occurring in the analyst-analysand dynamic, thereby setting themselves up as authorities on what is real and what is not. Analysts who encourage more personal or human engagement with their patients fall prey to what Hoffman sees as a stubborn adherence to the analyst as the authority figure with the patient as a supplicant; these analysts may be compassionate, but they call the shots as to what is actually going on. This characterization of so-called classical or orthodox analysts has been roundly criticized by Haynal (1997) for oversimplifying the complexity of the historical evolution of psychoanalytic theory and technique over the past century, especially in Europe.

I admit to being puzzled by Hoffman's criticisms. It would seem to me that a relational perspective that is firmly rooted in the Interpersonal tradition (initiated by Sullivan and subsequently developed by Fromm, Fromm-Reichmann, C. Thompson, O. Will, and numerous others) would privilege spontaneity *and* personal engagement by both analyst and analysand, a manner of engagement that cannot be reduced to technical interventions, however enlightened or perceptive such interventions may be. Hoffman complains that there is no way of distinguishing between personal and transferential aspects of the analytic dyad and says even Freud, with his conception of the unobjectionable transference,[1] observed that transference is ubiquitous in virtually all human relationships. Hoffman chastises Stone, for example, for claiming that the transferential and real relationships are distinct but intertwined when he says that "the transference will, under [certain] circumstances, include realistic perceptions of the analyst" (1983, p. 49). Hoffman argues that Stone cannot have it both ways, to say that one can distinguish between the two and yet insist they can commingle.

It seems to me that Hoffman is genuinely confused about the distinction between the personal and technical aspects of the analytic experience and, so, reduces it to unrelenting tech-ridden interventions that pervade the treatment situation. This problem probably originates from how Freud envisioned matters of technique and the subtle differences between real and transferential love, outlined in Freud's seminal and most exhaustive paper on the nature of love, "Observations on Transference-Love" (1915). Because Freud saw transference phenomena as contemporary editions of the patient's Oedipal, unrequited love, he recognized that so-called transference experiences occur in all human encounters, including outside the analytic situation. We only call this phenomenon transference (instead of love) in the context of analysis because no one can fall in love with their analyst as innocently as they might otherwise in the normal course of events. This is because the comportment of the analyst with whom the patient forms a positive transference is essentially a *contrivance*. The analyst does not show concern, curiosity, and compassion for the patient because of the compelling character traits the analysand happens to possess. He does so because that is what he is being paid to do; it is his job. That doesn't, however, mean that the feelings of concern and compassion he displays toward his patient are not genuine. They are. They are two human beings who spend a lot of time together, and the analyst feels these things because that is what makes him human. He may also harbor his own personal reasons for wanting to help people. Perhaps he took care of his mother when he was a child and developed a tolerance and ease with such uncommonly intimate and intense relationships that he has opted to turn this talent into a vocation. The patient is effectively thrown into an intensive relationship not unlike she might with a married colleague. Familiarity breeds intimacy, and the situation that brings people together may elicit emotional reactions that they would otherwise never experience with that person.

Another way of putting it is that transference is ubiquitous because our capacity for love is universal and always operative. If we were not capable of such feelings, we would not be effective practitioners. Indeed, it is a prerequisite for and the foundation of every intimate relationship we have. The personal and the transferential do blend, but they can be distinguished with effort. A patient may come to trust me because I remind him of his grandfather whom he loved and admired, but also because I treat him in such a way that invites such trust. The technique of non-judgmental neutrality is not just a technique: it speaks to my capacity to suspend judgment and keep an open mind, a personal attribute. When this furthers my patient's analytic attitude and his ability to free associate and reflect on my interpretations, I don't necessarily have to bring it to my patient's attention that "this is only transference, you know," even if that is true. On the other hand, it is a judgment call as to when and how often I feel the need to offer transference interpretations, be they of the genetic or here-and-now variety. But the technique of rendering such interventions occurs in the context of a personal relationship that is guided by our respective character traits, including our respective capacities for intimacy, candor, and affiliation. Hoffman seems so intent on bringing our attention to a favored technique that he ends up throwing out the baby of personal engagement with the bathwater of classical technique.

Hoffman advocates a less dogmatic and more sceptical manner of sharing interpretations with his patients, and I applaud him for that. Behaving more compassionately and sensitively with one's patients is a no-brainer. But in my view, the inherently personal aspects of the analyst-patient relationship should not necessarily be subject to analysis, nor should they always fall under the rubric of technique. That which is personal is, by its nature, generally taken for granted and permitted to pass as that dimension of the analytic relationship that is both genuine and authentic. *It is from this foundation of the ongoing personal relationship that transference phenomena derive.* The significance of this distinction will become more apparent below.

What accounts for this glaring dichotomy in our conception of the personal relationship, and why is there such reluctance to recognize and, in turn, systematically explore the vital role this relationship plays in the analytic process? Why does the word "personal" arouse so much concern that it has been more or less banished from our characterization of this process and relegated to psychoanalytic "psychotherapy"? Finally, what role does the psychoanalytic conception of the unconscious play in these considerations and how did our conception of transference as a strictly unconscious phenomenon become incompatible with the notion of a personal dimension to the analytic relationship?

It is a common assumption that the unconscious is the pivot around which psychoanalytic theory and practice orbit and that this distinguishes psychoanalysis from other kinds of psychotherapy, such as CBT, family therapy, or humanistic and psychodynamic therapies. It necessarily follows that one of the cardinal questions raised by the psychoanalytic conception of the unconscious is the role of the subject or person who is engaged in this therapeutic endeavor. Freud's earlier topographical model addressed this question in a somewhat ambiguous manner when he coined the term *Gegenwille* ("counter-will" in English) in order to locate the role of unconscious motivation and how intentions can be operative yet unknown to the subject (Leavy, 1988). The term will has been historically marginalized by psychoanalysts for a variety of reasons. Being a verb as well as a noun, the term always implies a subject. When I do something that I claim I didn't mean or intend to, it does no good to plead that blind, impersonal forces "did" the act. Those so-called unconscious forces are *me*.

Counter-will served as an early marker for how Freud conceived of the unconscious as a subject who *performs acts* about which the actor is, to varying degrees, unaware. Though this term endured for some twenty years, after 1912 it more or less disappeared as the generalization collapsed into concepts like resistance, repression, unconscious conflict, and drive. Freud's subsequent structural model cemented this process even further when he explicitly depersonalized unconscious agency in the language of id, superego, and defense mechanisms. But the gain in specificity was accompanied by the loss of a *personal*, as well as responsible, will. As Freud pursued his project of establishing the empirical causes of symptoms, his earlier notion of the unconscious as a secret agent or anonymous ego— i.e., counter-will—receded into the background.

The tendency to depersonalize the unconscious has been more or less adopted by virtually all subsequent schools of psychoanalysis and adapted to their myriad conceptions of the unconscious. Its explicitly *impersonal* status has persisted while accompanied by technical interventions that emphasize impersonal dimensions to the transference, motivation, and resistance to such a degree that the person engaged in the process has effectively ceased to exist. Increasingly abstract and ever more arid conceptions of the unconscious have led to more and more impersonal and disassociated conceptions of transference and the accompanying treatment relationship. Yet, the very concept of transference has not been completely embraced. It has even been criticized by some analysts as offering an all-too-convenient defense for practitioners who are uncomfortable with the unavoidable personal engagement with patients that the intimate psychoanalytic situation fosters. For example, Chertok and de Saussure (1979, p. 13) argue that Freud's conception of transference often serves "a defensive measure—a kind of prophylaxis that depersonalizes the relationship and interposes a 'third person' between the patient and the doctor, like the duenna-nurse who peers over the gynecologist's shoulder during examination." Thomas Szasz (1963), back in the days when he was still a psychoanalyst, also alluded to the role of transference as a mode of defense when he observed that "the concept of transference serves two separate analytic purposes: it is a crucial part of the patient's therapeutic experience, and a successful defensive measure to protect the analyst from too intense affective and real-life involvement with the patient" (p. 437). Szasz avers, "the idea of transference implies denial and repudiation of the patient's *experience qua experience*; in its place is substituted the more manageable construct of a *transference experience*" (p. 437). These authors suggest that the analysis of transference is frequently employed to help analysts who are uncomfortable with the personal intimacy aroused between themselves and their patients by attributing such feelings to transference instead of acknowledging the emotions they genuinely feel for each other or simply letting them be, sans interpretation.

I suspect that a significant part of the problem derives from our conception of unconscious process and its role in our repression of the personal dimension of the treatment relationship. The term person, or *persona*, was first invoked in Roman law to refer to citizens who possessed the right to vote in a democratic political process. To vote implied an agent who possessed sufficient autonomy to assume responsibility for the decision-making process in which he participated. Because a slave lacked such autonomy, he was not deemed a "person" and was accordingly denied the right to vote, as only persons (i.e., non-slaves) were granted these rights. Similarly, Freud, who saw the ego as a slave or servant to unconscious processes, decided over time that the unconscious is not personal but impersonal, meaning analytic patients could not be held responsible for acts, thoughts, or intentions they are unconscious of harboring or committing *at the time* they commit them. Unconscious ideation becomes impersonal precisely when and because it lacks agency. In principle, such thoughts can nevertheless become personal again (or for the first time) once they become conscious and the person in question accepts responsibility for them. Yet the trend in contemporary psychoanalysis is to maintain the impersonal conception of transference throughout the treatment experience, no matter what insights patients may have about the feelings they harbor for their analyst.

The psychoanalytic conception of the transference phenomena character-izes the patient's experience of and attributions about the person of the ana-lyst as an inherently unconscious process. Efforts by relational analysts to render this dynamic more democratic have subjected the analyst to the same kind of scrutiny as the patient, but the notion of an explicitly personal engage-ment of the kind I am describing that falls outside the purview of *technical interventions* is typically overlooked or rejected. The psychoanalytic litera-ture has consequently tended to focus on transference-countertransference phenomena, their specifically unconscious function, and the ways that ana-lysts are affected by their patients' projections. This has led to a consen-sus that analysts should focus their attention on analyzing such projections while avoiding interactions of a personal nature which, by implication, are defined as *non-interpretative* communications because they do not speak to unconscious processes. To return to the slave metaphor, for relational analysts, both analysand and analysts are *equally* enslaved by their respec-tive unconsciouses, in an endless to-and-fro of intersubjectivity and infinite regress.

Consequently, all vestiges of the personal relationship shared with patients have been transformed into aspects of the patient's transference with the analyst and the analyst's countertransference with the patient, both of which are systematically interpreted and analyzed. From a classi-cal perspective, transference is conceived as a rarefied, trance-like state of childlike hypnotic regression that places the patient in a one-down posi-tion from which she cannot extricate herself because she is always "in" the transference, which she cannot, by definition, escape. This has the chilling consequence of perceiving the analysand as never really being the author of his or her experience or a proper adult in an I-Thou relationship, but the "effect" of unconscious forces to which only the analyst is privy. The more recent relational and contemporary effort to extend this process to a similar analysis of the *analyst's* conscious and unconscious process only duplicates the problem but neither addresses nor resolves it.

These relatively recent developments fly in the face of a long history of analysts, going all the way back to Freud and Ferenczi, who embrace the concept of a personal or realistic component to the analytic relationship. Greenson, as Hoffman observed, focuses on what he calls the "real" relationship as distinct from the transference, which pertains to perceptions by the patient that are deemed realistic rather than fantastic or inappropriate. In Greenson's depiction of the real relationship, however, he tends to focus on the patient's experience of the analyst, neglecting the analyst's relationship with the patient. Because the relationship between analyst and analysand is not symmetrical, the correlation between their respective positions is not identical. Whereas the patient's experience of the analyst is couched in terms of varying degrees of transference phenomena, the analyst's experience of and behavior toward the analysand is typically couched in terms of technique, a circumscribed set of behaviors epitomized by interpretative strategies. The concept of countertransference similarly falls under the purview of technique, whether it is conceived as unconscious impediments to the analyst's optimal functioning in the analytic dyad or as aspects of the analyst's conscious experience that conform to technical scrutiny. Increasingly, countertransference phenomena are defined simply as the totality of the analyst's experience, including what used to be deemed "personal" reactions but, subsumed under technical oversight, effectively eliminating a genuinely personal component to the relationship.

In other words, most of what the analyst says nowadays is monitored by *technical* considerations, whereas anything of a personal nature—which is to say, anything that is uttered spontaneously and without calculated regard for its intended effect on the patient's transference—is virtually eliminated. Greenson and other analysts who are concerned with distinguishing between transferential and real components of the patient's experience of the process do not specifically address its correlate: *the technical and non-technical components of the analyst's behavior*. It is this aspect of the analyst-patient dyad that I am specifically concerned with in this chapter.

Even those relational analysts who object to the classical characterization of the patient's transference as nothing more than distortions of reality tend to conceive virtually all of the analyst's behavior as aspects of technique. For example, Renik (1999) advocates acts of self-disclosure by the analyst and characterizes such revelations as conforming to a technical strategy whose purpose is to exercise a desirable effect on the patient's transference, reminiscent of Alexander's advocacy of manipulating the transference in order to facilitate a corrective emotional experience. In such a scheme, the analyst's acts of self-disclosure are not, strictly speaking, personal but rather calculated to have a specific effect. In order for such interventions to be personal, they would have to emanate part and parcel from *who* the analyst is, not *what* the analyst does. Renik does not advocate self-disclosure simply because that is who he is and sees no harm in simply being himself. Instead, he specifically contrasts self-disclosure with the idiosyncratic foibles of a given analyst's personality traits and characterizes his self-disclosures as technical interventions. Renik argues that such self-disclosures should be adopted by all analysts *as a new standard of technique.*

Yet, like Hoffman, Renik seems genuinely confused about the difference between the technical and personal domains of the analytic relationship. For instance, Renik (1999) says:

> My own style as a person, and therefore as an analyst, is toward the active, exhibitionistic rather than the reserved end of the spectrum. All things being equal, I usually prefer to mix it up with a patient and field the consequences rather than risk missing out on an opportunity for productive interchange. By suggesting that the analyst play his or her cards face up, however, I am not rationalizing my personal style or elevating it into a technical principal. *Willingness to self-disclose, as a policy, can and should apply across the individual styles of various analysts.*
>
> (p. 531; emphasis added)

Despite Renik's claim that he is not elevating his personal style to a technique, as soon as he advocates this way of working for *all* analysts, he is not suggesting that they be like him but that they adopt a manner of working—by definition, technique—that he believes will bear greater analytic success. If Renik put his observations down to an attribute of his personality, that that is simply who he is and that he adapts his technique to fit his personality, then he would be explaining how conducting analysis suited *him*, period. But as soon as he advocates his interventions for all, he is advocating a technical intervention. As a technique that he advocates for others to follow, it is no longer a character trait but the application of his mind and comportment in the analytic situation.

The Specifically Personal Dimension to the Analytic Relationship

What would behavior of a specifically personal nature look like in contrast to a prescribed set of techniques? And how would such behavior be beneficial to the patient's treatment? Am I merely splitting hairs by attempting to distinguish between analytic behavior of a personal rather than technical nature? I don't believe so. The recognition and elaboration of the personal relationship should obviously *enhance* the therapeutic process, not compromise it. Acting from the analyst's person simply for the sake of it would not make much sense if it had a deleterious effect on the treatment relationship. On the other hand, if its aim is to benefit the analytic process, then why wouldn't such personal engagement—on par with Renik's definition of self-disclosure—entail a *technical* intervention, by definition?

The problem with conceptualizing the personal engagement that all analysts experience with their patients as a component of technique is that in order to come across as a genuine person, analysts need to be true to their given personality traits and behavioral characteristics, whatever they happen to be. In order to be genuine, the analyst's way of conducting him- or herself should be natural, spontaneous, and without guile. The most common complaint patients typically make about analysts who conform to classical technique is the *lack of genuineness* concerning the way they conduct themselves.[2] Yet, one of the principal goals of analytic treatment is to increase the patient's capacity for genuineness in their manner of relating to others, as well as themselves. On the other hand, those analysts who object to a classical or austere way of behaving with patients and advocate doing the opposite, e.g., affecting a more conversational and emotional engagement with their patients, invariably argue that *all* analysts would be advised to behave that way, even if such a way of behaving feels out of character or unnatural to a given analyst. It is my impression that most analysts are not naturally talkative nor do they wear their hearts on their sleeves. For them, being "themselves" might well entail remaining silent throughout most of their analytic sessions, not because their technique tells them to but because that is what they are comfortable doing with more or less everyone. To become talkative and responsive would not only feel unnatural to them, it would also be experienced by their patients as contrived and artificial, perhaps weird. Winnicott is a perfect example of an analyst who learned over many years the value of saying little yet was regarded by all who saw him in treatment as uncommonly considerate and genuine. Analysts typically connect with their patients in ways they are not entirely aware of because, in so doing, they are just being themselves, whatever that entails. By extension, an analyst cannot be him- or herself and conceive doing so as a *standard of technique*. Being oneself is, by definition, personal. As such, it is an act of creativity that is *uniquely one's own*.

So what are the criteria for being oneself that most analysts find so objectionable that they have been factored out of the psychoanalytic treatment perspective? Unlike the techniques that analysts adopt, *there cannot be universal standards* for how a given analyst uses his or her personality in the treatment of each patient. Freud wasn't even comfortable with mandating strict standards for his technical principles, let alone the personal ones! As a rule of thumb, what is deemed personal is basically common-sensical, if not immediately predictable or obvious. It is both outside technique and subject to individual variation. It cannot be codified because, just as analysts differ from person to person, each analyst's conception of the personal relationship will vary accordingly. Moreover, analysts are liable to form different conceptions of what the personal relationship entails at different stages of their careers and with different patients, when they succumb to this or that mood, the time of day, how long they have been working with a given patient, and so on.

For the personal relationship to be spontaneous, unpredictable, and authentic, it has to be free of contrivance and subterfuge, a manner of being that, for lack of a better word, comes from the heart. This is why the most common incidence of the personal relationship is often manifested in the form of *spontaneous conversations* that evolve between analyst and patient. Such conversations may include self-disclosures by the analyst, but not necessarily. The basic idea is that not everything the analyst says is limited to offering interpretations, eliciting data, or other technical considerations. Classical analysts tend to reject conversation out of hand because they believe "conversing" has no discernible role in the analytic process, whereas relational analysts tend to reduce such otherwise spontaneous conversations to a technique that can come across as contrived and manipulative. Conversations are obviously gratifying for patient and analyst alike and are necessarily restrained by the use of abstinence, but to abandon them entirely becomes artificial for those analysts who, like Freud and Ferenczi, are naturally conversational. For example, there are times when patients may want to muse about ideas, whether philosophical, literary, or spiritual, when reflecting on the human condition and their place in the scheme of things and ask their analysts to reciprocate. Analysts may, in turn, participate in such conversations without the need to reduce such musings to manifestations of transference and analyze them accordingly. Some analysts may even initiate such conversations when the spirit moves them to for reasons that are not necessarily apparent to them at the time. It is my sense that such spontaneous, inherently extra-analytic exchanges have a profound impact on the analytic relationship as well as the outcome of treatment, but in ways that we may be incapable of determining on a case-by-case basis, let alone moment-to-moment.

Permitting one's personality to become part of the constellation of elements that analysts utilize serves as an invaluable source for authentic relating with patients. *It is my thesis that these incidents of feeling genuinely connected to one's analyst are critical if unconventional, even controversial, components of every successful treatment experience.* Because each analyst's personality is unique, each analyst's manner of being personally engaged with patients will vary. Feeling free to converse spontaneously is only one personality trait among many that cannot be reduced to technical edicts. For example, a given analyst's capacity for affection, disaffection, concern, kindness, courage, consideration, compassion, curiosity, and wisdom are all personal characteristics that will fundamentally differ from one analyst to another. Moreover, such characteristics cannot be taught in psychoanalytic institutes nor can they be learned under supervision. You might say they are so personal that each analyst has to struggle in her own analysis to discover which ones epitomize the peculiarities of her own personality and determine those that are strengths and weaknesses by developing her clinical style accordingly. They are not only traits of personality, but part and parcel aspects of the analyst's *way of living* and operative in all aspects of it, including the relationships that are fashioned with one's patients.

The Role of Character in the Personal Relationship

Of all the psychoanalytic perspectives that have emphasized the role of the personal relationship, the interpersonal and existential perspectives are the most explicit in addressing this aspect of the analyst-analysand relationship. This is not to suggest that other perspectives have neglected this issue. On the contrary, there is a rich psychoanalytic literature that both addresses and advocates the role of the personal relationship in the analytic process, as I noted above.[3] The existential tradition has even questioned the efficacy of making clear-cut distinctions between the personal and transference relationships.[4] Existentialists have historically tended to avoid terms like technique and focused instead on those phenomena of which the patient is aware and those of which the patient is not aware, that which is accessible to awareness and that which is inaccessible.[5] The fact that analysts occupy a necessarily professional role in their work does not necessarily imply that the relationship fashioned with their patients is not personal. Yes, there are professional relationships that do not occasion a personal dimension. For example, x-ray technicians in a hospital setting may have little, if any, opportunity to engage in personal conversation with their subjects because they can carry out their role with minimal, if any, personal contact. Psychoanalytic relationships, however, cannot avoid such contact because the personal medium of engaging in conversation is the *essence* of their professional activities. The boundaries between the personal and professional are constantly evolving in ways of which we are not entirely aware.

It should be apparent by now that the character or person of a given analyst is of critical importance to how that analyst's patients will experience and benefit from that relationship. Whereas technical principles are indispensable to every analysis, the question I am addressing is the often neglected but equally important issue of the analyst's unique personality and attendant character traits. For some analysts—and I would include myself among them—the role of the analyst's character is of far greater importance than the technique a given analyst opts to employ. There is no way of empirically substantiating this claim, but I believe it, nonetheless.

That being said, the psychoanalytic conception of character has been historically pathologized as embedded structures of the personality that compromise the individual's ability to obtain maximum gratification from or adaptation to life. Freud employed the word character in two distinct ways. In his earlier writings, but also sporadically in later papers, he referred to character in the sense of a virtuous, upstanding individual, but the vast majority of his publications refer to it in the second sense as a form of psychopathology that is deeply embedded in the patient's personality. The first to catch his attention was the obsessional type, soon followed by a host of others and subsequently expanded on by a succession of a new generation of analysts. Because they are so deeply embedded, the individual is profoundly adapted to a given constellation of character types, e.g., hysterical, obsessive, schizoid, narcissistic, paranoid, and so on. The notion that character may refer to features of one's personality structure that are inherently *virtuous* is not a typical preoccupation of contemporary psychoanalytic literature or nomenclature. We speak in an offhand way of a person possessing good character or strong character to signify an individual of exemplary moral fiber who epitomizes excellent values, such as the ones I listed above, e.g., kindness, generosity, courage, integrity, honesty, resolve, and the like. But these examples of character are usually invoked only when employing non-technical terminology about the patient, somehow outside the analyst-patient dynamic.

Though Freud referred to his first use of character only fleetingly (see, for example, Freud, 1905), he never abandoned his belief that virtuous character traits are an indelible ingredient of every successful analytic treatment. He perceived the British, for example, as a culture he admired for possessing "excellent character." Moreover, he believed that candidates for analytic treatment should possess a degree of good character but the precise character traits they should exhibit are left for us to ponder. Since Freud, analysts have tended to remain silent about such expectations. As the treatment of severe psychopathologies (e.g., schizoid, narcissistic, and borderline character structure) has increasingly dominated the psychoanalytic literature, the question of analyzability has receded into the background. Freud questioned whether schizoid and narcissistic patients could be analyzed because he believed they were too self-absorbed, yet this assessment was based on their pathology, not their character specifically. Freud's focus, as we know, was on neurotics, yet many of them he deemed "good for nothing" and unsuitable for the kind of perseverance, honesty, and will that he expected analytic patients to embody. These character traits were, in his way of thinking, independent of the pathology (whether neurotic or psychotic) a given patient suffers.

Similarly, Freud (1913) expected analysts to possess an even higher degree of virtue than the patients they treat, most prominent among them honesty.[6] Freud didn't say a lot about honesty because it is not a matter of technique but concerns the analyst's personality. He or she has or hasn't got it, but it cannot be turned on or off like a switch or learned via a course of study. Moreover, analysts who do not possess a high degree of character will find the trials and demands of analytic work not to their liking. They may very well succeed in becoming analysts but it was Freud's opinion they would not be very good at it because they would serve as poor role models for their patients. Until recently, analytic institutes typically assessed character in screening prospective applicants for training, but increasingly this question is omitted from consideration because character is so difficult to measure and depends more or less entirely on the subjective opinion of the analysts conducting the interviews. Ironically, in order to make the admissions process less subjective and more democratic, the relevance of and preoccupation about the relation between the analyst's character and technique has receded into the background.

Even if personal virtue cannot be taught, the concept can be and should be included in the curriculum of psychoanalytic institutes. Though we cannot "learn" to be virtuous, we can raise our awareness of those aspects of our personalities that disclose our attitudes about our work and frustrations and the role our character plays in many of our notions about theory and technique, the kinds of patients we like to work with and those we do not. Given the vast amount of literature on character pathology, it would also be instructive to distinguish between the two types of character I have been discussing, including their relationship to personality (now employed more or less interchangeably with character) and what I have been depicting as the personal relationship.

In conclusion, the capacity to acknowledge the existence of a personal relationship with one's patients, and the wherewithal to freely engage it in a manner that complements the specific needs of each treatment situation, lends a dimension of genuineness and authenticity to the relationship that has profound implications for the way the analysis is experienced, and even how technical principles are applied. Fortunately, most analysts know this intuitively—if not deliberately—and conduct themselves accordingly.

Notes

1 Though this term is rarely invoked nowadays, it has been replaced here and there with terms such as the personal or real relationship, or the working or therapeutic alliance.

2 For an illuminating example of such complaints, see Daphne Merkin (2010) in a recent article in *The New York Times Magazine*, August 8, 2010, pp. 28–47.

3 For example, see Ticho, 1982; Ticho and Richards, 1982; Gill, 1988; Gitelson, 1962, 1952; A. Reich, 1958; Bouvet, 1958; Nacht, 1958.

4 See Laing, 1967; Tillich, 2000; and Buber, 1970, for informed discussions concerning the personal nature of every therapeutic encounter.

5 See Askey and Farquhar, 2006, for an illuminating review of existentialist and phenomenological critiques of the unconscious.

6 See Thompson, 2004, for more on Freud's views about honesty.

References

Askey, R. and Farquhar, J. (2006) *Apprehending the Inaccessible: Freudian Psychoanalysis and Existential Phenomenology*. Evanston, IL: Northwestern University Press.

Bouvet, M. (1958) Technical Variation and the Concept of Distance. *International Journal of Psychoanalysis,* Vol. 39: 211–221.

Buber, M. (1970) *I and Thou* (W. Kaufman, Trans.). New York: Free Press.

Chertok, L. and de Saussure, R. (1979/1981) The Therapeutic Revolution: From Mesmer to Freud. In J. Malcolm (Ed.), *Psychoanalysis: The Impossible Profession* (p. 13). New York: Alfred A. Knoph.

Davies, J. and Frawley, M. (1991/1999) Dissociative Processes and Transference-Countertransference Paradigms in Psychoanalytically Oriented Treatment of Adult Survivors of Childhood Sexual Abuse. In S. Mitchell and L. Aron (Eds.), *Relational Psychoanalysis: The Emergence of a Tradition*. Hillsdale, NJ: The Analytic Press.

Freud, S. (1905/1953) *On Psychotherapy*. Standard Edition (Vol. 7, pp. 257–268). London: Hogarth Press.

Freud, S. (1913/1958) *On Beginning the Treatment (Further Recommendations on the Technique of Psycho-Analysis I)*. Standard Edition (Vol. 12, pp. 121–144). London: Hogarth Press.

Freud, S. (1915/1958) *Observations on Transference-Love (Further Recommendations on the Technique of Psycho-Analysis III)*. Standard Edition (Vol. 12, pp. 157–171). London: Hogarth Press.

Freud, S. (1953–1973) *The Standard Edition of the Complete Psychological Works of Sigmund Freud* (24 vols; J. Strachey, Ed. & Trans.). London: Hogarth Press (Referred to in Subsequent References as Standard Edition).

Gill, M. (1988) Converting Psychotherapy into Psychoanalysis. *Contemporary Psychoanalysis*, Vol. 24, No. 2: 262–274.

Gitelson, M. (1952) The Emotional Position of the Analyst in the Psycho-Analytic Situation. *International Journal of Psychoanalysis*, Vol. 33: 1–10.

Gitelson, M. (1962) The Curative Factors in Psycho-Analysis. *International Journal of Psychoanalysis*, Vol. 194–205.

Haynal, A. (1997) A European View: *A Meeting of Minds: Mutuality in Psychoanalysis* by Lewis Aron (Hillsdale, NJ: The Analytic Press, 1996). *Psychoanalytic Dialogues*, Vol. 7: 881–884.

Hoffman, I. (1983/1999) The Patient as Interpreter of the Analyst's Experience. In S. Mitchell and L. Aron (Eds.), *Relational Psychoanalysis: The Emergence of a Tradition*. Hillsdale, NJ: The Analytic Press.

Laing, R. D. (1967) *The Politics of Experience*. New York: Pantheon.

Leavy, S. (1988) *In the Image of God: A Psychoanalyst's View*. New Haven and London: Yale University Press.

Maroda, K. J. (2007) Ethical Considerations of the Home Office. *Psychoanalytic Psychology*, 24: 173–179.

Merkin, D. (2010, August 8) My Life in Therapy: What 40 Years of Talking to Analysts Has Taught Me. *The New York Times Magazine.*

Mitchell, S. and Black, M. (1995) *Freud and Beyond: A History of Modern Psychoanalytic Thought.* New York: Basic Books.

Nacht, S. (1958) Variations in Technique. *International Journal of Psychoanalysis,* Vol. 39: 235–237.

Ogden, T. (1994/1999) The Analytic Third: Working With Intersubjective Clinical Facts. In S. Mitchell and L. Aron (Eds.), *Relational Psychoanalysis: The Emergence of a Tradition.* Hillsdale, NJ: The Analytic Press.

Reich, A. (1958) A Special Variation of Technique. *International Journal of Psychoanalysis*, Vol. 39: 230–234.

Renik, O. (1999) Playing One's Cards Face Up in Analysis: An Approach to the Problem of Self-Disclosure. *The Psychoanalytic Quarterly*, Vol. 68: 521–539.

Szasz, T. (1963) The Concept of Transference. *The International Journal of Psychoanalysis,* Vol. 44: 432–443.

Thompson, M. G. (2004) *The Ethic of Honesty: The Fundamental Rule of Psychoanalysis.* Amsterdam and New York: Rodopi.

Ticho, E. (1982) The Alternate Schools of the Self. *Journal of the American Psychoanalytic Association*, Vol. 30: 840–862.

Ticho, E. and Richards, A. (1982) Psychoanalytic Theories of the Self. *Journal of the American Psychoanalytic Association*, Vol. 30: 717–733.

Tillich, P. (2000) *The Courage to Be.* New Haven and London: Yale University Press.

Deception, Mystification, Trauma

Laing and Freud

R. D. Laing's impact on the mental health profession over the last half century has been both complex and diverse. There is, nevertheless, one consistent and prevalent theme that has persisted in all of Laing's books that is readily discernible to anyone who is familiar with his message. Simply put, Laing's work is epitomized by his opposition to the use of any intervention that runs the risk of alienating one's patients from the very people who are trying to help them. Laing believed that many of the tools customarily employed by psychiatrists and psychotherapists, unbeknownst to themselves, often objectify the patients they treat. Those patients are made to feel less like *persons* who are desperately seeking their emancipation than treatment "entities" who are molded into a preconceived scheme.

The most telling feature of Laing's clinical technique was his radical—some would say provocative—effort to eliminate the enormous gulf that customarily exists between therapists and their patients. This is why Laing insisted that it is important to behave in such a way that reassures one's patients that they're in the presence of another human being like themselves, a person who is no doubt more together but who nonetheless shares the same day-to-day concerns—and the same kind of pain.

To whom was Laing indebted for this markedly ethical imperative in his work? While his intellectual influences can be traced to a variety of sources—Eastern religions, the American family therapy movement, Marxism, existential philosophy, and phenomenology—in this essay, I would like to explore Laing's identification with psychoanalysis. Those who note the importance of Laing's analytic training typically refer to his supervision experience with D. W. Winnicott at the British Psychoanalytic Institute and secondarily to his fellow Scotsman, Ronald Fairbairn, as decisive influences. In America, the work of Harry Stack Sullivan is noted, if not for his psychoanalytic theories,

DOI: 10.4324/9781003429104-11

then for his uncommonly humane treatment of and regard for schizophrenic patients. While all of these influences are undeniable, the one that I believe was the most pervasive, though generally omitted, is that of Freud. It is to this much-neglected influence that I wish to direct my attention.

This is a debt that will undoubtedly surprise many since it is barely mentioned in any of Laing's writings. It is a debt, however, that was frequently noted in the seminars Laing gave at the Philadelphia Association in London, in numerous public lectures he delivered in the 1970s, and to students like myself who enjoyed the opportunity of being supervised by him in their analytic training. While the heart of Laing's teaching never wavered from his fidelity to existential-phenomenology, it was tempered by his identification with psychoanalysis. And it was through Freud, I believe, that his identification with psychoanalysis was principally realized.

In this variety of contexts, then, Laing alluded to Freud frequently. I know that Laing admired Freud, but, what's more, I believe he saw himself as Freud's intellectual heir. Laing never actually claimed to be Freud's successor as, for example, Jacques Lacan did in the 1950s. But, unlike Lacan, Laing was loathe to toot his own horn in terms of his relationship with the psychoanalytic tradition. Besides, Laing was a master of understatement. Even his style of writing owed a lot to the art of allusion. Moreover, he didn't think of himself as a *follower* of any thinker, philosopher, or analyst. Yet, I believe that Freud's influence is palpable and an ever-present force in Laing's writings and, more importantly, in his message.

Truth and Trauma

What is the principal feature that aligns Laing's work with Freud's? I believe that the greatest measure of Laing's debt to Freud concerns his preoccupation with the nature of deception and its relation to trauma. The employment of deception was a cornerstone of Freud's theory about the nature of psychical conflict and its role in virtually all forms of psychopathology. Freud—like most conventional psychiatrists today—initially believed that hysterical symptoms were the consequence of psychological *trauma:* sexual abuse by one of the child's parents. In his "History of the Psychoanalytic Movement," published in 1914, Freud acknowledged that he was initially influenced by Charcot's theory of hysteria. He says:

> Influenced by Charcot's view of the traumatic origin of hysteria, I was readily inclined to accept as true and etiologically significant the

statements made by patients in which they ascribed their symptoms to passive sexual experiences in the first years of childhood—to put it bluntly, to seduction.

(1914, p. 17)

However, the weight of contradictory evidence eventually demolished the efficacy of Charcot's theory. While sexual molestation was probably just as common in 1914 as it is now, it couldn't explain the prevalence of hysterical symptoms in patients who couldn't possibly have been molested. This conclusion was shattering, but it also provided Freud with an important insight. If some patients are capable of complaining about "traumas" that never occurred in reality, then mightn't the *fantasies* concerning those alleged traumas themselves account for the emergence of a neurotic conflict? Freud (1914) concluded that:

If hysterical subjects trace back their symptoms to traumas that are fictitious, then the new fact which emerges is precisely that they create such scenes in *phantasy*, and this *psychical* reality has to be taken into account alongside *practical* reality.

(pp. 17–18)

The implications of this discovery were explosive. It completely altered Freud's (and, with it, the psychoanalytical) conception of trauma. Literally meaning wound, the concept of trauma was adopted from medicine and the procedure that was used to treat injuries. When one thinks of trauma, the words violation, shock, and violence readily come to mind. Whereas Freud initially assumed that neurosis was the consequence of a traumatic experience—due to a painful or disappointing reality—his subsequent rejection of the "seduction theory" altered his way of conceiving the nature of disappointment and our reactions to it.

Freud concluded that the anticipation of trauma can be even more traumatic, in a manner of speaking, than trauma itself; which is to say, one's actual *experience* of trauma. Freud began to appreciate the degree to which young children are vulnerable to disappointment and how hard it is for them to cope with frustration. In fact, children are capable of repressing virtually anything that is too painful to bear, and it is relatively easy for them to replace an objectionable reality with a more inviting fantasy. By defending themselves from painful disappointments—i.e., "traumas"—in this way, children, in effect, don't experience those disappointments in the ordinary sense, even though their disappointments occur in reality and they suffer the effects of them at the time that they happen.

Having repressed what they can't permit themselves to take in, they subsequently become anxious that they will *discover something they mustn't permit themselves to know*. In other words, they intuitively fend off painful experiences that they unconsciously anticipate are about to happen; yet, in reality, they already have.

Truth and Deception

This view of trauma succinctly explains the nature of "psychical conflict" in Freud's model, whether the form of pathology one is talking about is neurosis or a form of psychosis. People who suffer such a conflict are essentially of *two minds:* they struggle against the intrusion of a reality that is too painful to accept on the one hand and harbor a fantasy that is incapable of being realized on the other. Consequently, their lives are always in abeyance. Following this conception of psychopathology, the goal of psychoanalysis is relatively straightforward. Analytic patients try to face up to realities they have always avoided—no matter how painful or disappointing—by *experiencing* them in the analytic situation. To paraphrase an axiom of Heidegger's in a different idiom, we allow the dreadful—which has already happened—to happen.

Ironically, if we can still speak in terms of trauma in the ordinary sense, the traumatic event would have to be redefined as that moment in history when we couldn't bear to experience something that was about to happen. By employing this form of deception on ourselves—in Lacanian terms, a *meconnaissance*—we contrive to delay a painful experience by splitting our existence in two.

Freud's analysis of Dora—though the treatment was a failure—was a prototypical example of the relationship between truth and deception in the etiology of neurosis (Freud, 1905). Dora, who was only eighteen when she began her analysis, had been subjected to the most extraordinary deceptions and intrigues imaginable. Her father had been involved in a love affair with a married woman right under Dora's nose—and presumably her mother's—for years. He even conspired to look the other way while his mistress's husband—the infamous Mr. K—attempted to seduce Dora, a child only fourteen years old.

Though he failed then, two years later, Mr. K tried again. This time Dora took the matter to her father, not realizing that he was aware of Mr. K's intentions and even supported them. Dora's father went through the motions of confronting Mr. K, who ostensibly denied everything. Dora subsequently fell into a prolonged depression, compounded by a host of related hysterical symptoms.

By the time she was eighteen and apparently suicidal, Dora's father took her to see Freud. Her brief analysis quickly uncovered the intrigues that Dora herself had "known" but repressed. Perhaps the most remarkable aspect of Freud's inquiry into the causes of Dora's condition concerned the question: what specifically drove Dora into her pathological condition, the traumatic events that transpired at the hands of her family, or the consequent *self-deceptions* Dora employed to protect herself from disappointment?

Freud suspected that Dora was actually in love with Mr. K but that her devotion to her father and the intense jealousy she felt over his affair with Mrs. K made it impossible for her to confront the reality of her situation. In other words, as unsettling as her family's duplicity must have been, it was Dora's unwillingness to face the truth—i.e., about her own feelings—that provoked the neurotic conflict she now suffered.[1]

One of the most edifying things about this case that strikes me as particularly significant concerns Freud's evolving conception of trauma. Whether the reality one is confronted with is so terrible that no one could be expected to accommodate it or whether the rejection of that reality simply doesn't suit the individual who happens to be faced with it, it still comes down to the same thing: *the rejection of reality, for whatever reason, always gives rise to a "dual reality" that manifests a pathogenic conflict.*

Let's take a moment to review where we are so far. Freud's conception of psychopathology was rooted in the notion that our intolerance of a frustrating (experience of) reality compels us to reject that reality and substitute in its place fantasies that compensate for what was denied us. This stratagem epitomizes the plight of neurotics, who are so attached to their fantasies that they will protect them from anything that threatens to intrude.

On the other hand, Freud thought that the graver forms of psychopathology—such as schizophrenia—follow a modified course. Like neurotics, schizophrenics also reject realities that elicit intolerable frustration. However, the schizophrenic's fantasies diverge from those of neurotics in significant ways. Freud believed that the psychotic process was essentially driven by narcissism, occasioning a withdrawal of libido into oneself which permits psychotics to obtain a measure of gratification that is denied them in reality. Yet, the fantasy life of psychotics—and this is even more pronounced in schizophrenia—is inherently *distressing*. Their fantasies are typically tormenting and delusional.

Why, if psychotics withdraw from reality in order to *relieve* suffering, does their defense against frustration occasion fantasies that are intrinsically unpleasurable? Freud compared this phenomenon to disturbing dreams, which, like pleasing ones, are a means of escaping reality. He conjectured that we experience distressing dreams as punishment for entertaining fantasies that are forbidden to us in waking life. Similarly, the psychotics' withdrawal from reality is untenable. A portion of the reality they seek to escape seeps in and—in life as in bad dreams—"punishes" them for their flight (Freud, 1924).

Laing and Freud

Laing accepted the basic premise of Freud's thesis but took it further. Following Sullivan and Frieda Fromm-Reichmann, he suspected that the reality schizophrenics are trying to get away from must be more harrowing than the one that engenders simple frustration. In other words, psychotics must have a good reason to be even more terrified of reality than neurotics, who, in turn, typically comply with reality but diminish its effects by repressing their desires instead.

He concluded that frustration alone couldn't explain the psychotic's extreme withdrawal. If Freud's principal thesis was correct—that the psychotic rejects reality because it's so painful—then what would compel someone to withdraw in such a radical fashion? Isn't it possible, Laing conjectured, that the reality psychotics reject is qualitatively different from the one we ordinarily encounter? This was the question that prompted Laing to seek an alternative to narcissism as the principal motive force in schizophrenia.

Laing proceeded to apply Freud's conception of psychic trauma to his own research into extreme forms of delusional confusion but in a more dialectical framework. While Freud emphasized the use of fantasy as a way of avoiding objectionable realities, Laing was interested in the means by which people systematically employ deception on one another in order to manipulate the *other* person's experience—and that person's reality as well. This dialectical dimension to my experience of others—what I think they think about me; and what they, in fact, think but conceal from me—comprised

Laing's definition of social phenomenology: *my internal critique of how others affect—and sometimes play havoc with—my experience.*

Laing concluded that schizophrenia is the consequence of deceptions that are employed on someone who assumes he is being told the truth—and who depends on what that person is telling him to be true. Whereas Freud conceived of trauma in terms of the frustration that thwarts an anticipated pleasure, Laing envisioned a different form of trauma that could specifically account for psychotic anxiety and withdrawal. He saw this in terms of states of confusion that follow when one's reality has been savaged, not through self-deception alone but as a consequence of being duped or deceived by another. While these two forms of deception (Laing's and Freud's) are not mutually exclusive—in fact, they typically interact—the frustration of pleasure is even more poignant when compounded by the loss of my hold on reality.

Laing and Deception

The nature of deception was a common theme in Laing's writings throughout the 1960s, his most prolific decade as an author. Ironically, *The Divided Self*—Laing's first and most famous book, published in 1960—is the only one in which deception *between* persons (as opposed to self-deception) doesn't play a major role. It was a classic existentialist study about the experience of going mad but said little about the social context that would subsequently play such a critical role in Laing's thinking. It did, however, presage what would come later with a compelling exploration of the relationship between self-deception and psychopathology.

Laing's next book, *Self and Others,* published the following year (1961), examined—as its title implies—the effect that human beings have on *each other* in the etiology of severe psychological disturbance. A telling prelude to what would come to epitomize Laing's clinical philosophy can be found in a brief reference in that work to Heidegger's essay, "On the Essence of Truth" (Heidegger, 1977; and see Thompson, 1994a, pp. 51–92). Noting Heidegger's reliance on the pre-Socratic term *aletheia*—which conceives truth as whatever emerges from concealment—Laing put his own twist on Heidegger's thesis by emphasizing the interdependency between candor and secrecy—an innovation that probably owes more to Sartre and Freud than to Heidegger's ontological preoccupations.

Many of the terms that Laing introduced in that book for the first time—e.g., collusion, mystification, attribution, injunction, untenable positions—were coined for the purpose of providing a conceptual vocabulary that could help explain how human beings, in their everyday interactions with each other, are able to distort the truth so effectively that they are able to affect each other's reality, and their sanity as well. It was just this vocabulary that Laing suggested was missing in Freud's psychoanalytic theories. Moreover, Laing believed that the subsequent object relations theories that followed Freud's lacked this more personal—in effect, existential—dimension to the etiology of psychosis.

All of Laing's books published in that decade expanded on this theme and developed it in a variety of ways. For example, in 1964 Laing and his research colleague, Aaron Esterson, published a study of eleven schizophrenic patients, emphasizing their interactions with members of their respective families. *Sanity, Madness and the Family* (Laing and Esterson, 1964) stands out as one of the most impressive phenomenological studies of this kind ever undertaken. Laing deftly demonstrated how, in every family they studied, massive forms of trickery, deception, and mystification were systematically employed against each of the schizophrenic family members—all daughters—by their parents. One of the patients, whom Laing called "Maya" (alluding to the Hindu term, meaning illusion), is typical of the families studied. Her parents, who come across as pretty disturbed themselves, believed that their daughter had special powers which enabled her to read their minds. The father spoke openly—when his daughter wasn't present—of having systematically employed "tests" on his daughter to confirm that Maya, indeed, could tell what her parents were thinking. Maya, in turn, suspected that something of the sort was being done to her, but when she actually confronted her parents in one of the family sessions, they coyly winked at Laing and denied it—as they had done all her life.

In case after case, Laing and Esterson unearthed a casual and often chilling array of deceptive maneuvers of this kind employed by the parents against their children. In effect, they were systematically distorting the truth about their efforts to manipulate their children and, by that distortion, twisted their hold on reality by hopelessly confusing them. Employing an argument that has come to epitomize the controversy that is now associated with Laing's reputation, he argued that even if their research didn't conclusively prove that acts of mystification "cause" schizophrenia, incidents of this kind were ubiquitous in all the families they studied. The reader is left to draw his or her own conclusions. Laing didn't specifically explore what might motivate parents of schizophrenics to manipulate their children in this fashion, nor did he argue that these forms of mystification are unique to such families. Indeed, mystification is inherent in the hypocrisy of everyday life. A casual glance through the cases studied, however, offers a fairly compelling picture of histrionic parents who employ any number of devices and manipulative stratagems in order to get their way. They remain oblivious to the effects that their behavior is having on their children, even if it is pointed out to them. Parents suffering from narcissistic, borderline, or paranoid personality organizations would presumably engender similar or even worse forms of mystification. Remaining faithful to phenomenological methodology, however, Laing resisted the temptation to speculate on these considerations.

His approach to this problem has nonetheless led many parents of schizophrenics to accuse Laing of blaming them for the plight of their children. In fact, Laing attributed this problem to the human condition. Human beings are devious and dishonest creatures who, without thinking, violate and betray one another as a matter of course. Schizophrenia is only one of the many consequences of this state of affairs. Laing believed it is our duty as members of society to do what we can to rise above our plight—and to be wary of those who know not what they do. He pointed out that psychiatrists and psychotherapists need to address this problem just like the rest of us and guard against committing similar mistakes with their patients. The history of psychiatric treatment is a testament to that community's sometimes callous failure to do so.

That same year (1964), Laing and another colleague, David Cooper, published a study of Jean-Paul Sartre, a major influence on Laing's thinking. Sartre's notion of "bad faith" resonated with Laing's growing awareness of the devastating effects of deviousness on the formation of the self and our subjective experience. Sartre's later efforts to merge his existentialist philosophy into a more social theory mirrored Laing's endeavors to develop a truly interpersonal conception of psychopathology (Laing and Cooper, 1964).

In 1966, Laing published another study with two colleagues at the Tavistock Institute, Russell Lee and Herbert Phillipson, which examined the frequently confused communication patterns of married couples—the same patterns evinced in magnified form among families of schizophrenics (Laing, Phillipson, and Lee, 1966). This now-neglected book is radical even now, offering a compelling method of working with couples that is generally lacking in the literature today. Phillipson a research psychologist, devised a testing device that could be used to "diagnose" a given couple's (mis)communication patterns, whereas Lee, a family therapist, contributed his knowledge of systems theory that was adopted by the American family therapy movement. The opening chapters, however, were clearly penned by Laing, who borrowed from Hegel's master/slave dialectic in order to expose the level of duplicity and deception that commonly exists in love relationships.

In 1967, Laing published a collection of papers that would contribute significantly to his growing fame: *The Politics of Experience*. In this book, Laing was less concerned with exploring the phenomenology of experience than with what he depicted as the everyday "politics" of one's experience of others.[2] He wanted to explore how other people invariably *affect* my experience and even determine what it is, whether, for example, they value my experience and confirm it or, on the contrary, are threatened by my experience and disavow it.

This was the book where Laing categorically insisted that severe forms of psychopathology are always the consequence of human deviousness and declared that all of us are really "murderers and prostitutes" when the mask of our social veneer is stripped away (Laing, 1967, p. *xiv*). The theme that emerged in every chapter was the same. Human beings—often unwittingly—employ acts of casual deception over one another in the name of altruistic motives, though the effects of their behavior are frequently violent and even "traumatic." The book had an explosive impact on an entire generation of psychology students by reminding them that what is most important in the therapeutic experience is the caring and straightforward manner in which clinicians treat their patients, not because of clever or convoluted techniques—a page that Laing obviously borrowed from both Harry Stack Sullivan and Freud, but geared to a new generation of students. This rather novel definition of violence—adapted from Hegel and Marx— became the cornerstone of all of Laing's subsequent books.

Finally, in 1970, Laing published a series of vignettes that dramatically conveyed the sense of being caught in a net or an impasse with persons to whom one is attached but who it seems are strangling one's existence (Laing, 1970). Laing called them "knots." Sartre's play, "No Exit," was undoubtedly an inspiration for Laing's efforts to create—like Freud's case history—this new literary genre. This device was introduced in order to depict, phenomenologically, the actual experience of being mystified, derived from the many hours Laing spent listening to his patients recount the knots that they were trapped in.

Laing and Dora

Ironically, Freud's analysis of Dora, the most famous analytic treatment ever published, is also a prototypical example of the kind of manipulation and deception that Laing believed is employed in families of schizophrenics. Laing once told me that the case had a profound impact on his thinking and that he was even startled, in subsequent readings of it, by the degree of mystification that Dora's father employed against her. In his analysis of the case, however, Freud argued that the deceptions Dora had employed *against herself* served as the etiological factors that eventually culminated in her neurotic condition. On the other hand, she was also subjected to relentless acts of subterfuge, deviousness, and outright lying, all for the purpose of denying what everybody knew was going on. The most extravagant incident of this kind of deception—i.e., mystification—was when Dora's father conspired with Mr. K (who had propositioned her to become his mistress) to convince her that she had only imagined Mr. K's attempt at seduction. In other words, what Dora had experienced in reality was reinterpreted back to her, by the two men whom she loved the most, as *mere inventions of a disturbed and oversexed imagination.* This is the kind of mystification—the reinterpretation of one's experience as fantasy—that Laing attributed to the etiology of psychotic disintegration.

If Laing's thesis is correct, why then did Dora not develop a psychosis instead of the most celebrated case of hysteria ever documented? In fact, Laing never said that mystification is exclusive to families of schizophrenics. Laing and Esterson had originally intended to follow up their study of schizophregenic families with one that examines the interactions of so-called normal ones. They conducted a portion of that study but never reported their findings. According to Laing (in a seminar he gave at the Philadelphia Association in the mid-70s), the normal families also employed mystification, but the implications of this observation, since the study was never completed, were inconclusive.

On the other hand, there are obvious factors that distinguished Dora's family from a schizophregenic one. For one thing, Dora was as devious with her family as they were with her. She was an exceptionally clever young woman and quite precocious for her age. In fact, she was so furious with her father that subsequent to her aborted analysis with Freud, she became devoted to exacting revenge against him as well as every other man she was subsequently involved with (Deutsch, 1985).

Dora's treatment with Freud opened her eyes to aspects of her history that she hadn't anticipated. She apparently wasn't prepared for the revelations that her analysis so suddenly disclosed. She was alternately shocked and dismayed at the many deceptions that had been employed against her, which Freud uncovered, one by one, as her history unfolded. Yet, Dora never lost her head throughout the analysis. What's more, she wasn't fooled for a minute by her father's (and Mr. K's) efforts at mystification. While the pre-psychotic will typically comply with the mystifying parent by abdicating his or her perception of reality in deference to that of the parents, Dora immediately assumed that Mr. K was lying when he contradicted her version of what had transpired between them. And when Freud suggested that her father must have been lying to her, too, she was able to accept this unsettling discovery in spite of its heartbreaking ramifications.

Another important distinction between the way Dora's family employed mystification and the way the family of a schizophrenic might is that, in Dora's case, the purpose of the mystification was simply to *deny Dora's accusations*. Dora's father and Mr. K colluded together in their deception of Dora in order to avoid the potentially embarrassing revelation of the secret agreement they had made between them. They just didn't want Dora—now that she had openly protested—to spoil their scheme.

On the other hand, the motives for which mystification is employed in families of schizophrenics entail a more subtle purpose: to actually subvert the child's experience of reality. Indeed, the person against whom the mystification is employed is desperately trying to *disengage* him or herself from the domination of parental figures who are endeavoring to control what their child *thinks and believes,* not merely the child's behavior (Thompson, 1985, pp. 88–117). In Dora's case, her father was only trying to get her out of the way. His ostensible goal wasn't to increase her dependency on him but to appease Mr. K, whose wife, after all, was his mistress! And unlike the pre-schizophrenic, Dora wasn't trying to emancipate herself from the situation she was in; she was actually trying to prolong her connection with her father, who had substituted in her place Mr. K's wife.

Laing hypothesized that the type of "traumas" neurotics and schizophrenics respectively suffer are categorically different, even if each coincidentally occasions familial deception. Being lied to isn't, in and of itself, enough to generate a psychotic reaction. One has to take into account the purpose for which one is being deceived and the effect that it has on one's (experience of) reality, phenomenologically speaking. Furthermore, there needs to exist a level of dependency in which the mystified child feels trapped—and from which that child cannot risk separation.

While mystification is employed in order to manipulate others to adopt an untenable point of view, not everyone is such easy prey to this form of deception. One has to *want* to believe the fabrication that is employed, even if it doesn't coincide with what one instinctively knows is true. Most of us either defend our perceptions in the face of opposition or we revise them in deference to the other person's. In effect, we give the other person the benefit of the doubt. We may subsequently discover that we were lied to, duped, deceived, or whatever, and when we realize we've been tricked, we may feel like a fool. Perhaps we're grateful for having discovered the truth about something that never seemed right in the first place. Or we might wish we hadn't learned the truth, but now that we have we accept it and try, for better or worse, to live with it.

This was the dilemma that confronted Dora. She discovered things about her father she didn't want to know and was in anguish because of her realization. Dora's problem, as Freud noted in his report, was that she *couldn't forgive* her father for having betrayed her. She was so bent on revenge that she devoted her existence, body and soul, to punishing every man with whom she became involved—including Freud. This is the kind of knot neurotics frequently tie themselves in. They feel betrayed by the object of their love but can't forgive *or* forget and move on with their lives (Thompson, 1994a, pp. 110–114).

Psychotics, however, lack the facility that was available to Dora to *openly protest* the deceptions that are employed against them. They know the truth but struggle with themselves to disavow it. They try to comply with the mystification, but they can't ignore their experience, either. They split their reality in two and pay the ultimate price for serving two masters. Their withdrawal from reality enables them to both comply with *and* oppose a reality they can't bring themselves to accept.

Mystification and Trauma

Laing didn't dispute Freud's distinction between neurotic and psychotic symptom formation; generally, he thought that Freud's conception of it, from a phenomenological point of view, was extraordinary. What he did question was the *nature* of reality that neurotics and psychotics encounter and whether their respective experiences of it are qualitatively different. While Laing agreed with Freud's view that reality is inherently experienced as being *difficult,* he also believed, because of the range of realities we are capable of experiencing, that the particulars of a given reality must play a critical role in the etiology of our respective reactions to it—whether for or against. What's more, some of us may be acutely aware of what is happening around us and, because of our precocious knowledge, pay a huge price for knowing what we lack the maturity to accept. The fact that many schizophrenics have exceptionally high IQs suggests that they may know too much for their own good.

Yet, some analysts have accused Laing of reverting to a pre-analytic conception of trauma when he proposed that mystification is etiologically decisive in people diagnosed as schizophrenic. The idea that schizophrenics are passive victims of deception would appear to overlook the importance of *agency* in those who fall prey to madness (if, indeed, "madness" genuinely characterizes their plight). Doesn't the so-called victim also play a role in his or her rejection of reality? In fact, Laing's first book, *The Divided Self,* adopted the more Sartrian view that madness is "chosen" as a way out of an unlivable situation; in effect, an existential choice.

But Laing never suggested that psychotic individuals adopt a strictly passive position (Thompson, 1985, pp. 88–117). He was simply pointing out, following Freud, that our hold on reality is fragile at best. We all struggle with reality to varying degrees. Whether we repress or deny reality, who can say with any certainty that being "out of touch" with it categorically depicts the pathological condition? After all, if we weren't aware of what a given reality was, how could we manage to "defend" ourselves against it so successfully?

Following Heidegger, Laing adopted the view that our *experience* of reality depends on what we *believe* is true. We have to develop some notion of what is true about a given situation in order to accept *or* reject it. But what if the situation we're in is such that reality keeps shifting and sliding away just when we thought we understood it? We would soon find ourselves in such a state of perplexity that we couldn't be sure what we're accepting or disavowing, whether it was real or fallacious. In effect, we would be so out of touch with our experience of "reality" that we couldn't be sure *what* our experience was.

In fact, Laing's advocacy of becoming more completely whom one is through experience owes less to a phenomenological critique of its nature—such as, for example, was performed by Hegel (see Heidegger, 1970, and Husserl, 1973)—than it does to his conviction that every human being has the fundamental right to his or her experience and not have it indifferently subverted or destroyed. This is vouchsafed in Laing's development of a politics of experience, in fact, an ethics of experience, a technical innovation that was as indebted to Laing's Scottish background as to Sartre's later philosophy. He saw therapy as a sort of "DMZ" where we're granted temporary asylum in order to explore experience and determine its unconscious determinants by coming to terms with the truths that experience discloses. In other words, to truly experience something, according to Laing, entailed an ethical endeavor: a call to develop our innate capacity for becoming more honest with ourselves.

Laing never wavered from his advocacy of remaining *faithful* to experience by being true to what, from the vantage of experience, is one's personal view. That doesn't necessarily mean that one is "correct" about one's beliefs or that those beliefs have to be correct in order to enjoy the privilege of having them, an example of healthy narcissism. Laing championed our inalienable right to experience things according to our predilections. We also have the right to be wrong by making mistakes and learning from them. Or maybe not. In other words, the task of therapy isn't a tool employed to adapt oneself to the expectations of others. Endeavoring to do so is one of the principal symptoms of neurosis. Instead, therapy aims to reconcile the split we have created in *ourselves*. In order to do that, we need to come to our senses and learn to accept who we are. Even if our struggle with reality gives rise to alienation, compromise and conciliation is no more a solution than isolating ourselves from others. If we ever hope to resolve this dilemma, we need to accommodate the disappointments and betrayals that are rife with living. But the first step in doing that is to have our experience of the past confirmed and not dismissed as symptomatic of "pathology."

The reason Laing took such pains to labor this aspect of human existence was because—like Freud—he believed that we, because we're so scared, take advantage of others in order to ease our frustrations. Children and mental health patients, the most vulnerable members of society, are the most frequent targets of these tactics. Sometimes therapists, in their zeal to effect change, resort to questionable tactics of their own. They become manipulative and, without knowing it, transform therapy into a sort of contest where the more clever protagonist "wins."

Freud was sensitive to the difficulty that every psychoanalyst faces in trying to bring about change without employing coercive maneuvers. He coined a number of terms—e.g., countertransference, neutrality, abstinence, therapeutic and educative ambition—that were intended to alert us to the inherent dangers that our power over patients occasions. Similarly, Laing's therapeutic technique could be reduced to a single preoccupying concern: how honestly are therapists really behaving with their patients, and how honest are therapists actually capable of being? Laing's devotion to these ethical considerations owes a considerable debt to Freud's "fundamental rule," the pledge exacted from each patient to be candid about whatever comes to mind. In other words, patients promise to reveal what they're thinking and try not to lie about it.

Of course, Freud discovered that this is the one thing patients are loathe to do. They're afraid of disclosing their well-kept secrets because of what, in turn, those secrets may reveal about *themselves*. On the other hand, Laing believed that many patients have good reason to be dubious about exposing themselves since their experience may have taught them that it's wrong to think or feel the way they do. Consequently, they've "forgotten" what they think and haven't a clue who they really are.

Laing, however, believed that the "fundamental rule" shouldn't be construed as simply a promise to verbalize one's thoughts. It entails a pledge to plumb the depths of experience while accepting responsibility for the person one turns out to be. That can't happen unless the therapist, in his or her neutrality, is completely accepting of who we reveal ourselves to be, warts and all. Though Laing was uncomfortable with the idea of exacting the kind of "oath" from his patients that Freud advocated, he nevertheless believed that some form of implicit understanding has to be reached between therapists and their patients, one that is rooted in mutual respect. Patients have to learn to put up with the idiosyncrasies of their therapist just as therapists should be gracious and put up with theirs.

Conclusion

When all is said and done, Laing believed that psychotics are not only more anxious than those who are not psychotic, they are also confused. If we want to help them find a way out of their confusion, it is imperative to understand what the nature of their confusion is about—and not do or say anything that might make them even more confused than they already are. What is the source of their confusion? What could possibly engender the kind of trauma that occasions psychotic disintegration? Basically, Laing attributed it to lying. Yet, mystification isn't the only form of deception that may subvert one's reality. Victims of duplicity, for example, are often confused about the truth but *don't realize how confused they are*. They may sense that something is wrong, but when they try to address it, they encounter evasion—just as Maya did in her family—compounding even further the deterioration of their hold on reality.

Laing suggested that this kind of deception can be devastating. When one finally discovers the truth about something that was concealed for many years, the victim of this deception may be so discombobulated that he feels his reality has been forcibly taken from his grasp. In his later writings and lectures, Laing recounted many vignettes of this sort, of people who had lost a chunk of their existence through having been deceived, who felt cheated out of a life they had accepted for what it seemed. When they turn to therapy, they desperately cling to the years that have been stolen from them. They feel lost between two worlds, the one they thought was real and the one that was suddenly thrust upon them, without any warning. The task of therapy, Laing suggested, is to help them mend the rupture that lies at the heart of their existence by letting go of their failed disappointments and starting over. This is perhaps the last thing that people in therapy really want to do, but it's the only way out of the impasse.

Laing's work was rooted in his uncanny sensitivity to the effects of deception on our relations with others. Like Freud, he believed that fidelity to one's personal truth was the royal road to psychic freedom. Laing saw his role as a clinician as one of helping people "untie" the knots they were in. He believed that the best way of helping them do that was by doing the opposite of what, they believed, had been done to them in the past. He didn't question whether their experience of the past was correct or delusional. He gave them the benefit of the doubt. Like Freud, he treated them as honestly as he was capable of doing.

Laing has been taken to task for suggesting that mental health professionals are less invested in being truthful with their patients than they are with "adapting" them to conventional norms by any means possible—even against their will. Yet, we should remember that Laing wasn't the first to make this accusation. Freud made similar comments about his psychiatric colleagues in Vienna. In fact, Freud distinguished psychoanalysis from conventional medical treatment on precisely these grounds when he reminded us that "psychoanalytic treatment is founded on truthfulness" and that "it is dangerous to depart from this foundation" (1915, p. 164). If there were any doubt as to what his intentions were when he made these remarks, he added that "anyone who has become saturated in the analytic technique will no longer be able to make use of the lies and pretenses which a doctor normally finds unavoidable" (p. 164).

By the time Laing appeared on the scene in the 1950s, he had begun to suspect—and was later convinced—that even psychoanalysts had begun to depart from Freud's admonition, an observation he alluded to in many of his lectures and that informs his gradual estrangement from the psychoanalytic community. It seemed to Laing that most analysts had become so taken with the complicated nature of unconscious fantasy and its interpretation that they had forgotten how to be real with their patients when it was indicated. Though Laing valued interpretations and employed them in his practice, he believed that the psychoanalyst's principal task is to *validate our patient's experience*. The goal of therapy should be to help others find their way to the ground of their experience through their relationship with their therapist.

Ironically, many psychoanalysts today perceive therapy as a respite from reality, where patients are protected even from any kind of contact with their therapists that may make them feel the least bit uncomfortable. It's surprising that Freud has come to epitomize the standard for this aloof, "classical" technique when, in fact, he advocated a balance between the real and the symbolic that Laing believed is disappearing in contemporary analytic practice across the board. How, he asked, does one propose to exclude the realness of the patient-analyst relationship from the treatment experience? Who, he pondered, is actually more frightened of the reality in question, patients or their analysts? That is a thought worth pondering.

Notes

1 See my *The Truth About Freud's Technique: The Encounter with the Real* (1994a, pp. 93–132) for a comprehensive discussion of Freud's analysis of Dora.
2 For an appraisal of the explicitly phenomenological dimension to Laing's conception of experience and its clinical application see my "The Fidelity to Experience in Existential Psychoanalysis" (1994b).

References

Deutsch, F. (1985) A Footnote to Freud's 'Fragment of an Analysis of a Case of Hysteria.' In C. Bernheimer and C. Kahane (Eds.), *In Dora's Case: Freud-Hysteria-Feminism* (pp. 35–43). New York: Columbia University Press.

Freud, S. (1905/1953) *Fragment of an Analysis of a Case of Hysteria.* Standard Edition (Vol. 7, pp. 3–122). London: Hogarth Press.

Freud, S. (1914/1957) *On the History of the Psychoanalytic Movement.* Standard Edition (Vol. 14, pp. 3–66). London: Hogarth Press.

Freud, S. (1915/1958) *Observations on Transference-Love (Further Recommendations on the Technique of Psychoanalysis III).* Standard Edition (Vol. 12, pp. 157–171). London: Hogarth Press.

Freud, S. (1924/1961) *The Loss of Reality in Neurosis and Psychosis.* Standard Edition (Vol. 19, pp. 183–187). London: Hogarth Press.

Freud, S. (1953–1973) *The Standard Edition of the Complete Psychological Works of Sigmund Freud* (24 vols; J. Strachey, Ed. & Trans.). London: Hogarth Press (Referred to in Subsequent References as Standard Edition).

Heidegger, M. (1970) *Hegel's Concept of Experience.* San Francisco: Harper and Row.

Heidegger, M. (1977) *Basic Writings.* San Francisco: Harper and Row.

Husserl, E. (1973) *Experience and Judgement.* Evanston: Northwestern University Press.

Laing, R. D. (1960) *The Divided Self.* New York: Pantheon.

Laing, R. D. (1961) *Self and Others.* New York: Pantheon.

Laing, R. D. (1967) *The Politics of Experience.* New York: Pantheon.

Laing, R. D. (1970) *Knots.* New York: Pantheon.

Laing, R. D. and Cooper, D. L. (1964) *Reason and Violence.* London: Tavistock.

Laing, R. D. and Esterson, A. (1964) *Sanity, Madness and the Family.* New York: Basic Books.

Laing, R. D., Phillipson, H. and Lee, A. R. (1966) *Interpersonal Perception.* London: Tavistock.

Thompson, M. G. (1985) *The Death of Desire: A Study in Psychopathology.* New York: New York University Press.

Thompson, M. G. (1994a) *The Truth About Freud's Technique: The Encounter With the Real.* New York: New York University Press.

Thompson, M. G. (1994b) The Fidelity to Experience in Existential Psychoanalysis. In K. Schneider and R. May (Eds.), *The Psychology of Existence: An Integrative, Clinical Perspective* (pp. 233–247). New York: McGraw-Hill.

Chapter 12

Free Association

A Technical Principle or Model for Psychoanalytic Education?

I would like to begin with a dogmatic statement that is intended solely for the sake of discussion and, hopefully, will not alienate my many friends who teach in either psychoanalytic or academic institutions. I know that many of them are involved in training psychoanalysts in universities, that they probably owe a great deal to such institutions, and are understandably grateful for the education they obtained from that experience. Others who are not involved in academia as such may be associated with free-standing psychoanalytic institutes that are nevertheless modeled on academic education and, for that reason, they may feel identified (at least in principle) with the academic model of education.

Though my psychoanalytic training was not at a university, I was educated, like everyone else, at a university in my undergraduate education and, like many, obtained a PhD in psychology at a graduate institute. So my experience is not that alien to yours, though I confess I sometimes wonder if I have lost my memory of having traveled here from another galaxy when I realize how out-of-step I feel when I have the occasion to teach at a graduate school, which I do now and then in California. Be that as it may, I believe that psychoanalytic education of some sort belongs in academic institutions, even if I am about to share with you my reservations about conceiving psychoanalytic training along academic lines.

What I wish to explore isn't the pros and cons of academic education but rather psychoanalytic training and the relationship between the technique of free association and the process of becoming a psychoanalyst. Having said that, I shall preface my remarks with a statement that I hope will put my sentiments into perspective. That statement is:

> The academic model of education is ill-suited to train and educate people to become psychoanalysts.

DOI: 10.4324/9781003429104-12

Why do I say this? The first reason is perhaps the most obvious one because *psychoanalysts are essentially concerned with the way human beings treat each other*. Psychoanalysts are human beings who help others come into their own by treating them as they would like to be treated themselves, with a modicum of respect, compassion, and honesty. After all, their patients are people who are simply struggling to survive in a difficult world by trying to come to terms with who they are while endeavoring to get along with others the best they can. This sounds simple enough, so I probably haven't said anything thus far that anyone would necessarily object to, though I am aware that what I am saying could be said another way, one that would place more emphasis on other aspects of the treatment experience that arises in the course of it, such as, for example, relief from mental anguish, the critique of one's fantasy life, increasing one's capacity to love, resolution of inner conflicts, making the unconscious conscious, and so on.

Such agendas are nevertheless less likely to succeed if the analyst reduces the cause of a patient's suffering to some "condition" or other that entails a lot of know-how and expertise in order to "treat" it effectively. Psychology programs in universities, for example, assume that students can learn how to be therapists by studying it in books. This, after all, is fundamental to academic education: a tautology, as it were. One reads the theory and what others claim to know about its application in treatment and then is evaluated on how well the material has been absorbed before finally being permitted to treat a patient oneself.

Now I'm going to add something that you may feel is even more provocative than what I said a moment ago: I don't believe that this way of preparing to be a psychoanalyst is feasible. That's right; I'm not suggesting that it is a less "desirable" way of training to be a psychoanalyst or even a more "impoverished" way, but that it is *not even possible to become a psychoanalyst by this method*. Though some people indeed become psychoanalysts in this fashion—and many of them become exemplary analysts who have contributed immeasurably to the field—the *becoming* of the psychoanalyst they have become has nothing to do with the academic component of their education. Let me explain what I mean by this apparently absurd statement.

The basis of my argument is based on a simple observation, yet one that many educators seem to have ignored in spite of having noted this observation themselves. That observation is:

We learn about human misery from our own suffering, and we learn to relieve it by coming to terms with the suffering that we have experienced and continue to experience every day of our lives.

Training in psychoanalysis should be concerned with helping students get in touch with the roots of their suffering by devoting themselves to the practical task of alleviating that suffering from a psychoanalytic perspective. Once they have managed to do this, they will have obtained the necessary authority to help other people with such a task, the nature of which they will have experienced first-hand. Why are academic institutions ill-equipped to provide the rudiments of this experience? Indeed, why are psychoanalytic institutes, which are modeled on academic education, not as suited for this form of education as they once were? On the other hand, by what criteria can one claim that psychoanalytic institutes are doing such a bad job of it when, after all, they have educated nearly all of the psychoanalysts who are practicing today? I would be the first to admit that the enormous success that the institution of psychoanalysis has enjoyed—until recently—can be explained by the fact that most psychoanalysts have been educated in psychoanalytic institutes. On the other hand, in some people's minds, this also accounts for the terrible mess that psychoanalysis is currently facing, not only in the United States but, with the odd and perhaps momentary exception (Argentina), all over the world.

I'm not trying to lay all of psychoanalysis's woes at the doorstep of its training institutions—there is no question in my mind that recent developments in psychopharmacology partially account for its current malaise—but I have formed the opinion over the past quarter of a century that the untold numbers of exemplary psychoanalysts who have been educated in those very institutions and are eminent members of their field have achieved such renown, not *because* of their educational experience, but *in spite of it*. Moreover, it is they who have given their institutions the good name they enjoy—not the reverse.

Don't misunderstand me: the last thing I want to do is engage in a tirade against psychoanalytic institutions. As I have already intimated, some of my best friends have been educated in them, and I am a member of one myself. What I do wish to do is simply share my observations with you and the implications I have derived from them. The principal lesson that I have drawn from these observations is this: psychoanalytic *education* should mirror the experience of psychoanalytic *therapy*, yet the analytic training experience is, in virtually every case that I know, a fundamentally different animal from the experience of psychoanalysis itself. But, if psychoanalytic training is to be modeled on psychoanalysis, what feature of psychoanalysis is essential to one's experience of it?

Simply, psychoanalysis revolves around the experience of "free associa-tion." Without any agenda in mind and with no ostensible goal or plan, a space is created in the consulting room wherein analytic patients are free to roam around, deepen, and gain access to previously unacknowledged dimensions of their experience while confiding its mysteries to another per-son. This is a process that obviously invites and, in turn, depends on self-disclosure. Though there are currently many schools of psychoanalysis, and each has a different notion about how such disclosures should be treated, the essential element that binds all the analytic schools together, no matter what their theoretical orientation may be, is that free association is an indis-pensable element of every analytic encounter. Whether one perceives in this experience the mutative element of analytic therapy or simply a method for gaining access to the unconscious, virtually all psychoanalytic practitioners employ free association in their treatment scheme, even if they disagree as to what free association is. What, then, *is* free association? Like so many of the technical rules that govern psychoanalytic technique (e.g., neutral-ity, abstinence, working-through, analysis of resistance, handling of the transference, confidentiality, the art of interpretation), there isn't a defini-tive description of what free association entails anywhere in the psycho-analytic literature, not even in Freud. It means different things to different people. Typically, Freud said next to nothing about free association, so one may interpret the basis of its method and the rules of its application in any number of ways, given the paucity of instruction that Freud offered about it. Therefore, all I can offer are highlights of what the irreducible elements of free association are for me and how these elements inform the manner in which psychoanalysts and psychoanalytic candidates learn:

> The process of self-disclosure, to which the act of free association refers, provides analytic patients the freedom to simply speak their own minds and to think their own thoughts while making whatever sense of their experience they are able to, for whatever length of time it may take, for however long that may be.

One of the cardinal principles of psychoanalysis is that the analyst doesn't direct the treatment or coerce the patient to follow one course of action over another. Yet, upon entering a typical psychoanalytic institute, little of this atmosphere is in evidence. Indeed, everything that will be learned is more or less determined in advance. Students are told what is important to know and what isn't, and candidates are evaluated according to how well they have learned what the instructor thinks they should know. *My thesis is that this manner of instruction is more suited to academic education than to training analysts.* Whereas academic institutions are obliged to quantify the knowledge they profess to know and disseminate it accordingly, the training of psychoanalysts follows virtually the *opposite* direction. Analysts are taught—if this is the right word—to "forget" what they think they know and, when this is accomplished, to learn what they can, not from this supervisor or that, but from the patients in their care.

The key to analytic education isn't the acquisition of knowledge but the cultivation of naïveté.

So why isn't this the model that has been adopted for the way analysts are actually trained? In fact, analysts *were* trained this way in its infancy, before vast amounts of analytic literature had been accumulated and before the psychoanalytic community was dominated by analysts who were determined to make psychoanalysis more acceptable to the scientific (read, "academic") community. Over time, as the ideas that began to emerge from analysts were collected, disseminated, and published, the institutes that followed in their wake were organized, initially in a haphazard fashion but eventually in a direction that was specifically modeled on academic principles. Though institutes are quite small when compared to academic institutions, and the size of their classes offers the potential for an aura of intimate informality, the attitude that is typically fostered is—forgive this generalization—antithetical to the way psychoanalysis is practiced.

The atmosphere in analytic institutes isn't "free" but *compulsory*. If they possess a character, I would diagnose it as obsessional. There are rules for the sake of having them, and the educational experience is run, not like a journey, but a tight ship, to borrow a Naval metaphor. This is apt, I believe, due to the air of military precision that one invariably encounters there, one that is diametrically opposed to the enigmatic nature of the typical treatment experience. Moreover, the comparison to the obsessional character type is descriptive of how psychoanalytic treatment is taught. This observation is not news to you, I know. The analytic community's identification with the obsessional view of the world has been noted by numerous analysts over the better part of the past century, none more eloquently than Hans Loewald (1980):

> In psychoanalytic theory we are accustomed to think of the relationship between ego and reality as one of adjustment and adaptation. . . . This conception of the relationship between ego and reality presupposes a fundamental antagonism that has to be bridged or overcome in order to make life in this reality possible. . . . [Hence the psychoanalyst's conception of] culture and the external world are representative of . . . a hostile-defensive integration of reality. It is a concept of reality as it is most typically encountered in the obsessive character neurosis, a neurosis so common in our culture that it has been called the normal neurosis.
>
> (p. 30)

Loewald, like many analysts before him, recognized that the psychoanalytic conception of reality is essentially obsessional in nature, but I would go even further. I would add that *the way psychoanalytic training is conceived and conducted has inadvertently followed suit.* I have noted elsewhere (Thompson, 1994, pp. 205–212) that psychoanalysts seem drawn to fostering for themselves a culture that is obsessional in spirit. Often, the candidate in analytic training can be identified as an obsessional type: serious, determined to succeed, dedicated to a mission, self-sacrificing, humorless, resourceful, studious, and ambitious. Indeed, many of the features that characterize psychoanalytic theory and writing are consistent with the obsessional type. The most obvious feature of this trait among analytic institutes is the rigid manner in which psychoanalysis is generally taught and the way psychoanalysis itself is conceived. I'm not the first to suggest that it more closely approximates the preservation of Church doctrine than the open-ended exploration of a discipline that is, given its nature, impossible to define.[1]

The question is this: is there an alternative to the "tight ship" model of training, one that more closely approximates the spirit in which psychoanalytic treatment is conceived? I believe there is, and I cannot think of a better example on which to base such a model than the free association method, adapted from a confidential treatment experience to a milieu environment in which candidates come together with a view of applying the instrument to which they have already been inured.

In 1988, at the invitation of a group of students who were seeking psychoanalytic training but were unsatisfied with the strictures of conventional psychoanalytic institutes, a group of colleagues and I formed a psychoanalytic *salon* in San Francisco for the purpose of educating psychoanalysts in this fashion. We called it *Free Association*, a double entendre because it was not only a school devoted to helping students learn the free association method but an organization that saw itself as an association of equals devoted to the free dissemination of ideas. The group included psychoanalysts, philosophers, historians, and other educators who had backgrounds in phenomenology or psychoanalysis, or both, and who viewed psychoanalysis as a philosophy in the Socratic sense of the term. In other words, rather than attempting to delineate the potential interface *between* philosophy and psychoanalysis, we saw psychoanalysis as inherently philosophical already, a form of philosophy that saw its roots in the ancient Socratic, sceptic, and Stoic philosophical traditions when ethics was conceived as a therapy whose purpose was the relief of psychological suffering.

While our principal purpose was to train analysts, we believed that the conversation in which the fundamental issues of psychoanalysis occur should be situated in an historical context that not only takes into account the historical roots of psychoanalysis but learns from those traditions (whether medical, philosophical, or religious) that, throughout history, have tackled the same problems that contemporary psychoanalysts are endeavoring to address. Moreover, we saw psychoanalysis as merely the most recent development in a long history of antecedents that were concerned with the relief of human suffering, one that has necessarily absorbed into itself the fruits of its pre-history while situating the lessons learned in a contemporary context.

Naturally, our curriculum didn't resemble the curricula of conventional analytic institutes because we didn't have one. We specifically decided not to organize our seminars in conformity with curricula that adhered to an academic model, a model that, no matter how innovative or cutting-edge it imagines itself to be, is nevertheless interchangeable with the curriculum from any other psychoanalytic institute. This is hardly a model to engender original thinking. Instead, we tried to create an atmosphere in which students would be invited to grapple with the *unexpected, the unexplained, and the ambiguous* by approximating to a considerable degree the experience of a typical psychoanalytic session. With no curriculum or course outlines to follow, we believed that students were more likely to approach the seminars with a sense of apprehension, fueled by an attitude of curiosity. Because students weren't prejudiced with the comfort of reading assignments, we hoped they would be more likely to follow what was presented with an "emptied," which is to say, open state of mind.

The meetings were organized according to the predilections of the instructors who convened them, based on the vicissitudes of their professional interest, in other words, what happened to be of interest on the given day of their seminar. In lieu of a fixed, generalized curriculum that could be taught by any number of qualified instructors, the content of each seminar was derived from the unique and, by necessity, unrepeatable, here-and-now experiences of the faculty who were involved with the program. If there was a bias, the more seasoned the analyst (or instructor), the better. Consequently, the education offered more closely approximated an apprenticeship or mentorship model than a more typical academic one, a model that is typical in art academies but virtually absent in conventional psychoanalytic institutes. This, it seemed to us, was the basis on which any of us could offer what we had to offer, so why pretend to be conveying knowledge that is presumed to be derived from "science" when the only thing that we knew with confidence was what we had ourselves *experienced*, that which moved us personally, and which by its nature was constantly evolving? By abandoning a dogma of literature that students were expected to integrate into their education, seminars were conceived as a source of provocation, controversy, and inspiration for further, independent study, a catalyst, as it were, to think for oneself.

A typical seminar may be devoted, for example, to the phenomenological method, the principles of intentionality, intersubjectivity, and self-disclosure, with a view to determining the origins of the free association method, including antecedents that could be traced to forms of meditation, the Christian mystics (such as Meister Eckhart), and the essays of Michel de Montaigne. Other seminars may be devoted to tracing the origins of the technical principles that guide psychoanalysts, by locating the origins of the rule of neutrality, for example, in the Ancient sceptics, or the rule of abstinence in German Romanticism, and so on. In other words, whatever the topic explored, the idea was to offer depth to the concepts discussed that is typically lacking in psychoanalytic institutes, which, with their inordinately narrow focus, treat methodology as if it was invented by the latest psychoanalytic guru. With an appreciation for the history and pre-history of psychoanalysis to call upon, we found that students are more likely to grasp the importance of history, for example, in principle, offering a framework from which the historical significance of their patients' lives could also be appreciated. History was conceived of not as a series of facts or events that are assessed in terms of their accuracy or chronology but as a *living dimension* to everything one experiences in the present.

Because there is no agreement in the international psychoanalytic community as to what psychoanalysis is, we invited our candidates the opportunity to answer that question themselves by virtue of their own experience and practice. The criteria for acceptance into training was, like analysis, more or less self-selecting. Anyone was free to join the seminars if they wished, whether they intended to pursue analytic training or had other, more intellectual agendas, with whomever they pleased, and seek supervision with whomever they wished to, and so on. As to whether the patients they treated were invited to adopt the supine position or attend sessions so many times a week was left to the discretion of the students and their patients.

Some have suggested that without discernible criteria on which to assess one's performance, there could be no acceptable standards with which to determine what students had learned, if anything. Others have protested that without even minimal requirements for graduation, one's education would become so unremittingly *laissez-faire* that there would be little incentive to improve oneself *via* the ordeal of rigorous assessment.

I can only say in response to such objections that, in my experience, it doesn't seem to work that way. It is true that the notion of assessment would necessarily be compromised by such an educational schema, but our point of departure was that such standards are ultimately arbitrary and, so, ineffectual. Candidates are typically graduated because institutes have a commitment to graduating them, whether they have accomplished such and such in the interim or not. In fact, it would seem that completion of training—at any institute—is just as ambiguous a process as the termination of a typical analytic treatment. Each of us entertains different criteria for how treatments should be ended and when, and, in retrospect, it is never that obvious who has benefited or not, and how much. Personally, I believe that treatment has effectively ended (whether we recognize it or not) when a patient has had enough. Similarly, education reaches its terminus when a student reaches a similar conclusion.

This is the same principle, after all, that governs the termination of every treatment. We allow the patient's conscience to be his or her guide, no matter how developed or impoverished that patient's conscience may be. At the end of the day, a person's conscience is the only authority that counts because it is the only authority, when all is said and done, that the analyst is able to call upon when alone in the consulting room with a patient.

Admittedly, the model I am proposing stands or falls on the principles of self-reliance, self-motivation, and an inordinate sense of personal responsibility. Many analysts today had no access to training institutes when they sought training, and they were obliged to more or less train themselves. They got themselves into therapy, arranged for supervision, and, if they were resourceful, gathered around themselves a group of peers with whom they could meet and share their experiences together. This is not the easiest way to become an analyst, to be sure, but it is no less effective than any other. Section I (psychoanalytic clinicians) of Division 39 (psychoanalysis) of the American Psychological Association was established on precisely this principle, viz., that there are many roads to Rome, and each is just as valid, in principle, as the other. But whereas Section I nevertheless inclines toward conventional, institutional training if it is available, I doubt whether conventional psychoanalytic institutes are adequate to the task for which they were conceived, for the reasons I have just stated.

For those who pursue the more conventional psychoanalytic model, once an institute is created and the first class of candidates has graduated, the institute becomes a self-perpetuating organism. Even if the experience of that first group was fresh, vital, and alive, as succeeding groups of candidates are admitted and educated, the noose systematically tightens until it is only the shadow of how vital, open, and alive it was at its inception. We all know that the principal function of such institutes is not solely for the purpose of training future analysts but to serve as a cash cow for those same analysts once they have graduated. The politics of every psychoanalytic institute in the world revolves around who gets to be a training analyst and who doesn't, and who gets to teach those candidates, because the ones that get to enjoy an undeniable advantage over everyone else due to their access to affluent and properly impressed patients. Once an institute comes into being, it is obliged to survive and to perpetuate itself, and this obligation insidiously compromises the selection of candidates to be trained, thereby corrupting the very process by which those candidate's analysts and supervisors are selected, and so on. The waters of therapeutic excellence become inexorably diluted so that those who do not make the cut will be excluded from "training analyst" status. Where has the educational integrity gone when the principal purpose of institutes is to increase the income and prestige of a handful of select individuals whose connection with the real problems of the typical analytic patient is increasingly compromised?

These are only some of the reasons the Free Association experiment was conceived, as a compromise between a conventional institute with its undeniable ability to foster as sense of fellowship and a self-directed model which imposes extraordinary self-discipline on the candidates who are able to manage it. I wish I could claim some originality for this model but, ironically, the credit for that would have to go to Freud, who thought of it first. What I have just described is more or less how analysts were trained in Vienna when the first circle of Freud's followers gathered around him. Institutes were subsequently formed years later in a variety of locations and followed parallel paths, which in turn developed alternative standards until they finally coalesced into what has become the contemporary psychoanalytic institute, modeled on the academic standard first fashioned in Berlin. From a scientific perspective, it is argued that psychoanalytic training has improved and evolved over the years and that the treatment instrument has also improved for the better. But if you reject the claim that psychoanalysis is a science—hard, soft, or otherwise—it could just as persuasively be argued with as much veracity that the task analysts have set themselves does *not* necessarily improve (like medical technology, for example) over time, with ever-increasing newer and more effective discoveries on the horizon. If our principal concern is with *how human beings experience themselves and why*, then this very process must be rooted in the discipline of self-discovery, beginning and ending with the fruits of one's personal self-examination.

I am not suggesting that we should do as Freud did because Freud got it right, and we can't do it better. On the contrary, I am suggesting that we shouldn't ignore him as we have become prone to simply because he is no longer the latest fashion. There are other analytic schools besides Freud's that evolved along similar, non-academic lines, far removed from the rarefied atmosphere of Vienna. Another example of this design was personally related to me by Otto Allen Will, Jr. (1998), who received his training from Harry Stack Sullivan and Frieda Fromm-Reichmann in this fashion during the embryonic days of the Washington School of Psychiatry. By Will's account, contemporary analytic training today is a radical departure from the more relaxed, *laissez-faire* attitude that characterized Sullivan's milieu in the 1930s and 40s. But the influence to which I am most personally indebted was my own analytic training experience with R. D. Laing and his colleagues in London at the Philadelphia Association. For Laing, it was imperative that students discover what psychoanalysis is about for themselves, taking into account other disciplines throughout history, East and West, that have sought to relieve human beings of the angst of simply being human. While Free Association has chartered its own course and is a product of the people who have taught there, it is also profoundly indebted to Sullivan's and Laing's respective experiments (The school of Jacques Lacan was founded on similar principles in Paris).

What Freud, Sullivan, and Laing shared in common was that *they founded their respective schools themselves.* They were extraordinary and original thinkers who possessed the charisma and wherewithal to collect around themselves students who wanted to learn from them. When they died, their survivors created institutes in their name and, over time, they, too, grew into the "institutions" that they are today. Perhaps this is inevitable. It may be that the only way to preserve the psychoanalytic instrument is to periodically create it anew by forming new institutes and dismantling the old, permitting successive generations of analysts to discover its uncanny uniqueness for themselves.

This is what we decided to do at Free Association from the outset. There would be no line of succession, no hierarchy of good students demarcated from the bad ones, separated by the promise of spoils that, by their nature, engender competition, envy, jealousy, and unbridled ambition. Our aim was to train the group of students we had collected around ourselves, however long that might entail, and disband that moment in history when it was completed. Those who graduated were free to found their own schools or join others, but their fate, like the patient who has finished analysis, would rest in their hands. Over the past thirty odd years, Free Association has reconvened a number of cohorts to engage in such a training experience, and we are currently embarking upon a new one under the aegis of the New School for Existential Psychoanalysis, conducted worldwide on a virtual basis.[2]

I know that ours is a necessarily isolating profession and that we bear this alienation to degrees that we may not have expected, and at times we no doubt wish it were otherwise. If this is the case, then it is only prudent to remain vigilant against our inherently corrupting, all-too-human nature, wherever and whenever it arises, however tempting it may be to capitulate to our incurable sense of loneliness by compromising our best efforts to be true to ourselves.

Notes

1 For a recent example of how psychoanalytic institutes are typically organized, see Kirsner, 2000.
2 It so happens that due to Covid a new group of colleagues and I, under the auspices of Free Association, Inc., have decided to start a new training group, NEW SCHOOL FOR EXISTENTIAL PSYCHOANALYSIS, that will be taught exclusively on Zoom, with candidates as well as faculty spread all over the world, under the same criteria as the original 1988 group, beginning September 2022.

References

Kirsner, D. (2000) *Unfree Associations: Inside Psychoanalytic Institutes*. London: Process Press.
Loewald, H. (1980) *Papers on Psycho-Analysis*. New Haven and London: Yale University Press.
Thompson, M. G. (1994) *The Truth About Freud's Technique: The Encounter With The Real*. New York: New York University Press.
Thompson, M. G. and Thompson, S. (1998, April) Interview with Dr. Otto Allen Will, Jr. *Contemporary Psychoanalysis*, Vol. 34, No. 2.

Chapter 13

The Rule of Neutrality

If there is one concept that epitomizes the specificity of psychoanalytic technique, it would undoubtedly be the term "neutrality." Outside of analytic nomenclature, the term is rarely used, and within the analytic community, it is the technical principle most frequently invoked to distinguish classical psychoanalysis from its "friendlier," user-friendly cousins. Since Freud first invoked it in the last of his six papers on technique ("Observations on Transference-Love" [1915]), neutrality has become *the raison d'être* for what we have since come to embrace as "psychoanalysis."

Yet the application of this technical rule has changed dramatically since it was originally conceived. The first indications of this shift occurred after the Second World War, in the late 1940s and early 1950s, when Freud's analytic cases were characterized by some of his own followers as ineffectual (Kanzer and Glenn, 1980; Kris, 1951). Ironically, the most frequently heard criticism of Freud's analytic cases, then and now, is the alleged *absence* of classical analytic interventions. I believe these criticisms help demonstrate the extent to which analytic technique has changed over the course of the past century and how much it has diverged from Freud's conception of it. The term "classical technique," as it is now conceived, only vaguely depicts Freud's clinical behavior. What accounts for this remarkable transformation in such a critical aspect of his treatment philosophy? More importantly, how have these developments altered the actual practice of psychoanalysis? These are some of the questions I wish to explore in this chapter. I shall begin by reviewing representative characterizations of neutrality in the literature, then compare and contrast them with Freud's depiction of neutrality, gleaned from a variety of sources. I hope to demonstrate an inherent misunderstanding about what Freud intended to convey by this concept.

DOI: 10.4324/9781003429104-13

In *The Analytic Attitude* (1983), Roy Schafer depicts neutrality as the following:

> The analyst remains neutral in relation to every aspect of the material being presented by the analysand. . . . In his or her neutrality, the analyst does not crusade for or against the so-called id, superego or defensive ego. The analyst has no favorites and so is not judgmental. The analyst's position is, as Anna Freud (1936) put it, "equidistant" from the various forces at war with one another. The simplistic, partisan analyst, working in terms of saints and sinners, victims and victimizers, or good and bad ways to live, is failing to maintain the analytic attitude.
>
> (p. 5)

In other words, analysts who fail to employ neutrality in response to *every aspect* of their patient's material fail to maintain the requisite "analytic attitude."

> In contrast, the analyst who remains neutral is attempting to allow all of the conflictual material to be fully represented, interpreted and worked through. The neutral analyst is also attempting to avoid both the imposition of his or her personal values on the analysand and the unquestioning acceptance of the analysand's initial value-judgements.

> It is particularly important to maintain his neutrality in relation to parental figures and spouses for, to some extent, the analysand is identified with them and is vulnerable to the same value judgments that may be passed on them. Also, the analysand may be referring to other people in order to represent indirectly, as in a dream, some disturbing feature of his or her own self. For this reason too the analyst must take care to regard these others neutrally. . . . To achieve neutrality requires a high degree of subordination of the analyst's personality to the analytic task at hand.
>
> (p. 6)

Subordination of the analyst's personality should be understood "in terms of the analyst's appropriate moderation, regulation and often simply curtailment of any show of activity of a predominantly narcissistic sort" (p. 6). Schafer allows, however, that there are times when analysts can't be expected to maintain neutrality, when they are permitted to abandon their

neutral attitude and reveal the feelings, criticisms, and expectations that
they harbor about their patients. However, those exceptions are allowed
only on those occasions when the patient's behavior

> may seriously disrupt the continuity or effectiveness of the analysis or
> threaten the basic welfare of the analysand. These factors include the
> analysand's constant precipitation of life crises, prolonged absences,
> non-payment of fees, acts of gross delinquency, physical illness, toxic-
> ity, suicidal depression, schizophrenic regression, etc.
>
> (p. 6)

What are the basic elements of Schafer's views about the nature of
neutrality? First, he conceives it as an attitude that every analyst should
endeavor to adopt *throughout* the course of each session. Neutrality entails,
but isn't necessarily limited to: a) remaining non-judgmental; b) taking care
to hide from one's patients those personality traits that the analyst doesn't
customarily conceal; and c) maintaining a naive and unexpectant attitude
toward everything that patients say.

I agree with many of the points that Schafer emphasizes about the nature
of neutrality. However, he arrives at certain conclusions which I question.
The principal point I object to is the axiomatic nature of Schafer's conception of neutrality and his insistence that it should be employed relentlessly throughout the course of treatment. According to Schafer, whenever
neutrality is breached, "analytic treatment," properly understood, is inter-
rupted. "Non-analytic" moments should be minimized accordingly. One
could conceivably employ a graph that quantifies analytic incidents against
non-analytic ones to determine "how much" analysis is taking place. At a
certain point, one may breach the criteria of the prescribed analytic experience and lapse into a diluted—no doubt, inferior—form of psychotherapy.
Worse, one may have polluted the *therapeutic* experience beyond repair.

Schafer (1983) suggests that the most obstinate foil to neutrality is therapeutic ambition, a direct consequence of the analyst's narcissism. Though
he doesn't spell out what narcissism entails, he more or less implies that
analysts who behave in an overtly friendly manner are "narcissistic"
because: a) expressions of affection aren't germane to analytic work, and b)
the only reason analysts would be so motivated is to compel their patients to
love them. Such a strategy would fuel the patient's narcissism, in turn, and
dilute the quota of frustration needed to effect psychic change. Hence, the

employment of neutrality should thwart the patient's narcissistic impulses by keeping the analyst's narcissism in check. I shall return to Schafer's characterization of analytic neutrality later.

Now I would like to turn to the American Psychoanalytic Association's compendium of analytic terms, *Psychoanalytic Terms and Concepts* (1990). This book is an official publication of the American Psychoanalytic Association and serves as a reference for analytic candidates in training. They define neutrality as:

> The stance of the analyst generally recommended for fostering the psychoanalytic process. Central to psychoanalytic neutrality are keeping the countertransference in check, avoiding the imposition of one's own values on the patient, and taking the patient's capacities, rather than one's own desires as a guide. . . . The concept also defines the recommended emotional attitude of the analyst, one of professional commitment for helpful, benign understanding that avoids extremes of detachment and overinvolvement. The analyst's neutrality is intended to facilitate the development, recognition and interpretation of the transference neurosis and to minimize distortions that might be introduced if he or she attempts to educate, advise or impose values on the patient based on the analyst's countertransference. . . . Avoiding the imposition of values upon the patient is an accepted aspect of psychoanalytic neutrality. However, there is increasing recognition that the analyst's values are always operative, especially those involving the search for truth, knowledge, and understanding, and those emphasizing orientation toward reality, maturity, and change.
>
> (1990, p. 127)

According to this definition, analysts should be particularly wary of imposing their personal values onto patients. The authors nevertheless qualify this aspect of neutrality by allowing that the search for truth, respect for reality, and even seeking change are values that all analysts "impose" on their patients as a matter of course. To summarize: a) the analyst's countertransference intrudes on his or her capacity for neutrality; b) the analyst's values—excepting the qualifications noted above—should be concealed from one's patient; c) the patient should set the agenda for the course of analysis, not the analyst; and d) neutrality is an "emotional attitude" every analyst is expected to adopt, characterized by benign understanding.

The necessity for qualifying the imposition of this rule is obvious. Since the goal of treatment is at least indirectly "imposed" on patients, the need to impose goals—even when they aren't spelled out—must be exempted from neutrality. Treatments without any goal whatsoever—no matter how understated that goal may be—would have no ostensible purpose. The authors realistically qualify the axiomatic nature of neutrality by accounting for this critical point.

One wonders, however, how the authors are able to reduce one's capacity for benign understanding to an "emotional attitude"? Even if our capacity for compassion and understanding could be relegated to emotion, how could it be regulated or controlled? Surely our capacity for benign understanding lies outside emotions and even serves as a foil against their imposition when manifested, for example, in the analyst's countertransference.

The third reference to analytic neutrality I shall examine is provided by the French analysts Jean Laplanche and J.-B. Pontalis. In *The Language of Psychoanalysis* (1973), they suggest that neutrality is:

> One of the defining characteristics of the attitude of the analyst during the treatment. The analyst must be *neutral* in respect of religious, ethical and social values—that is to say, he must not direct the treatment according to some ideal, and should abstain from counseling the patient; he must be *neutral* too as regards manifestations of transference (this rule usually being expressed by the maxim, "Do not play the patient's game"). And finally, he must be *neutral* towards the discourse of the patient. . . . Freud gives the clearest indication of how neutrality should be understood in his "Recommendations to Physicians Practising Psycho-analysis" (1912b/1958). In this paper, he castigates "therapeutic ambition" and "educative ambition" and deems it wrong to set a patient tasks, such as collecting his memories or thinking over some particular period of his life. The analyst should model himself on the surgeon who has one aim and one aim only, ". . . performing the operation as skillfully as possible."
>
> (p. 115)

In fact, Freud's "Recommendations to Physicians Practising Psycho-analysis" (1912b) offers his most exhaustive discussion on the nature of analytic neutrality. Ironically, Freud had not yet introduced the actual term for it when the paper was written.[1] The paper is devoted entirely to the appropriate mental attitude—"neutrality"—psychoanalysts should endeavor to adopt with their patients.

One of six papers on technique published between 1911 and 1915, Freud conceived the series as a technical manual for the clinical practice of psychoanalysis. It was the only time in his career he was ever tempted to do so. Though he returned to the subject now and then during the remaining course of his life, the principal elements of what he had to say about the matter are contained in those six papers.[2]

"Recommendations to Physicians Practicing Psycho-analysis" is the third paper in the series. It is preceded by a brief discussion on dream interpretation (1911) and an exhaustive examination of transference published a year later (1912a), then followed by the three remaining papers—"On Beginning the Treatment" (1913), "Remembering, Repeating and Working-Through" (1914), and "Observations on Transference-Love" (1915)—all of which share the same subtitle. Hence the "Recommendations to Physicians" paper is the anchor of the others and is essential to understanding the entire series.

"Recommendations to Physicians" is divided into nine parts, each pertaining to a facet of neutrality. Freud devotes the entire paper to advocating a most unusual form of attentiveness entailing an "evenly suspended attention," the nature of which is probably more familiar to practitioners of Buddhist meditation than the typical physician. Analysts are advised against striving to remember everything their patients say because "as soon as anyone deliberately concentrates his attention to a certain degree, he begins to select from the material" instead of giving everything equal weight (Freud, 1912b, p. 112). Besides, analysts who think that they know what is important to remember and what isn't are invariably mistaken because "the things one hears are for the most part things whose meaning is only recognized later on" (p. 112).

Freud equates this paradoxical mode of attentiveness with the fundamental rule of analysis,[3] the patient's pledge to be candid. It is important to appreciate the degree to which Freud's conception of the fundamental rule dominated his analytic technique in order to grasp the centrality of his rule on neutrality. After discovering that neurotic conflicts are derived from repressed secrets, Freud realized that the patient's free associations could be interpreted to reveal what those secrets were. By uttering whatever comes to mind in a random and haphazard fashion, patients inadvertently divulge crucial clues about what comprises their unconscious wishes. This procedure, however, is incumbent on obeying the "fundamental rule": the pledge to utter the contents of one's associations without censorship. In effect, patients are expected to *be honest* when complying with this rule. From this time forward, the thrust of analytic technique was predominantly concerned with the mutative ramifications of *instilling rapport* and only tangentially with the need to determine causation of symptoms. Given the overriding importance that rapport had assumed in analytic treatment, Freud asked how analysts could expect their patients to obey the fundamental rule unless they, in turn, behave in a reciprocal manner. If analysts want their patients to treat their thoughts, feelings, and inclinations with equal weight, then analysts must treat everything they're told in a complementary frame of mind: with equanimity. Freud believed this recommendation was so crucial he even claimed that everything "achieved in this manner will be sufficient for all requirements during the treatment" (1912b, p. 112).

The rule of neutrality also explains Freud's admonition against taking notes during analytic sessions. Writing notes necessarily entails the critical use of one's mind and detracts from the "evenly suspended attentiveness" neutrality is intended to foster. Though keeping notes is a habit that is difficult for scientifically trained analysts to break, Freud was merciless in his insistence on this recommendation. Analysts who argue that psychoanalysis must conform to the criteria of empirical science find this recommendation especially hard to swallow. One of the champions of science himself, Freud nonetheless dismissed the notion that analysis could ever be subjected to anything like a "scientific" study or report (1912b, pp. 113–114). Deep down, we all know that scientific reports prove nothing except to air the beliefs of the scientists who write them. Since data can be "cooked" this way or that, Freud questioned why analysts should be expected to engage in such a facile game. Though Freud was a great admirer of science, he apparently believed that the treatment situation must be protected from the potential for abuse that academic institutions commit as a matter of course. In fact, Freud (1912b) offers his most eloquent depiction of neutrality when arguing against mingling science with treatment objectives:

Cases which are devoted from the first to scientific purposes and are treated accordingly suffer in their outcome; while the most successful cases are those in which one proceeds, as it were, without any purpose in view, allows oneself to be taken by surprise by any new turn in them, and always meets them with an open mind, free from any presuppositions.

(p. 114)

Even the intention of publishing a case would contaminate the delicate balance of attentiveness and relaxation that Freud urges analysts to adopt. While he doesn't explicitly say so, this was probably one of the lessons brought home to Freud as a consequence of his failed analysis of Dora, which he had decided to publish at the beginning of her treatment (Thompson, 1994, pp. 97–98). The point he is trying to make is that analysts need to protect themselves from knowing too much about matters that are inconsequential by encumbering themselves with details that will subvert their principal task: keeping an open mind to everything their patients have to say.

As noted above, Laplanche and Pontalis (1973) cited Freud's admonition against succumbing to "therapeutic ambition," which Freud was no doubt alluding to when he suggested (here for the first time) that analytic candidates should themselves undertake analysis to help mitigate their countertransference tendencies. Though Laplanche and Pontalis cite therapeutic ambition in the context of Freud's counsel to model oneself on surgeons, this recommendation is usually taken out of context to infer that Freud coldheartedly suppressed any feeling of sympathy for his patients whatsoever (Gay, 1988, p. 249; Thompson, 1994, pp. 122–124). Let us examine this recommendation in its entirety:

I cannot advise my colleagues too urgently to model themselves during psychoanalytic treatment on the surgeon who puts aside all his feelings, even his human sympathy, and concentrates his mental forces on the single aim of performing the operation as skillfully as possible. Under present day conditions, the feeling that is most dangerous to a psychoanalyst is the therapeutic ambition to achieve by this novel and much disputed method something that will produce a convincing effect upon other people. This will not only put him into a state of mind which is unfavorable for his work, but will make him helpless against certain resistances of the patient, whose recovery, as we know, primarily depends on the interplay of forces in him. The justification for requiring this emotional coldness in the analyst is that it creates the most advantageous conditions for both parties: for the doctor a desirable protection for his own emotional life and for the patient the largest amount of help that we can give him today. A surgeon of earlier times took as his motto the words, "I dressed the wounds, God cured him." The analyst should be content with something similar.

(Freud, 1912b, p. 115)

As one can see, Freud's admonition to "model oneself on the surgeon" assumes an altogether different connotation than is typically characterized when the rule is not read in its entirety. The so-called emotional coldness that he is frequently accused of advising was offered solely in the context of reminding analysts that it isn't they who perform miracles but the interplay of "forces" in the patients themselves, forces that are as inaccessible to manipulation by analysts as the will of God. In other words, if one examines the context where Freud invoked the "model of the surgeon" analogy, he was merely steering analysts from committing hubris: the temptation of acting like "gods" who would pretend to shape the course of their patients' lives. Maintaining such a degree of modesty isn't as simple as it seems. Obviously, psychoanalysts are extraordinarily ambitious people. They have to be in order to survive the enormous sacrifices that are required to undertake the necessary training. This experience, however, is just as likely to arouse hubris as to instill a modicum of humility.

Similarly, educative ambitions arouse another example of hubris when analysts claim they could possibly know what patients should do with their lives when the treatment comes to an end. No doubt, all analysts are occasionally disappointed with the choices some patients opt for when the analysis reaches its terminus. They frequently find themselves walking a thin line between inadvertently "supporting" a foolish decision by saying nothing or indirectly "advising" against an alternate course of action by exploring its unconscious motives. Maintaining silence in the course of analysis, as in life, can speak volumes, and one never knows what patients read into those moments. Freud believed that analysts inadvertently abandon their neutrality when they presume to know what is "good" for their patients, as though they are blessed with a capacity for seeing into the future that is denied other mortals. These are the occasions when hubris is a manifestation of countertransference, when analysts seek the role of "savior" instead of settling for that of interlocutor. A few years later, Freud (1919) expanded on this aspect of neutrality when contrasting it with an attitude he suspected depicted the Zurich school:

We refused most emphatically to turn a patient who puts himself into our hands in search of help into our private property, to decide his fate for him, to force our own ideals upon him, and with the pride of a Creator to form him in our own image and see that it is good. I still adhere to this refusal, and I think that this is the proper place for the medical discretion which we have had to ignore in other connections.

(p. 164)

Another example of neutrality can be found in the fourth paper of the series, "On Beginning the Treatment" (1913). According to Laplanche and Pontalis (1973), the development of a viable transference relationship depends entirely on the correct handling of neutrality. They quote Freud:

> It is certainly possible to forfeit the first success if from the start one takes up any other standpoint than one of sympathetic understanding, such as a moralizing one, or if one behaves like the representative or advocate of some contending party.
>
> (Freud, 1913, p. 140)

Let's examine this quotation in its entirety to avoid any possible misunderstanding. Freud was apparently concerned with a very practical matter: how soon in the treatment should analysts begin to interpret their patients' communications?

> The next question with which we are faced raises a matter of principle. It is this: When are we to begin making our communications to the patient? When is the moment for disclosing to him the hidden meaning of the ideas that occur to him, and for initiating him into the postulates and technical procedures of analysis? The answer to this can only be: Not until an effective transference has been established in the patient, a proper *rapport* with him. It remains the first aim of the treatment to attach him to it and to the person of the doctor. To ensure this, nothing need be done but to give him time. If one exhibits a serious interest in him, carefully clears away the resistances that crop up at the beginning and avoids making certain mistakes, he will of himself form such an attachment and link the doctor up with one of the imagos of the people by whom he was accustomed to be treated with affection. It is certainly possible to forfeit this first success if from the start one takes up any standpoint other than one of sympathetic understanding, such as a moralizing one, or if one behaves like a representative or advocate of some contending party—of the other member of a married couple, for instance.
>
> (Freud, 1913, pp. 139–140)

Freud's characterization of "sympathetic understanding" as epitomizing neutrality no doubt confuses those analysts who equate the neutral attitude with the "coldness of the surgeon," noted by Laplanche and Pontalis. The two technical recommendations, written a year apart, seem to contradict each other. In the first recommendation (1912b, p. 115), Freud emphasizes the need to withhold sympathy (in the service of neutrality), while in the second (1913, p. 140), he advocates the expression of sympathetic understanding. Laplanche and Pontalis (1973) imply that an attitude of sympathy nonetheless epitomizes neutrality when they cite a reference that can be found in Freud's *Studies on Hysteria* where he, in perhaps his earliest depiction of neutrality, characterized it as an attitude in which . . .

> One works, to the best of one's power, as an elucidator [*Aufdlarer*] (where ignorance has given rise to fear), as a teacher, as a father confessor who gives absolution, as it were, by a continuance of his sympathy and respect after the confession has been made.
>
> (Freud & Breuer, 1893–95/1955)

On the other hand, Schafer (1983) appears to believe that the expression of sympathetic understanding diverges from analytic neutrality when he advises against becoming entangled in a patient's domestic quarrels. According to this view, if one's patient is embroiled in an argument with a spouse, for example, neutrality requires that the analyst avoid "taking sides." Repeating what Schafer said earlier:

> It is particularly important to maintain his neutrality in relation to parental figures and spouses for, to some extent, the analysand is identified with them and is vulnerable to the same value judgements that may be passed on them.
>
> (1983, p. 6)

Schafer construes neutrality as an attitude that requires analysts to be opaque with their patients, to subordinate their personalities and conceal from patients their personal opinions, not only when it seems appropriate but throughout the course of treatment. Yet, when Freud warns against adopting a "moralizing" tone in the recommendation just noted, he says nothing about taking *no* sides (as Schafer does). On the contrary, he advises against becoming an advocate for *the contending party*, such as the patient's spouse. The idea of neutrality isn't, strictly speaking, served by taking no sides; the neutral analyst gives the impression of always being *on the patient's side*, irrespective of the foolishness one's patient is bound to commit.

How could analysts appear to be sympathetic if they were noncommittal to everything their patients complain about? The expression of sympathy— i.e., commiseration—shows that analysts are supportive by not insinuating a note of "disapproval" about the nature of their patients' tribulations, however biased or confused they may be. Whereas Freud construed neutrality as a vehicle for instilling rapport, Schafer conceives the term literally as exemplifying a "neutered," non-position from which analysts are forbidden to either commiserate with or condemn the patient's prejudices. In practice, strict adherence to this technique would be experienced by patients not as unintrusive and cautious but as distinctly *disinterested* in the everydayness of their concerns—the very attitude that analysts erroneously attribute to Freud's surgeon analogy! I don't believe this distinction is simply a matter of how much or little sympathy one should express at a given moment; it epitomizes how "classical" analysis is currently conceived.

One of the barriers to integrating Freud's extraordinarily subtle conception of neutrality into one's clinical practice is its proximity to the rule of abstinence: refusing to comply with the patient's demand for love. Many analysts equate the two as separate concepts while others—such as Laplanche and Pontalis (1973)—characterize abstinence as "a simple consequence of neutrality," implying a kinship that can be misleading (p. 3). Adding to the confusion, Freud didn't bother to provide definitions for either term, the consequence of a writing style in which he preferred to allow the context where terms were invoked to imply their meaning. In fact, though the "Recommendations to Physicians" paper was devoted entirely to neutrality and abstinence, *it was three more years before their recommended application was explicitly linked to their respective technical terms.*

Freud also had the habit of weaving a discussion of one concept into his treatment of the other, but without saying so. For example, in the analyst-as-surgeon analogy where Freud admonishes analysts to "put aside all [their] feelings, even human sympathy," he is actually invoking abstinence, not the rule of neutrality (1912b, p. 115). Then, in the very next sentence when he warns that "the feeling that is most dangerous to a psychoanalyst is the therapeutic ambition to achieve . . . something that will produce a convincing effect upon other people," he is invoking the rule of neutrality (p. 115). Due to the confusion that persists about the two concepts, the prevalent view of neutrality is rooted in the assumption that it entails keeping the analysts' affect in check. In fact, neutrality isn't specifically concerned with affect but with the way analysts divide their attention during the analytic hour. It pertains to the analysts' *state of mind* and the manner in which they bring their minds to bear on what their patients confide. Feelings enter the picture only when they inhibit the analyst's capacity to adopt a neutral attitude.

On the other hand, abstinence is concerned with the analyst's affect, but not in the manner that Schafer's (1983) term, "subordination of the personality," implies. The rule of abstinence pertains exclusively to those feelings that prompt analysts to behave seductively. Nothing in Freud's conception of neutrality or abstinence calls for analysts to subordinate their personalities in the sense of *disguising* their feelings about the things their patients say. The expressions of anger, impatience, disappointment, irritation, and concern are actually tangential to the rule of abstinence, as well as the rule of neutrality. One of the principal myths about neutrality is that one is supposed to adopt an "affect-less" attitude, assuming that it is even possible to do so.

Another reason the distinction between neutrality and abstinence has become so muddled is that both terms were introduced in the same technical paper, "Observations on Transference-Love" (1915), only a few sentences apart. In that paper, Freud was trying to help analysts cope with the extraordinary demands that their patients impose during the course of treatment. But the nature of those demands was actually quite narrow: the sometimes explosive and unpredictable erotic longings patients "transfer" onto their analysts. This phenomenon led Freud to conjecture that transference feelings are instigated by our unfulfilled longing for love, which axiomatically crop up in the course of analysis as they do in virtually all relationships. What sets analytic transference feelings apart from non-analytic ones is that, in the former, analysts a) aren't in a position to relieve their frustration; and b) mustn't allow themselves to behave indifferently when they arise. It is in this context that analysts are supposed to assume a so-called neutral perspective.

While analysts mustn't make it their business to satisfy their patients' longings, neither should they play their hands too close to their chest. That being said, it isn't so easy to grapple with the intense demands every analyst encounters. It requires enormous confidence and tact to fulfill one's role honestly without resorting to guile or manipulation. Some analysts, Freud discovered, resorted to lecturing their patients that it would be "wrong" to return their love and hoped that would end the matter forever. Others took the opposite tack and misguidedly assumed that their patients were somehow obligated to fall in love with them in order to evoke the "analytic experience." Some even encouraged their patients to do so at the beginning of treatment, as though they could manufacture such feelings on command. Freud observed that either extreme would breach neutrality by violating the ethical standard on which analytic relationships are founded. If analysts expect their patients to comply with the fundamental rule of analysis—to bare all without censorship—they, in turn, must learn to accept the entire range of their patients' experience without losing their equilibrium.

Why did Freud choose this paper to finally give neutrality its proper name? What was it about the nature of erotic demands that prompted him to devote an entire paper to a technical principle he had treated at length already? Freud was apparently startled by the degree of duplicity that some analysts engaged in when confronted with their patients' transference behavior, not unlike the startled reaction of Joseph Breuer to Anna O.'s declaration that he had fathered her child. It wasn't long after that famous treatment that Freud replaced hypnosis with the free association method. The unprecedented innovation of speaking spontaneously without reservation gave neurotic patients, for the first time, the responsibility for serving as authors of their own destiny, unconscious parapraxes and all. It wasn't until much later, however, in 1912, that Freud introduced the "fundament rule." Contrary to conventional wisdom, this rule was not identical to the free association method (Thompson, 1994, pp. 155–174). The following year, Freud explicitly outlined how the two rules should be distinguished from each other (1913, pp. 134–135). Whereas free association is a verbal form of meditation by which patients utter the thoughts that come to mind, the fundamental rule is the patient's explicit pledge to verbalize those thoughts without censorship. In the absence of one's actual pledge to "free associate"—a unique blend of conscious motivation and unconscious associations—the dynamics of the patient's resistance to this rule would be moot.

The imposition of this rule—the only one, Freud adds, that patients are asked to follow (1913, p. 134)—suggests that analytic treatment is rooted in a commitment to honesty. This commitment, however, applies to analysts as well; otherwise, patients would lose whatever respect they had for their analysts in the first place. Freud was particularly sensitive to the standard of morality practiced by society in general and the casual duplicity that the public expected from physicians. This was the context in which Freud conceived the ethical standard that analysts were expected to follow. Some analysts apparently wondered what the harm would be in bending the truth just a little for the sake of expediency. After all, why should analysts be expected to restrict themselves to the same terms as their patients when it wasn't they who were in treatment? Finally, what would be wrong with giving patients the love they craved initially, then weaning them off it when they became independent? Freud's reaction to these rationales for deception was typically blunt:

> My objection to this expedient is that psychoanalytic treatment is founded on truthfulness. In this fact lies a great part of its educative effect and its ethical value. It is dangerous to depart from this foundation. Anyone who has become saturated in the analytic technique will no longer be able to make use of the lies and pretenses which doctors normally find unavoidable; and if, with the best intentions, he does attempt to do so, he is very likely to betray himself. Since we demand strict truthfulness from our patients we jeopardize our whole authority if we let ourselves be caught out by them in a departure from the truth.
>
> (1915, p. 164)

This was the context in which Freud introduced the actual term "neutrality" by virtue of the analyst's commitment to seeking *and* speaking the truth:

> Besides, the experiment of letting oneself go a little way in tender feelings for the patient is not altogether without danger. Our control over ourselves is not so complete that we may not suddenly one day go further than we had intended. In my opinion, therefore, we ought not to give up the neutrality towards the patient, which we have acquired through keeping the counter-transference in check.
>
> (1915, pp. 163–164)

Having now invoked neutrality for the first time, Freud turned his attention to abstinence. If analysts treat their patients honestly and keep an open mind to everything they say, they will eventually unleash in those patients a newfound freedom which, in turn, elicits greater demands on themselves.

In fact, they may err in behaving too openly and lead their patients to surmise that their uncompromising acceptance of everything they fantasize about is silently encouraged. Patients may conclude that their analysts are secretly in love with them and, armed with this source of gratification, their motivation to change will be compromised accordingly. This is the principal reason why

> the treatment must be carried out in abstinence. . . . I shall state it as a fundamental principle that the patient's need and longing should be allowed to persist in her, in order that they may serve as forces impelling her to do work and to make changes, and that we must beware of appeasing those forces by means of surrogates.
>
> (1915, p. 165)

One of the reasons, then, for introducing the rule of abstinence was to compensate for the consequences of neutrality. Some patients hoped to substitute their analyst's role as "elucidator" with the more pleasing one of lover. Freud treated these developments as axiomatic of the patient's resistance to treatment and introduced abstinence as a prophylactic against inadvertently succumbing to seduction. Abstinence serves to *moderate* how much openness ("neutrality") analysts should employ, depending on the circumstance. Abstinence also serves as insurance against expressing more sympathy than is prudent. Though Laplanche and Pontalis (1973) depict abstinence as a subsidiary of neutrality, abstinence often serves as a *foil* to neutrality and *vice versa*. Because the essence of neutrality is rooted in openness, this is frequently construed by patients as a demonstration of the analyst's love. In transference, this is taken personally as though intended for that patient alone. On the other hand, when analysts withhold sympathy for fear of encouraging erotic fantasies, they risk inhibiting that aspect of transference that is epitomized by the capacity for candor.

How, then, can analysts hope to reconcile the seeming contradiction between neutrality and abstinence? The answer is actually quite simple. Despite the impression given by Schafer (1983), neutrality was never intended to be employed *universally*. It should be applied with discretion, depending on the forces at play in each patient. The rule of neutrality solely entails the analyst's openness to the patient's experience in all its variety and device. Whereas the rule of abstinence admonishes analysts to hold their feelings in check, neutrality serves as a prophylactic against becoming too clever, manipulative, coercive, deceptive, therapeutically ambitious, and controlling. On the other hand, neutrality can be carried too far. Were it feasible for analysts to engage in neutrality full bore—an impossibility—their role would become so compromised that they would be relegated to the part of permissive patron. Patients would interpret their inactivity as a sign of "agreement," and the analysis would lose its tension.

This is why neutrality *needs to be employed selectively but not sparingly*. Analysts inadvertently breach neutrality whenever they offer interpretations because, by their nature, interpretations often undermine the patient's most treasured assumptions. Carried to extremes, the use of interpretation may hinder the patient's capacity for inquiry by situating the analyst in too active a role. This dilemma prompted both Winnicott and Lacan to dispense with interpretations more or less entirely in order to expand the range of neutrality they could employ with patients. Yet, Freud warned against ignoring common sense by taking this strategy to extremes. In his "Recommendations to Physicians" paper, he explicitly advocated alternating a neutral frame of mind with an ordinary one by "swinging over according to need from the one mental attitude to the other" (1912b, p. 114). The same principle applies to the rule of abstinence. Some patients, for example—especially hysterics—may require the employment of more abstinence, whereas obsessional patients may require considerably less.[4]

In fact, Freud's analysis of the Rat Man is a perfect example of how neutrality and abstinence should be alternated. More recent conceptions of neutrality have diverged so markedly from Freud's that he is now criticized for not having exercised more neutrality than he customarily employed. For example, Freud committed a number of gestures in his treatment of the Rat Man that most analysts now find objectionable, even "un-analytic," such as sending his patient postcards while on holiday, loaning him a book, asking to see photographs of his girlfriend, and offering him food when he was hungry (Thompson, 1994, pp. 205–240). Langs reflects the opinion of a great number of contemporary analysts in suggesting that Freud's gestures were deviations from strict analytic neutrality (in Kanzer and Glenn (Eds.), 1980, pp. 215–216). He even argues that Freud's display of sympathy and concern "endangered" the analytic frame by unnecessarily gratifying his patient (p. 227). Mahony (1986) concurs with this view and concludes that Freud was "frequently intrusive [and] reassuring," talked too much, and was "aggressively helpful" (p. 90).

Some of Freud's critics condemn the poverty of transference interpretations in virtually all of his published cases, including that of the Rat Man. Gill (1982), for example, suggested that the preponderance of genetic interpretations over transferential ones, compounded by the short duration of his analytic cases, culminated in a superficial treatment experience at best. Together, these criticisms portray Freud as someone who failed to attend to the unconscious dynamics of the patient's current situation, breached analytic neutrality through overinvolvement, and was prone to investigating the underlying causes of neurotic conflict while neglecting to help patients work through their transference neurosis.

Virtually all these criticisms are founded on the erroneous notion that neutrality is intended to promote an experience of *deprivation* in the analytic situation. On the contrary, Freud promoted a vision of neutrality that was rooted in the principle of *non-interference*. It was never intended to serve as a vehicle for withholding gratification but as a means of facilitating free associations. Allowing this distinction, Freud's analysis of the Rat Man is a perfect example of how neutrality should be employed.

For example, at a critical point in the Rat Man's analysis, he suddenly turned against Freud in a moment of delusional fury and accused him of trying to marry him off to his daughter, Anna. Shocked at his own outburst, he was subsequently worried that Freud would summarily terminate his analysis. A tense period ensued, during which Freud remained noncommittal about the meaning of his patient's outburst. Many analysts would have interpreted the emergence of the negative transference in order to "ease" the intensity of the situation. By suggesting that the patient's feelings do not, in fact, pertain to them (the analyst) personally, they hope to nullify the patient's aggression and ensure continuation of treatment.

Compared with current standards, it is all the more remarkable that Freud chose to say nothing. He had said nothing earlier to encourage the emergence of his patient's negative feelings (by behaving in a remote manner, for example), nor, once the feelings spontaneously erupted, did he say anything to discourage them. Instead, Freud invoked neutrality by: a) tolerating his patient's feelings and accepting them at face value; b) not "interpreting away" the power of the moment; and c) giving his patient time to come to terms with his feelings himself. Soon after this interlude, the Rat Man's symptoms disappeared.

What was specifically "neutral" about Freud's handling of the Rat Man's negative transference feelings? The most significant feature of his reaction was that Freud offered *no interpretations*. As a rule, Freud almost never used transference interpretations because he believed they encouraged patients to intellectualize their feelings instead of working them through. Freud preferred genetic interpretations instead because they supported the educational goal of helping patients to appreciate the unconscious forces of their existence. While genetic interpretations are just as liable to breach neutrality as transferential ones, Freud apparently felt they were less likely to inhibit the patient's capacity to work through the transference neurosis by persevering with the fundamental rule (Thompson, 1994, pp. 192–204).

Freud's gestures of friendship and support served to facilitate the spirit of openness that neutrality is intended to foster. Besides, Freud was generally friendly with all of his patients. He was a gracious and outgoing person who unreservedly enjoyed the company of his fellow human beings. The examples of "extra-analytic" behavior that Freud's critics accuse him of committing were hardly momentary lapses, nor were they rare. Freud was notorious for being both amiable and talkative with patients when measured by conventional standards (Lipton, 1977). Haynal (1989) quotes numerous examples from former patients who reported that Freud engaged in straightforward dialogues with them. And Racker (1968) bemusedly concluded that if neutrality is intended to impose limitations on how much analysts should say, Freud couldn't possibly be characterized as a "classically neutral" analyst! (pp. 34–35).

Whatever neutrality was intended to foster when Freud conceived it, it was never meant to prohibit analysts from simply *being themselves*. As Freud himself demonstrated, neutrality should never inhibit analysts from behaving in a friendly and overtly sympathetic manner when it is in their nature to do so. Even when such behavior challenges the criteria of abstinence—and it will—the employment of abstinence shouldn't be so severe that it deprives analysts of their intrinsic humanity.

One should bear in mind that neutrality is a state of mind whose sole purpose is to complement the fundamental rule of analysis. It is probably best characterized by the sceptic notion of *epoché:* the disciplined suspension of judgement (Annas and Barnes, 1994). Ironically, the act of interpretation itself is essentially a sceptical notion because it assumes that knowledge cannot be determined through scientific examination. Knowledge, by its nature, is mysterious, ambiguous, and inexact. It is never precise, but it can approximate precision. We can never really "know" what it is. By suspending judgement about the nature of what is going on around and within ourselves, we become wary of our assertions and less invested in proving that they are right. The sceptics concluded that truths can never be proved because they are intrinsically *personal*. The only truths we ever really know are based on experience, so they are meaningful only to ourselves. According to the sceptics, we try to escape the weight of our experience by seeking objective truths that, once established, we argue against. This, they believed, is the principal cause of mental anguish, what we today label anxiety. Therapeutically, the sceptics suggested it is possible to obtain happiness by systematically abandoning our search for certitude. The extent to which we succeed in doing so helps to cure us of the need for argumentation, a precursor to neurotic ambivalence.

Freud was a sceptic in the spirit by which he advocated neutrality. By keeping an open mind to the other's experience and not imposing solutions on what is ultimately unknowable, analysis helps patients obtain relief from their conflicts. Free association and neutrality serve the same purpose: they promote the peace of mind that can only be obtained by treating everything with equal weight.

If patients can be expected to be truthful about the nature and variety of their experiences, analysts must learn to be open to what those experiences are. Freud advised that the principal means of doing so was through "keeping the counter-transference in check" (1915, pp. 163–164). But what does that specifically entail? If analysts hope to employ neutrality with a modicum of diligence, flexibility, and common sense, then they need to have mastered the task of being neutral *with themselves*. Their own experience of analysis and self-analysis should have fostered a capacity for learning to accept their own idiosyncrasies, limitations, jealousies, fears, anxieties, in effect, the totality of the person they have become. If they are unable to do so—if, in fact, they are at odds with themselves and the weight of their everyday existence—they will impose the same grief onto their patients, regardless of what their training has advised.

Like free association, neutrality is a kind of "meditation." It employs a vigilance that is consuming but paradoxically accepting of how we situate ourselves in the world. It entails nothing more complicated than learning to be honest with ourselves and, so, with others. That is why Freud's conception of neutrality isn't so much a matter of technique as a person's *manner of being* in the world.

The dialectic of analytic knowledge—when the analyst should say something and when to let others do the talking—encapsulates the sense of play that is inherent in Freud's approach to neutrality. He knew that psychoanalysis, unlike science, could never aim at precision, let alone approximate it, because it is rooted in our ability to be patient. It instills in us a capacity for *non*-intervention in the face of insurmountable pressures to do something, to demonstrate signs of success. It is paradoxical in that doing nothing is our principal means of effecting change. That is why the efficacy of analysis cannot be measured by determining how much or how little neutrality to employ but by knowing when it's prudent to be neutral and when to take a position.

Notes

1 He only introduced it three years later in the last of his technical papers, "Observation on Transference-Love" (1915), apparently the only time he ever invoked it.
2 See my critique of the technical papers in Thompson, *The Truth About Freud's Technique: The Encounter With the Real* (1994).
3 This was only the second time that Freud used this term; the first was in "The Dynamics of Transference" published the same year (1912a).
4 See my discussion of Freud's employment of neutrality with the Rat Man in Thompson, 1994, pp. 230–240.

References

Annas, J. and Barnes, J. (1994) *Sextus Empiricus: Outlines of Scepticism*. Cambridge: Cambridge University Press.

Freud, A. (1936) *The Ego and the Mechanisms of Defense*. New York: International Universities Press.

Freud, S. (1911/1958) *The Handling of Dream-Interpretation in Psycho-Analysis*. Standard Edition (Vol. 12, pp. 89–96). London: Hogarth.

Freud, S. (1912a/1958) *The Dynamics of Transference*. Standard Edition (Vol. 12, pp. 97–108). London: Hogarth.

Freud, S. (1912b/1958) *Recommendations to Physicians Practising Psycho-analysis*. Standard Edition (Vol. 12, pp. 109–120). London: Hogarth.

Freud, S. (1913/1958) *On Beginning the Treatment (Further Recommendations on the Technique of Psycho-Analysis I)*. Standard Edition (Vol. 12, pp. 121–144). London: Hogarth.

Freud, S. (1914/1958) *Remembering, Repeating and Working-Through (Further Recommendations on the Technique of Psycho-analysis II)*. Standard Edition (Vol. 12, pp. 145–156). London: Hogarth.

Freud, S. (1915/1958) *Observation on Transference-Love (Further Recommendations on the Technique of Psycho-analysis III)*. Standard Edition (Vol. 12, pp. 157–171). London: Hogarth.

Freud, S. (1919) *Lines of Advance in Psycho-Analytic Therapy*. Standard Edition (Vol. 17, pp. 157–168). London: Hogarth Press.

Freud, S. (1953–1973) *The Standard Edition of the Complete Psychological Works of Sigmund Freud* (24 vols; J. Strachey, Ed. & Trans.). London: Hogarth Press (Referred to in Subsequent References as Standard Edition).

Freud, S. and Breuer, J. (1893–95/1955) *Studies on Hysteria*. Standard Edition (Vol. 2). London: Hogarth.

Gay, P. (1988) *Freud—A Life for Our Time*. New York: Basic Books.

Gill, M. (1982) *Analysis of Transference, Vol. 1: Theory and Technique*. New York: International Universities Press.

Haynal, A. (1989) *Controversies in Psychoanalytic Method*. New York: New York University Press.

Kanzer, M. and Glenn, J. (Eds.). (1980) *Freud and his Patients*. New York: Aronson.

Kris, E. (1951) Ego Psychology and Interpretation in Psychoanalytic Therapy. *Psychoanalytic Quarterly*, Vol. 20: 15–30.

Laplanche, J. and Pontalis, J.-B. (1973) *The Language of Psychoanalysis* (D. Nicholson-Smith, Trans.). London: The Hogarth Press.

Lipton, S. (1977) The Advantages of Freud's Technique as Shown in His Analysis of the Rat Man. *International Journal of Psycho-Analysis*, Vol. 58: 255–273.

Mahony, P. (1986) *Freud and the Rat Man*. New Haven: Yale University Press.

Moore, B. and Fine, B. (1990) *Psychoanalytic Terms and Concepts*. New Haven, CT: American Psychoanalytic Association, Yale University Press.

Racker, H. (1968) *Transference and Countertransference*. New York: International Universities Press.

Schafer, R. (1983) *The Analytic Attitude*. New York: Basic Books.

Thompson, M. G. (1994) *The Truth About Freud's Technique: The Encounter With the Real*. New York: New York University Press.

Chapter 14

The Existential Dimension to Working Through

Of all the papers Freud published on the technical principles of psychoanalysis, his conception of working through is arguably the most subtle. Compounding the inherent difficulty of the concept itself is the little he had to say about it (less than one page of text in the 23 volumes of his publications) and the fact that he conceived it relatively late in the evolution of his treatment philosophy. Freud invoked the term for the first time in "Remembering, Repeating and Working Through" (1914), one of six papers he devoted to technique between 1911 and 1915. The term subsequently crops up now and then, but this seminal paper was the only occasion where Freud set out to define what the term is intended to mean. More remarkable still, working through has no precise definition. Like so many of the technical principles that comprise Freud's treatment philosophy (e.g., neutrality, abstinence, free association, transference, countertransference, resistance), a close examination of what Freud actually had to say about this term reveals a different picture from the one we are often led to believe. In fact, the very concept of working through has suffered increasing criticism from contemporary analysts, and there is a surprising lack of interest in the concept as a whole. One possible explanation for the rule's neglect by contemporary practitioners is probably due to what I perceive as its inherently existential nature, which I shall set out to explore in this paper.

In general terms, working through is applicable in the context of the patient's resistance to treatment. One of the questions that invariably arises when resistance is broached is what, precisely, is the patient resisting? What, in turn, is the patient supposed to "work through"? In addressing these questions, I shall begin with representative comments from the analytic literature depicting how working through is typically conceived.

DOI: 10.4324/9781003429104-14

Beginning with the glossary of the American Psychoanalytic Association, *Psychoanalytic Terms and Concepts*, Moore and Fine (1990) propose:

> It is the goal of working through to make insight more effective, that is, to bring about significant and lasting changes in the patient. . . . It may involve merely repeating and elaborating the usual analytic work, extending and deepening the analysis of the resistances, which need to be overcome repetitively and progressively and, in some cases, require special intervention. Prior interpretations often require expansion or modification so, they become more comprehensive or to the point, identifying basic themes or highlighting countless ways in which the conflictual situations are imbedded in [the patient's] character structure.
>
> (p. 210)

Moore and Fine depict working through as the act of repetitiously "working over" an intractable issue with the aim of persuading the patient to embrace an unpleasant reality by finally accepting the analyst's interpretation despite the patient's reluctance to do so. In effect, they conceive working through as simply complying with an interpretation that the patient was heretofore unable or unwilling to accept. It should be noted that this depiction of working through relies more or less entirely on a given patient's capacity for rationality, brought to bear in order to overcome his or her resistance to the analyst's conception of reality. The intellectual feature of this characterization of working through is obvious and is readily contrasted with others that perceive it in a more ambiguous light. Compare, for example, Moore and Fine's definition of working through with one offered by Laplanche and Pontalis (1977). In their view, Freud. . .

> [S]eems to suggest that working-through constitutes as fundamental an aspect of the treatment as do recollection of repressed memories and the repetition that occurs in the transference. In point of fact the article in question leaves us in considerable doubt as to what Freud means exactly by working-through. Some points, however, are made clear:
>
> a. Working-through applies to resistances.
> b. It generally follows the interpretation of a resistance that has apparently had no effect . . .
> c. Working through permits the subject to pass from rejection or merely intellectual acceptance to a conviction based on lived

experience (*Erleben*) . . . In this sense, it is by 'becoming *more conversant* with this resistance that the patient is enabled to carry out the working-through.

(p. 488; emphasis added)

Compared with the definition offered by Moore and Fine, Laplanche and Pontalis emphasize the critical importance of the patient's subjective experience, the nature of which psychoanalytic treatment endeavors to deepen. In their view, working through entails the act of getting past a purely intellectual understanding of something and becoming more or less "convinced" of it, which is to say, to *experience* it, heart and soul. Consequently, the experience of working through is transformative in that it changes one's way of seeing the world. More recently, some have taken the process of working through to include the behavior of the analyst as well as the patient. According to Laplanche and Pontalis (1977):

In the Freudian texts . . . working-through is unquestionably treated as a form of work accomplished by the *analysand*. Those authors since Freud who have insisted on the necessity for working-through have also emphasized the part invariably played in this process by the *analyst*. Witness, for example, this passage from Melanie Klein: "The necessity to work through is again and again proved in our day-to-day experience: for instance, we see that patients, who have at some time gained insight, repudiate this very insight in the following sessions and sometimes even seem to have forgotten that they had ever accepted it. It is only by drawing our conclusions from the material as it reappears in different contexts, and is interpreted accordingly, that we gradually help the patient to acquire insight in a more lasting way."

(p. 489)

Klein's treatment of working through reflects the increasingly popular convention that it pertains to something that is repetitiously manifested throughout the treatment experience and requires considerable effort (by the analyst) in order to affect a weakening of the patient's resistance. Viewed from this perspective, working through amounts to a "reworking" of the same interpretation, repeated over and over, until the patient finally gets it. Whereas Laplanche and Pontalis adopt a more ambiguous tone toward the nature of working through, their citation of Klein is more or less consistent with the view offered by Moore and Fine, which reduces working through to a rationalist form of activity. The Kleinian conception of working through entails the capacity to obtain insight into the nature of one's unconscious symptom formation by "understanding" the role it plays in one's psychical reality. Though Klein is not alone in this, she represents a group of analysts who advocate a conception of the analytic process that is governed by the patient's capacity to: a) *understand* the reasons for one's resistance to change; and b) *effect change* by virtue of such understanding. Working through is conceived of as a "wearing down" of the patient's resistance by the intellectual force of the analyst's interpretation and, ultimately, his or her insistence on it.

I now turn to Freud's comments about the nature of working through and compare his treatment of this phenomenon with the preceding. Recall that Freud's comments pertaining to working through appear at the very end of a lengthy discussion about the nature of memory and the repetition compulsion, a concept that Freud introduced in this paper for the first time.[1] For the sake of preserving the context in which Freud's conception of working through arose, I shall begin my discussion at the point where Freud is in the process of reviewing the dynamics of resistance and the recommended means for overcoming it. Freud (1914) begins with this observation:

> First and foremost, the initiation of analytic treatment in itself brings about a change in the patient's conscious attitude to his illness. He has usually been content with lamenting it, despising it as nonsensical and under-estimating its importance; for the rest, he has extended to its manifestations the ostrich-like policy of repression which he adopted towards its origins. Thus it can happen that he does not properly know under what conditions his phobia breaks out or does not listen to the precise wording of his obsessional ideas or does not grasp the actual purpose of his obsessional impulse. The treatment, of course, is not helped by this.
>
> (p. 152)

Despite the caveat that patients go into analysis in order to relieve their suffering, they are nevertheless reluctant to address the basis of such suffering wholeheartedly. Instead, they prefer to, as Freud says, "lament" their suffering, even though complaining has no discernible effect on the suffering itself. In light of the above, Freud suggests that if patients genuinely hope to benefit from the treatment, they must first find the means to *change their attitude* about what their suffering is about.

[The patient] must find the courage to direct his attention to the phenomena of his illness. His illness itself must no longer seem to him contemptible, but must become an enemy worthy of his mettle, a piece of his personality, which has solid ground for its existence and out of which things of value for his future life have to be derived.

(1914, p. 152)

Freud observed that the symptoms patients complain about—the same symptoms that brought them into therapy initially—are paradoxically gratifying. The symptom about which patients complain is nothing less than a contrivance[2] created for the purpose of relieving a form of suffering that is even more intolerable than the symptom itself. Whichever guise a symptom assumes—whether, for example, anxiety, depression, hypochondria, sexual inhibition, etc.—it also serves as a source of comfort that one comes to cherish and protect. This is presumably the reason patients instinctively resist the analyst's efforts to get to the bottom of what prompted their symptoms by discussing it relentlessly.

This ingenious conception of the symptom alerts us to the paradoxical role that Freud's notion of working through entails. In fact, working through and the "work" of analysis are essentially the same thing, phenomenologically speaking. The only work patients are asked to perform in the course of their treatment is deceptively elusive. Patients are not asked, nor are they expected, to change the behavior they complain about, nor are they admonished to improve their manner of living or to adopt one course of action in place of another. Such devices would only exacerbate the guilt they already suffer. All they are asked to do, to the best of their ability, is to adopt the fundamental rule of analysis as their guiding principle: to disclose whatever comes to mind and to endeavor, to the degree one is able, to ponder its significance. Yet no sooner do patients begin to disclose the manifest content of the hidden motives that foster their symptoms than the act of free associating breaks down. Every effort to inquire into the nature of their suffering and the purpose it ostensibly serves is evaded, and they persist in acting out their unconscious motives in place of examining them. Consequently, the source of their complaint remains protected from exposure and continues to serve its secretive aim, the perpetuation of the gratifying symptom. This is why, according to Freud, "[The analyst] celebrates it as a triumph for the treatment if he can bring it about that something that the patient wishes to discharge in action is disposed of through the work of remembering [instead]" (1914, p. 153).

But what does "remembering" actually entail? Contrary to conventional wisdom, the patient's capacity to remember shouldn't be confused with the simple act of recollection. Remembering, in the sense that Freud employs, entails *the ability to recognize the historical dimension of what the patient is currently experiencing.* In order to genuinely experience the here and now of the analytic moment, we have to situate our experience in an historical context. In other words, if I hope to make sense of the way I have become the person that I am, I have to submit to the work of determining my origins.

Yet the act of remembering isn't as simple or straightforward as it may seem. There is a knack to remembering that belies the logic of a good memory because the only way we are able to approximate it is through the experience of free associating, i.e., speaking my mind. Free association is a state of mind—remembering—that is at one turn succumbed to, and the next resisted because what every patient would prefer to do, despite protestations to the contrary, is not to remember but to *forget*. Resistance to remembering is unavoidable because the kind of thinking that all of us are accustomed to (the rational use of the mind) is resistance in its essence.[3]

Though patients are invited at the beginning of therapy to be as candid as they can, every analyst allows the privilege of circumventing this injunction to the degree that we are inclined. It is axiomatic that patients are indeed "free" (in the political sense, if not the psychical one)[4] to indulge their impulses (and defenses) as they please, so long as they commit themselves to observing the rule of candor *in principle*, if not consistently. According to Freud:

[The analyst does not hinder the patient] from carrying out unimportant intentions even if they are foolish; one does not forget that it is in fact *only through his own experience and mishaps* that a person learns sense. There are also people whom one cannot restrain from plunging into some quite undesirable project during the treatment and who only afterwards become ready for, and accessible to, analysis.

(1914, p. 153; emphasis added)

There is an unavoidable tension between the need to get things off one's chest while simultaneously resisting the obligation to reveal whatever comes to mind. One of the ways of easing the pressure is to act out one's torment in roundabout ways. Freud wasn't interested in circumventing the (patient's) resistance but sought instead to capitalize on the tension that the treatment engenders and even thrives upon.

Yet the handling of resistance is paradoxical because the treatment confers upon every patient the unfettered freedom to employ it. Some analysts aspire to surmount this paradox by resorting to analytic methods that dispense with the fundamental rule altogether, substituting in its place the so-called analysis of resistance (Gray, 1994). One wonders what such analysts conceive resistance to entail if they feel obliged to circumvent the very conditions that elicit its manifestation. It seems to me that without the tension that the fundamental rule engenders, there would be nothing for the patient to resist. The capacity to endure the paradoxical nature of the treatment situation is the key to resolving the conflict from which pathogenic conflicts and such are derived. Instead of merely "analyzing" the resistance as an end in itself, Freud (1914) argued that patients should endeavor to overcome their resistance as well. But how?

> The first step in overcoming resistance is made, as we know, by the analyst's uncovering the resistance, which is never recognized by the patient, and acquainting him with it. Now it seems that beginners in analytic practice are inclined to look on this introductory step as constituting the whole of their work. I have often been asked to advise upon cases in which the [analyst] complained that he had pointed out his resistance to the patient and that nevertheless no change had set in; indeed, the resistance had become all the stronger, and the whole situation was more obscure than ever. The treatment seemed to make no headway. This gloomy foreboding always proved mistaken. The treatment was, as a rule, progressing most satisfactorily.
>
> (p. 155)

The act of bringing a patient's attention to an incidence of resistance seldom, in and of itself, prompts the resistance to disappear. Whereas non-analytic interventions that rely on suggestion simply encourage patients to adopt more desirable behavior, Freud conceived the analytic method in fundamentally different terms. How did he characterize the key to this perspective?

> One must allow the patient time to become more conversant with this resistance with which he has now only become acquainted, to *work through* it, [and] to overcome it, by continuing, in defiance of it, the analytic work according to the fundamental rule of analysis.
>
> (1914, p. 155)

This deceptive and highly condensed passage contains the essence of what Freud envisioned the principle of working through to entail. For him, the "work" of working through should never be confused (as Klein insisted) with working over one's resistance; instead, it merely entails the task of *persevering* when the work of analysis (compliance with the fundamental rule) breaks down. In effect, working through is a form of recovery, the nature of which overcomes my resistance to submitting to the task I am engaged in already. Ironically, the term "overcome"—*Überwinden* in German—has aroused objections from some analysts who suggest it introduces a combative element into the otherwise neutral stance that analysts are encouraged to adopt. Gray, for example, characterizes Freud's conception of working through as basically overbearing and even un-analytic. According to Gray (1994):

> To "work upon," to "overcome," [and] to "deal with" resistances involve technical measures that are often different from those used in *analyzing* defenses. Yet Freud was unequivocal in his recognition that the key to effective, lasting therapeutic results lay in reversing the pathological alterations that the defense mechanisms have wrought on the [patient's] ego. This is illustrated by his observation: "Indeed, we come finally to understand that the overcoming of these resistances is *the essential function of analysis and is the only part of our work that gives us the assurance that we have achieved something with the patient.*"
>
> (p. 38; quoted citation attributed to Freud; emphases added by Gray)

Gray interprets Freud's citation (above) as confirmation that Freud was the first to introduce the analysis of defense, implying that the technical innovation of "resistance analysis" advocated by ego psychology has its source (and implicit justification) in Freud himself. Yet, in seeming contradiction to his own contention, Gray hastens to question, "What was it that Freud, if he was not *analyzing* defenses, had primarily relied on to influence the ego?" (1994, p. 38). Gray raises this question not once but repeatedly. After all, if Freud invented resistance analysis (as Gray claims), then why did Freud fail to actually analyze the resistance of the patients he treated? At a loss to offer a credible answer, Gray admits to his puzzlement at this (his own) question. In my view, the problem is not whether Freud failed to practice what he preached but what Freud took the proper handling of resistance to entail. Apparently, it meant something altogether different to Freud than it did to Gray and a generation of ego psychologists. The tendency among analysts today involves increasingly ingenious methods of subverting the patient's resistance by pointing it out and discussing it. The analyst is advised to address the resistance when this occurs, explore the feelings that have prompted it, elicit whatever associations come to mind, and so on. Analysts who "analyze" the resistance try to turn the tables on it by making the resistance not merely an artifact of and obstacle to therapy but the focus of it. During the course of such "analysis," the patient is obliged to momentarily halt free associating while the analyst, having temporarily suspended neutrality, interrogates the patient about what he or she is resisting and why. Once the resistances have been pinpointed, labeled, and analyzed accordingly, the patient is left with what is presumed to be a better understanding of the resistance in question, even if comprehension of it does little, if anything, to diminish it.

Though Gray insists that this form of intervention was sanctioned by Freud himself, there is nothing I can find in Freud's technical papers or the many accounts of his treatment philosophy that give credence to Gray's contention. On the contrary, Freud's writings suggest he was relatively passive in his treatment methodology. The work of analysis, as was stated unequivocally, is not the responsibility of the analyst but rather the task—indeed, the obligation—of the patient. According to Lohser and Newton (1996):

Working through the resistance [for Freud] did not mean, as it does today, that the analyst engaged in its lengthy exploration and interpretation but, rather, that the patient was to work through it by aggressively pushing *through* it, or acting in spite of it, and re-dedicating himself or herself to free association. The purpose of the analyst's interpretation of resistance is not to examine the content of the resistance or the nature of the anxiety underlying it but, rather, to point out to the patient that some behavior that he or she does not understand to be resistance *is* [in fact] resistance.

(p. 166)

When faced with a patient's opposition to therapy (which is to say, to engage in candid self-disclosure), Freud preferred to simply wait for the patient to resume free associating whenever the patient was ready to, thereby permitting the patient's unconscious to disclose itself by its own accord, in its own time, over however much time it entailed, but within limits. He believed patients need to actually come up against their resistance by learning to struggle with it and, eventually, learn to accommodate the anxieties that their defenses aim to suppress until a time when they are able to accommodate their anxieties to the degree they are able to tolerate. Yet Gray perceives in Freud's conservative prescription a treatment strategy that is allegedly intrusive, if not outright abusive. According to Gray (1994):

Dropping full-scale hypnosis or hypnotic trance from psychoanalytic technique did not result in the exclusion of suggestion . . . to *influence* the patient. Just as strong positive transference was the earlier vehicle for the trance-hypnosis which entirely excluded the ego's participation, so positive transference became the vehicle for *influencing* the patient's participation in the analytic process. The *authoritarian* element, although applied with a different emphasis, was nevertheless preserved.

(p. 38)

Gray (1982) argues that Freud's conception of working through amounts to nothing more than a disguised form of suggestion. Overcoming one's resistances, by his definition, entails the act of employing one's will to abandon them simply because that is what the analyst wants the patient to do. Moreover, Gray maintains that Freud: 1) relied solely on suggestion in his handling of resistances; 2) used his authority as a means of coercing his patients to abandon them; and 3) relied exclusively on positive transference as the vehicle for working through them. If this is indeed what Freud proposed, Gray would be correct in characterizing such tactics as pre- or un-analytic devices. But does this depiction of working through accurately characterize Freud's analytic method?

I don't believe it does. Perhaps the reason Gray arrives at this conclusion is his failure to appreciate the subtlety with which Freud envisioned the experience of working through at the deepest level. An example of Gray's oversight is his (mis)understanding of how Freud intended overcoming (*Überwinden*) one's resistances to work. In German, *Überwinden* means "to get over something" by finally facing it and eventually "coming to grips" with it. It has the same connotation, for instance, as when overcoming a loss by accepting the loss as a new facet of one's existence. The philosopher who most passionately rhapsodized about the need for overcoming painful aspects of life by facing them was Friedrich Nietzsche, who, by Freud's admission, anticipated many of his most radical ideas. The capacity (or virtue) for overcoming one's fears was a prominent feature of Nietzsche's conception of the ideal or "super" man, the *Übermensch* in German, or "overman." For Nietzsche, the ideal person is one who resolves to overcome the weight of existence by accepting reality for what it is. Similarly, overcoming one's resistance to unanticipated and oftentimes unwelcome interpretations hinges on the ability to accommodate the anxieties elicited when broadsided by an alternative point of view. Overcoming the resistance to unveiling ourselves to others entails "working through" the inescapable fear of coming to terms with who we are by taking in what others (embodied in what the analyst) make of us, wherever the chips may fall.

This doesn't mean that once we accept our vulnerability and make our bed in it, our resistance to this state of affairs lets up. In the treatment, working through simply entails the wherewithal to persevere with the "work" of analysis the best one can, despite one's inevitable resistance to it. In counterpoint, the analyst endeavors, as best he is able, to adopt an inherently *passive* role in the treatment—not, as Gray proposes, an active one. When communication breaks down, as it invariably does, or when an interpretation fails to elicit more inquiry, Freud (1914) reminded us:

> The [analyst] has nothing else to do than to wait and let things take their course, a course which cannot be avoided nor always hastened. If he holds fast to this conviction he will often be spared the illusion of having failed when in fact he is conducting the treatment on the right lines.
>
> (p. 155)

Freud never implied that adopting such a passive role—a feature of neutrality—was supposed to be easy. He readily acknowledged that the demands of the treatment situation are just as arduous for analysts as for their patients:

> This working-through of the resistances may in practice turn out to be an arduous task for the subject of the analysis and a trial of patience for the analyst. Nevertheless it is a part of the work which effects the greatest changes in the patient and which distinguishes analytic treatment from any kind of treatment by suggestion.
>
> (1914, pp. 155–156)

It is ironic that Freud would characterize his conception of working through as the single most feature of technique that distinguishes it from alternative, more "suggestive," forms of treatment when Gray's account characterizes it as the most suggestive feature of Freud's treatment philosophy. What could explain such a blatant misunderstanding of Freud's tightly-wound description of this technical principle? One possible explanation is that analysts today tend to conceptualize resistance in the broadest possible terms, whereas Freud conceived it in the most narrow terms. Whereas contemporary analysts tend to situate resistance as resisting any aspect of the treatment that is believed to be in the patient's interests, Freud restricted its occurrence to that of resisting candor, in effect halting one's participation in the act of *self-disclosure*.

Yet, self-disclosure is epitomized by nothing more onerous than disclosing what happens to be on one's mind. The most extreme (and stereotypical) example of resistance is probably opting to say nothing, but we know it is more complicated than that because resistance cannot be reduced to silence alone. On the contrary, some patients talk *ad nauseam*; they freely "dissociate" in place of associating and effectively say nothing, keeping the content of their revelations as close to the surface as possible. To genuinely free associate requires more than simply speaking out loud because it assumes compliance with the spirit of the rule as well as the letter of it. To authentically "free" associate assumes nothing less than—forgive me—opening one's heart to another person by taking that person into one's confidence and confessing one's innermost experience. "Working through" resistance entails the ability to recover the capacity for candor that was momentarily lost. If, in the final analysis, resistance is nothing more than a "loss of heart," then working through is the wherewithal to open one's heart again, by succumbing, in spite of one's reluctance to do so, to the dialectic of free associating.

Obviously, this takes time. Working through relies on the passage of time and the time it takes to let time assume its proper function in the treatment. When Freud insists that analysts must "wait and let things take their course," he is invoking a conception of time that is existential in nature. Indeed, *psychoanalysis is essentially a device that arranges for time to employ its effect upon us*. The couch, the inexorable pace, and the pregnant pauses that epitomize its odd conversational conventions are all contrivances that Freud devised in order to resurrect our neglected relationship with time. Few analysts have recognized this inherently phenomenological dimension to Freud's treatment philosophy.[5] This isn't a matter of imposing suggestion or authority but of revealing those aspects of ourselves that we are finally able to disclose by submitting to our experience of the moment. But how can one's resistance to experience be altered if the analytic situation is, by its nature, beyond one's control? Given the importance of experience in this endeavor and how one's experience is affected, there is a striking absence of inquiry into the nature of experience in the psychoanalytic literature. Freud and his followers grasped the significance of experience from a "common sensical" perspective but saw little reason to explore its philosophical implications. Yet the enigmatic nature of free association and the patient's resistance to it is impossible to grasp without recourse to the role experience contributes to the treatment situation.

Nowhere is its relevance more obvious than in Freud's conception of working through, a principle that speaks specifically to the experience of free associating and the resistance patients mount against it. Perhaps its neglect in the literature is due to the emphasis customarily reserved for investigating the unconscious, which, due to its latency, is effectively impossible to *experience per se*. Instead, analysts typically rely on conjecture and inference (both of which comprise "experience-distant" activities) in order to guess what its contents and machinations might be. Yet, it is the conscious, experiencing agent who submits to analysis in the first place and who uncovers (or resists) what is hidden by eliciting spontaneous verbalizations as they occur. This explains why the task of analysis cannot be reduced to one of deciphering what is obstinately hidden but of finally coming to grips with one's unconscious in the singular act of disclosing it. It is nevertheless easy to resist experience and even suppress it by engaging in intellectualization, repression, splitting, denial, projection, and other defensive maneuvers. Given the forces we mount against it, what can we say about the role experience properly entails, and how can one succeed in deepening one's experience in the to-and-fro of the analytic encounter?

According to the Oxford English Dictionary, experience derives from the Latin *experientia*, meaning "to try" or "a trial." It is also cognate with the word "peril," implying danger or risk. Experience is, in turn, defined as "the fact of being the subject of a state or condition;" "of being consciously affected by an event;" and "to feel, suffer, and undergo." On a deeper level still, a properly phenomenological rendering of experience implies both intentionality and intersubjectivity, since it is the subject—"I"—who experiences that which is inherently "other" than myself. In effect, my experience is *me* in the context of my being-in-the-world. Experience also pertains to a quality of consciousness, since I can experience something only to the degree that I am aware of it. This is the quality of experience Freud was invoking when he said, "it is only through [one's] own experience (*Erfahrung*) and mishaps that a person learns sense."

Is that all there is to say about it? Is it all or nothing, a matter of being aware or unaware of the topic at hand? Or are there greater or deeper degrees of experience I am capable of obtaining but neglect to avail myself of? We alluded to these questions earlier when we examined the experience of free associating and the degree of candor it entails. In fact, free associating entails more than permitting one's thoughts to come to mind because I never merely "observe" what occurs to me but I also experience it, dread, and avoid it; otherwise, I would have nothing to resist. It should be obvious to us by now that the psychoanalytic conception of experience fails to account for the elasticity of the phenomenon. The concept of experience is as perennial as it is enigmatic, going all the way back to the fourth century B.C. and the sceptics who were the first philosophers to reject rationality as the arbiter of wisdom, by substituting in its place the primacy of one's originary experience.[6] Since then, a host of philosophers, theologians, and thinkers from other disciplines explored the nature of experience and made it the cornerstone of their inquiry into the human condition.

Despite the attention given to experience, there is a tendency in psychoanalysis to dispense with the concept altogether or to retain it as a hollow principle that has abandoned its sense of relevance and proportion. In a critique of Susan Isaacs' views concerning the relationship between fantasy and experience, R. D. Laing challenged Isaacs' (and, with her, the psycho-analytic) characterization of unconscious fantasy as a *mode of experience*. According to Isaacs:

> Through external experience, phantasies become elaborated and capable of expression, but they do not depend upon such experience for their existence.
>
> (Quoted in Laing, 1969, p. 4)

Isaacs avers that our conscious, waking experience of the external world elicits both conscious and unconscious fantasies (as a means of relieving the frustrations encountered in experience) but that such fantasies are nevertheless not exclusively dependent on experience for their existence. She argues:

> Unconscious phantasies form the operative link between instincts and mechanism. When studied in detail, every variety of ego-mechanism can be seen to arise from their origin in instinctual impulses. . . . [Hence] a "mechanism" is an abstract general term describing certain mental processes *which are experienced by the subject as unconscious phantasies.*
>
> (Ibid, p. 5; emphasis added)

Laing wonders how it is possible to experience something the nature of which one is completely *unaware* (i.e., unconscious) of experiencing. The implications of such a thesis for the use of psychoanalytic interpretation are significant. One of the basic principles of Isaacs' theory, for example, is that the patient is always at the mercy of defense mechanisms that, even after they have been interpreted, continue to act upon the patient and always will. In turn, such defenses are conceived as fundamentally alien to the patient's agency and will always remain so. The purpose of interpretation is to alert the patient to the existence of such defenses so that one may account for their effects. This is consistent with Gray's (1994) view that the aim of the treatment situation is one of "reversing the pathological alterations that the defense mechanisms have wrought on the [patient's] ego" (p. 38). It is little wonder that, given their respective conceptions of "defense," these authors are unable to account for the nature of experience as such because, by it, the very notion of experience is virtually negated. In a study devoted to the exploration of experience from a phenomenological perspective, Laing (1967) set out to "translate" the psychoanalytic conception of mechanism into a language of personal experience:

> Under the heading of "defense mechanism," psychoanalysis describes a number of ways in which a person becomes alienated from himself. For example, repression, denial, splitting, projection, introjection. These "mechanisms" are often described in psychoanalytic terms as themselves "unconscious," that is, the person himself appears to be unaware that he is doing this to himself. Even when a person develops sufficient insight to see that "splitting," for example, is going on, he usually experiences this splitting as indeed a mechanism, an impersonal process, so to speak, which has taken over and which he can observe but cannot control or stop.

> There is thus some phenomenological validity in referring to such "defenses" by the term "mechanism." But we must not stop there. They have this mechanical quality because the person as he experiences himself is dissociated from them. He appears to himself and to others to suffer from them. They seem to be processes he undergoes, and as such he experiences himself as a patient, with a particular psychopathology.

> *But this is so only from the perspective of his own alienated experience.* As he becomes de-alienated he is able first of all to become aware of them, if he has not already done so, and then to take the second, even *more crucial step of progressively realizing that these are things he does or has done to himself.* Process becomes converted back to praxis, [and] the patient becomes an agent.
>
> (1967, pp. 17–18; emphasis added)

Another analyst influenced by Klein, Hans Racker, employs Klein's notion of unconscious fantasy (here elaborated by Isaacs) in his interpretation of the analyst's countertransference "experience" of the patient's unconscious fantasies. Because the very concept of experience has been relegated to nonsense, analysts such as Racker and Isaacs are free to distort its meaning to serve their clinical end: that of becoming the arbiter of what the patient's experience is and what that experience is said to be up to. More disturbing still is their conviction that their respective patients will never be afforded the opportunity of ever finally *recovering* their experience because they assume to do so is not even possible. Returning to Isaacs, Laing (1969) counters:

> In my experience, self does not experience the experience of other directly. . . . [Yet] from the perspective of self seeing other, Isaacs infers from her experience of the other's actions certain things about the other's experience, [in the same way that] an adult infers what a baby experiences.
>
> (p. 6)

In other words, Isaacs conceives the interpretive process along the lines of a mother who is endeavoring to make sense of her baby's experience, since the baby is unable to *tell* the mother what the baby's experience is. While allowing adult patients are able to tell us about their experience, Isaacs is convinced that such patients *are* nonetheless capable of experiencing feelings and ideas *they are unaware of experiencing*, and which, by this reasoning, require the analyst to tell them what such experiences are. Laing continues:

> Isaacs, in referring not simply to imagination, daydreams, or reveries, but to "unconscious phantasy," is making two types of inference . . . namely: she is inferring something about the other's experience, *and* she is inferring that this is something of which the other is unaware. This seems to mean that there is a whole *type* of experience, as well as specific "content" *of* experience, of which the other who "has" the imputed experience knows, or may know, nothing. From her premises, corroboration of her self's inferences by explicit testimony from other is not necessary to confirm these particular inferences.
>
> (p. 6)

As far as Isaacs is concerned, confirmation of such inferences about the patient's "unconscious" experience is supported solely by: a) the "correctness" of her theory; and b) the patient's "progress" in analysis. Whatever that means. By dent of this theory, the patient is *ipso facto* incapable of ever actually "knowing" what his unconscious experience is since such experience is, by definition, unconscious. Laing remarks at the marvel of such a thesis in the way it leaves the patient out of the loop, so the speak, whenever the analyst endeavors to determine the content of the patient's experience by ignoring the patient's account of what his experience is. According to Isaacs, it is unnecessary to wait for or expect one's patient to undergo, let alone suffer, his own experience, to be moved by it, and finally come to terms with it because the analyst and the analyst alone is able to do this for him or her. Isaacs concludes that it is virtually impossible for patients to ever *experience* their experience themselves—or even to corroborate the accuracy of the analyst's interpretations that purport to determine what their experience is said to be.

One of Laing's favorite examples of how this conception of experience translates into psychoanalytic interpretation is taken from one of Wilfried Bion's most famous clinical vignettes. Whereas Laing would say that the purpose of interpretation is to help the patient get in touch with his or her experience, the early Bion (following Klein's perspective) uses interpretation to "translate" to the patient what the patient is (said to be) experiencing "in" his or her unconscious. The following vignette is what Bion (Klein, Heimann, and Money-Kyrle (Eds.), 1957) characterizes as "the essentials" of two sessions with a schizophrenic patient whom he had been treating for five years in psychoanalysis. Interpretations, says Bion, should be offered in language that is simple, exact, and mature:

Patient: I picked a tiny piece of my skin from my face and feel quite empty.

Bion: The tiny piece of skin is your penis, which you have torn out, and all your insides have come with it.

Patient: I do not understand . . . penis . . . only syllables and now it has no meaning.

Bion: You have split my word 'penis' into syllables and now it has no meaning.

Patient: I don't know what it means, but I want to say, 'if I can't spell I can't think.'

Bion: The syllables have now been split into letters; you cannot spell— that is to say you cannot put the letters together again to make words, so now you cannot think.

The following day, the exchange goes as follows:

Patient: I cannot find any interesting food.

Bion: You feel it has all been eaten up.

Patient: I do not feel able to buy any new clothes and my socks are a mass of holes.

Bion: By picking out the tiny piece of skin yesterday you injured yourself so badly you cannot even buy clothes; you are empty and have nothing to buy them with.

Patient: Although they are full of holes they constrict my foot.

Bion: Not only did you tear out your own penis but also mine. So today there is no interesting food—only a hole, a sock. But even this sock is made of a mass of holes, all of which you made and which have joined together to constrict, or swallow and injure, your foot.

(pp. 229–230)

I grant there is a fine line between employing interpretations for the purpose of enlivening the patient's experience, on the one hand, and with the consequence of intellectualizing that experience, on the other. The analyst has no control over which of the two a given patient is more likely to be inclined, nor how a given patient will respond to interpretations in principle. All patients are prone to intellectualizing their treatment experience because doing so serves to protect them from precisely those experiences they are wont to avoid. The ultimate outcome of a given treatment is impossible to predict; try as we may to influence it to the degree that providence permits. Laing's reaction to Bion's work with this patient pertains less to the "correctness" of such interpretations than to what it says about what the patient appears to be experiencing and how Bion responds to it.

By all appearances, Bion ignores what the patient is telling him about his experience because Bion doesn't think the patient has a clue what his experience is. Instead, Bion "interprets" to the patient what *he* feels confident is going on in the patient's unconscious and what the patient is "really" experiencing. Yet, when his patient responds with obvious consternation to Bion's interpretations, Bion simply construes such comments as evidence of how confused his patient is about his experience. The confusion that Bion attributes to his patient is not, in Bion's opinion, a consequence of his interpretations, mind you, but a product of the patient's *failure to recognize and, so, experience his own experience*, as it is understood by Bion. What is the consequence of this dramatic innovation in Klein's, Isaacs,' and Bion's and, by extension, the psychoanalytic conception of experience? Basically, it has done away with it. I am no longer conscious or in any discernible sense aware of what my most important experiences are and, according to Klein, I never will be. Consequently, I must rely on others to tell me what is going on in my own mind and explain the content of my own experience.

Despite the views of mainstream psychoanalysts, such as Klein, Isaacs, Racker, and Bion, experience has been the object of fascination for philosophers from ancient times to the present. Even Hegel, an idealist in other respects, argued that change is possible only to the degree that we are capable of accounting for our experience of the ideas with which we typically wrestle. Hegel rejected the common sense notion of experience that reduces it to the simple awareness of an event, in the manner, for example, that I experience writing this sentence, by arguing that when I truly experience something, I am also *affected* by it because it comes as a shock.[7] Experience necessarily confronts me with frustration because it violates my familiar view of things by forcing something new into consciousness. Due to its intrinsically unsettling nature, Hegel concluded that experience also elicits despair because it disturbs my previous accommodation of reality. Consequently, my capacity to experience subverts what is familiar by changing my point of view, and "who" I am.

More recently, Heidegger examined the revelatory aspects of experience in addition to its strictly transformative role emphasized by Hegel. Heidegger focused on the interplay between experience and self-discovery by proposing that experience doesn't merely change the world I inhabit but also reveals things I hadn't realized before. Consequently, experience elicits truths about myself and my view of the world. Moreover, Heidegger was drawn to the inherently practical task of determining the ground of personal existence and how to make peace with it, honestly and authentically. Heidegger discovered that if a person is prepared to employ a degree of forethought and discipline to the task, experience can be nudged in a certain direction in order to achieve a specific goal. By anticipating my experience with a conscious aim in mind, I can use that experience to gain insight into the person I am and the world I inhabit.

Experiences don't just "happen" in random, haphazard fashion; I am also capable of resisting experience, avoiding the weight of it, and even forgetting painful experiences I have suffered in the past. In turn, the degree to which I am able to experience something to the core of my being—whether eating a meal, falling in love, even undergoing psychoanalysis—is determined by how willing I am to submit (i.e., give myself over) to the experience in question. This means there are degrees to experience; it isn't all or nothing. These considerations about the nature of experience offer profound implications for the role of the psychoanalyst and the means by which interpretations are used in order to transform what the patient experiences and how. Laing observed that Heidegger's conception of experience already presupposes an act of interpretation that, in turn, determines what I am inclined to experience in the first place:

> Our experience of another entails a particular interpretation of his behavior. To feel loved is to perceive and interpret, that is, to experience, the actions of the other as loving.

> In order for the other's behavior to become part of self's experience, self must perceive it. *The very act of perception [and hence experience] entails interpretation.*
> (Laing, Phillipson, and Lee, 1966, pp. 10–11; emphasis added)

According to Laing, everything a patient experiences in analysis is the end result of "interpretations" the patient has already surreptitiously given to all he is capable of experiencing throughout the course of the analytic relationship.[8] What the analyst says is never actually "heard" in the way the analyst necessarily intends it because it is unconsciously interpreted by the patient according to his or her interpretative schema, a culmination of everything the patient has previously experienced (and understood by those experiences) in the course of a lifetime. In other words, every analytic patient experiences the world according to a personal bias that is prone to resisting anything that is foreign to it. The dogmatic nature of the patient's views, held together by a lifetime of neurotic impasse maneuvers, serves to account for the resistances that analysts invariably encounter when employing an interpretation. Because both the analyst and patient are always already (i.e., unconsciously) interpreting everything the other says, what is actually *heard* by each and, in turn, experienced is impossible to communicate directly, because every account of one's experience entails the use of words which, when uttered, are *de facto* "interpretations" of that experience. This constantly changing interplay of speech, recognition, and misunderstanding accounts for the extraordinary difficulty analysts encounter in their endeavor to effect change since the change they aspire to effect is at the mercy of the patient's ability to question and, ultimately, reframe her originary experience, the nature of which is, for the most part, impervious to change and no less difficult to determine.

This is why analysts need to be wary of the temptation to offer interpretations at random with the hope that some will simply "stick," and should endeavor instead to learn the means by which such interpretations actually affect the patient (transference) and, in turn, how the patient's reactions affect the analyst (countertransference) the way that they do.[9] In every communication with a patient, the analyst aims to: 1) learn what the patient's interpretative framework is; 2) determine the means by which that interpretative framework constructs a "world" (the transference neurosis) that the patient attributes to the analyst; and 3) offer the patient a wider range of interpretations to consider. The analyst's task is one of helping patients overcome their innate resistance to experiencing something new, strange, or forgotten. In their resistance to this process, patients employ alternative "interpretations" of their own that serve to distance them further from experiences they construe as particularly painful while substituting other, more pleasing experiences in their place. If an experience of unexpected force slips through the patient's carefully wrought net of defenses, he will nevertheless instinctively limit the degree to which he is ready to permit the experience to affect him and, so, transform one kind of experience into another.

Heidegger concluded that experience never simply "occurs" in the abstract but is necessarily *suffered* in the existential sense. Because I always have a hand in what I experience and the degree to which I permit my experience to affect me, no one can ever impose an experience on another person willy-nilly. It is nevertheless possible, through coercion, intimidation, or seduction, to engender an experience that the other person may, in hindsight, wished not to have succumbed to. Such experiences can, in turn, be repressed and harbored unconsciously, i.e., without thinking about them. This conception of experience is perfectly consistent with Freud's formulation of free association and the painstaking dynamics of working through one's resistance to changing one's experience.

These considerations may help to explain why the act of interpreting the patient's disclosures with the aim of aligning them with past or repressed experiences is a slippery slope upon which every analyst has tripped. The likelihood of transgressing the boundaries that designate the respective roles assigned to analyst and patient alike is built into the fabric of the analytic relationship because the outcome often depends on the manner in which such interpretations are offered. Interpretation is an undeniably invaluable and no doubt indispensable resource, but only when employed with a view to helping patients gain access to a dimension of their experience that is dormant, affecting the opportunity of coming to terms with a lost, unincorporated dimension of experience, however painful such experience may be.

It seems to me too many analysts employ interpretation as a means of translation and indoctrination instead of the more frustrating goal of revelation and discovery. Some analysts seem to believe only they have the means of determining what is latent because only they know the theories that can decipher what it means. Some analytic schools are admittedly more invested in this form of sorcery than others. When analysts choose to dispense with interpretations altogether or effect a more sceptical perspective, they are sometimes accused of abandoning psychoanalysis altogether. Freud probably instigated this bias, and every subsequent analytic school has embellished it further. To give Freud his due, however, he eventually realized after trial and error that the underlying purpose of interpretation is a necessarily modest one: that of simply helping patients to hear and, so, experience what they are themselves capable of saying in their own words. When employed with such caution, the interpretive act is less likely to elicit the depth of resistance that the Kleinian approach (for example) often engenders. Every analytic patient is alone in this endeavor, not because it implies a one-person psychology, but because only the patient can speak from his or her experience because only the patient can say what that experience is.

In the final analysis, psychic change is effected, not through insight alone, but by the wherewithal to relinquish designs that are not tenable to begin with. Because we all suffer from the burden of an existence that frustrates and disappoints at every turn, psychoanalysis was never cut out to serve as a mechanism for "success." Its greatest resource is rather the change it is capable of fostering, if not in the social arena in which we live then, perhaps, within ourselves. What patients work through during the course of their therapy is nothing less than a grudging acceptance of who they are and, more importantly, who they are not in a world in which they are "thrown" because the world is never entirely their own making. It is perhaps fitting to give Freud (1910) the last word on the matter, in a passage where he offers the choice—existential, to be sure—every analytic patient must face at the terminus of their treatment:

> A certain number of people, faced in their lives by conflicts which they have found too difficult to solve, have taken flight into neurosis and in this way won an unmistakable, although in the long run too costly, gain from illness. What will these people have to do if their flight into illness is barred by the indiscreet revelations of psychoanalysis? They will have to be honest, confess to the [forces] that are at work in them, face the conflict, fight for what they want, or go without it.
>
> (pp. 149–150)

This is bitter medicine, indeed, but one that therapy patients are never obliged to swallow because it is always their option to accept these terms or decline. Yet although they are never obliged to, they are nevertheless obligated, whether they like it or not, to live with the choices they make.

Notes

1 See Thompson, 1994, pp. 192–204, for an exhaustive critique of Freud's paper.
2 See my discussion about the role of "contrivance" in the analytic setting in Thompson, 1994, pp. 78–87.
3 See Thompson, 1985, pp. 1–23, for a more exhaustive discussion on the relation between rationality and resistance.
4 See Merleau-Ponty, 1962, pp. 434–456, for more on this point.
5 For a singular exception, see Loewald, 1980, pp. 43–52; 138–147. See also Leavy, 1988.
6 See Thompson, 2000a and 2000b, for a more detailed exploration of how the sceptic treatment of experience anticipated the modern invention of psychoanalysis.
7 See Thompson, 1996 and 1997, for a more detailed account of the phenomenology of experience.
8 This view of interpretation has been called hermeneutic by some but the hermeneutic literature does not emphasize the role of experience to the degree that the phenomenological perspective developed by Husserl or Heidegger does.
9 Here I employ "transference" and "countertransference" in the generic sense of pertaining to the patient's and analyst's subjective experience, respectively.

References

Freud, S. (1910/1957) *The Future Prospects of Psycho-Analytic Therapy*. Standard Edition (Vol. 11, pp. 139–151). London: Hogarth Press.

Freud, S. (1914) *Remembering, Repeating and Working Through (Further Recommendations on the Technique of Psycho-Analysis II)*. Standard Edition (Vol. 12, pp. 145–156). London: Hogarth Press.

Freud, S. (1953–1973) *The Standard Edition of the Complete Psychological Works of Sigmund Freud* (24 vols; J. Strachey, Ed. & Trans.). London: Hogarth Press (Referred to in Subsequent References as Standard Edition).

Gray, P. (1982) Developmental Lag in the Evolution of Technique for Psychoanalysis of Neurotic Conflict. *Journal of the American Psychoanalytic Association*, Vol. 30: 621–655.

Gray, P. (1994) *The Ego and Analysis of Defense*. Northvale, NJ: Jason Aronson.

Klein, M., Heimann, P. and Money-Kyrle, R. E. (Eds.). (1957) *New Directions in Psychoanalysis*. New York: Basic Books.

Laing, R. D. (1967) *The Politics of Experience and the Bird of Paradise*. Harmondsworth: Penguin.

Laing, R. D. (1969) *Self and Others*. 2nd Revised Edition. London: Tavistock Publications.

Laing, R. D., Phillipson, H. and Lee, A. R. (1966) *Interpersonal Perception: A Theory and a Method of Research*. London: Tavistock Publications.

Laplanche, J. and Pontalis, J.-B. (1977) *The Language of Psychoanalysis*. London: Hogarth Press.

Leavy, S. (1988) *In the Image of God: A Psychoanalyst's View*. New Haven, CT and London: Yale University Press.

Loewald, H. W. (1980) *Papers on Psychoanalysis*. New Haven, CT and London: Yale University Press.

Lohser, B. and Newton, P. (1996) *Unorthodox Freud: The View From the Couch*. New York: The Guilford Press.

Merleau-Ponty, M. (1962) *Phenomenology of Perception* (C. Smith, Trans.). London: Routledge & Kegan Paul.

Moore, B. E. and Fine, B. D. (1990) *Psychoanalytic Terms and Concepts*. New Haven: Yale University Press.

Thompson, M. G. (1985) *The Death of Desire: A Study in Psychopathology*. New York and London: New York University Press.

Thompson, M. G. (1994) *The Truth About Freud's Technique: The Encounter With The Real*. New York and London: New York University Press.

Thompson, M. G. (1996, December) Deception, Mystification, Trauma: Laing and Freud. *The Psychoanalytic Review*, Vol. 83, No. 6.

Thompson, M. G. (1997, October) The Fidelity to Experience in R. D. Laing's Treatment Philosophy. *Contemporary Psychoanalysis*, Vol. 33, No. 4.

Thompson, M. G. (2000a, January) The Crisis of Experience in Contemporary Psychoanalysis. *Contemporary Psychoanalysis*, Vol. 36, No. 1.

Thompson, M. G. (2000b, July) The Sceptic Dimension to Psychoanalysis: Toward an Ethic of Experience. *Contemporary Psychoanalysis*, Vol. 36, No. 3.

Index

For Product Safety Concerns and Information please contact our EU
representative GPSR@taylorandfrancis.com
Taylor & Francis Verlag GmbH, Kaufingerstraße 24, 80331 München, Germany